Competitiveness and Solidarity in the European Union

AF835200

Starting in the 1980s, competitive pressures and the ideology of competitiveness have shaken and transformed traditional models of development, public policy, and governance in Europe.

This edited book carries out a comprehensive, interdisciplinary, and innovative analysis of the relationship between competitiveness and solidarity in the contemporary European Union. It offers an original contribution to the scholarly debates on the current developments and challenges of welfare states, social and economic policies, and forms of governance in the European Union. Bringing together an international team of cutting-edge scholars in the social sciences and the humanities, *Competitiveness and Solidarity in the European Union* sheds light on the conceptual richness and policy relevance of these relationships, pointing to important avenues to make the European Union more economically successful and socially fairer.

This book will be of key interest to scholars and students of European Union studies and, more broadly, of EU Law, Public Policy, Economics, Sociology, Political Science, Geography, and Contemporary History.

Paolo Chiocchetti has a PhD in European Studies from King's College London. His research focuses on the transformation of Western European party systems, comparative politics, Italian politics, European governance, and socio-economic policy.

Frédéric Allemand is Principal Investigator of the RESuME project (resume.uni.lu) at the Faculty of Law, Economics and Finance of the University of Luxembourg. His research focuses on EU law, Economic and Monetary Union, and European economic governance.

Routledge/UACES Contemporary European Studies

The primary objective of the new Contemporary European Studies series is to provide a research outlet for scholars of European Studies from all disciplines. The series publishes important scholarly works and aims to forge for itself an international reputation.

Edited by Chad Damro, University of Edinburgh, UK, Elaine Fahey, City University London, UK, and David Howarth, University of Luxembourg, Luxembourg, on behalf of the University Association for Contemporary European Studies.

Editorial Board: Grainne De Búrca, European University Institute and Columbia University; Andreas Føllesdal, Norwegian Centre for Human Rights, University of Oslo; Peter Holmes, University of Sussex; Liesbet Hooghe, University of North Carolina at Chapel Hill, and Vrije Universiteit Amsterdam; David Phinnemore, Queen's University Belfast; Ben Rosamond, University of Warwick; Vivien Ann Schmidt, University of Boston; Jo Shaw, University of Edinburgh; Mike Smith, University of Loughborough, and Loukas Tsoukalis, ELIAMEP, University of Athens and European University Institute.

Commercial Realism and EU Trade Policy
Competing for Economic Power in Asia and the Americas
Katharina L. Meissner

Parties, Power and Policy-making
From Higher Education to Multinationals in Post-Communist Societies
Silvana Tarlea

Competitiveness and Solidarity in the European Union
Interdisciplinary Perspectives
Edited by Paolo Chiocchetti and Frédéric Allemand

For more information about this series, please visit: www.routledge.com/Routledge-UACES-Contemporary-European-Studies/book-series/UACES

Competitiveness and Solidarity in the European Union

Interdisciplinary Perspectives

Edited by Paolo Chiocchetti and Frédéric Allemand

Routledge
Taylor & Francis Group
LONDON AND NEW YORK

UACES

First published 2019 by Routledge

2 Park Square, Milton Park, Abingdon, Oxfordshire OX14 4RN
52 Vanderbilt Avenue, New York, NY 10017

Routledge is an imprint of the Taylor & Francis Group, an informa business

First issued in paperback 2020

Copyright © 2019 selection and editorial matter, Paolo Chiocchetti and Frédéric Allemand; individual chapters, the contributors

The right of Paolo Chiocchetti and Frédéric Allemand to be identified as the authors of the editorial matter, and of the authors for their individual chapters, has been asserted in accordance with sections 77 and 78 of the Copyright, Designs and Patents Act 1988.

All rights reserved. No part of this book may be reprinted or reproduced or utilised in any form or by any electronic, mechanical, or other means, now known or hereafter invented, including photocopying and recording, or in any information storage or retrieval system, without permission in writing from the publishers.

Notice:
Product or corporate names may be trademarks or registered trademarks, and are used only for identification and explanation without intent to infringe.

British Library Cataloguing-in-Publication Data
A catalogue record for this book is available from the British Library

Library of Congress Cataloging-in-Publication Data
Names: Chiocchetti, Paolo, editor. | Allemand, Frédéric, editor.
Title: Competitiveness and solidarity in the European Union : interdisciplinary perspectives / edited by Paolo Chiocchetti and Frédéric Allemand.
Description: Abingdon, Oxon ; New York, NY : Routledge, 2019. | Series: Routledge / UACES contemporary European studies | Includes bibliographical references and index.
Identifiers: LCCN 2018036714| ISBN 9781138545878 (hardback) | ISBN 9781351001809 (ebk) | ISBN 9781351001793 (web pdf) | ISBN 9781351001786 (epub) | ISBN 9781351001779 (mobipocket/kindle)
Subjects: LCSH: European Union countries–Economic policy. | European Union countries–Economic integration. | Competition–European Union countries. | European Union countries–Social policy.
Classification: LCC HC241 .C576 2019 | DDC 338.6/048094–dc23
LC record available at https://lccn.loc.gov/2018036714

ISBN: 978-1-138-54587-8 (hbk)
ISBN: 978-0-367-66446-6 (pbk)

Typeset in Times New Roman
by Wearset Ltd, Boldon, Tyne and Wear

Contents

Figures

Tables

Contributors

Karl Aiginger is Director of the Policy Crossover Centre: Vienna – Europe (www.querdenkereuropa.at). He is also Professor of Economics at the Vienna University of Economics and Business, honorary Professor at the University of Linz, Austria, and co-editor-in-chief of the *Journal of Industry, Competition and Trade* (JICT). In the recent past he has worked as Director of the Austrian Institute of Economic Research (WIFO) and as coordinator of the research project WWWforEurope (www.foreurope.eu). His research focuses on competitiveness, industrial policy, and economic policy.

Frédéric Allemand is Research Fellow of the Robert Schuman Institute of European Affairs and Principal Investigator of the RESuME project (resume.uni.lu) at the Faculty of Law, Economics and Finance of the University of Luxembourg, Luxembourg. He is also associate researcher at the Geostrategy Centre of the École Normale Supérieure (ENS) in Paris and lecturer at Sciences Po in Paris and at the ENA in Strasbourg. His research focuses on EU law, Economic and Monetary Union, and European economic governance. He is the author of more than 50 scholarly publications, including *Gouverner la zone euro après la crise* (Gualino, 2016). Since 2017, he has been the chief editor of the *Revue de l'euro*, an interdisciplinary journal on European economic governance.

Annette Bongardt is Visiting Senior Fellow in European Political Economy at the London School of Economics. She is also a professor and coordinates International and European Studies at the National Institute for Public Administration in Lisbon and is Visiting Associate Professor at University Fernando Pessoa in Porto, Portugal. Her research focuses on EU policy, European economic governance, competitiveness, and sustainability.

Paolo Chiocchetti has a PhD in European Studies from King's College London. His research focuses on the transformation of Western European party systems, comparative politics, Italian politics, European governance, and socio-economic policy. He is the author of *The Radical Left Party Family in Western Europe, 1989–2015* (Routledge, 2017).

Bolesław Domański is Professor of Human Geography and Dean of the Faculty of Geography and Geology at the Jagiellonian University in Krakow, Poland.

His research focuses on issues of local and regional development, restructuring of industrial towns and regions, urban regeneration, post-socialist transformation, foreign direct investment, and regional policy.

Klaus Dörre is Chair for Labour, Industrial and Economic Sociology at the Friedrich Schiller University Jena, Germany, co-director of the DFG-Research Group on Post-Growth Societies, and co-editor of the journals *Berliner Journal für Soziologie* (BJS) and *Global Dialogue*. His research focuses on the theory of capitalism and of financial market capitalism, precarious employment, strategic unionism, digitalization, and right-wing populism. He is the author of *Capitalism and Labor: Towards Critical Perspectives* (Campus, 2018).

Jennifer Eschweiler is a Postdoctoral Researcher at Roskilde University, Denmark, where she works on the SOLIDUS project (solidush2020.eu). Her research focuses on solidarity, the third sector, deliberative democracy, and social movements.

Sacha Garben is Professor of EU Law at the College of Europe, Bruges, Belgium. Her recent research focuses on the constitutional and substantive aspects of the division of competences between the EU and the Member States and on the balance between social and economic interests in the EU legal and political order. She is the co-editor of *The Division of Competences between the EU and the Member States: Reflections on the Past, the Present and the Future* (Hart, 2017).

Lars Hulgård is Professor of Social Entrepreneurship at Roskilde University, Denmark. He is also founder and co-chair of the Centre for Social Entrepreneurship at Roskilde University, permanent Visiting Professor at the Tata Institute of Social Sciences in Mumbai, and co-founder of the EMES International Research Network. His research focuses on social entrepreneurship, the social economy, social innovation, and social policy. He is the co-editor of *Social Enterprise and the Third Sector: Changing European Landscapes in a Comparative Perspective* (Routledge, 2014).

Susana Muñoz is Research Scientist at the Faculty of Law, Economics and Finance at the University of Luxembourg. She holds a PhD in Law. Her current activities include teaching EU law and research focused on fundamental social rights in post-crisis Europe.

Laura Polverari is Senior Research Fellow at the European Policies Research Centre (EPRC), School of Government and Public Policy, University of Strathclyde, UK. Her research focuses on the design, implementation, and evaluation of public policy, EU cohesion policy, regional policy in Italy, administrative capacity and capacity-building, the mainstreaming of gender equality, cross-national policy transfer in regional and urban development, and public accountability. She is the co-editor of *Handbook on Cohesion Policy in the EU* (Edward Elgar, 2016).

Hicham Rassafi-Guibal holds a PhD in Public Law from the University of Valenciennes. His doctoral research explored the concept of economic evidence in French and European Public Law. His current research focuses on European administrative law and public economic law.

Francisco Torres is Visiting Senior Fellow in European Political Economy at the London School of Economics. He is also Visiting Professor at the Católica Lisbon School of Business & Economics and PEFM Associate at St Antony's College, University of Oxford, UK. His research focuses on international and European political economy. He is the co-editor of *Governance of the European Monetary Union* (Routledge, 2016).

Laurent Warlouzet is Professor of History at the Université du Littoral-Côte d'Opale, France. A specialist in the history of the European Union, he is the author of *Governing Europe in a Globalizing World: Neoliberalism and its Alternatives Following the 1973 Oil Crisis* (Routledge, 2018).

Acknowledgements

The present volume is the fruit of the research conducted in the framework of the RESuME project ('Ressources sur le modèle socio-économique européen'), a three-year research project of the Centre Virtuel de la Connaissance sur l'Europe (CVCE) and of the University of Luxembourg, led by Frédéric Allemand and co-financed by the Erasmus+ Programme of the European Union. The project was conceived to develop an innovative body of scholarship, scientific and educational resources, and digital tools on the European socio-economic model. Its results are openly accessible at https://resume.uni.lu.

This book would not have been possible without the invaluable work of the many people involved in the RESuME project, in particular: its core staff (Frédéric Allemand, Paolo Chiocchetti, Daniele Guido, Susana Muñoz, Hicham Rassafi-Guibal, and Alessia Virone); its support staff (Estelle Bunout, Sarah Cooper, Sergio De la Parra, and Karine Delval); its scientific committee (Susanna Cafaro, Kenneth Dyson, Jean-Marc Ferry, David Howarth, Manuel Lopez Escudero, Nikos Scandamis, and Blanche Sousi); its partners from the Sapienza University of Rome (Maria Felice Arezzo, Raimondo Manca, and Donatella Strangio), the Arendt House (Philippe-Emmanuel Partsch), and the Fondation IDEA (Muriel Bouchet and Michel-Edouard Ruben) in Luxembourg; the contributors to its other publications (especially Serge Allegrezza, José Caballero, Louis Chauvel, Mark Hunyadi, Juho Korhonen, Florent Legrand, Agnieszka McCaleb, Thomas Moretto, Laurence Potvin-Solis, Erik S. Reinert, and Igor Tkalec); and other collaborators. To all of them go our heartfelt thanks. We also gratefully acknowledge the generous financial and infrastructural support of the European Commission, of the CVCE, and of the University of Luxembourg.

Our biggest debt is to the 14 contributors of the volume, who have engaged with intellectual vigour and an open and critical spirit with the variety of disciplinary fields, national traditions, theoretical perspectives, and policy issues involved in the project. In addition, we and the contributors have greatly benefitted from the intellectual exchange with the invited scholars who took part in two international conferences at the University of Luxembourg: the workshop on 'European Competitiveness' on 29–30 March 2017 and the conference on 'Competitive Europe and the Transformation of the Welfare State' on 24 November 2017.

Finally, we would like to express a special thank you for their support, constructive feedback, and hard work to the series editors of the Routledge-UACES Contemporary European Studies book series, to Andrew Taylor and Sophie Iddamalgoda of Routledge, to the production team at Routledge and Wearset, to our copy-editor Susan Dunsmore, and to the anonymous reviewers of our book proposal.

Paolo Chiocchetti and Frédéric Allemand
Esch-sur-Alzette
25 October 2018

Abbreviations

AG	Advocate General
ANPAL	*Agenzia Nazionale per le Politiche Attive del Lavoro* (National Agency for Active Labour Market Policies)
ARS	Regional Health Agencies
ASEAN	Association of Southeast Asian Nations
BCG	Boston Consulting Group
BLI	Better Life Index
BRIC	Brazil, Russia, India, and China
CAP	Common Agricultural Policy
CEPS	Economic Committee for Health Products
CETA	Comprehensive Economic and Trade Agreement
CIPE	*Comitato Interministeriale per la Programmazione Economica*
CJEU	Court of Justice of the European Union
CLLD	community-led local development
CSF	Community Support Framework
DAX	*Deutscher Aktienindex*
DPS	*Dipartimento per lo Sviluppo e la Coesione Economica*
DRG	diagnosis-related group
EAEC	European Atomic Energy Community
EAFRD	European Agricultural Fund for Rural Development
EBIT	earnings before interests and taxes
EC	European Commission
ECB	European Central Bank
ECJ	European Court of Justice
ECSC	European Coal and Steel Community
EEC	European Economic Community
EESC	European Economic and Social Committee
EIB	European Investment Bank
EMFF	European Maritime and Fishery Fund
EMS	European Monetary System
EMU	Economic and Monetary Union
EPSCO	Employment, Social Policy, Health and Consumer Affairs (Council of the EU)

EPSR	European Pillar of Social Rights
ERDF	European Regional Development Fund
ESF	European Social Fund
ESIF, ESI Funds	European Structural and Investment Funds
ESM	European Stability Mechanism
EU	European Union
EU-15	the 15 Member States of the European Union before 2004
EU-28	the 28 Member States of the European Union since 2013
EVA	economic value added
FAS	Fund for the Underutilised Areas
FDI	foreign direct investment
FSC	*Fondo Sviluppo e Coesione*
FTA	free trade area
GATT	General Agreement on Tariffs and Trade
GDP	gross domestic product
GEMU	Genuine Economic and Monetary Union
GHM	*groupe homogène des malades*
GHS	*groupe homogène de séjour*
GHTs	*groupements hospitaliers territoriaux*
GVA	gross value added
ICT	information and communication technologies
IGRUE	General Inspectorate for the Management of Financial Relations with the EU
ILO	International Labour Organization
IMF	International Monetary Fund
ITI	Integrated Territorial Instrument
MERRIs	teaching, research, reference and innovation mission
MFA	Multi-Fibre Agreement
MIG	mission in the general interest
NIEO	New International Economic Order
NOP	National Operational Programme
NSRF	National Strategic Reference Framework
NUTS	Nomenclature of territorial units for statistics
NUVAP	*Nucleo di valutazione e analisi per la programmazione*
NUVEC	*Nucleo di verifica e controllo* (Verification and Control Unit)
OCA	optimum currency area
OECD	Organisation for Economic Co-operation and Development
OEEC	Organisation for European Economic Cooperation
OJ	*Official Journal* of the EU
OMC	Open Method of Coordination
OMT	outright monetary transactions
ONDAM	*Objectif national de dépenses d'assurance maladie*
OP	Operational Programme
PA	Partnership Agreement
PMSI	*Programme de médicalisation des systèmes d'information*

R&D	research and development
ROP	Regional Operational Programme
SE	solidarity economy
SEDA	Sustainable Economic Development Assessment
SGP	Stability and Growth Pact
T2A	*tarification à l'activité*
TEEC	Treaty establishing the European Economic Community
TEU	Treaty on European Union
TFEU	Treaty on the Functioning of the European Union
TNC	transnational corporation
TSCG	Treaty on Stability, Coordination and Governance in the Economic and Monetary Union
UK	United Kingdom of Great Britain and Northern Ireland
UN	United Nations
US, USA	United States of America
UVAL	evaluation unit
UVER	verification unit
WTO	World Trade Organization

1 Introduction

Paolo Chiocchetti and Frédéric Allemand

Since the 1980s, the intensification of economic competition (globalisation, rise of new industrial powers, European integration, liberalisation, privatisations) has been transforming the constraints and nature of public policy-making, while the language of competitiveness has been colonising the scholarly and popular discussion on business strategy, public policy, and public governance. Solidarity, as embodied in complex national systems of social protection, redistribution, and market-correcting regulation (such as the welfare state, taxation, industrial and regional policy, industrial relations, and the third sector), has had to adapt to this challenge. The result has been a progressive move from a 'protective and redistributive' towards a 'competitive and productive' form of solidarity (Streeck 1999), whose concrete content, however awkwardly, oscillates between a surrender to the logic of the markets and intelligent efforts to harness them for public goals. The Great Recession of 2007–09 and the subsequent Eurozone crisis have further exacerbated the pressure on national systems of solidarity, leading to massive social problems and wide-ranging reforms in the name of competitiveness.

These global trends, and their implications for European societies, are the object of an immense body of literature, including some excellent recent interdisciplinary (Crespy and Menz 2015; Dølvik and Martin 2014; Schiek 2013; Vandenbroucke *et al.* 2018) and specialist (Barbier *et al.* 2015; Countouris and Freedland 2013; De la Porte and Heins 2016; Matthijs and Blyth 2015; Moreau 2011; Talani 2016) overviews. Two important aspects, however, are insufficiently explored in the relevant scholarship. The first is the role played by the theories and discourses of competitiveness in the transformation of public policy-making, which is more often tackled from the point of view of economic and institutional constraints or of ideational change rooted in neo-liberal or third-way ideas. The second is an explicit discussion of the variety of different, and often contradictory, ways in which the relationship between competitiveness and solidarity can be conceptualised in theory and embodied in practices.

The present volume sets itself the task of starting to fill these gaps and to provide an interdisciplinary and pluralist investigation of the interplay between competitiveness and solidarity from both a theoretical and an empirical or policy-oriented point of view. Its scope will be limited to developments and debates within the territory of the European Union. This choice is due to the particularly developed nature of European economies, of European systems of social regulation and protection, and of European regional integration, a fact which enables the study of the tensions and synergies between competitiveness and solidarity in their most advanced state. The chapters will thus include theoretical investigations, analyses of EU, national, and regional policies (and of their interaction), and case studies of developments in the EU as a whole, in its Member States, and in specific regions. It is our intention to contribute to a richer understanding of the concepts of competitiveness, of solidarity, and of their relationship, and we will shed new light on various aspects of social life and policy-making in contemporary European societies.

Competitiveness and solidarity in theory

The idea of solidarity has a long history. The term was introduced into the social sciences and the humanities in the 1840s from an older legal meaning, it gradually gained the upper hand over the closely related terms of Christian love, civic friendship, and revolutionary brotherhood, and ultimately became a key concept in scholarly and political discussions on ethics, political philosophy, social analysis, and social and economic policy. Its importance derives from the widespread belief that the natural evolution of modern societies, if left to their own devices, is bound to produce unacceptable levels of inequality, exclusion, and anomie and, ultimately, a breakdown of social order; to prevent this outcome, individuals, social groups, and states must introduce protective and compensatory measures to control the untrammelled workings of the capitalist mode of production, of competition, and of individualism. The idea of solidarity, thus, has gradually come to serve as the normative justification and the synthetic cover for a large variety of attitudes, behaviours, policies, mechanisms, and systems. These include, notably: individual altruism and mutual aid; the promotion of intermediate groups (e.g. families, churches, voluntary associations, trade unions, cooperatives, and political parties); the creation of complex systems of social protection and redistribution (e.g. family support, clientelism, charity and philanthropy, mutualism, and welfare states); the implementation of public policies; and the production and socialisation of values, beliefs, norms and ideologies (e.g. human, civil, and social rights, civic religion, nationalism, and socialism).

The idea of competitiveness is much more recent, but equally relevant to public policy. The term was first mentioned around 1916 but was rarely used before the Second World War. In the 1950s and the 1960s, it gained some popularity in the analysis of international trade and related policies. In the 1980s and the 1990s, finally, it was developed into a key concept for the analysis of any kind of public policy issue and its use became ubiquitous in both scholarly and popular publications. As will be shown in Chapter 2, this polysemic term hides three distinct and potentially contradictory meanings. The first meaning of the term, *competitiveness as competition or rivalry*, directly connects it with the above-mentioned concern of economics, the social sciences, political philosophy and beyond: the very same problematic that caused the emergence of the idea of solidarity in the first place as a counterweight to social injustice and disintegration. The second meaning of the term, *competitiveness as relative performance*, allows it to latch onto a myriad of technical debates aimed at identifying the most effective mechanisms, strategies, and contexts ensuring the success of an individual, a firm, a territory, or an institution in the competitive struggle. The third meaning of the term, *competitiveness as absolute performance*, emerged in the 1990s as a reaction to the negative associations of the other two meanings and gives competitiveness entry into a further fundamental area of the economic and socio-political scholarship (welfare, development, modernisation).

Given these premises, it is no wonder that question of the relationship between competitiveness and solidarity has been gaining traction in scholarly debates on the most diverse kinds of theoretical problems, societal developments, and public policy issues. With reference to international trade and globalisation, the desire to improve the competitive position of a given firm, industry or territory is often met with accusations of unfair competition and lack of concern for the consequences on weaker foreign countries (e.g. dumping, beggar-thy-neighbour policies, deindustrialisation, unequal development, race to the bottom in social and environmental standards); moreover, the overall economic benefits of increased competitive interaction are highly concentrated and leave behind substantial groups of 'losers' in need of protection or compensation. With reference to social policy, the pressure of global competition is one of the main drivers of the transformation of the welfare state (together with political choices and structural factors, such as population ageing, the feminisation of the workforce, tertiarisation, lower growth, looser family structures, higher unemployment, and precariousness); in this domain, a satisfactory balance between alleviating the fiscal burden on the competitiveness of firms (low taxation) and enhancing national solidarity (high social provisions) is hard to find. With reference to economic policy, the solidarity-enhancing measures typical of the post-war boom and of its aftermath (e.g. rising wages and social standards, fiscal redistribution, Keynesian public spending, state-led industrialisation, economic planning, financial repression) are less and less common, allowing economic inequality and social exclusion to rise in developed economies. With reference to individual and group behaviour, the pressures of intense competition may give rise to social pathologies, protective counter-movements, and exclusionary or aggressive ideologies. More generally, the tension between competitiveness and solidarity plays out across virtually all policy domains, as the promotion of competition and relative performance in management, infrastructure, public administration, foreign policy, education, culture, and so on may conflict with the imperatives of solidarity and undermine the cohesion of social groups and societies as a whole.

In defining the relationship between competitiveness and solidarity, the literature is essentially divided into two main camps. The first camp argues that competitiveness and solidarity are fundamentally contradictory: pursuing the former means neglecting the latter, and vice versa. For some authors (Arnsperger 2011; Petrella 1996), the competitiveness embodied in possessive individualism, group rivalry, free market capitalism, and globalisation undermines solidarity and corrodes social ties. The competition between individuals, firms, groups, and nations naturally creates winners and losers: solidarity must kick in to protect and compensate the latter. Moreover, competition may lead to undesirable forms of interaction (e.g. overexertion, extreme egoism, or immoral strategies) or outcomes (e.g. the mutual destruction of the competitors): solidarity-based regulations must intervene to ensure a 'fair' and productive game. Finally, competition may be inefficient: alternative forms of social interaction such as bottom-up cooperation or top-down organisation, besides being far more in tune with the spirit of solidarity, may even lead to superior outcomes. For other authors (Hayek 1960; Hunt 2000), conversely, the pursuit of individual interest and the competition between autonomous individuals are both the moral basis of a free society and the source of its material wealth and overall development. Intrusive solidarity-inspired constraints to competition are therefore considered both economically ill-advised and morally unjustified, except for those geared at ensuring the continued functioning of the system itself (e.g. a legal system protecting personal freedom and property rights, the enforcement of some basic rules of the game, a minimal safety net for the losers). For most authors, finally, the question becomes one of maintaining an (unstable) acceptable compromise between the two principles (Garben 2017; Stjernø 2005; Streeck 1999).

The second camp, instead, argues that competitiveness and solidarity are actually mutually reinforcing: pursuing the former means automatically strengthening the latter, and vice versa. On the one hand, a standard argument in the economic and policy literature is that more economic competition should lead to a higher level of productivity, innovation, and economic growth, thereby increasing the resources potentially available for solidarity-inspired redistribution (e.g. higher wages, improving social standards, a more generous welfare state). On the other hand, solidarity may be used as a lever to improve the external competitiveness of a system. Growing wages can stimulate productivity by raising workers' motivation and efficiency (Murphy and Topel 1990), by encouraging the introduction of labour-saving technologies (Storm and Naastepad 2013), and by boosting aggregate demand, which in turn is conducive to economies of scale and innovation (Verdoorn 2002). A developed welfare state may have the same effect, as it improves the quality of the labour force (e.g. through healthcare and education), it ensures the survival and continued integration of citizens temporarily not employed but who may be needed in the future (e.g. through unemployment benefits and basic incomes), it reduces crime and social tensions, and it serves a macroeconomic stabilisation function (Gough 1996). Specific social policies geared at enhancing skills, raising employment and labour participation, and reducing social exclusion can be understood as 'social investment', which pays over time in terms of increased productivity and economic growth (Morel *et al.* 2012). More generally, inclusion and relative equality may lead to purposely cohesive firms and societies, with beneficial effects on their competitive potential.

Competitiveness and solidarity in the European Union

In the European Union, the relationship between competitiveness and solidarity has gradually come to dominate the political and policy debates over the last three decades, flanking older conceptual couplets such as freedom and equality, individual rights and the public interest, national interest and supranational cooperation, economic growth and social cohesion (Jepsen and Serrano Pascual 2005), liberalisation and social regulation (Scharpf 2010), or the market and the social (Garben 2017). These two concepts, however, are explicitly or implicitly deployed in a variety of different and often contradictory ways.

In the two core EU Treaties, the Treaty on European Union (TEU) and the Treaty on the Functioning of the European Union (TFEU), since the 1990s, both competitiveness and solidarity have progressively achieved the status of important programmatic principles, although their value as legally justiciable norms vary. The noun 'competitiveness', always used in the sense of competitive success, was first mentioned in the 1992 Maastricht Treaty and now appears in six articles of the consolidated version of the two treaties. The adjective 'competitive', mostly used in the sense of degree of competition, has been present since the 1951 Treaty of Paris and now appears in eight articles. The noun 'solidarity', which usually refers to the mutual behaviour of Member States, was only present in the TEEC preamble before the 1992 Maastricht Treaty but can now be found in 12 articles or preambles; solidarity towards disadvantaged citizens is usually given other names (social cohesion, development, progress, protection, or security). Particularly interesting are two articles. Art. 3 TEU lists the goals of the European Union as follows, prescribing a balance between the economic and the social, the market and social progress, and competitiveness and solidarity:

> The Union shall establish an internal market. It shall work for the sustainable development of Europe based on balanced economic growth and price stability, a highly competitive social market economy, aiming at full employment and social progress, and a high level of protection and improvement of the quality of the environment. It shall promote scientific and technological advance. It shall combat social exclusion and discrimination, and shall promote social justice and protection, equality between women and men, solidarity between generations and protection of the rights of the child. It shall promote economic, social and territorial cohesion, and solidarity among Member States.…

Art. 151 TFEU, in turn, explicitly frames the question of wages and social protection in terms of a compromise between social rights and competitiveness constraints:

> The Community and the Member States, having in mind fundamental social rights such as those set out in the European Social Charter signed at Turin on 18 October 1961 and in the 1989 Community Charter of the Fundamental

> Social Rights of Workers, shall have as their objectives the promotion of employment, improved living and working conditions, so as to make possible their harmonisation while the improvement is being maintained, proper social protection, dialogue between management and labour, the development of human resources with a view to lasting high employment and the combating of exclusion. To this end the Community and the Member States shall implement measures which take account of the diverse forms of national practices, in particular in the field of contractual relations, and the need to maintain the competitiveness of the Community economy. They believe that such a development will ensue not only from the functioning of the common market, which will favour the harmonisation of social systems, but also from the procedures provided for in this Treaty and from the approximation of provisions laid down by law, regulation or administrative action.

Detailed legal analyses of the role played by solidarity in EU law abound (Müller 2010; Sangiovanni 2013); a comprehensive legal analysis of the role played in EU law by competitiveness, instead, has yet to be written.

The economic strategies produced by the European Union over the last three decades are also centred on the goal of simultaneously enhancing European competitiveness and solidarity. In 1993, the White Paper on 'Growth, competitiveness, employment' already sought to combine the pursuit of competition, growth, and social protection (EC 1993). In 2000, the Lisbon Strategy was presented as a 'positive strategy which combines competitiveness and social cohesion' and set the strategic goal for the EU of becoming 'the most competitive and dynamic knowledge-based economy in the world capable of sustainable economic growth with more and better jobs and greater social cohesion' (European Council 2000). In 2010, in turn, the Europe 2020 Strategy was portrayed as 'a strategy for smart, sustainable and inclusive growth' and set three mutually reinforcing priorities for the EU: 'Smart growth: developing an economy based on knowledge and innovation. Sustainable growth: promoting a more resource-efficient, greener and more competitive economy. Inclusive growth: fostering a high-employment economy delivering social and territorial cohesion' (EC 2010). Both strategies were inspired by a vision that we can summarise as 'competitive solidarity', seeing improved competitiveness as a necessary precondition for the maintain of the European welfare state and considering social investment (notably in employability, education, and social inclusion) as an important resource – beyond innovation, competition, fiscal consolidation, infrastructural investment, and a favourable business climate – to raise the relative and absolute performance of the European economy (Copeland and Papadimitriou 2012; Zeitlin and Vanhercke 2018).

The Eurozone crisis led to a renewed attention by European states and institutions to competitiveness, but to the clear detriment of national solidarity. Competitiveness differentials between euro area countries measured by current account balances, relative inflation rates, relative unit labour costs, or relative productivities obsessively dominated public discussion (Draghi 2012). The 2011 Euro Plus Pact (originally called the 'Competitiveness Pact'), geared at achieving a 'stronger economic policy for competitiveness and convergence', similarly saw the main road to restore competitiveness in a (relative) reduction of wages and social expenses in the countries living beyond their own means. Meanwhile, financial assistance programmes and overall reforms of the framework of European economic governance institutionalised the policy orientation of radical fiscal tightening ('austerity') and 'structural reforms', which again generally resulted in a compression of prices, wages, labour protection, and welfare provisions in most Eurozone countries (Agostini *et al.* 2017; Allemand *et al.* 2016; De la Porte and Heins 2016; Wallace 2015).

European solidarity is routinely invoked in the discussion of existing EU policies or of reform proposals in direct opposition to narrow national self-interest and egoism. On Eurozone reform, economically stronger countries are urged to accept a degree of solidarity in the form of common risk-sharing and fiscal mechanisms to support and complement responsible national policies aimed at restoring fiscal discipline and competitiveness (Van Rompuy *et al.* 2012). When discussing the EU budget, poorer countries generally push for a larger and more 'social' budget while richer countries prefer a stronger focus on competitiveness-related expenditures such as research and infrastructural investment (Hix and Høyland 2011; Laffan and Lindner 2015). On asylum, finally, countries hosting many asylum-seekers plead for their 'redistribution' in the name of solidarity while countries hosting few of them oppose such plans in the name of the law (Dublin II) or of national interest (Müller 2015).

Finally, social and political actors in all fields and in all countries (academics, practitioners, policy-makers, ministries and agencies, research centres, judges, political parties, professional associations, interest groups, etc.) naturally compete to push forward their own specific notions of competitiveness, solidarity, their best indicators, their appropriate balance, and their productive reconciliation in innovative policy designs.

In general terms, the antagonistic or mutually reinforcing interaction between competitiveness and solidarity plays out in three major domains within the European Union: (1) European and national competitiveness imperatives and policies affect the degree of *national solidarity*, often resulting in pressures for a compression of existing levels of social protection and provisions; (2) the desire to strengthen *intra-European solidarity*, notably through the achievement of greater socio-economic convergence of territories, improved policy coordination, and deeper pooling of competences, is confronted by the desire of each nation state and sub-national unit to enhance its own competitiveness (relative performance); and (3) the improvement of the overall competitiveness of the European economy may lead to positive or negative consequences for the rest of the world, thereby affecting *extra-European solidarity*. In each of these domains, the concrete interplay between competitiveness and solidarity may lead to dangerous imbalances, acceptable compromises, or virtuous circles.

Structure of the book

To explore the above-mentioned issues in detail, we have brought together a pluralist and interdisciplinary team of European experts on competitiveness and solidarity from various areas of the social sciences and the humanities. The authors have been asked to investigate the ways in which competitiveness and solidarity are conceptualised and concretely interact in different disciplinary traditions, policy domains, and historical contexts. The result is a mixture of theoretical and practical case studies addressing many burning issues of the contemporary European policy and political debate.

In Chapter 2, 'Competitiveness, solidarity, and their relationship: a theoretical framework', Paolo Chiocchetti provides a novel theoretical framework for the analysis of competitiveness, solidarity, and their relationship. A comprehensive analysis of the fortune, conceptual history, and meaning of the terms 'competitiveness' and 'solidarity' shows that, while the latter has different but complementary meanings, the former has three independent and contradictory faces: competition, relative performance, and absolute performance. This fact has important repercussions on the relationship between competitiveness and solidarity, which can be conceptualised as antagonistic, as mutually reinforcing, and even as coinciding. Awareness of this conceptual complexity is essential for both theoretical research and empirical and policy-oriented analysis

In Chapter 3, 'European competitiveness: competition, cooperation, solidarity', Frédéric Allemand discusses the implications for public policy-making of the progressive adoption – from the 1980s onwards – of a competitiveness-centred paradigm by all major states around the world. Primarily a response to a changed international economic environment (globalisation, European integration, the rise of new industrial powers, economic stagnation, fears over the sustainability of the welfare state), this embrace did not mark the retreat to a minimal state and the end of public policy but meant, on the contrary, the reconfiguration and 'revitalisation' of public action within the constraints of a liberal economy. Within the European Union, this process also involved a partial transferral of macro-economic policies at the European level and the requirement for stronger coordination between countries and levels of governance. The economic success and political sustainability of this strategy, however, rest on its ability to guarantee an effective balance between competition, cooperation, and solidarity.

In Chapter 4, 'Competitiveness and solidarity in the history of the European Union, 1957–2017', Laurent Warlouzet provides a broad historical overview of the interplay between competitiveness and solidarity in the evolution of socio-economic policies in the EEC/EU since its creation in 1957, identifying three major types of policy orientation: (1) social-oriented; (2) neo-mercantilist; and (3) market-oriented. The three models have coexisted over time in a shifting and dynamic balance. The chapter charts their evolution across five main historical phases: (1) 'embedded liberalism'; (2) 'the shock of the global'; (3) the 'Single Market' period; (4) the 'end of history'; and (5) 'the crisis of Western globalization'. Although the weight of market-oriented and neo-liberal policies has dramatically risen since the mid-1980s, reactions to the current economic crisis, which has been lingering since 2007–08, may again shift the balance in unexpected directions.

In Chapter 5, 'Competition, cooperation, and solidarity in EU law: a federal perspective', Sacha Garben explores the role played by competition, cooperation, and solidarity in federal legal frameworks in general, and in the 'federal' legal order of the European Union, in particular. She shows that concrete legal outcomes with regard to the balance between competition and solidarity do not derive from the abstractly 'cooperative' or 'competitive' nature of the federal model, but rather from its specific constitutional configuration and substantive competences. The EU legal order, in particular, not only creates destabilising conflicts between solidarity and competition but often decides them in favour of the latter. This undesirable and unsustainable imbalance should be corrected through a reform programme informed by a two-step 'reciprocity-based solidarity' framework.

In Chapter 6, 'Harnessing competitiveness for social and ecological goals: high-road competitiveness is necessary and feasible', Karl Aiginger argues for a conceptualisation of competitiveness as the ability to achieve broad economic, social, and ecological goals and details the advantages of 'high-road' economic strategies based on innovation, skills, product quality, the embrace of markets and of 'responsible globalisation', and the active compensation/retraining of the 'losers' of competition. An alternative both to a narrow focus on price competition and to a populist retreat towards economic nationalism, the new perspective of 'competitiveness 4.0' can reconcile economic growth, solidarity, and ecological sustainability, helping the European Union to move forward towards a more prosperous and fairer future.

In Chapter 7, 'The social and solidarity economy sector: a bottom-up alternative?', Jennifer Eschweiler and Lars Hulgård summarise the history, theoretical foundations, and broader implication of the social and solidarity economy. Developing beside, beyond, or – for its radical supporters – against state and market, this multifaceted sector has been attracting increasing interest since the 2008 economic crisis. Its 'constructed solidarity', based on voluntary initiative, reciprocity, democratic participation, and original forms of economic production and consumption, makes it an interesting bottom-up alternative to both market-based competition and bureaucratic solidarity. This potential, however, can only be realised by a combination of a supportive institutional environment and of pressures from below.

In Chapter 8, 'Social capitalism is a thing of the past: competition-driven *Landnahme* and the metamorphosis of the German Model', Klaus Dörre surveys the recent metamorphosis of the 'German Model'. He argues that, during the 1990s and the 2000s, a process of competition-driven *Landnahme* – a kind of ceaselessly repeated primitive accumulation – transformed the nature of the German economy from a paradigmatic example of Fordist 'social capitalism' to an export-oriented capitalism based on 'competitive solidarity'. The main features of this transformation are, domestically, the dispossession and selective integration of the workforce in a 'precarious full-employment society', and externally, the establishment of a half-hegemonic economic dominance which exacerbates European asymmetries. For the German working class, this shift meant a radical change in material conditions, subjectivity (notably, with the development of forms of 'exclusive solidarity'), and forms of industrial regulation and conflict, challenging traditional perspectives of both trade union work and labour sociology.

In Chapter 9, 'Competitiveness in public hospitals: the case of France', Hicham Rassafi-Guibal explores the paradoxical problem of competitiveness in French public hospitals, where the provision of a quality, universal health care is traditionally understood as a public service based on the fundamental right to health and the notion of national solidarity. This notwithstanding, public hospitals increasingly are finding themselves exposed to internal and external competitive pressures and pushed by legislators and regulatory authorities to increase efficiency, thereby reducing their costs. This creates tensions but also interesting compromises, and it may have contributed to the evolution of the concept of competitiveness towards a more inclusive logic.

In Chapter 10, 'Competitive solidarity and regional development: the case of Italy', Laura Polverari examines the interplay between competitive solidarity and regional development through the case study of the Italian *Mezzogiorno*. In response to a persistent lagging behind of Southern regions, the Italian state (since the late 1940s) and the European Union (since the 1970s) have deployed regional policies of varying intensity, focus, and institutional design. These have benefitted the *Mezzogiorno* with important flows of public investment and social spending, but they have failed to reduce its developmental gap in relation to the rest of the country. The main causes of this failure are multiple, including the overall weakness of national development over the last decades, insufficient resources, the lack of linkages with wider supporting policies and reforms, policy design flaws, political problems, and a weak administrative capacity.

In Chapter 11, 'Competitive solidarity and regional development: the case of Poland', Bolesław Domański examines the interplay between competitive solidarity and regional development through the case study of Polish regions. As in Italy, the relative gap between metropolitan areas and the historically underdeveloped Eastern regions continues to widen. Contrary to Italy, however, the growing competitiveness of the Polish economy since 1993 massively enhanced economic prosperity and social welfare in all regions, leading to a gradual convergence with Western European countries in economic, social, and environmental terms. The Polish experience shows both the path dependency of territorial development, reproduced in the interaction between historical patterns and new opportunities, and the advantages of FDI- and export-led growth strategies for low- and middle-income countries. In addition, it shows that territorial differences in non-material aspects of social well-being are easier to correct than those in material aspects; as a consequence, regional policy should focus less on promoting local economic development and more on supporting local well-being, including via the integration of weaker areas with dynamic centres through increased connectivity and mobility.

In Chapter 12, 'The road towards a genuine Economic and Monetary Union: more competitive and fairer', Annette Bongardt and Francisco Torres assess the evolution of Economic and Monetary Union (EMU) and its chances of becoming a 'genuine' EMU (GEMU), thus reconciling competitiveness and solidarity. The creation of Economic and Monetary Union (EMU) in the 1990s triggered a qualitative change in European integration, but its functioning remains unsatisfactory and vulnerable to external shocks. While structural reforms and ownership-building at the national level are essential, they need to be guided by a broader and more balanced reform narrative. The authors therefore argue that the sustainability and continued development of both the Eurozone and the European Union hinge on further reform of EMU, inspired by a future-oriented, fairer, and more democratic European socio-economic model.

In Chapter 13, 'Striking a balance between competitiveness and social fairness: what can we expect from the European Pillar of Social Rights?', Susana Muñoz discusses the emergence, nature, and implications of the European Pillar of Social Rights, a new legal instrument of the European Union geared at moving towards a fairer and more socially balanced model of European competitiveness. Announced in November 2017, the Pillar lacks legally binding force and perhaps ambition, and its implementation rests on the premise of a converging political will and close collaboration of EU, national, regional, and local levels of governance. Despite these problems, its 'integrated, dynamic, and action-oriented approach' has the potential to build momentum for change and to lead to a significant strengthening of the EU's social dimension.

In Chapter 14, 'Conclusion', Paolo Chiocchetti and Frédéric Allemand summarise the main theoretical, methodological, and empirical findings of the volume and discuss their broader implications.

Conclusion

The contributions in the present edited book – in-depth analyses of specific theoretical or empirical problems, written by leading scholars of different disciplines in the social sciences and the humanities in a spirit of interdisciplinary dialogue – shed new light on the way in which competitiveness is transforming contemporary European societies, on the nature of the relationship between competitiveness and solidarity, and on how this relationship concretely plays out across policy domains and historical and geographical cases. They will therefore be of interest both to specialists in European Union Studies, EU Law, Public Policy, Economics and Political Economy, Sociology, Political Science, Geography, and Contemporary History and to a general readership passionate about the state of the European Union and of contemporary European societies.

The evidence and arguments presented throughout the book also have distinctive broader policy and political implications. Has competitiveness been pursued too far, fatally undermining the fairness, cohesion, and sustainability of our socio-economic systems? Should competition and competitiveness be rolled back in the name of solidarity? Which kind of balance between competitiveness and solidarity is desirable and feasible? Or, on the contrary, can European societies simultaneously become *more competitive and more solidary*? The answer to these questions depends, of course, not only on technical considerations (the nature of the issue at hand, the design of specific policy solutions, a trade-off analysis), but also on each individual politically and philosophically informed vision of the 'good society'.

References

Agostini, Chiara, Valentina Lisi, David Natali, and Sebastiano Sabato (2017). *Balancing protection and investment: structural reform in five countries.* Brussels: ETUI.

Allemand, Fréderic, Mathieu Bion, and Jean-Luc Sauron (2016). *Gouverner la zone euro après la crise: l'exigence d'intégration.* Paris: Gualino.

Arnsperger, Christian (2011). 'No competition without solidarity? The normative frameworks for analyzing the fairness of competition', *Ethical Perspectives* 18(3): 355–83.

Barbier, Jean-Claude, Ralf Rogowski, and Fabrice Colomb (eds) (2015). *The sustainability of the European Social Model.* Cheltenham: Edward Elgar.

Copeland, Paul and Dimitris Papadimitriou (eds) (2012). *The EU's Lisbon Strategy: evaluating success, understanding failure*. Basingstoke: Palgrave Macmillan.

Countouris, Nicola and Mark Freedland (eds) (2013). *Resocialising Europe in a time of crisis.* Cambridge: Cambridge University Press.

Crespy, Amandine and Georg Menz (eds) (2015). *Social policy and the Eurocrisis: quo vadis social Europe?* London: Palgrave Macmillan.

De la Porte, Caroline and Elke Heins (eds) (2016). *The sovereign debt crisis, the EU and welfare state reform.* London: Palgrave Macmillan.

Dølvik, Jon Eric and Andrew Martin (eds) (2014). *European social models from crisis to crisis: employment and inequality in the era of monetary integration.* Oxford: Oxford University Press.

Draghi, Mario (2012). Competitiveness of the euro area and within the euro area. Speech, Paris, 13 March. Available at: www.ecb.europa.eu/press/key/date/2012/html/sp120313.en.html

EC (European Commission) (1993). 'Growth, competitiveness, employment: the challenges and ways forward into the 21st century', White Paper. COM(93) 700. Brussels: European Commission.

EC (European Commission) (2010). 'Europe 2020: a strategy for smart, sustainable and inclusive growth', Communication from the Commission. COM(2010) 2020 final. Brussels: European Commission.

European Council (2000). 'Presidency Conclusions'. Lisbon European Council, 23 and 24 March 2000. Available at: www.europarl.europa.eu/summits/lis1_en.htm

Garben, Sacha (2017). 'The constitutional (im)balance between "the Market" and "the Social" in the European Union', *European Constitutional Law Review* 13(1): 23–61.

Gough, Ian (1996). 'Social welfare and competitiveness', *New Political Economy* 1(2): 209–32.

Hayek, Friedrich A. von (1960). *The constitution of liberty.* Chicago: University of Chicago Press.

Hix, Simon and Bjørn Høyland (2011). 'Expenditure policies', in Simon Hix and Bjørn Høyland, *The political system of the European Union.* 3rd edn. Basingstoke: Palgrave Macmillan.

Hunt, Shelby D. (2000). *A general theory of competition: resource, competences, productivity, economic growth.* London: SAGE.

Jepsen, Maria and Amparo Serrano Pascual (2005). 'The European Social Model: an exercise in deconstruction', *Journal of European Social Policy* 15(3): 231–45.

Laffan, Brigid and Johannes Lindner (2015). 'The budget. Who gets what, when, and how?', in Helen Wallace, Mark Pollack, and Alasdair Young (eds). *Policy-making in the European Union*. 7th edn. Oxford: Oxford University Press, 220–42.

Matthijs, Matthias and Mark Blyth (eds) (2015). *The future of the Euro*. Oxford: Oxford University Press.

Moreau, Marie-Ange (ed.) (2011). *Before and after the economic crisis: what implications for the 'European Social Model'?* Cheltenham: Edward Elgar.

Morel, Nathalie, Bruno Palier, and Joakim Palme (2012). *Towards a social investment welfare state? Ideas, policies and challenges*. Bristol: Policy Press.

Müller, Andreas T. (2010). 'Solidarität als Rechtsbegriff im Europarecht', in Clemens Sedmak (ed.). *Solidarität: vom Wert der Gemeinschaft*. Darmstadt: Wissenschaftliche Buchgesellschaft, 77–104.

Müller, Andreas T. (2015). 'Solidarität in der gemeinsamen europäischen Asylpolitik', *Zeitschrift für öffentliches Recht* 70(2): 463–89.

Murphy, Kevin M. and Robert H. Topel (1990). 'Efficiency wages reconsidered: theory and evidence', in Yoram Weiss and Gideon Fishelson (eds), *Advances in the theory and measurement of unemployment*. London: Palgrave Macmillan, 204–40.

Petrella, Riccardo (1996). *Le bien commun. Éloge de la solidarité*. Charleroi: Éditions Labor.

Sangiovanni, Andrea (2013). 'Solidarity in the European Union', *Oxford Journal of Legal Studies* 33(2): 213–41.

Scharpf, Fritz W. (2010). 'The socio-economic asymmetries of European integration: or why the EU cannot be a "social market economy"', *European Social Analysis* 10: 1–8.

Schiek, Dagmar (ed.) (2013). *The EU economic and social model in the global crisis: interdisciplinary perspectives*. London: Routledge.

Stjernø, Steinar (2005). *Solidarity in Europe: the history of an idea*. Cambridge: Cambridge University Press.

Storm, Servaas and C.W.M. Naastepad (2013). 'Wage-led or profit-led supply: wages, productivity and investment', in Marc Lavoie and Engelbert Stockhammer (eds). *Wage-led growth: an equitable strategy for economic recovery*. Geneva: ILO, 100–24.

Streeck, Wolfgang (1999). 'Competitive solidarity: rethinking the "European Social Model"', MPIfG Working Paper 99/8. Köln: Max-Planck-Institut für Gesellschaftsforschung.

Talani, Leila (ed.) (2016). *Europe in crisis: a structural analysis*. London: Palgrave Macmillan.

Vandenbroucke, Frank, Catherine Barnard, and Geert De Baere (eds) (2018). *A European Social Union after the crisis*. Cambridge: Cambridge University Press.

Van Rompuy, Herman, José Manuel Barroso, Jean-Claude Juncker, and Mario Draghi (2012). 'Towards a genuine Economic and Monetary Union ("Four Presidents' Report")'. Available at: www.consilium.europa.eu/media/23818/134069.pdf

Verdoorn, Petrus J. (2002). 'On the factors determining the growth of labor productivity', in John McCombie, Maurizio Pugno, and Bruno Soro (eds). *Productivity growth and economic performance: essays on Verdoorn's law*. London: Palgrave Macmillan, 28–36.

Wallace, Paul (2015). *The Euro experiment*. Cambridge: Cambridge University Press.

Zeitlin, Jonathan and Bart Vanhercke (2018). 'Socializing the European Semester: EU social and economic policy co-ordination in crisis and beyond', *Journal of European Public Policy* 25(2): 149–74.

2 Competitiveness, solidarity, and their relationship

A theoretical framework

Paolo Chiocchetti

This chapter provides a novel theoretical framework for the analysis of competitiveness, solidarity, and their relationship. The first section discusses the fortune, conceptual history, and meanings of the concept of competitiveness, showing that it has three contradictory faces (competitiveness as competition, as relative performance, and as absolute performance). The resulting tensions are theoretically brought to coherence by a 'mainstream' interpretation, but they remain fully operative in real-world situations. The second section discusses the fortune, conceptual history, and meanings of the concept of solidarity, showing that its various connotations are largely compatible. The third section explores the relationship between competitiveness and solidarity, showing that this can be conceptualised in divergent ways: as antagonistic, as mutually reinforcing, and as coinciding. This variety of solutions has important policy implications: in most situations, however, the two concepts do conflict to some degree, and a (productive) balance between the two must be sought.

Competitiveness

Conceptual history

No systematic enquiry into the origin and development of the term *competitiveness* exists in the literature. Its etymology is relatively clear, but neither the date of first use nor detailed discussion of its usage is available. According to the Online Etymology Dictionary (Harper 2017), the noun was derived at an unknown date from the adjective 'competitive' (first attested in 1826) and, via English (competition, around 1600; to compete, 1610) and possibly Middle French (*compéter*, fourteenth century), from the Latin *compĕto* ('come together', 'strive together', 'rival'). Knowledge on its later development is similarly scant. Most scholars of competitiveness suggest an occasional use in the 1960s, followed by a boom in popularity in the 1980s and 1990s (Chopplet 2007; Eagleton-Pierce 2016). Belabes (1999), in his detailed discussion of competitiveness debates in the United States, backdates the initial use of the term to the immediate aftermath of the Second World War; however, no information on the pre-First World War period is provided. Altogether, both review and original research articles tend to focus on the evolution of a distinctively economic concept of competitiveness first developed by economists and management scholars and later imported into neighbouring fields such as political economy, economic geography, public policy, and governance, ignoring the multiplicity of alternative uses of the term in other contexts and disciplines. Finally, assessments of the rising fortune of the term remain vague and impressionistic.

A preliminary analysis of the appearance of the noun 'competitiveness' in the four largest databases of English-language scholarly and popular publications (Web of Science, Google Scholar, Google Books, and Google Ngram)[1] sheds new light on the fortune and conceptual development of the term.

The term was possibly introduced into the English language during the First World War. Its first verified appearance in the databases is in a 1916 scientific article by the American psychologist Herman H. Young (1916: 16).[2] Early occurrences seem to be not conscious word creations but extemporaneous nominalisations of the adjective 'competitive', which featured prominently in both scholarly and popular discourse throughout the nineteenth century. Its introduction with reference to microeconomic and trade questions (Wolfe 1919: 32–5), however, may also have been inspired by the German usage, where *Konkurrenzfähigkeit* is already attested in the 1850s and *Wettbewerbsfähigkeit* in the 1890s (Born 1850; Sympher 1900).

The history of the term can be divided into three broad stages. In the first half of the twentieth century, the term was sparsely used by psychologists and economists to express a variety of facts related to competition. Four distinct meanings can be singled out. Young (1916: 160), discussing the psychological development of children, defines it as 'spirit of competition or rivalry'. Wolfe (1919: 32–5) broadly equates it with the 'ability to compete in the international trade'. Hicks and Allen (1934: 59) employ it to describe the degree of competition and substitutability extant between two commodities, following Edgeworth's distinction between rival and complementary goods. Stigler (1942: 2), finally, uses it to indicate the actual degree of competition present in a market or economy, its position in the continuum ranging from 'perfect competition to perfect monopoly'. These meanings gained some currency in their specialist fields, but the popularity of the term remained altogether low.

From the 1950s to the 1970s, the term acquired conceptual depth and a systematic use in the field of international economics, where it was employed by scholars (Balassa 1962; Fleming and Tsiang 1956; Hirsch 1967; Kravis and Lipsey 1971; McGeehan 1968; Tyszynski 1951) and policy-makers (Belabes 1999) to define the relative performance of industries and countries in exports or foreign trade. The use of the term also grew in other fields, such as psychology (Argote *et al.* 1976), political science (Almond and Coleman 1961), and biology (Fried 1971), where it continued instead to refer to the degree of competition in a system or to the positive attitude towards competition of an actor.

From the 1980s onward, finally, the trade-related concept of competitiveness progressively broadened its meaning and its popularity boomed among scholars and policy-makers in a variety of disciplinary fields. Three interrelated shifts can be noted. First, as a result of the rapid liberalisation and growth of world trade, direct investment, currency markets, and financial flows (in short, globalisation), the traditional meaning of performance on the international markets acquired an objectively enhanced relevance for domestic actors. Export-oriented sectors became larger and more vital for the overall health of each national economy; domestically oriented sectors became less shielded from external pressures and considerations, which imposed themselves through greater imports, foreign investments, foreign borrowing, and take-overs; and traditional remedies against the loss of national competitiveness such as protectionism, managed devaluations, and capital controls became more difficult to deploy (Held *et al.* 1999). Second, the concept of competitiveness started to refer not only to export success or a favourable trade balance, but also to broader economic goals – such as the attraction of investments or a sustained growth of productivity, employment, gross domestic product (GDP), standards of living, and social welfare – as well as to a variety of non-economic goals – such as a fair distribution of income and wealth, environmental sustainability, or a self-determined life (Aiginger 2006; Aiginger and Vogel 2015; Porter 1990). Third, the focus of authors increasingly shifted from descriptive assessments of the competitiveness of a given industry or economy to an active interest in developing effective competitiveness strategies for firms, territories, institutions, and states (Bristow 2010; Genschel and Seelkopf 2015; Pedersen 2010; Porter 1990).

As a result of these shifts, the concept of competitiveness became ubiquitous. All aspects of social life previously understood as bearing on the productivity and profitability of firms and on the economic growth or broader development of territories started to be discussed in terms of competitiveness: comparative and competitive advantages, technology and innovation, the features of markets, the behaviour of economic actors (firms, workers, consumers, and public authorities), economic policy at large, education and training, welfare systems, good governance, cultural norms, and many other issues. Competitiveness escaped the narrow confines of trade issues to became a prominent object of study in large areas of the social sciences and humanities, particularly management (Hitt *et al.* 2008; Lee and Peterson 2000), economics (Aiginger 2006; Berger 2008; Collignon and Esposito 2014; Fagerberg 1988; Mosconi 2015), geography (Audretsch *et al.* 2016; Bristow 2010; Martin 2011), political economy (Cerny 1997, 2010; Scharpf and Schmidt 2000; Streeck 1999), economic policy (Copeland and Papadimitriou 2012), social policy (Gough 1999; Van Kersbergen and Hemerijck 2012), and education (Jessop 2008; Sahlberg 2006). In older senses, it is alive in areas such as microeconomics (Lau 1982), psychology (Smither and Houston 1992), sociology (Wetzel 2015), or party politics (Kitschelt 2011). At the level of non-academic discourse, the concept came to dominate discussions of economic and social questions by policy-makers, policy experts, and the public at large (Bruno 2009; Fougner 2006, 2008; Sum 2009). Governments set up competitiveness commissions and councils, commissioned reports, and developed strategies.[3] Public and private organisations started to publish yearly reports with competitiveness indicators, league tables, and recommendations.[4]

And, particularly in the European Union and its Member States, the concept made its way into the legal realm, for instance, in the Maastricht Treaty (TUE 1992) and in the Fiscal Compact (TSCG 2012).

Fortune

The growing fortune of the term can be gauged by looking at the quantitative evolution of its occurrence in the above-mentioned databases over time. The relative frequency of the term in Google Ngram (scholarly and non-scholarly books, from 1900 to 2000) shows a very rare use before 1935, a slow growth until 1970 (below 0.0001 per cent), an explosive growth from 1970 to 1995 (over 0.0007 per cent), followed by stability at high levels until 2000 (see Figure 2.1). The absolute frequency of the term in the Web of Science corpus (scholarly publications excluding books, from 1975 to 2016), in turn, shows a delayed but even more impressive growth: from 16 publications in 1975 to 111 in 1990, 366 in 1992, 938 in 2006, 2,360 in 2011, and an astonishing 3,948 in 2016 (see Figure 2.2).

Despite its relatively recent fortune, the term 'competitiveness' has achieved, thanks to this rapid rise, a status in the English language that does not compare too unfavourably with that of most key economic and social concepts in the same semantic field (Table 2.1). A search for competitiveness returns two million total hits in Google Scholar (publications), 516,000 total hits in Google Books (books), 36,561 total hits in the Web of Science (records), and a value in 2000 of 0.0007 per cent in Google Ngram (books). These values are less than one-fifth those of concepts such as productivity and innovation, but broadly similar to those of concepts such as profitability and specialisation.

The frequencies of the foreign-language equivalents of competitiveness in three other major European languages (German, French, and Italian) in Google

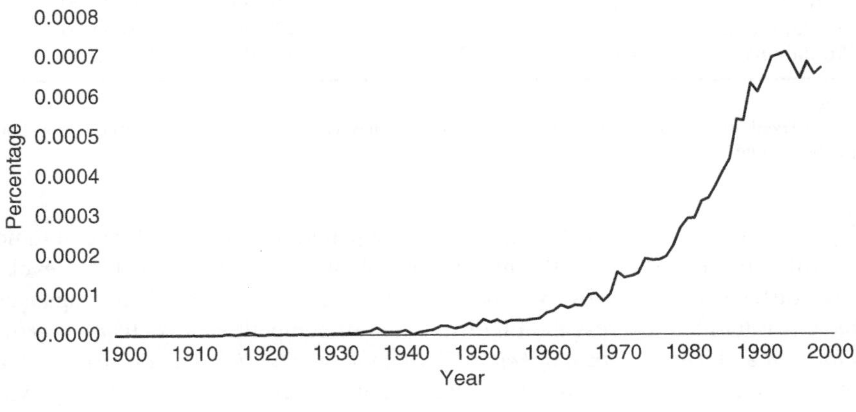

Figure 2.1 Frequency of 'competitiveness' in the Google Books Ngram English corpus, 1900–2000.

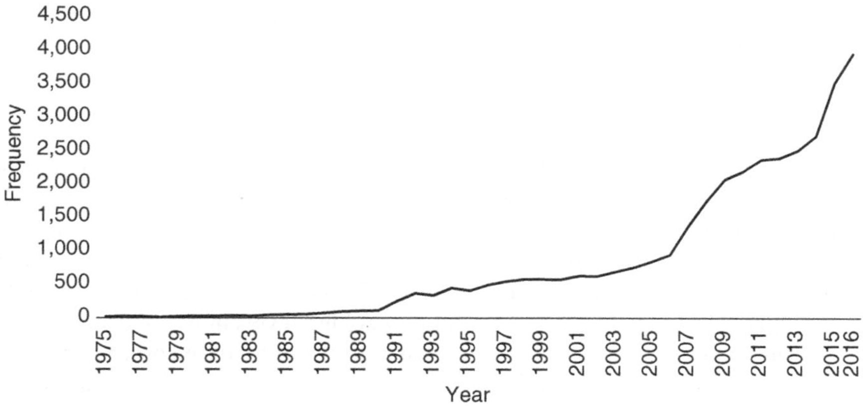

Figure 2.2 Frequency of 'competitiveness' in the Web of Science corpus, 1975–2016.

Table 2.1 Frequency of 'competitiveness' and related concepts in various corpora

	Google Ngram (2000, %)	*Web of Science (all)*	*Google Books (all)*	*Google Scholar (all)*
Development	0.0365	3,303,035	51,600,000	7,760,000
Growth	0.0173	2,671,494	18,500,000	6,400,000
Performance	0.0155	3,199,262	13,100,000	6,530,000
Competition	0.0053	267,391	8,410,000	3,120,000
Efficiency	0.0041	1,333,697	7,830,000	5,540,000
Productivity	0.0028	210,570	3,120,000	3,540,000
Innovation	0.0023	194,028	2,890,000	3,870,000
Capability	0.0016	470,286	2,470,000	4,330,000
Modernisation	0.0010	21,756	1,471,000	1,892,000
Competitiveness	0.0007	36,561	516,000	2,010,000
Specialisation	0.0007	41,567	929,000	1,800,000
Profitability	0.0006	26,784	1,820,000	1,570,000

Note
As retrieved on 30 October 2017. Some search results may vary as much as 10 per cent over a short period of time.

Ngram, broadly follow, with some delay, the pattern of the English one: a rapid growth from the 1960s to the mid-1990s followed by stability at high levels. Two differences must, however, be noted. On the one hand, all three languages have two terms to express the English notion of competitiveness (*Wettbewerbsfähigkeit* and *Konkurrenzfähigkeit* in German, *compétivitité* and *concurrentialité* in French, *competitività* and *concorrenzialità* in Italian): both are essentially synonymous, and the second version is much less commonly used than the first one. On the other hand, the terms started to be used at very different times: already in the eighteenth century in German, but only in the 1950s in French (Piatier 1955) and Italian (Rossolillo 1956).

To sum up, the relatively recent term of competitiveness (about 100 years old) has progressively risen since the 1970s from the condition of obscure technical term to the status of one of the key terms of scholarly and popular discussions of economic and societal problems. But what is competitiveness, exactly?

A conceptual anatomy: three faces, one 'mainstream' interpretation

Despite its growing academic popularity, competitiveness is often regarded as a problematic, dangerous, or meaningless concept. Standard glossary entries dub it 'elusive' (Lee 2001) and 'vague, fuzzy' (Rubalcaba 2017), and literature reviews point to a myriad of distinct, sometimes unconnected, and often contradictory usages and operationalisations (Aiginger 2006; Altomonte *et al.* 2013; Berger 2008; Cellini and Soci 2002; Debonneuil and Fontagné 2003; Siggel 2006). Moreover, many mainstream economists tend to use it sparingly or avoid it altogether, opting instead for more precise and theory-based alternatives such as competition, comparative advantage, productivity, or growth. Critics deny the relevance of competitiveness indicators for an assessment of the health of an economy. Paul Krugman (1994), for instance, famously argued that 'the growth rate of living standards essentially equals the growth rate of domestic productivity', irrespective of a country's competitive success on international markets, and that a loss of relative competitiveness does not necessarily affect a country's welfare, as countries 'have no well-defined bottom line', trade is 'a small factor in the economy', and international trade 'is not a zero-sum game'. Many authors point out that the pursuit of competitiveness may lead to a variety of wrong and harmful policy prescriptions: for instance, an excessively outward-oriented focus, which may operate to the detriment of inward-oriented sectors, domestic demand, and services (Krugman 1994), or competitive devaluations, deflations, and protectionism, which may initiate self-reinforcing spirals of falling demand, growth and employment. Finally, it is often alleged that, rather than being an empirical phenomenon or a coherent scientific concept, competitiveness is rather a 'discourse' (Sum 2009), a Foucauldian 'discipline' (Bruno 2009) or an 'ideology' (Rinehart 1995) serving specific socio-political interests.

Are these criticisms convincing? An in-depth analysis of the existing literature shows that behind the term 'competitiveness' lurk neither one nor countless, but three distinct and potentially contradictory meanings. These three faces of competitiveness, in turn, are usually given coherence by a dominant 'mainstream' interpretation, which defines them in compatible or mutually reinforcing terms.

There is no doubt that competitiveness can be conceptualised, operationalised, and measured in a wide range of different ways. A survey of the theoretical and methodological literature shows that a specification of the concept of competitiveness depends on choices over at least ten fundamental criteria: meaning, field, scope, comparison, subject, actor, type of competition, stage, dynamism, benchmark, and type of indicator (Table 2.2). Their combination may lead to

Table 2.2 The concept(s) of competitiveness: an overview

Criterion	*Operationalisation*	*Example of definitions*	*Example of indicators*
Meaning	Three types	Competition	Effective number of firms
		Relative performance	Share of world exports
		Absolute performance	GDP growth
Field	Selection of a field and subject-matter (unlimited number)	Sport	Victory margin
		Psychology	Houston's index
		Microeconomics	Market share
		Macroeconomics	GDP per capita
		Education	Pisa results
		Politics	Index of electoral competitiveness
Scope	Narrow to broad	Trade	Value of exports
		Growth	Gross domestic product
		Social welfare	UNDP's human development index
Comparison	None to general	Self-centred	Absolute performance
		Limited comparison	Performance vs selected competitors
		General comparison	Performance vs all competitors
Subject	Actor or process	Actor	Psychological competitiveness
		Process	Selectivity of a hiring process
Actor	Individual to collective	Individual	Productivity of a worker
		Organisation	Profitability of a firm
		Collective	Value-added in a region
Type of competition	Real to hypothetical	Real zero-sum-game	Wins and losses in a poker game
		Mental zero-sum-game	Shares of world exports within a growing world trade
		Hypothetical competition	Position in the world happiness ranking
Stage	Input to output	Input/ex-ante	Comparative advantage, shadow $
		Throughput/ex-nunc	
		Output/ex-post	Competitive advantage, current $
Dynamism	Static or dynamic	Static	Position in a ranking
		Dynamic	Position change over time
Benchmark	Low to high	Participation/survival	Qualification for a game
		Average performance	Better than half of participants
		Best performance	Winner of a game
Type of indicator	Single to composite	Single	Export growth
		Multiple	GDP growth with balanced trade
		Composite	WEF's global competitiveness index

hundreds or thousands of distinct definitions and alternative indicators.[5] However, this fact in itself does not speak against the validity of the concept of competitiveness: it may just indicate that we are talking about a very general concept (such as development or performance) which can usefully be applied to a broad range of empirical problems, provided that its use is adequately specified and contextualised.

What is problematic, however, is that the term competitiveness is indeed used in three distinct and potentially contradictory meanings: an issue that has largely escaped the secondary literature (Table 2.3).

The first and older meaning of competitiveness includes a variety of related notions describing the high *degree of competition* of process and sector or the *competitive attitude* of an actor. Thus, we talk of the competitiveness of a market, an industry, an election, a sport, or a recruiting process to refer to their purpose (selective vs non-selective), the number of actual competitors (many vs few), the nature of their interaction (competitive vs cooperative), the barriers to the entry of potential competitors (low vs high), the overall distribution of resources (dispersed vs concentrated), the likely outcome of the race (open vs pre-determined), or other similar attributes. Similarly, we talk of a competitive individual or firm if she/he or it shows a strong psychological propensity to engage in competitions (and to win), actively participates in (as opposed to withdrawing from) competitive endeavours, or exhibits a behaviour characterised by rivalry (as opposed to cooperation or solidarity). The notion can have either positive or negative connotations. On the one hand, competition tends to stimulate individual effort, skills, performance, and excellence. In economics, for instance, it can lead to a better fit between products and needs, lower prices, higher efficiency and productivity, and innovation. On the other hand, competition may turn out to be inappropriate or harmful. Many situations call for cooperative and solidaristic, instead of competitive, behaviour: for instance, in relations within a given social group (family, firm, class, or nation), where competition among individual members may harm their collective welfare and runs against ethical norms. Actors may start to compete with the 'wrong' means: think about the use of

Table 2.3 The three faces of competitiveness

Face	*Synonyms*	*Antonyms*
1. Competitiveness as competition	Rivalry Individualism Egoism Competitive interaction Market Competition	Cooperation Collectivism Altruism Isolation Organisation Monopoly
2. Competitiveness as relative performance	Relative success	Relative failure
3. Competitiveness as absolute performance	Absolute success	Absolute failure

performance-enhancing drugs. Finally, an excessive level of competition and rivalry may force players to harm others or themselves, for instance, when athletic overexertion leads to the development of injuries and professional diseases, when market rivalry leads to a profit squeeze, or when political competition between states turns to mutual destruction in war.

The second meaning of competitiveness, derived from the first, refers to the success of an actor or product in a competitive process or, more precisely, to her/his or its *relative performance*. It describes the ability of someone or something to perform better than one's rivals, on a given respect, according to a given benchmark. Thus, we talk of a competitive product if it is qualitatively better, cheaper, more profitable, or more popular than its alternatives; of a competitive firm, if it is more technologically advanced, efficient, profitable, or has a larger market share; a worker, if she/he is more qualified, productive, paid, or demanded; an army, if it is bigger and stronger; a territory, if it can export more, attract more investments, or create more value and incomes than other territories. This meaning clearly dominates both in the scientific literature and in the popular usage, particularly in the discussion of trade and microeconomic and economic policy questions. Importantly, determining success and failure is generally an ambiguous and partially subjective enterprise, depending on the specific choices made in selecting the reach of the comparison, the measure and indicator used, the threshold of acceptability, and other factors. A comparative and actor-centred concept, this second meaning of competitiveness stands in a paradoxical relation with the first. On the one hand, the pursuit of success and the fear of failure are the two mechanisms that motivate actors to engage in a competition and push them to increase their competitive efforts. On the other hand, the more the competition increases, the fewer chances to win and fewer benefits of a good performance will be. The surest way to prosper in a long-term competition is, indeed, to eliminate dangerous rivals and to prevent the entry of new competitors.

The third meaning of competitiveness, which tentatively emerged from the 1970s onwards, refers to the satisfactory *absolute performance* of an actor or product against the yardstick of her/his or its own past performance, expectations, or conscious goals, without regard to any consideration of external competition and relative performance. This use is surprising, because it entirely severs the connection between competitiveness and competition and transforms the term in an awkward synonym of existing concepts such as productivity, growth, development, or social welfare; nevertheless, the literature has been moving precisely in this direction. At first, authors tried to remedy the narrow and sometimes counterproductive focus of existing trade-based definitions of competitiveness focused on relative performance by broadening them through the inclusion of elements of absolute performance (growth, employment, living standards). In the European Economic Community, for instance, the Uri Report claimed that true competitiveness (there called '*capacité concurrentielle*', a calque of the German *Wettbewerbsfähigkeit* meaning 'ability to compete') cannot be reduced to a neutral or positive current account balance, but 'is on the contrary characterised by an equilibrium attained between full employment, price stability, growth, and the highest possible living standard for the mass of the population' (Uri 1972: Annexe 1:1). In the United States, similarly, the 1985 Young Report defined competitiveness as the 'degree to which a nation can, under free and fair market conditions, produce goods and services that meet the test of international markets while at the same time maintaining or expanding the real incomes of its citizens' (Young 1986: 502). Later on, most influential definitions of competitiveness entirely embraced a focus on absolute performance, at least at first sight. The seminal article by Michael Porter (1990) stated that 'the only meaningful concept of competitiveness at the national level is productivity'. The World Economic Forum ultimately adopted the same orientation, defining competitiveness as 'the set of institutions, policies, and factors that determine the level of productivity of a country' (Sala-i-Martin *et al.* 2008). Karl Aiginger, in turn, defined competitiveness as the 'ability to create welfare' (Aiginger 2006) and, more specifically, the 'ability of a country (region, location) to deliver Beyond GDP goals' (Aiginger and Vogel 2015). The revolutionary implications of this move were in practice often dampened by converting absolute indicators of performance into relative ones through comparisons (e.g. by measuring relative productivity or relative economic performance) and rankings. Nevertheless, it is clear that the concerns, strategies, and efforts of many actors often remain geared at improving absolute performance (e.g. a faster GDP growth) or achieving arbitrary goals (e.g. fulfilling the Millennium Development Goals). This third meaning of competitiveness is theoretically unrelated to the previous two: the improvement of absolute performance can be achieved within a highly competitive context or in full isolation; it can be coupled with relative gains or relative losses.

To sum up: competitiveness has three faces, and each of them alludes to features of social life which may be unrelated or even antagonistic. Success in a competition can be the outcome of an improvement in absolute performance or of strategies aimed at restricting the competition and hindering the progress of the competitors. A player who is too successful will end up spoiling the competitiveness of the game, as her/his rivals will either drop out or will not be able to catch up; in turn, an increase of competition will worsen individual relative performances, reduce the chances of winning, and constrain the benefits of a victory. Internally, a cohesive and cooperative structure often puts a given organisation at an advantage in the pursuit of relative or absolute performance. Externally, relative and absolute gains may happen in the absence of any real competitive interaction: for instance, when competition is only hypothetical (say, life expectancy rankings), when the interaction is actually cooperative (say, development aid), or when improvements are driven by other kinds of causes and motivations (say, path dependence, chance, or the pursuit of domestic socioeconomic goals). Finally, improvements in absolute performance can be coupled with relative decline, if competitors improve faster.

All these contradictions also apply to the specific issue of the economic competitiveness of nations. The patterns of economic growth during the 'golden age of capitalism' (1945–73), for instance, were not based on the model of a cut-throat competition between companies within a private sector-based, laissez-faire, and open global economy, but were structured around relatively isolated national economies combining elements of competition and cooperation, private initiative and state intervention, openness and closure (Aglietta 2000 [1979]; Maione 2001). Technological innovation, product differentiation, and economies of scale may produce temporarily unassailable positions for companies, sectors, and countries, which then benefit from monopoly rents to the detriment of the rest of the world. A nation can pursue relative economic gains at the expense of its own overall growth: a good example is the 1979–81 'Volcker shock' in the United States, which reflated the US share of nominal world GDP while causing a sharp domestic and global recession.[6] Finally, a nation can pursue absolute economic development by sacrificing its relative economic power. In the post-Second World War decades, for instance, the United States promoted or tolerated the rapid reconstruction of Western Europe and Eastern Asia and the growth of large parts of the developing world: the benefits of these policies in absolute terms (new trade and investment opportunities, foreign profits, higher domestic growth) generally outweighed in the minds of American businessmen and policy-makers their adverse consequences in relative terms (a sharp decline of the US share of world GDP).[7]

In consideration of their logical and practical independence, it may be advisable to restrict the use of the term competitiveness to its second face (competitiveness as competitive success or relative performance) and to replace it with less ambiguous terms with reference to its first (competitiveness as competition) and third (competitiveness as absolute performance): respectively, with competition and development. The reason why this solution has not generally been adopted is that, in the minds of most academic and non-academic proponents of the concept, the three faces of competitiveness are on the contrary intimately linked, either as elements that necessarily stand or fall together or as equally worthy goals that *can* be reconciled with appropriate policies and strategies. The thrust of this 'mainstream' group of interpretations of competitiveness can be illustrated by looking at two influential early examples, one drawn from the academic and the other one from the policy-oriented literature.

Michael Porter's (1990) article 'The competitive advantage of nations' starts by equating national competitiveness with absolute performance: a 'high and rising standard of living for its citizens', which in turn fundamentally depends on the 'productivity' of its firms. Productivity and prosperity, however, are premised on developing the relative potential ('competitive advantage') and performance ('competitive success') of firms and territories: only the technological and economic leaders can secure high incomes and continuous improvements. Both relative and absolute performance, finally, cannot be achieved by any means. They are the necessary outcome of the pressure of competition between domestic firms ('domestic rivalry, like any rivalry, creates pressure on companies to innovate and improve'), between national firms and their international competitors ('thousands of struggles for competitive advantage against foreign rivals in particular segments and industries'), and between states (which must 'create an environment in which companies can gain competitive advantage').

The European Commission's (EC 1993) White Paper on 'Growth, competitiveness, employment', similarly, is fundamentally concerned with absolute performance, although conceived in broader terms: it looks for ways to ensure the 'sustainable development' of European economies, which includes sustained GDP growth, full employment, social integration, environmental sustainability, and other non-economic goals. The report is concerned about the disappointing economic performance of the European Economic Community since the 1970s, characterised by mass unemployment, low growth, and a loss of competitive edge in relation to the US, Japan, and the emerging economies. To counteract these trends, it proposes a broad range of policies geared at improving productivity and profitability, encouraging adaptability and innovation, boosting investment, and stimulating exports. Crucially, these policies aim at improving not only absolute, but also relative performance, for instance, by lowering production costs (e.g. wages, labour taxation, public expenditures, interest rates, and red tape) and by improving the European share of world exports and of high value-added products. These policies, finally, should be pursued – and can only be pursued effectively – in a framework characterised by increased internal competition, undistorted market mechanisms, and international openness: 'for the level of employment in the Community to improve, firms must achieve global competitiveness on open and competitive markets, both inside and outside'.

As both examples show, the 'mainstream' interpretation of competitiveness is the result of a sustained theoretical and rhetorical effort to find a synthesis between three key traditional goals of economic policy (economic liberalism, relative economic success, and domestic development) while anchoring them within a general market- and competition-based framework. It thus reflects both the rise of neo-liberal ideas and the need to leave some room for manoeuvre for alternative neo-mercantilist and developmentalist/welfarist perspectives. Competitiveness is therefore an ambiguous concept but, like Jabko's (2006) 'market', its ambiguity is desired and productive, as it allows a broad ideological convergence while discrediting unwanted solutions (e.g. protectionism or state-led development) and favouring specific kinds of outcomes. Whether this 'mainstream' interpretation can stand the test of reality is questionable. In specific situations, competition, relative performance, and absolute performance can be successfully pursued by a country at the same time and without negative externalities. In other situations, as shown above, the three faces of competitiveness conflict with each other and with the welfare of other countries: priorities must be chosen, compensation mechanisms developed, or alternative solutions deployed.

Solidarity[8]

Conceptual history and fortune

The conceptual history of the term 'solidarity' has been explored in detail in the literature (Bayertz 1999; Brunkhorst 2002; Stjernø 2005; Wildt 1995, 1998).

The term 'solidarity' emerged in eighteenth-century France with a legal-commercial meaning derived from Roman law (*obligatio in solidum*: joint and several liability for an obligation). It assumed the broader meanings of interdependency, mutual obligation, and fraternity in the 1840s in the works of Saint-Simonian and Fourierist authors (Pierre Leroux, Hippolyte Renaud, August Comte) and the activity of socialists and labour activists during the 1848 revolutions. Nevertheless, 'the phenomenon of solidarity existed before the idea was formulated. The idea existed before the term became widespread' (Stjernø 2005: 25). Closely related precursors were the Biblical ideas of love and brotherly love (*agape/caritas*, *philadelphia/fraternitas*), the Graeco-Roman idea of civic friendship (*philia/amicitia*), and the French Revolutionary idea of fraternity (*fraternité*).

Since the 1850s, the concept has enjoyed a broad, albeit uneven, reception. It is worthy of note that, although the initial choice of the term was explicitly motivated by the pursuit of an 'objective' alternative to notions of Christian love, civic friendship, and revolutionary fraternity, its lingering charge of emotional, moral, and particularistic connotations made it generally unappealing to mainstream modern thought (Bayertz 1999). Its success has thus been particularly strong among currents reacting against classic liberalism, such as socialism (Fourier, Marx), Catholic social thought (the solidarity principle), French radicalism (Léon Bourgeois' *solidarisme*), the labour movement (workers' solidarity), particularistic communities (national solidarity, women's solidarity, black solidarity), debates on social policy (social solidarity as expressed in the welfare state), and 'third sector' organisations (the social and solidarity economy). Within the humanities and social sciences, solidarity has been discussed as a central concept by several important authors (Émile Durkheim, Nicolai Hartmann, Max Scheler, Talcott Parsons, Jürgen Habermas, Michael Hechter, Richard Rorty, and Hans Küng), but has more often been discarded in favour of more neutral and specific terms. Nevertheless, the concept of solidarity has gradually acquired a widespread popularity in scholarly and popular discussions of social and political issues. According to Google Ngram data, its frequency in the English language has continually grown from the 1840s to the early 1980s and stabilised afterwards, with values of 0.0002 per cent in 1900, 0.0007 per cent in 1950, 0.0011 per cent in 1979, and 0.0012 per cent in 2000 (Figure 2.3). The last value compares favourably with traditional alternatives (same frequency as charity, much higher frequency than brotherhood, fraternity, and altruism) and is almost double than that of competitiveness.

Meaning

Just like competitiveness, the term 'solidarity' does not have a clear and unequivocal content. A 'wavering, inexact and often suggestive use of the term' is widespread; a variety of 'different and sometimes very contradictory' meanings exists (Bayertz 1999: 3–4); and its differentiation from neighbouring concepts (interdependence, cooperation, social integration and cohesion, group identification, altruism, social justice, redistribution) is often unclear.

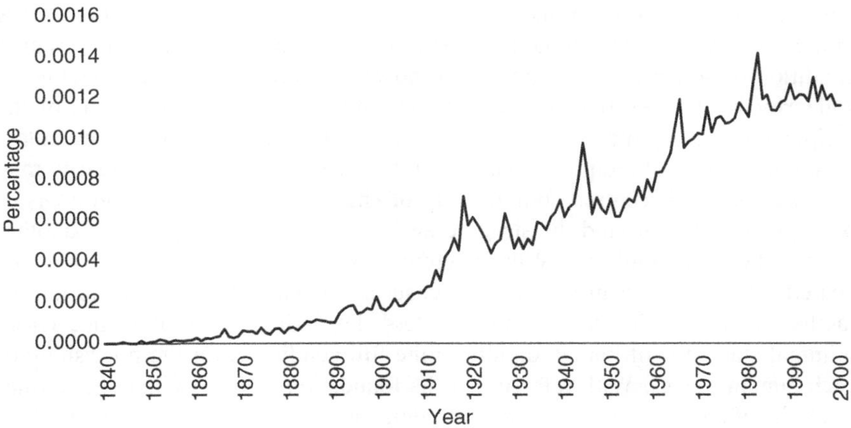

Figure 2.3 Frequency of 'solidarity' in the Google Books Ngram English corpus, 1840–2000.

I would argue that it is possible to identify at least four partially distinct meanings. First, solidarity may refer to the strength of the *feeling of belonging* of the members of a given group towards the collective. Second, it may refer to the factual *degree of cooperation and mutual support* within the said group. Third, it may refer to the *emotional or moral imperative* that compels a person to help other group members by sharing one's attention, time, and resources with them, particularly when they are in need or are perceived as victims of an injustice or an unjust condition. Fourth, it may refer to a *socio-political principle* guiding public policy (such as social legislation, social protection, public services, and redistribution) or alternative systems of correctives to the 'natural' outcomes of untrammelled economic competition (such as philanthropy, cooperatives and mutuals, trade unions, churches, and the 'third sector'). Unlike in the case of competitiveness, however, these different meanings are largely compatible. The general definition of solidarity as 'a mutual attachment between individuals, encompassing two levels: a factual level of actual common ground between the individuals and a normative level of mutual obligations to aid each other, as and when should be necessary' offered by Bayertz (1999: 3) covers well all facets of the concept.

Solidarity can also vary according to its scope, agonism, function, foundation, and subject (Arnsperger and Varoufakis 2003; Bayertz 1999; Laitinen and Pessi 2014; Stjernø 2005). With reference to its scope, it is not clear if solidarity should refer only to interactions between members of a common group or include interactions with persons outside the group. Most authors argue that solidarity, unlike pure altruism, always implies a degree of group closure and identification. However, the extensiveness of the said group may vary from very narrow (a football team) to universal (the human race). Civic solidarity among citizens of the same polity naturally plays a key role here, as it is backed not only by interpersonal ideas and emotions but also by the authority and resources of the state. Actual or potential reciprocity is also widely considered an essential condition of solidarity: this contention, however, is not entirely convincing, as solidarity is often exerted or deemed due simply because of the status of the recipient as a group member, as a victim, or as a fellow human being, regardless of any likelihood of reciprocation. With reference to its agonism, solidarity may be based on a self-centred commonality of characteristics, values, and goals or be explicitly built around the struggle against an enemy (an oppressor, another nation, the non-members). With reference to its function, solidarity may be geared at maximizing group interest, ensuring social order and integration, or facilitating the attainment of more or less demanding ideas of justice (from minimal standards of human dignity to the full conditions for the flourishing of each human being). With reference to its foundation, solidarity may be normatively justified on various grounds (religious, republican, universalistic, utilitarian) and can be empirically driven by different motives (empathy, emotions, rational calculus, moral reasoning, socialization, legal obligations). The subject of solidarity, finally, tends to vary from discipline to discipline: for the moral philosopher and the psychologist, it is always the individual with her/his reasoning, emotions, and behaviour; for the sociologist, it is generally the social group or society with its factual or emotional internal cohesion; for the legal, political, and policy-oriented scholar, finally, it is often the state, implementing the principle of solidarity in its laws, policies, and institutions (e.g. the welfare system). This view is, however, not uncontested, as many liberal, Christian, and left-libertarian authors warn – from different perspectives – of the negative effects of top-down, bureaucratic, and impersonal processes on the vitality of the solidaristic feelings and activities of individuals and intermediate organizations (Gorz 1980; John Paul II 1991; Tocqueville 1835).

The relationship between competitiveness and solidarity

The contradictory nature of the concept of competitiveness described in the first section has important consequences for the *relationship* between competitiveness and solidarity. This can be conceptualised in three divergent ways: as antagonistic, as mutually reinforcing, and as coinciding (Figure 2.4).

The first and most common group of solutions thinks of competitiveness as *antagonistic* to solidarity. From an actor-centred perspective, a competitive behaviour based on rivalry, individualism and egoism represents the polar opposite of a solidaristic one based on cooperation, collectivism and altruism: the former is guided by the maximisation of one's narrow interest and forbids collaboration with or aiding others, while the latter is guided by the pursuit of the common good and prescribes joining forces with others and actively helping the less successful. From a system-centred perspective, a competitive society based on many independent units (firms and individuals) fiercely competing on free and open markets is also often criticised as ethically questionable, corrosive

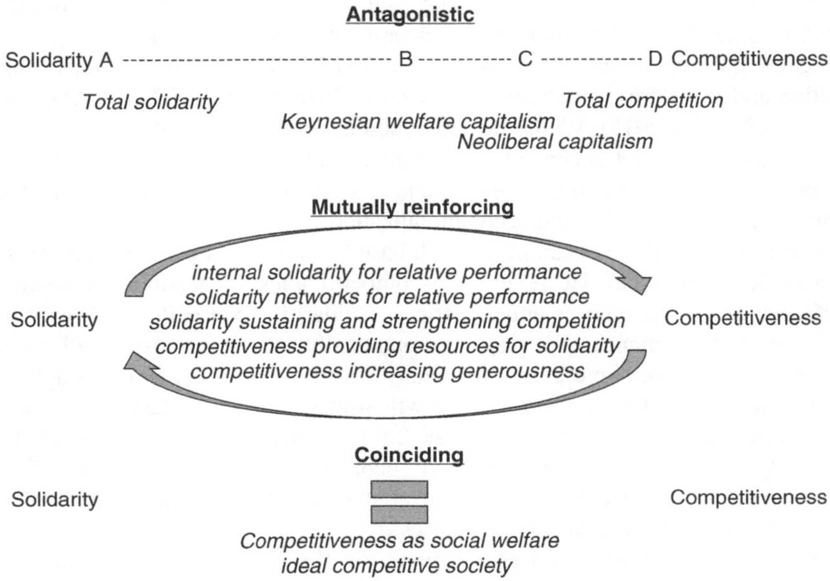

Figure 2.4 Relationships between competitiveness and solidarity.

of social bonds, threatening the weak, and inimical to equality and institutionalised solidarity. Conversely, supporters of competition may often regard many forms of social collaboration and social protection as unjustifiable restrictions on individual freedom and as obstacles to economic development. Therefore, solidarity stops where competition begins: the more competition there is, the less solidarity, and vice versa. From the point of view of public policy, the question then becomes that of the appropriate balance between these two opposing principles: how to regulate competition, how to delimit its field of action, and how to compensate its negative consequences.

In this continuum of mixtures of solidarity and competitiveness, several relevant historical or ideal types have been identified in the literature.[9] Radical leftist authors have argued for a progressive radicalisation of the welfare state or of community-based solidarity mechanisms and the ultimate withering away of competition (Bukharin and Preobrazhensky 1969 [1920]; Fourier 2009 [1841]; Hudis 2012; Kropotkin 1926 [1892]). Radical free-market supporters, on the contrary, have argued for minimising or eliminating non-voluntary solidarity, extolling the virtue of individual initiative and competition (Hayek 1960; Nozik 1974; Rothbard 1970). The model of the Keynesian welfare capitalism, prevalent in Western Europe and beyond, from the 1940s to the 1970s, sought to chart a middle course between the extremes of an untrammelled competitive capitalism and of a fully cooperative and egalitarian utopia, trying in different ways to preserve the dynamic force of competition and of the market while ensuring a high level of growth, redistribution, and social protection (Albert 1993; Boccara 1971; Esping-Andersen 1985, 1990; Hall and Soskice 2001; Hay and Wincott 2012; Offe 1984; Radice 2000; Ruggie 1982). The model of neo-liberal capitalism, which has been gradually gaining the upper hand from the 1980s onwards, moved the bar towards competition and away from solidarity (Cahill *et al.* 2018; Cerny 1997; Duménil and Lévy 2013; Palier 2013). While regulation and intervention have not significantly decreased – and the retrenchment of the welfare state has been slow and partial – the promotion of competition, markets, and risk has gradually overshadowed the former focus on protection and decommodification.

The above-mentioned examples are all based on a view of competitiveness as competition (first face). However, also competitiveness understood as relative performance can be seen as antagonistic to solidarity. Externally, each gain in the relative performance of a player automatically means the loss of all other players. In addition, some games are really zero-sum: in a context of stagnant world trade, for instance, export-led growth strategies directly damage the economies of one's neighbours (Bernaciak 2015; Collignon and Esposito 2014). Internally, the pursuit of international economic competitiveness is often achieved at the expense of domestic social standards by reducing wages, other costs, and 'unproductive' welfare expenses.

A second important group of solutions, on the contrary, thinks competitiveness and solidarity are *mutually reinforcing*. There are many situations where this applies. First, internal solidarity is an important resource for external competitive success. If the competing unit is a collective actor (e.g. a family, a team, a firm, a party, an army, a nation), its internal functioning can hardly be entirely based on individualism, competitive interaction, and market mechanisms: collective identification, cooperation, and planning are always present to a certain degree and often very extensive. Second, external solidarity networks are another key resource for competitive survival and success. An individual or collective actor competing with everybody else, all the time, and in all social spheres would not survive long: permanent allies, temporary alliances, neutral relationships, rules of the game, and competition-free spaces are required. Third, solidarity mechanisms are often necessary to make the competition possible, preserve it over time, and intensify it. Without some form of solidarity between players, for instance, an agreement on certain rules of the game, competition would be brutal and short, soon leading to the mutual destruction of all players or their abandonment of the field. Moreover, in the typical situation of a long-term competitive game where the winner is allowed to accumulate resources (e.g. money, market shares, skills), the natural outcome is often the creation of an unassailable predominance of one player; to prevent this, mechanisms to reduce the impact of the acquired advantage, to ensure the survival of the losers, to encourage the entry of new players, and even to periodically restore a level playing field are necessary. In addition, comprehensive social safety nets (e.g. family support, welfare policies, debt relief) can increase the propensity and the ability of individuals and groups to engage in the economic competition in the first place. Fourth, relative and absolute success in the competition increases the amount of resources available for internal redistribution and social investment, although there is no certainty that they will be used to this end. Finally, the achievement of a substantial degree of relative and absolute success may increase the generosity of a player: the successful player has less need and desire to resort to brutal competitive methods and less fortunate players, who are no longer perceived as a threat, are more likely to be (temporarily) helped. In all these cases, competitiveness and solidarity need each other and, under appropriate conditions, strengthen each other: the more solidarity there is, the more competitiveness, and vice versa.

In this respect, it is important to note that a large number of the theories and models developed since the 1990s in the field of economics, business strategy, economic policy and social policy – which we can group under the heading of 'competitive solidarity' – are based precisely on the assumption that both strong competition and solidary mechanisms, particularly investment in education and training, regional development, labour market participation, and social inclusion, are necessary for relative and absolute economic success (competitiveness). Endogenous growth theory (Aghion and Howitt 1998; Lucas 1988; Romer 1990), for instance, traces economic success back to firm-level investments in innovation, R&D, and human capital. Research on firm and territorial competitiveness (Boschma 2004; Ketels 2006; Nathan and Overman 2013) and on new industrial policy (Aiginger 2007; O'Sullivan *et al.* 2013) similarly emphasises the key role of innovation, industrial clustering, infrastructure, an educated and skilled workforce, sustainability, 'good government', and public-private partnerships. 'Third way' social democratic arguments on welfare state reform put forward the perspective of a 'social investment state' (Giddens 1998; Morel *et al.* 2012; Van Kersbergen and Hemerijck 2012) investing massively in education, research, flexicurity, and activating social policies not to shelter people from the market, but to increase their participation and chances of success in the economic competition. All these theories ideally point to a new form of 'competitive solidarity' or 'competitive and productive solidarity' (Streeck 1999) reconciling the imperative of competitiveness with the desire to improve social protection and social cohesion. In practice, however, there are limits to this virtuous circle. On the one hand, the degree of competitiveness achieved still generally represents a constraint on the degree of solidarity that a system can afford: thus, successful firms, regions, and countries can embrace high wages, adopt socially responsible behaviour, and make large investments in human capital, research, and inclusion, while unsuccessful ones are forced to limit or even reduce their levels of social provisions. This problem is compounded by the fact that competitiveness as absolute performance (e.g. GDP growth) is not a zero-sum game, but competitiveness as relative performance (e.g. place in the global value chain) is: in the latter sense, only a few territories can be 'winners', and each advance of a territory means the retrogression of all others. On the other hand, in an open and globalised economy public authorities are hard put to ensure that social and other investments will actually benefit their own local economies, as high-value firms and skilled workers can always leave in pursuit of better locations. Finally, the model of competitive solidarity is only interested in social expenditures insofar as they directly improve competitiveness, leading to a skewing of public policy to the detriment of valuable but non-marketable goals (e.g. creating jobs regardless of their adequateness and conditions, fighting poverty instead of boosting wages, educating for employability instead of for personal and civic development, investing in potential workers rather than in permanent invalids and pensioners).

A third group of solutions, finally, thinks of competitiveness as largely *coinciding* with solidarity. This can happen in two main ways. On the one hand, competitiveness understood as absolute performance can be directly conceptualised as a synonym for social welfare (Aiginger 2006; Aiginger and Vogel 2015). Therefore, an increase of living standards or 'Beyond GDP' goals automatically becomes an increase in competitiveness, while development strategies based on social and ecological dumping may increase a country's GDP but actually decrease its overall competitiveness. On the other hand, competitiveness understood as competition can be theoretically shaped in such a radical way that makes solidarity redundant, because it leads to an almost-perfect equality and viability of all (surviving) economic actors. For neo-classical authors, in a perfectly competitive economy in a state of long-term equilibrium, there are no monopolistic rents. All demand is satisfied, all productive factors are used, all firms have the same technology, commodities are produced at the costs of production, there is no profit, and all workers are equally employed, equally efficient, and paid the same wages (Walras 2003 [1874]). If this were not the case, existing actors or new entrants would flow into the deviant product, sector, profession or economy and homogenise its returns. The result is that firm and individual are fiercely competing, but all of them – at least, the one who survives the initial selection – obtain the same minimal return (save for eventual effort- and risk-seeking preferences). As perfect equality and inclusion are reached, solidarity becomes inessential, except for possible support to the 'surplus' population not fit to take part in the competition.

Conclusion

This chapter has explored in detail the history, fortune, and polysemy of the ideas of *solidarity* and *competitiveness*. Rising from relatively humble origins, both ideas have gradually become commonplace in the English language (since the 1910s and the 1990s, respectively), extended their influence and depth, and ultimately achieved the status of key concepts in the social sciences and in the broader societal discussion.

The concept of competitiveness has been shown to possess three independent and contradictory faces: competitiveness as competition, competitiveness as relative performance, and competitiveness as absolute performance. These three meanings are generally reconciled in 'mainstream' interpretations, which posit a virtuous circle between competition, competitive success, and self-improvement. In many real-world situations, however, the three meanings conflict with each other: priorities must be chosen, compensation mechanisms developed, or alternative solutions deployed.

The chapter has also provided a novel theoretical framework for the analysis of the relationship between competitiveness and solidarity. This can be conceptualised in a variety of ways: some antagonistic, some mutually reinforcing, and some coinciding. In the first and most common case, competitiveness and solidarity conflict: either one or the other must give in, and acceptable compromises between the two must be sought. In the second and most interesting case, competitiveness and solidarity sustain and strengthen each other: an increase in solidarity leads to more competitiveness and vice versa. In the third and most abstract case, competitiveness is defined as synonymous with solidarity or, conversely, solidarity is subsumed in the working of an ideal perfect competition.

Two main policy-oriented implications can be derived from this analysis. On the one hand, scholars and practitioners are well advised to pay the utmost attention to the conceptual complexity and richness of the idea of competitiveness, of the idea of solidarity, and of the relationships between them. On the other hand, the same scholars and practitioners might find it judicious, when investigating societal problems or designing policy solution, to probe for both positive feedbacks and negative externalities between competitiveness and solidarity.

Notes

1 The scope and composition of the databases are varied. The Web of Science covers the bibliographic record of over 90 million scholarly publications excluding books published between 1975 and the present; Google Scholar includes over 160 million (mostly scholarly) books and publications published at any time; Google Books includes over 25 million scholarly and non-scholarly books published at any time; the Google Ngram Viewer English corpus includes a full-text representative selection of over five million scholarly and non-scholarly books drawn from Google Books. Google Ngram results are relative frequencies (percentage of occurrences on the total corpus) while the other three databases provide absolute frequencies. Each source has its problems and limitations, particularly regarding accuracy, size, completeness, and balance – see, for instance, Pechenik *et al.*'s (2015) critique of the Google Ngram Viewer corpus. In the following analysis, the use of Google Ngram is limited to the period 1900–2000, as later changes in its composition linked to the rise of cheap electronic editions of old books led to a massive conservative bias in its frequencies.

2 Earlier occurrences in Ngram Viewer and Google Scholar refer to incorrectly dated items.

3 Particularly noteworthy are the 'Global competition – the new reality' report (Young 1986), four reports by the Competitiveness Policy Council (e.g. CPC 1992), and the 'Building the American dream' report (Kantor 1996) in the United States and the 'Rapport sur la capacité concurrentielle de la Communauté européenne' (Uri 1972), the 'Growth, competitiveness, employment' White Paper (EC 1993), four reports by the Competitiveness Advisory Group (Ciampi 1996; Jaquemin and Pench 1997), the Sapir Report (Sapir *et al.* 2004), and the Lisbon and Europe 2020 strategies (European Council 2000, EC 2010) in the European Union.

4 In particular, the World Economic Forum's *Global Competitiveness Report* (since 1979), the IMD's *World Competitiveness Yearbook* (since 1996), various competitiveness indicators by the Council on Competitiveness in Washington (discontinuously

since 1988), and the EU's *European Competitiveness Report* (since 1995). In addition, the measurement and benchmarking of national economic, financial, institutional, educational, social, political, and other performances by statistical offices (e.g. the UN, the IMF, the OECD, the World Bank, the ILO, Eurostat), NGOs and research institutes (e.g. Freedom House, Quality of Government Institute, Transparency International), universities, and private companies (e.g. QS, THE, Moody's, S&P) are also increasingly framed, to some degree, in terms of competitiveness.

5 For instance, the World Economic Forum measures 'broad' country competitiveness with a composite index made up of 117 individual indicators (Schwab and Sala-i-Martin 2014) and the project Mapcompete has identified 140 distinct indicators for the field of economic competitiveness alone (Altomonte *et al.* 2013).

6 Largely as a consequence of the appreciation of the dollar set off by the interest rate hikes decided by the Federal Reserve Chairman Paul Volcker, the US share of nominal world GDP rose from 24.0 per cent in 1979 to 32.2 per cent in 1985. Meanwhile, the US real GDP growth fell from 3.6 per cent (1970–79) to 2.7 per cent (1979–85), while the world real GDP growth fell from 4.0 per cent to 2.5 per cent. On the episode, see Duménil and Lévy (2004).

7 What was crucial, however, was the impact of geopolitical, political, and meta-economic goals (containing the threat of the Soviet Union and left-wing movements and anchoring 'the West' within a US-led international political and economic system), which made the relative sacrifices necessary and acceptable.

8 This section is partially based on Chiocchetti (2017).

9 See also the interesting distinction of Arnsperger (2011) between emergent (neo-liberal), redistributive (social democratic), and reconstructive (radical) solidarity.

References

Aghion, Philippe and Peter Howitt (eds) (1998). *Endogenous growth theory.* Cambridge, MA: MIT Press.

Aglietta, Michel (2000 [1979]). *A theory of capitalist regulation: the US experience.* London: Verso.

Aiginger, Karl (2006). 'Competitiveness: from a dangerous obsession to a welfare creating ability with positive externalities', *Journal of Industry, Competition and Trade* 6(2): 161–77.

Aiginger, Karl (2007). 'Industrial policy: a dying breed or a re-emerging phoenix', *Journal of Industry, Competition and Trade* 7(3–4): 287–323.

Aiginger, Karl and Johanna Vogel (2015). 'Competitiveness: from a misleading concept to a strategy supporting Beyond GDP goals', *Competitiveness Review* 25(5): 497–523.

Albert, Michel (1993). *Capitalism against capitalism.* Hoboken, NJ: Wiley and Sons.

Almond, Gabriel A. and James S. Coleman (1961). *The politics of developing areas.* Princeton, NJ: Princeton University Press.

Altomonte, Carlo, Marco Antonielli, Michael Blanga-Gubbay, and Silvia Carrieri (2013). *Competitiveness indicators report.* Budapest: Mapcompete, Hungarian Academy of Sciences.

Argote, Linda M., Joan E. Fischer, Peter J. McDonald, and Edgar C. O'Neal (1976). 'Competitiveness in males and females: situational determinants of fear of success behavior', *Sex Roles* 2(3): 295–303.

Arnsperger, Christian (2011). 'No competition without solidarity? The normative frameworks for analyzing the fairness of competition', *Ethical Perspectives* 18(3): 355–83.

Arnsperger, Christian, and Yanis Varoufakis (2003). 'Toward a theory of solidarity', *Erkenntnis* 59: 157–88.

Audretsch, David, Albert Link, and Mary Walshok (eds) (2016). *The Oxford handbook of local competitiveness.* Oxford: Oxford University Press.

Balassa, Bela (1962). *Recent developments in the competitiveness of American industry and prospect for the future.* New Haven, CT: Yale University Press.

Bayertz, Kurt (1999). 'Four uses of solidarity', in Kurt Bayertz (ed.) *Solidarity.* Dordrecht: Kluwer, 3–28.

Belabes, Abderrazak (1999). 'Myth and paradox of "US competitiveness" debate from the end of World War II to nowadays', GREQAM Working Paper No. 99C07. Marseille: GREQAM. Available at: www.amse-aixmarseille.fr/sites/default/files/_dt/greqam/99c07.pdf

Berger, Thomas (2008). 'Concepts of national competitiveness', *Journal of International Business and Economy* 9(1): 91–111.

Bernaciak, Magdalena (ed.) (2015). *Market expansion and social dumping in Europe.* London: Routledge.

Boccara, Paul (1971). *Le capitalisme monopoliste d'Etat.* Paris: Editions Sociales.

Born, David (1850). *Denkschrift: über den Einfluß der Mahl- und Schlachtsteuer auf die gewerblichen Verhältnisse Berlins, besonders in Bezug auf die Arbeitslöhne und auf die Konkurrenzfähigkeit anderen Städten gegenüber.* Berlin: Buchdruckerei der Reform.

Boschma, Ron (2004). 'Competitiveness of regions from an evolutionary perspective', *Regional Studies* 38(9): 1001–14.

Bristow, Gillian (2010). *Critical reflections on regional competitiveness: theory, policy, practice.* London: Routledge.

Brunkhorst, Hauke (2002). *Solidarität: von der Bürgerfreundschaft zur globalen Rechtsgenossenschaft.* Berlin: Suhrkamp.

Bruno, Isabelle (2009). 'The "indefinite discipline" of competitiveness benchmarking as a neoliberal technology of government', *Minerva* 47: 261–80.

Bukharin, Nikolai and Evgenii Preobrazhensky (1969 [1920]). *The ABC of communism.* London: Penguin. Available at: www.marxists.org/archive/bukharin/works/1920/abc/.

Cahill, Damien, Melinda Cooper, Martijn Konings, and David Primrose (eds) (2018). *The SAGE handbook of neoliberalism.* London: SAGE.

Cellini, Roberto and Anna Soci (2002). 'Pop competitiveness', *BNL Quarterly Review* 44(220): 71–101.

Cerny, Philip G. (1997). 'The paradoxes of the competition state: the dynamics of political globalization', *Government and Opposition* 32(2): 251–74.

Cerny, Philip G. (2010). 'The competition state today: from *raison d'État* to *raison du Monde*', *Policy Studies* 31: 5–12.

Chiocchetti, Paolo (2017). Solidarity. *RESuME*, 28 June 2017. DOI:10.25517/RESuME-YxjevDV-2017.

Chopplet, Marc (2007). 'Compétitivité', *Quaderni* 63: 23–4.

Ciampi, Carlo Azeglio (1996). 'Enhancing European competitiveness', *Banco Nationale del Lavoro Quarterly* 49(197): 143–64..

Collignon, Stefan and Piero Esposito (eds) (2014). *Competitiveness in the European economy.* London: Routledge.

Copeland, Paul and Dimitris Papadimitriou (eds) (2012). *The EU's Lisbon Strategy: evaluating success, understanding failure.* London: Palgrave Macmillan.

CPC (Competitiveness Policy Council) (1992). *Building a competitive America: first annual report to the President and Congress.* Washington, DC: Competitiveness Policy Council.

Debonneuil, Michèle and Lionel Fontagné (2003). *Compétitivité.* Paris: La Documentation française.

Duménil, Gérard and Dominique Lévy (2013). *The crisis of neoliberalism.* Cambridge, MA: Harvard University Press.

Eagleton-Pierce, Matthew (2016). 'Competition', in Matthew Eagleton-Pierce *Neoliberalism: the key concepts.* London: Routledge.

EC (Commission of the European Communities) (1993). 'Growth, competitiveness, employment: the challenges and ways forward into the 21st century', White Paper. COM(93)700. Brussels: European Commission.

EC (European Commission) (2010). 'Communication from the Commission. Europe 2020. A strategy for smart, sustainable and inclusive growth', COM(2010) 2020 final. Brussels: European Commission.

Esping-Andersen, Gøsta (1985). *Politics against markets: the social democratic road to power.* Princeton, NJ: Princeton University Press.

Esping-Andersen, Gøsta (1990). *The three worlds of welfare capitalism.* Princeton, NJ: Princeton University Press.

European Council (2000). 'Lisbon European Council, 23 and 24 March 2000, Presidency Conclusions'. Available at: www.europarl.europa.eu/summits/lis1_en.htm

Fagerberg, Jan (1988). 'International competitiveness', *The Economic Journal* 98(391): 355–74.

Fleming, John M. and Sho-Chieh Tsiang (1956). 'Changes in competitive strength and export shares of major industrial countries', *IMF Staff Papers* 5(2): 218–48.

Fougner, Tore (2006). 'The state, international competitiveness and neoliberal globalisation: is there a future beyond "the competition state"?', *Review of International Studies* 32: 165–85.

Fougner, Tore (2008). 'Neoliberal governance of states: the role of competitiveness indexing and country benchmarking', *Millennium* 37(2): 303–26.

Fourier, Charles (2009 [1841]). *Théorie des quatres mouvements et des destinées générales.* Dijon: Les presses du réel.

Fried, Maurice (1971). 'Determination of sterile-insect competitiveness', *Journal of Economic Entomology* 64(4): 869–72.

Genschel, Philipp and Laura Seelkopf (2015). 'The competition state: the modern state in a global economy', in Stephan Leibfried, Evelyne Huber, Matthew Lange, *et al.* (eds). *The Oxford handbook of transformations of the state.* Oxford: Oxford University Press, 237–52.

Giddens, Anthony (1998). *The third way: the renewal of social democracy.* Cambridge: Polity.

Gorz, André (1980). *Adieux au proletariat: au delà du socialism.* Paris: Éditions Galilée.

Gough, Ian (1999). 'Social welfare and competitiveness: social versus system integration?', in Ian Gough and Gunnar Olofsson (eds). *Capitalism and social cohesion: essays on exclusion and integration.* Basingstoke: Palgrave Macmillan.

Hall, Peter A. and David Soskice (2001). *Varieties of capitalism: the institutional foundations of comparative advantage.* Oxford: Oxford University Press.

Harper, Douglas (2017). 'Competitiveness', 'Competitive', 'Competition', 'Compete'. In *Online etymology dictionary.* Available at: www.etymonline.com/

Hay, Colin and David Wincott (2012). *The political economy of European welfare capitalism.* Basingstoke: Palgrave Macmillan.

Hayek, Friedrich A. von (1960). *The constitution of liberty.* Chicago: University of Chicago Press.

Held, David, Antony McGrew, David Goldblatt, and Jonathan Perraton (1999). *Global transformations: politics, economics and culture*. Cambridge: Polity Press.

Hicks, John R. and Roy G.D. Allen (1934). 'A reconsideration of the theory of value. Part I', *Economica* 1(1): 52–76.

Hirsch, Seev (1967). *Location of industry and international competitiveness*. Oxford: Clarendon Press.

Hitt, Michael, R. Duane Ireland, and Robert E. Hoskisson (2008). *Strategic management: competitiveness and globalization: cases*. 10th edn. Mason, OH: South Western.

Hudis, Peter (2012). *Marx's concept of the alternative to capitalism*. Leiden: Brill.

Jabko, Nicolas (2006). *Playing the market: a political strategy for uniting Europe, 1985–2005*. Ithaca, NY: Cornell University Press.

Jaquemin, Alexis and Lucio R. Pench (1997). *Europe competing in the global economy: reports of the Competitiveness Advisory Group*. Cheltenham: Edward Elgar.

Jessop, Bob (2008). 'A cultural political economy of competitiveness and its implications for Higher Education', in Bob Jessop, Norman Fairclough, and Ruth Wodak (eds). *Education and the knowledge-based economy in Europe*. Rotterdam: Sense, 13–40.

John Paul II (1991). *Centesimus annus*. Rome: Libreria Editrice Vaticana.

Kantor, Michael (1996). *Building the American dream. jobs, innovation, and growth in America's next century*. Washington, DC: US Department of Commerce.

Ketels, Christian H.M. (2006).'Michael Porter's competitiveness framework – recent learnings and new research priorities', *Journal of Industry, Competition and Trade* 6: 115–36.

Kitschelt, Herbert (2011). 'Party systems', in Robert E. Goodin (ed.). *The Oxford handbook of political science*. Oxford: Oxford University Press.

Kravis, Irving B. and Robert E. Lipsey (1971). *Price competitiveness in world trade*. Cambridge, MA: NBER.

Kropotkin, Pyotr (1926 [1892]). *The conquest of bread*. New York: Vanguard Press. Available at: www.gutenberg.org/ebooks/23428

Krugman, Paul (1994). 'Competitiveness: a dangerous obsession', *Foreign Affairs* 73(2).

Laitinen, Arto and Birgitta Pessi (2014). 'Solidarity: theory and practice: an introduction', in Arto Laitinen and Birgitta Pessi (eds), *Solidarity: theory and practice*. Lanham, MD: Lexington Books, 1–29.

Lau, Lawrence (1982). 'On identifying the degree of competitiveness from industry price and output data', *Economics Letter* 10(1–2): 93–9.

Lee, Sang M. and Suzanne J. Peterson (2000). 'Culture, entrepreneurial orientation, and global competitiveness', *Journal of World Business* 35(4): 401–16.

Lee, Simon (2001). 'Competitiveness of nations', in R.J. Barry Jones (ed.), *Routledge encyclopedia of international political economy*. London: Routledge, 224–7.

Lucas, Robert E. (1988). 'On the mechanics of economic development', *Journal of Monetary Economics* 22(1): 3–42.

Maione, Giuseppe (2001). *Le merci intelligenti: miti e realtà del capitalism contemporaneo*. Milan: Bruno Mondadori.

Martin, Ron (2011). 'Regional competitiveness: from endowments to externalities to evolution', in Philip Cooke, Bjørn Asheim, Ron Boschma, *et al.* (eds) *Handbook of regional innovation and growth*. Cheltenham: Edward Elgar, 234–45.

McGeehan, Joy M. (1968). 'Competitiveness: a survey of recent literature', *The Economic Journal* 78(310): 243–62.

Morel, Nathalie, Bruno Palier, and Joakim Palme (2012). *Towards a social investment welfare state? Ideas, policies and challenges*. Bristol: Policy Press.

Mosconi, Franco (2015). *The new European industrial policy: global competitiveness and the manufacturing renaissance.* London: Routledge.
Nathan, Max and Henry Overman (2013). 'Agglomeration, clusters, and industrial policy', *Oxford Review of Economic Policy* 29(2): 383–404.
Nozik, Robert (1974). *Anarchy, state, and utopia.* New York: Basic Books.
Offe, Claus (1984). *Contradictions of the welfare state.* Cambridge, MA: MIT Press.
O'Sullivan, Eoin, Antonio Andreoni, Carlos López-Gómez, and Mike Gregory (2013). 'What is new in the new industrial policy? A manufacturing systems perspective', *Oxford Review of Economic Policy* 29(2): 432–62.
Palier, Bruno (2013). 'Social policy paradigms, welfare state reforms and the crisis', *Stato e mercato* 33(1): 37–66.
Pechenick, Eitan A., Christopher M. Danforth, and Peter S. Dodds (2015). 'Characterizing the Google Books corpus: strong limits to inferences of socio-cultural and linguistic evolution', *PLoS ONE* 10(10): e0137041.
Pedersen, Ove Kaj (2010). 'Institutional competitiveness: how nations came to compete', in Glenn Morgan, John L. Campbell, Colin Crouch *et al.* (eds) *The Oxford handbook of comparative institutional analysis.* Oxford: Oxford University Press, 625–58.
Piatier, André (1955). 'L'économie française, est-elle competitive?', *Politique étrangère* 20(2): 141–78.
Porter, Michael (1990). 'The competitive advantage of nations', *Harvard Business Review* March–April: 71–91.
Radice, Hugo (2000). 'Globalization and national capitalisms: theorizing convergence and differentiation', *Review of International Political Economy* 7(4): 719–42.
Rinehart, James (1995). 'The ideology of competitiveness', *Monthly Review* 47(5): 14–23.
Romer, Paul M. (1990). 'Endogenous technological change', *Journal of Political Economy* 98(5): S71–102.
Rossolillo, Francesco (1956). 'Recensione di *L'Europa senza dogane*', *Il Politico* 21(3): 704–6.
Rothbard, Murray (1970). *Power and market: government and the economy.* Arlington, VA: HIS.
Rubalcaba, Luis (2017). 'Competitiveness', in Douglas Richardson, Noel Castree, Michael F. Goodchild, *et al.* (eds) *The international encyclopedia of geography.* Hoboken, NJ: Wiley and Sons.
Ruggie, John G. (1982). 'International regimes, transactions and change: embedded liberalism in the postwar economic order', *International Organisation* 36(2): 379–415.
Sahlberg, Pasi (2006). 'Education reform for raising economic competitiveness', *Journal of Educational Change* 7(4): 259–87.
Sala-i-Martin, Xavier, Jennifer Blanke, Margareta Drzeniek Hanouz, *et al.* (2008). 'The global competitiveness index: prioritizing the economic policy agenda', in Michael E. Porter and Klaus Schwab. *The global competitiveness report, 2008–2009.* Geneva: the World Economic Forum, 3–42.
Sapir, Jacques (2004). *An agenda for growing Europe: the Sapir Report.* Oxford: Oxford University Press.
Scharpf, Fritz W. and Vivien A. Schmidt (2000). *Welfare and work in the open economy.* Oxford: Oxford University Press.
Schwab, Klaus and Xavier Sala-i-Martin (2014). *The Global Competitiveness Report 2014–2015.* Geneva: World Economic Forum.
Siggel, Eckhard (2006). 'International competitiveness and comparative advantage: a survey and a proposal for measurement', *Journal of Industry, Competition and Trade* 6: 137–59.

Smither, Robert D. and John M. Houston (1992). 'The nature of competitiveness: the development and validation of the competitiveness index', *Educational and Psychological Measurement* 52(2): 407–18.

Stigler, George J, (1942). 'The extent and bases of monopoly'. *The American Economic Review* 33(2, Supplement): 1–22.

Stjernø, Steinar (2005). *Solidarity in Europe: the history of an idea.* Cambridge: Cambridge University Press.

Streeck, Wolfgang (1999). 'Competitive solidarity: rethinking the "European Social Model"', MPIfG Working Paper No. 99/8. Köln: Max-Planck-Institut für Gesellschaftsforschung.

Sum, Ngai-Ling (2009). 'The production of hegemonic policy discourses: "competitiveness" as a knowledge brand and its (re-)contextualizations', *Critical Policy Studies* 3(2): 184–203.

Sympher, Leo (1900). *Die wirtschaftliche Bedeutung der Kanalfrage*. Berlin: L. Simmon.

Tocqueville, Alexis de (1835). *Mémoire sur le pauperisme.* Available at: http://classiques.uqac.ca/classiques/De_tocqueville_alexis/memoire_pauperisme_1/memoire_pauper isme_1_texte.html

Tyszynski, Henry (1951). 'World trade in manufacturing commodities, 1899–1950', *The Manchester School* 19(3): 272–304.

Uri, Pierre (1972). *Rapport sur la capacité concurrentielle de la Communauté européenne*, Rapport Uri. Vol. 1. Brussels: Commission of the European Communities.

Van Kersbergen, Kees and Anton Hemerijck (2012). 'Two decades of change in Europe: the emergence of the social investment state', *Journal of Social Policy* 41(3): 475–92.

Walras, Léon (2003 [1874]). *Elements of pure economics.* London: Routledge.

Wetzel, Dietmar J. (2015). *Soziologie des Wettbewerbs: eine kultur- und wirtschaftssoziologische Analyse der Marktgesellschaft.* Wiesbaden: Springer VS.

Wildt, Andreas (1995). 'Solidarity', in Joachim Ritter and Karlfried Gründer (eds). *Historisches Wörterbuch der Philosophie.* Vol. 9. Darmstadt: Wissenschaftliche Buchgesellschaft, 1004–15.

Wildt, Andreas (1998). 'Solidarity: its history and contemporary definition', in Kurt Bayertz (ed.). *Solidarity*. Dordrecht: Kluwer, 209–20.

Wolfe, Archibald J. (1919). *Theory and practice of international commerce*. New York: International Book Publishing Company.

Young, Herman H. (1916). 'Physical and mental factors involved in the formboard test', *The Psychological Clinic* 10(6): 1–19.

Young, John A. (1986). 'Global competition – the new reality. Results of the President's Commission on Industrial Competitiveness', in Ralph Landau and Nathan Rosenberg (eds). *The positive sum strategy: harnessing technology for economic growth.* Washington, DC: The National Academies Press.

3 European competitiveness

Competition, cooperation, solidarity

Frédéric Allemand

The call for total commitment

Competitiveness is an obsession (Krugman 1994).[1] It informs all human activities, providing a basis for assessment and comparison: states and territories, public authorities, companies, individuals, industry sectors, R&D activities, the labour market, products, services and capital, education and health systems, institutions – the list goes on. Competitiveness is deeply embedded in the organisation and management of economic and social activities, resulting at the individual level in what may be seen as a general duty to perform (Chopplet 2007). In this respect, as reflected in the index developed by the World Economic Forum (WEF 2016), competitiveness has now become all-consuming or integrated.[2]

The far-reaching nature of competitiveness makes it hard to provide a univocal, unanimous definition of the concept (Cellini and Soci 2002: 73).[3] Used advisedly, it has as many meanings as there are fields and areas to which it can be applied (Feurer and Chaharbaghi 1994). As a neologism derived from the Latin *compĕto*, meaning 'to try to obtain, to attempt to attain',[4] the concept was first recorded in 1829 in English in its adjectival form 'competitive'[5] and in 1907 in French in *Le Nouveau Larousse Illustré*, meaning 'relating to a competition'. It became a term used in economics from the 1950s, meaning 'the ability to withstand competition'.[6] Competitiveness is relative: it expresses the comparison of individual performances with those of other competitors, with the primary aim of acquiring or maintaining a position (Deutsch 1949). It is developed with reference to an external audience.[7] It contains an element of antagonism in terms of the relationship with the other protagonists and the outcome of the competition. The inability to be competitive puts the economic operator, company or employee 'out of business', to use Paul Krugman's expression (Krugman 1994: 31).

When observed at the level of a territory or state, competitiveness is seen as a metaphor for political ranking, status or power (ibid.: 35). It contributes to a Darwinian interpretation of economics: competition enables a process of 'natural' selection among different agents, with the best winning and the losers being eliminated or weakened (Dollfus 1995; Hay 2007). Any loss of competitiveness can be seen as a threat to national security and justifies leveraging all the country's resources to tackle the situation:

> [I]n a somewhat paradoxical fashion, international competitiveness has been constituted both as a (if not the) central objective in relation to which more or less all state policies should be considered, and as a (if not the) central means to the resolution of more or less all other problems that the state is confronted with.
>
> (Fougner 2006: 165)

Competitiveness is a vital requirement, demanding total commitment with the unswerving aim of developing the most competitive, dynamic economy in the world.[8]

The revitalisation of the economic and social action of public authorities

The notion that states, territories and companies are obliged to change because of the constraints of competitiveness should not skew the debate. Competitiveness guides, organises, and sheds light on changes whose fundamental reasons can in fact be traced back to developments in the global economic and geopolitical environment, technological innovations, and the changing expectations of society since the mid-1960s.

Reacting to a changing environment

It is worth noting that debates on competitiveness became more pronounced in the United States from 1983–84 onwards. The severe recession that had been affecting the country for the past three years – marked by a sharp rise in unemployment and the weakening of the strategic pillars of the economy such as the steel, automotive and textile industries – was seen as a crisis of international competitiveness (Quayle 1983). In 1985, the Deputy Secretary of Commerce, Clarence J. Brown, stated that in this context: 'The United States' competitive position in world trade will dominate the national agenda for the rest of this century' (Brown 1986: 1075). In Europe, the first comprehensive study on the European Community's ability to compete, published by the European Commission, examined three turning points: (1) trade liberalisation following the Kennedy Round (1964–67); (2) the mobility of companies, especially North American companies; and (3) the development of information technologies (EC 1971). These three points prompted the Community to embark on a process of reflection on its own competitiveness, fearing that an insurmountable gap was opening up between Europe and America in terms of influence and living standards.

At the beginning of the 1980s, widespread unemployment, low productive investment, and high inflation all pointed to a major structural crisis. Resolving the crisis involved implementing an economic strategy associating the Community and the Member States with the aim of 'combating unemployment and restoring economic growth while preserving monetary stability and ensuring the competitiveness of their economies' (European Council 1982).[9] Twenty years later, the reconfiguration of global trade with the emergence of the BRIC countries (Brazil, Russia, India and China) on the world stage, the ICT revolution, and persistent structural unemployment represented new challenges that, in the EU's view, justified the setting of a new strategic objective focused on competitiveness (European Council 2000).

Competitiveness is both a reaction to a changing environment and a response to concerns over the role of the state in the economic and social field. This has been summed up as follows:

> With international economic links more extensive now than ever before, making it difficult for individual countries to achieve their economic and social objectives in isolation, it is perfectly rational to wonder ... whether the nation state has reached the end of its useful existence.
>
> (Panić 1997: 29)[10]

More specifically, it appears that the welfare state model as developed from the 1950s onwards is in crisis (Rosanvallon 1992 [1981]) and needs to be redesigned (Sauvé 2014). The influence of traditional drivers for action by states in the markets is being contested or even refuted by the liberalisation of trade and regions.[11]

According to Tiirmaa-Klaar:

> [D]uring Keynesian welfare capitalism the state was able to regulate, redistribute, and control economic activities on its soil and to own certain strategic industries. The growing economic openness and the third industrial revolution, more specifically the internationalisation of production, the advance in technologies and the growth of global financial markets have limited the autonomous policy making capacity of the state.
>
> (2006: 157)

States are subject to economic constraints (*Pouvoirs* 2012). This phenomenon is aggravated in Europe as a result of the European integration process. As the French Council of State observed in its 2015 public report on the economic action of public entities, the interdependence established between Member States as a result of European integration is resulting in most macroeconomic drivers being transferred to the European Union (Conseil d'État 2015). In this context, Patrick Le Galès asks the question 'What is the future of the state?', inasmuch as it has lost 'the exercise of political authority and [is] incapable of effectively controlling a considerable number of transnational phenomena' (Le Galès 2014: 2). Greece, denied the possibility of refinancing itself on the market by these phenomena, is a good example in this respect. The question goes beyond economic and social concerns; the vitality of democracy itself is at issue:

> [I]f it [the government] fails to live up to this challenge [of competitiveness], it leaves its nation's economic prospects to be determined by market forces alone, which will result in the neglect of many significant aspects of the country's long-term economic development.
>
> (Tiirmaa-Klaar 2006: 156)

Another expression of state power

Competitiveness is consequently another expression of state power with regard to market forces (Chopplet 2007). Competitiveness constitutes the main argument for economic revitalisation in light of globalisation (Panić 1997) or, in other words, for a rejustification of economic and social action by the state at a time when it may appear to be out of its depth and at risk of being swallowed up by a globalised environment (Badie 1999; Thirion 2007). It is a means of reassessing and redefining the state's drivers for action (Cerny 1990) with the aim of preserving the state's role as chief guarantor of public welfare. It indicates a 're-embedding' of the economy in the state, to use Karl Polanyi's (1983 [1944]) expression. The situation of the European banking industry reflects this development. In response to the 2008–09 crisis, states reasserted their role in this sector by taking action to support weakened institutions and thoroughly reorganizing banking regulation and surveillance at European level. In the singular case of Greece, we witnessed not just the transformation of a state but the building of a new state that met the institutional and economic standards of so-called 'developed' countries.

At the same time, the restoration of the economic and social role of the state does not mean that the powers exercised today can be the same as those exercised in the nineteenth century, especially in Europe.[12] To be more precise, European integration offers the possibility of preserving the role of the state via a redistribution of drivers for action at the most appropriate levels. As indicated in the first general report by the Commission on the competitiveness of the European Community (the Uri Report, 1972), this is the very 'objective and purpose of European integration' (EC 1971: 9).[13] This view is in line with the interpretation of the European motivations of states proposed by Alan S. Milward in his major work, *The European Rescue of the Nation-State*:

> The European nation-state rescued itself from collapse, created a new political consensus as the basis of its legitimacy, and through changes in its response to its citizens which meant a sweeping extension of its functions and ambitions reasserted itself as the fundamental unit of political organization.
>
> (1992: 3)

This rescue of the state by European integration involves two aspects. Drivers for action have been redistributed between the European and national levels: for reasons of efficiency, macroeconomic policies have been transferred to the

European level (Le Galès 2014: 8), while the state pursues microeconomic (structural) policies (Cerny 1997: 270). Each country is therefore free to develop policies that are best suited to its economic, social, and historical context. National performances are measured and compared, fostering the exchange of best practices.[14] At the same time, growing interdependence between policies pursued at national level, as well as between national and EU policies, means that close cooperation between member states is vital. The EU's economic policy is based on the coordination of national economic policies and policies adopted by the EU, including the completion of the internal market.[15] This harmonisation of micro- and macroeconomic policies is one of the main challenges of the new economic governance: improving the functioning of Economic and Monetary Union (EMU) will require the development of a more effective policy mix between macroeconomic policies (Allemand and Martucci 2012), if it is to improve European competitiveness.[16]

The harmonisation of national and European economic and social objectives

When it comes to interpersonal and intergroup relationships, it has been observed that 'competition or co-operation is directed toward the same social end' (May and Doob 1937). The reorganisation of states' powers within the framework of the EU does not, per se, determine the direction of the policies adopted.

A concept to encourage growth and employment

Based on the preliminary articles of the Treaties of the European Economic Community (EEC), the European Coal and Steel Community (ECSC) and the European Atomic Energy Community (EAEC), Pierre-Henri Teitgen noted that

> the ultimate aim of our treaties is therefore economic expansion, the development of living standards across the Community and closer relations between the member countries; from the outset, the common market is presented as a means to achieve this aim.
>
> (1971: 78)

In its first annual report on economic and social cohesion, the Commission set out the specific nature of the European social and economic model:

> [T]he organisation of society in European countries reflects the values of the social market economy. This seeks to combine a system of economic organisation based on market forces, freedom of opportunity and enterprise with a commitment to the values of internal solidarity and mutual support which ensures open access of all members of society to services of general benefit and protection.
>
> (EC 1996: 13)

These factors, which can be found in Article 3 of the Treaty on European Union (TEU), provide both meaning and direction for competitiveness in the EU. A country's competitiveness is not simply determined by its balance of payments equilibrium or the size of its budget surplus, and even less so by the desire to keep wages as low as possible. 'On the contrary, being genuinely competitive means being in a position to pay the highest salaries,' explains the Uri Report (EC 1971: 7). Forty years later, the Commission's approach has not changed, as confirmed by Jean-Claude Juncker in his opening statement at the European Parliament plenary session in 2014. 'Competitiveness is often confused with one-sided social regression,' noted the candidate for President of the European Commission, 'but competitiveness is not achieved through social regression' (Juncker 2014). Indeed, since the 1982 Copenhagen European Council, competitiveness has followed the same twofold pattern: lasting growth with high job creation (EC 1993). The Euro-Plus Pact adopted on 25 March 2011 by the Heads of State or Government of the Member States of the euro area and six other states retains this link: '[c]ompetitiveness is essential to help the EU grow faster and more sustainably in the medium and long term, to produce higher levels of income for citizens, and to preserve our social models' (European Council 2011).

The intractable economic and social dimension

The dual economic and social considerations of competitiveness have given rise to considerable theoretical discussions in all disciplines. Without attempting to summarise all the different positions, it is worth pointing out the criticism levelled at the discrepancy between the objectives and the policies implemented. Some authors claim that we are witnessing a transformation of the post-war Keynesian welfare state into a Schumpeterian state focused on policies of supply, competitiveness and innovation. They see the main effects as being a reduction in social spending and the exercise of state authority in order to maintain order, silencing interest groups opposed to capitalism and finding jobs for as many people as possible, regardless of their employment conditions. According to this model, the action of the state ultimately confirms and strengthens the legitimacy of natural market functioning (Jessop 2002). Political scientist Jonah Levy (1999) is one of many to observe that states are no longer aiming to direct the economy and the markets, but to build markets ('market-making states'). This would turn countries from welfare states into 'competition states' (Cerny 1997: 265),[17] using the mechanisms within market structures to improve their economic performances (Tiirmaa-Klaar 2006).

But this change in the relationship between the state and the market does not suggest a return to the 'naturalist naivety' of traditional liberals and the illusion of an 'invisible hand'. Nicolas Thirion (2014) emphasises:

> Advocates of this new approach refute the principle of *laissez-faire, laissez-passer*, believing that it is not state abstention that will best guarantee

> market logic, but rather state intervention whenever necessary to establish, reestablish, stimulate and boost competition in the markets, even if it means providing safeguard mechanisms for the markets to preserve the balances deemed essential for society.

In this context, the market economy and the state are not incompatible; quite the opposite. 'The state must govern for the market' (ibid.: 250). In the same way, Nicolas Jabko, while recognising that the market served as the basis for the development of Europe, highlights the ambiguous status of the market in the recent history of European integration:

> European unification is not taking place according to a predetermined scenario of wholesale liberalisation – nor is it naturally expected to serve as a rampart against market globalisation. The EU is a multinational, multipartite construct that cannot allow itself to support such clear-cut political tendencies.
>
> (2009: 3)

The market should be seen at once as a tool for liberalisation, an instrument for managing external threats and a new means of organising a shared socio-economic order (ibid.: 3).

The role played by the market in achieving the aim of competitiveness raises questions as to the methods used to implement social policies and preserve the heritage of the welfare state. Some have emphasised the process of 'social deprotection' at work since the early 1980s (Ferry 2000: 187). They decry the fact that, in their view, social Europe will never happen (Denord and Schwartz 2009). But the social question is more complex than it might seem; the terms have changed since the period of the *Trente Glorieuses* (Baverez 2000).[18] The welfare state has not been dismantled, but its organisational principles are being substantially reviewed (Pierson 2001).

In the context of the European Union, social policy remains largely a national prerogative.[19] The same goes for employment policy and social protection.[20] The respective development of these policies is mainly carried out at the national level, which encourages competition between the various social models. Yet this has not given rise to a generalised model (Esping-Andersen 1994). While some developments suggest a convergence of social protection regimes, it can be observed that path dependence and other local circumstances have resulted in national systems remaining confined within their idiosyncrasies (Pierson 1994). At the very most, hybrid models emerge, especially in the labour market:

> In the field of labour market policies, the general approach, which was previously geared towards maintaining revenues and status in employment, has veered towards an entirely different objective, namely boosting employment by the activation and institutionalisation of more labour-friendly standards.
>
> (Burgi 2009: 202)

This is the transition from the welfare state to the 'workfare state', in other words, the ideological entrenchment of the working society (Ferry 2000: 187). Work becomes an element in the adaptation of the market (the 'adaptive diversion of the market') and no longer reflects the inclusive values with which it is traditionally associated.

The economic and monetary integration initiated in 1994 revived the debate on the adaptation of the welfare state (Hemerijck 2012). By eliminating exchange rate variations and stepping up the free movement of capital, economic and monetary union (EMU) transfers the burden of adapting economic systems to an open competitive environment from the most mobile factors (capital) to the least mobile factors: labour and state efficiency. The idea is that competition will lead to a fall in costs, an improvement in services and a rise in innovation, and that growth in industry sectors exposed to competition will stimulate job creation. This will then benefit the entire economy, including protected sectors, via a knock-on effect. When it comes to job losses, greater flexibility on the labour market is intended to encourage recruitment or retraining in sectors that have been able to seize the opportunities created by opening up to European and/or international competition. Support for productive investment and the increased flexibility of the labour market should help remove obstacles to job creation.[21]

This general supply-side approach is not without risks at individual level. The Schumpeterian process of creative destruction may reveal a partial mismatch between the qualifications of those workers facing international competition and the new opportunities associated with the opening up of the economy to international markets, and it may also highlight an unequal redistribution of job creation between countries and regions via a polarisation of resources and wealth. The funds available for state operating costs and public services are also subject to the constraints of free capital movement. The tax burden is not the only condition governing investment decisions, but it represents an important factor. Concerns that the potential for company start-up should not be over-burdened by profits being skimmed off to fund insurance mechanisms have led to a transfer of taxation from capital to employment. Budgetary constraints have resulted in a rethink of the risk coverage service provided by the welfare state, as seen in the geographical redistribution of local public services, a preference for pension schemes involving a two-pillar system (state pension contributions and personal pension funds) and the tightening up of conditions for unemployment benefits.

These consequences of EMU on the welfare state have not been ignored; they have been incorporated into the EU agenda by Member States and the Community institutions under plans for a European social model. The aim of this concept is to create a social counterpart to the Single Market and EMU.[22] In his first address on the thrust of Commission policy, given to the European Parliament on 14 January 1985, Jacques Delors referred to the objectives enshrined in the Treaty establishing the European Community and the attainment of 'economic, social, and monetary integration'. The unification of the economic area had to go hand in hand with the unification of the social area (Delors 1985: 5, 10). In 1987, when the European Parliament gave its views on the priorities of a

European strategy for growth, it linked social policy with macroeconomic policies, territorial cohesion and the business environment. It particularly emphasised that it was impossible to separate progress in economic integration and progress in the social sphere leading to the creation of a social area (European Parliament 1987: 192). As Jacques Delors speculated, '[w]hat will happen without this minimal harmonisation of social rules? … Member States and firms trying to gain an advantage over their competitors, at the cost of what can only be described as social decline' (1985: 11).

The EU has taken several measures to reduce the phenomenon of social dumping. The aim is to contribute to economic stability and the strengthening of productive investment, even if the EU needs to take some responsibility in this area. Juncker's investment plan is the most recent example. Vocational training schemes have been strengthened and encouraged, especially from the mid-1990s onwards. Vocational training is seen as 'a crucial means of responding to accelerating economic and social change and of promoting employment, social cohesion and competitiveness' (EC 2004). To this end, a series of initiatives have been promoted with the aim of adapting skills to the needs of sectors considered to be growth industries, such as ICT and biotechnology.[23] Alongside these initiatives, regulatory efforts have been made to harmonise social rules, in close cooperation with the European 'social partners'. In a fragmented, heterogeneous environment, involving the partners (employers' organisations and trade unions) in the European social dialogue – an approach that was revived following the Val Duchesse dialogue in March 1985 – helps ensure compliance with social democracy and the integration of specific local needs (Delors 2004; Lapeyre 2015). The introduction of EMU involved a strengthening of economic and social cohesion via the inclusion in the Maastricht Treaty of a protocol on cohesion in addition to the provisions on EMU.

The expression of an 'order of competitiveness'

In EU terms, competitiveness helps revive the usefulness of action at national level while preserving the relevance of wide-ranging, strategic action at European level. In so doing, it informs and justifies the distribution of powers and responsibilities between the EU and the states. Competitiveness does not indicate a disengagement of the state in favour of the EU but rather a redefinition of the drivers available for state authorities to carry out more effective action for the sound functioning of the markets.

Moreover, competitiveness cannot merely be seen as the phenomenon of different territories engaging in competition against each other. It also serves an integrative purpose, creating a basis for the establishment of new methods of cooperation between national and European levels and soliciting action from both public and private stakeholders. Finally, competitiveness is a means and not an end in itself. It should serve to encourage sustainable growth and welfare for the countries of Europe. Competitiveness is only acceptable if it retains a sufficient degree of solidarity and cohesion among its members. Here we recognise the triptych behind the Single European Act, described by Delors in his own terms in his memoirs: 'Competition that stimulates, cooperation that strengthens, and solidarity that unites' (2004: 326). In our view, this triptych characterises an 'order of competitiveness'.

Acknowledgements

Many thanks to Sarah Cooper for the translation of this chapter from French.

Notes

1 For a similar analysis of the 'diktat' of competitiveness, see Rinehart (1995).
2 Competitiveness is defined here (WEF 2016) as 'the set of institutions, policies, and factors that determine the level of productivity of a country'. See also EC (2003).
3 Some authors point out that this 'abusive' generalisation of the concept strips it of its explanatory function. See Cellini and Soci (2002: 71).
4 See the entry 'compěto' in Olivetti and Olivetti (2016).
5 See the entry 'competitive' in Simpson and Weiner (2016).
6 See the entry 'compétitivité' in *Dictionnaire de l'Académie française*.
7 The original use of the concept of competitiveness is closely linked to the development of international trade theories from the 1950s onwards, reflecting changes in the terms of trade between the United States and other developed countries or countries in the process of economic catch-up. See, for example, Narvekar (1960).
8 See the central objective of the Lisbon Strategy (European Council 2000). The aim was put in virtually identical terms by President Obama in his State of the Union Address on 20 January 2015:

> So no one knows for certain which industries will generate the jobs of the future. But we do know we want them here in America. We know that. And that's why the third part of middle-class economics is all about building the most competitive economy anywhere, the place where businesses want to locate and hire.

9 The period 1981–83 saw a growing number of cross-cutting and sectoral communications from the Commission on competitiveness. For a summary list, see EC (1983).
10 See also the renowned book *The Rise and Fall of Great Powers* by Paul Kennedy (1988). Taking a long-term approach, the author describes a gradual decline of the United States and a rise of China or even of the European Economic Community. This decline may be slowed if appropriate policies are adopted.
11 As emphasised by Jean-Paul Fitoussi (2012: 64), this divestment of the state with respect to the market was less the result of any phenomenon of market transcendence and more a deliberate decision by interested parties. This point should be linked to the crisis affecting the welfare state from the 1970s onwards. To what extent did liberalisation represent a way of prompting a reform of the welfare state and guaranteeing its continued existence, albeit in a new form?
12 For an enlightening study of the legal dynamics at work in the process of distribution of responsibilities in favour of the EU and, ultimately, the 'strengthening of state influence', see Michel (2003).
13 For a detailed analysis of French concerns in the area of competitiveness and the competitive situation, see Kipping (2002).
14 See the many indicators established as part of the Lisbon Strategy and partly rationalised in the Europe 2020 Strategy. For a critical analysis, see Allemand (2005).
15 Article 119 of the TFEU. For a recent presentation of the need for coordination and the development of the coordination framework, see Allemand *et al.* (2016: 23ff).

16 See the explanatory memoranda concerning the legislative proposals of the Commission under the Six Pack, for example, EC (2010). See also the Euro-Plus Pact (European Council 2011).
17 Three distinctive factors are used by Cerny to qualify competition states: (1) a belief in the capacity of competitiveness to generate growth and improve living standards; (2) the priority placed on supply-based policies as opposed to demand-based policies; and (3) less distinction made between national and international policy. On the subject, see also Palan and Abbott (1996) and Palan (1998).
18 The author invites us to reconsider the social link from three angles: (1) a form of work structuring production; (2) a system of collective negotiations influencing the distribution of added value; and (3) social governance.
19 Articles 4 (2)(b), 5(3), and 151ff. of the TFEU.
20 Articles 5(2) and 145–50 of the TFEU concerning social policy; Article 153 of the TFEU concerning social protection.
21 For a description written some time ago but still relevant to this process, see EC (1971: 10).
22 See the emphasis placed by Jacques Delors on the development of the social question in preparations for the White Paper on completing the internal market and during the drafting of the Delors Report (Delors 1989), especially point 22.
23 See, for example, EC (1985). Note also that since 1975 there has been a European Centre for the Development of Vocational Training (Council Regulation (EEC) no. 337/75, of 10 February 1975).

References

Allemand, Frédéric (2005). 'La France face à la stratégie de Lisbonne: un bilan mitigé', *Futuribles* 310: 40–50.

Allemand, Frédéric, Matthieu Bion, and Jean-Luc Sauron (2016). *Gouverner la zone euro après la crise: l'exigence d'intégration*. Paris: Gualino.

Allemand, Frédéric and Francesco Martucci (2012). 'La nouvelle gouvernance économique européenne', *Cahiers de droit européen* 1: 15–99.

Badie, Bertrand (1999). *Un monde sans souveraineté: les États entre ruse et responsabilité*. Paris: Fayard.

Baverez, Nicolas (2000). 'La nouvelle question sociale', *Commentaires* 92(4): 799–806.

Brown, Clarence J. (1986). 'U.S. competitiveness in world markets', *N.Y.U. Journal of International Law and Politics* 18: 1075–86.

Burgi, Noëlle (2009). 'La construction de l'État social minimal en Europe', *Politique européenne* 27(1): 201–32.

Cellini, Roberto and Anna Soci (2002). 'Pop competitiveness', *BNL Quarterly Review* 220: 73.

Cerny, Philip G (1990). *The changing architecture of politics: structure, agency, and the future of the state*. London: Sage.

Cerny, Philip G. (1997). 'Paradoxes of the competition state: the dynamics of political globalization', *Government and Opposition* 32(2): 251–74.

Chopplet, Marc (2007). 'Compétitivité', *Quaderni* 6: 22–4.

Conseil d'État (2015). *Étude annuelle 2015. L'action économique des personnes publiques*. Paris: La Documentation française.

Delors, Jacques (1985). 'The thrust of Commission policy', speech by Jacques Delors, President of the Commission, to the European Parliament and extracts from his reply to the ensuing debate. Strasbourg, 14 and 15 January 1985. *Bulletin of the European Communities*, Suppl. 1/85.

Delors, Jacques (1989). *Report on Economic and Monetary Union in the European Community [Delors Report]*. Luxembourg: OPOCE.

Delors, Jacques (2004). *Mémoires*. Paris: Plon.

Denord, François and Antoine Schwartz (2009). *L'Europe sociale n'aura pas lieu*. Paris: Raison d'Agir.

Deutsch, Morton (1949). 'A theory of cooperation and competition', *Human Relations* 2: 129–52.

Dictionnaire de l'Académie française (1992–2016). 9th edn. Paris: Académie française, ATILF.

Dollfus, Olivier (1995). 'Mondialisation, compétitivités, territoires et marchés mondiaux', *Espaces géographiques* 24(3): 270–80.

EC (European Commission) (1971). *Rapport sur la capacité concurrentielle de la Communauté européenne* (Rapport Uri)]. Vol. 1. Brussels: Commission of the European Communities.

EC (European Commission) (1983). 'Communication from the Commission to the Council – Discussion paper for the special Council meeting of 20–21 September on the question of improving the international competitive position of European firms. Brussels, 14 September 1983. COM(83) 547 final. Brussels: Commission of the European Communities.

EC (European Commission) (1985). 'Vocational training and new information technologies – work programme for the period 1985–1988, Communication, Brussels, 18 April 1985', COM(85) 167 final. Brussels: Commission of the European Communities.

EC (European Commission) (1993). 'Growth, competitiveness, employment. The challenges and ways forward into the 21st century', White Paper. *Bulletin of the European Communities*, Suppl. 6/93.

EC (European Commission) (1996). 'First report on economic and social cohesion,' COM(96) 542 final, 6 November 1996. Brussels: European Commission.

EC (European Commission) (2003). 'Communication to the Council and to the European Parliament: some key issues in Europe's competitiveness: towards an integrated approach', COM(2003) 704 final. Brussels: European Commission.

EC (European Commission) (2004). 'Explanatory memorandum concerning the Proposal for a Council Regulation amending Regulation (EEC) No 337/75, Brussels, 8 January 2004', COM(2003) 854 final. Brussels: European Commission.

EC (European Commission) (2010). 'Proposal for a Regulation of the European Parliament and of the Council on the prevention and correction of macroeconomic imbalances, Brussels, 29 September 2010', COM(2010) 527 final. Brussels: European Commission.

Esping-Andersen, Gøsta (1994). 'After the golden age: the future of the welfare state in the new global order', UNRISD Occasional Paper No. 7. Geneva: United Nations Research Institute for Social Development.

European Council (1982). 'Conclusions of sessions of the European Council', Brussels, 29 and 30 March 1982.

European Council (2000). 'Lisbon European Council 23 and 24 March 2000: conclusion of the Presidency', Brussels: European Council.

European Council (2011). 'Euro Plus Pact: Stronger economic policy coordination for competitiveness and convergence, 25 March 2011: conclusions of the Brussels European Council, 24 and 25 March 2011, Annex I', EUCO 10/1/11 REV 1. Brussels: European Council.

European Parliament (1987). 'Resolution of 20 November 1987 closing the procedure for consultation of the European Parliament on the proposal for a Council Decision adopting the annual report on the economic situation in the Community and laying down economic policy guidelines for 1988', A2–182/87. OJ C 345, 21 December 1987. Brussels: European Parliament.

Ferry, Jean-Marc (2000). *La question de l'État européen*. Paris: Gallimard.

Feurer, Rainer and Kazem Chaharbaghi (1994). 'Defining competitiveness: a holistic approach', *Management Decision* 32(2): 49–58.

Fitoussi, Jean-Paul (2012). 'La marge de manœuvre des États. Des démocraties sans souveraineté?', *Pouvoirs* 142(3): 61–70.

Fougner, Tore (2006). 'The State, international competitiveness and neoliberal globalisation: is there a future beyond the "competition state"?', *Review of International Studies* 32(1): 165–85.

Hay, Colin (2007). 'What doesn't kill you can only make you stronger: the Doha Development Round, the Services Directive and the EU's conception of competitiveness', *Journal of Common Market Studies* 45: 25–43.

Hemerijck, Anton (2012). 'Two or three waves of welfare state transformation?', in Nathalie Morel, Bruno Palier, and Joakim Palme (eds), *Towards a social investment welfare state?* Bristol: The Policy Press, 33–60.

Jabko, Nicolas (2009). *L'Europe par le marché. Histoire d'une stratégie improbable*. Paris: Presses de Sciences Po.

Jessop, Bob (2002). *The future of the capitalist state*. Cambridge: Polity Press.

Juncker, Jean-Claude (2014). 'A new start for Europe. Opening statement in the European Parliament plenary session. Strasbourg, 15 July 2014'. Available at: http://europa.eu/rapid/press-release_SPEECH-14-567_en.htm

Kennedy, Paul (1988). *The rise and fall of great powers*. New York: Random House.

Kipping, Matthias (2002). *La France et les origines de l'Union européenne*. Paris: Comité pour l'histoire économique et financière de la France.

Krugman, Paul (1994). 'Competitiveness: a dangerous obsession', *Foreign Affairs* 73(2): 28–44.

Lapeyre, Jean (2015). 'Dialogue social européen: 30 ans d'expérience et de progrès, pour quel avenir?', Notre Europe, Policy Paper No. 124. Paris: Notre Europe – Institut Jacques Delors. Available at: http://institutdelors.eu/wp-content/uploads/2018/01/dialoguesocialeuropeen-lapeyre-ijd-jan15.pdf

Le Galès, Patrick (2014). 'Que devient l'Etat?', *Cahiers français* 379: 2–8.

Levy, Jonah D. (1999). *Tocqueville's revenge: state, society, and the economy in contemporary France*. Cambridge, MA: Harvard University Press.

Olivetti, Enrico and Francesca Olivetti (eds) (2016). *Le grand dictionnaire latin*. Paris: Olivetti Media Communication.

May, Mark Arthur and Leonard Doob (1937). 'Competition and cooperation', *Bulletin: Social Science Research Council* 25.

Michel, Valérie (2003). *Recherche sur les compétences de la Communauté*. Paris. L'Harmattan.

Milward, Alan S. (1992). *The European rescue of the nation state*. Berkeley, CA: University of California Press.

Narvekar, Prabhakar R (1960). 'The role of competitiveness in Japan's export performance, 1954–1958', *IMF Staff Papers* 8(1): 85–100.

Palan, Ronen (1998). 'Luring buffaloes and the game of industrial subsidies: a critique of national competitive policies in the era of the competition state', *Global Society* 12(3): 323–41.

Palan, Ronen and Jason Abbott (1996). *State strategies in the global political economy*. London: Pinter.

Panić, Mica (1997). 'The end of the nation state?', *Structural Change and Economic Dynamics* 8: 29–44.

Pierson, Paul (1994). *Dismantling the welfare state? Reagan, Thatcher and the politics of retrenchment*. Cambridge: Cambridge University Press.

Pierson, Paul (ed.) (2001). *The new politics of the welfare state*. Cambridge, MA: Harvard University Press.

Polanyi, Karl (1983 [1944]). *La grande transformation*. Paris: Gallimard.

Pouvoirs (2012). 'Les États sous contrainte économique', special issue, 142(3).

Quayle, Dan (1983). 'United States international competitiveness and trade policies for the 1980s', *Northwestern Journal of International Law & Business* 5(1): 1–12.

Rinehart, James (1995). 'The ideology of competitiveness', *Monthly Review* 47(5): 14–23.

Rosanvallon, Pierre (1992 [1981]). *La crise de l'État-providence*. Paris: Éditions du Seuil.

Sauvé, Jean-Marc (2014). 'Transformations et permanence de l'État', *Cahiers français* 379: 9–15.

Simpson, John and Edmund Weiner (eds) (2016). *Oxford English Dictionary*. Oxford: Oxford University Press.

Teitgen, Pierre-Henri (1971). *Cours de droit institutionnel communautaire*. Paris: Le cours de droit.

Thirion, Nicolas (2007). *Le marché et l'Etat à l'heure de la mondialisation*. Brussels: Larcier.

Thirion, Nicolas (2014). 'Des rapports entre le marché et la puissance publique: de l'État-providence à l'État régulateur', in Nicolas Thirion (ed.). *Crise et droit économique*. Brussels: Larcier, 237–57.

Tiirmaa-Klaar, Heli (2006). 'International competitiveness and the role of government in the globalised world economy', in Andres Kasekamp (ed.), *The Estonian foreign policy yearbook 2005*. Tallin: Estonian Foreign Policy Institute, 155–74.

WEF (World Economic Forum) (2016). *Appendix: Methodology and Computation of the Global Competitiveness Index, 2015–2016*. Davos: WEF.

4 Competitiveness and solidarity in the history of the European Union, 1957–2017

Laurent Warlouzet

While some scholars consider that the European integration process has always had a strong neo-liberal component, which has grown over the years,[1] this contribution will argue that, on the contrary, the development of the EU has always been characterized by a balance between the principle of competitiveness and the principle of solidarity. This contribution will shed light on a 60-year long history, from the 1957 Treaty of Rome creating the European Economic Community (EEC), which was then superseded by the European Union (EU) with the 1992 Maastricht Treaty, to now. It focuses on the EEC/EU, as this institution is by far the most influential in terms of economic cooperation.

According to the typology developed in Warlouzet (2018), throughout those 60 years, Western Europeans leaders have strived to implement three types of socio-economic models of Europe at the EEC/EU level.[2] The first, building a 'social Europe', aims at fostering solidarity, either by redistributive policies intended to reduce inequalities, or by taking measures targeted as the least favoured groups (the poor, the sick, women, or those suffering from dire working conditions, or from a degraded environment). The second type of policy is the neo-mercantilist one. Its aim is to maximize national industrial output by focusing on strengthening competitiveness through non-free market measures. Neo-mercantilism comes from the mercantilist impetus of protecting national companies and of fostering export. In this vision, world trade is a zero-sum game: the gains of one actor correspond to the losses of another. The prefix 'neo' is added to underline the fact that those policies were embedded in an international economic order based on a commitment to free trade dating back to 1945. In contrast to promoters of social policies, neo-mercantilists do not aim at protecting the poorest, even if this could be a side effect of shielding industry from international competition. The final category regroups 'market-oriented' policies which aim at promoting competitiveness by removing obstacles to the economic liberties of individuals and of firms, both at the national and at the international levels. Neo-liberal policies are a radical variant of market-oriented policies. They put the emphasis on a massive retrenchment of the welfare state combined with regressive fiscal policies, whereas those two elements are not present among moderate promoters of market-oriented policy.

The advantage of this threefold classification is double. First, it points out that the EEC/EU was not only market-oriented or neo-liberal right from the start. Second, it underlines that the goal of improving competitiveness can be attained either by neo-mercantilist or by market-oriented policies. Third, it provides a precise definition of neo-liberal Europe which is based on a set of clearly identifiable policy measures.

This contribution, based on a vast array of literature in history and in political science,[3] and on forays into various European primary sources,[4] will examine the unfolding of those three models of economic cooperation during five periods: (1) 'embedded liberalism' (1957–73); (2) the 'shock of the global' (1973–84); (3) the 'Single Market' (1985–92); (4) the 'end of history' (1992–2006); and (5) the crisis years (2007–present). They will all be examined chronologically, the last two sections being only sketched out since a historical perspective is lacking for such recent events.

'Embedded liberalism' (1957–73)

The first period (1957–73) was characterized by a relation between competitiveness and solidarity that was captured by the expression 'embedded liberalism', coined by John Ruggie in 1982. He defined it as a regime under which 'multilateralism and the quest for domestic stability were coupled and even conditioned by one another' (Ruggie 1982: 398). By 'domestic stability', Ruggie meant that the General Agreement on Tariffs and Trade (GATT) was founded on international free trade, but it included many exemptions, both permanent (for regional trade agreements) and temporary (in case of balance of payments problem or trade disputes). Ruggie went on to quote the famous economist Jacob Viner, a specialist in trade agreements, who asserted in early 1947, during the GATT negotiations: 'There are few free traders in the present-day world, no one pays any attention to their views, and no person in authority anywhere advocates free trade.'[5] In other words, the post-1945 international economic regime was not a pure laissez-faire approach that temporarily tolerated exemptions, but rather a comprehensive association of free market, neo-mercantilist and social policies.

'Embedded liberalism' was predicated on a rejection of the nationalism of the 1930s. Initially, it was the most liberal states who unleashed economic nationalism, first, the United States with trade protectionism in 1930 (the famous Smoot–Hawley Tariff Act), and then the United Kingdom with currency devaluation in 1931 (Boyce 2009). Combined with harsh deflation policies, this approach contributed to increase and to spread the economic crisis. Later on, in certain countries, economic nationalism fuelled political nationalism with the advent of Hitler in 1933. In reaction, after 1945, Atlantic elites fostered a radically different combination of international economic cooperation based on free trade (even if barriers to trade remained important until 1959 due to the reconstruction) and an internal priority on full employment. According to Ruggie:

> This was the essence of the embedded liberalism compromise: unlike the economic nationalism of the thirties, it would be multilateral in character; unlike the liberalism of the gold standard and free trade, its multilateralism would be predicated upon domestic interventionism.
>
> (1982: 393)

In other words, despite inevitable local differences, most leaders shared the conviction that the 1930s, and in particular Hitler's aggressive mercantilist policy, were a counter-model.

This translated into the Treaty of Rome of 25 March 1957 which created the European Economic Community. Detailed historical analysis of the early years of the EEC demonstrate that the Treaty of Rome was negotiated and implemented during its early years by a blend of Christian Democrats (Adenauer, Fanfani), of socialists (Spaak, Mollet) and of conservative politicians who were not neo-liberals (De Gaulle) (Parsons 2003; Varsori 2010; Warlouzet 2011b). Most of them signed or implemented the Treaty of Rome while at the same time strengthening their national welfare state. They put an emphasis on the EEC whereas a more market-oriented alternative, the Free Trade Area (FTA), was available. The FTA was rejected first and foremost by the French government, but many other actors, such as the European Commission, were sceptical about it (Warlouzet 2011a, 2011b). Only the most neo-classical and the least enthusiastic about European integration prioritized the FTA over the EEC: in particular, the German Minister of Economics Ludwig Erhard, who was outmanoeuvred by Adenauer (Löffler 2002: 563).

The Treaty of Rome of 1957 proved flexible enough to accommodate many kinds of national economic policies, as its extensive Articles 2 and 3 EEC stating its objectives demonstrate. Article 2 promotes a 'harmonious development of economic activities, a continuous and balanced expansion, an increased stability, an accelerated raising of the standard of living'. Article 3 lists a series of tasks to be completed, with an emphasis either on a market-oriented approach (items a, b, c, f), or on a social-oriented one (i, j, k), with a third category being unspecific (d, e, f, g, h) (see Box 4.1).

Whereas the Treaty of Rome certainly promoted market-oriented dynamics, it was by no means neo-liberal. Rather, it followed the style of a long tradition of promoters of a unified market in Europe in order to increase efficiency, and hence growth. As early as 1919, Keynes had defended in *The Economic Consequences of the Peace*, the necessity to lower the tariff barriers in Europe to spur growth and peaceful relations in Europe (Keynes 1919). Setting up a common market in Europe had been promoted by many moderate politicians and intellectuals in order to emulate the gigantic US internal market, which was associated with higher productivity and higher growth.

Setting up a European free trade zone was not incompatible with promoting solidarity. This was the idea behind the first Organization of European Economic Cooperation (OEEC) of 1948: massive American financial assistance was granted (through the Marshall Plan) and combined with the progressive opening

Box 4.1 Treaty establishing the European Economic Community (Treaty of Rome), 1957, article 3

For the purposes set out in the preceding Article, the activities of the Community shall include, under the conditions and with the timing provided for in this Treaty:

a the elimination, as between Member States, of customs duties and of quantitative restrictions in regard to the importation and exportation of goods, as well as of all other measures with equivalent effect;
b the establishment of a common customs tariff and a common commercial policy towards third countries;
c the abolition, as between Member States, of the obstacles to the free movement of persons, services and capital;
d the inauguration of a common agricultural policy;
e the inauguration of a common transport policy;
f the establishment of a system ensuring that competition shall not be distorted in the Common Market;
g the application of procedures which shall make it possible to co-ordinate the economic policies of Member States and to remedy disequilibria in their balances of payments;
h the approximation of their respective municipal law to the extent necessary for the functioning of the Common Market;
i the creation of a European Social Fund in order to improve the possibilities of employment for workers and to contribute to the raising of their standard of living;
j the establishment of a European Investment Bank intended to facilitate the economic expansion of the Community through the creation of new resources; and
k the association of overseas countries and territories with the Community with a view to increasing trade and to pursuing jointly their effort towards economic and social development.

Source: https://europa.eu/european-union/sites/europaeu/files/docs/body/treaties_establishing_the_european_communities_single_european_act_en.pdf

of European markets. The European Coal and Steel Community (ECSC) and then the EEC pushed this logic further. In 1956, the Ohlin report, requested by the ILO, considered that the setting up of a common market would naturally unleash growth. Only targeted measures to foster the mobility of workers were deemed useful (Mechi 2013: 26). The harmonization of social legislation was considered unnecessary, especially since the six founding members of the EEC had roughly the same level of GDP per capita in 1957 (except for Southern Italy), and since all of them had rather extensive welfare state provisions. Besides, most of these welfare states were of the 'Bismarckian' sort which meant that the social benefits depended on the type of work performed (as opposed to 'Beveridgian' welfare states where provisions are universal). As a result, social benefits varied a lot even within a single state, so harmonizing them at the European level seemed pointless (Palier 2009).

Moreover, the Treaty of Rome included provisions designed to offset the detrimental consequences of free trade. Some of them were general, such as safeguard clauses allowing a country to close its market temporarily. Article 117 EEC was rather ambitious from the social point of view, as it underlined 'the necessity to promote improvement of the living and working conditions of labour so as to permit the equalization of such conditions in an upward direction'. Other provisions were more specific, such as the establishment of a fund to develop 'overseas territories' (colonies and former colonies), various articles aimed at favouring the mobility of workers, and the creation of a 'European Investment Bank' (EIB) to promote economic development, particularly in less developed regions. The last two measures were especially targeted at Italy's *Mezzogiorno*.

Lastly, national neo-mercantilist policies were protected by Article 222 EEC, which explicitly allowed companies to be state-owned, and by rather ambiguous articles about state aid, which were implemented with great tolerance during the first 25 years (Warlouzet 2018). Specific provisions were devised to preserve the neo-mercantilist features of agriculture's regulation.

During the EEC's early years (1958–73), competitiveness was ensured primarily through the establishment of a genuine Common Market entailing the elimination of internal custom duties and quotas (completed on 1 July 1968, in 10 years instead of the 12–14 forecast in the Treaty of Rome) and the setting up of a common external tariff. The EEC negotiated as a single unit in international trade negotiations, the first being the Kennedy Round (1964–67) (Coppolaro 2013). Nevertheless, neo-mercantilist and social features were visible with the Common Agricultural Policy (CAP), since it was devised to alleviate the burden of the rural communities' adjustment to a more urban consumer society. The CAP was considered a sort of 'agricultural welfare state' (Knudsen 2009). Since the Treaty of Rome specified rather general and conflicting policy goals, it was the Commission and the Council which shaped them in 1962 and gave them strong neo-mercantilist features: the EEC market was protected from imports by specific duties and export aids was systematic. Under German pressure, cereal prices were fixed at very high levels in 1964, thus triggering fiscal imbalances in the 1970s. Social Europe was limited to targeted social measures such as the European Investment Bank (designed to fund economic investment in the poorest regions, such as the *Mezzogiorno*), the European Social Fund (which fostered the mobility of workers), the European Development Fund (which channelled aid to former imperial territories, before being replaced by the Yaoundé Convention in 1963), and the protection of migrant workers. Nevertheless, the priority for actors enmeshed in this 'embedded liberalism' framework remained the development of welfare states at the national level. This explains that Social Europe was limited to specific areas.

The 'shock of the global' (1973–84)

The 1973–84 period was characterized by the 'shock of the global' (Ferguson *et al.* 2010), defined both as a major economic crisis and as a new form of globalization. From the macro-economic point of view, growth rates plummeted all over the developing world in 1973 and in 1979, including in Japan, while unemployment rose. This was the end of the 'Golden Age'. Moreover, while the crisis of 1929 had triggered deflation, prices skyrocketed following the oil shocks. This rendered Keynesian-inspired policy of stimulus more difficult to implement, since they ended by fuelling inflation without decisively denting unemployment (Chélini and Warlouzet 2016). In terms of globalization, a new era unfolded during those years with the rise of non-Western producers, both Middle Eastern oil producers and East Asian industrial exporters. The word 'globalization' was popularized in 1983 to designate an integration of markets at the world scale, driven by technology (the lowering of transportation and communication costs) and by the emergence of new industrial producers (Sargent 2010: 53). The current application of the term goes beyond this narrow definition to include not only industrial goods but also, to some extent, agricultural products, services, people, ideas, and cultural norms. Rather than a centre-periphery dynamic, this phenomenon is characterized by multiple interactions which engender hybridization and cross-fertilization. Crucially, the notion of globalization put an emphasis on interconnectedness and on interdependence. Western European leaders devised three types of European approaches to cope with this challenge of globalization: social, neo-mercantilist, and market-oriented.

First, the project to build a comprehensive 'Social Europe' emerged at the political level with the German Chancellor Willy Brandt (1969–74) and subsequent official declarations by EEC leaders adopted at the Paris summits of 1972 and of 1974. The economic crisis and the division among member-states eventually shattered those bold ambitions. Social Europe materialized only in a very gradual and piecemeal way through two main channels. The first was specific legislation in new areas such as the protection of workers, gender equality, environmental protection, and health and security legislation. More daring ventures such as the creation of a European control of multinationals failed (Petrini 2013; Warlouzet 2018: 57–77). The second was the setting up of an original tool in 1975: a regional policy designed to establish a solidarity mechanism between rich and poor region all over Europe. However, in its early years, regional policy was mostly managed in an intergovernmental way and redistributed only a relatively limited amount of funding.

Second, neo-mercantilism was on the rise at the international level in those days. Many projects designed to organize international trade by a coordination of outputs and of prices were devised (Warlouzet 2018: 78–98). This was related to the North–South issue and the proclamation of a 'new international economic order' (NIEO) by the countries of the so-called 'South' in 1973 (Garavini 2012). Some of these ideas were implemented by the EEC, in several domains. In 1975, the EEC concluded the Lomé Agreement with 46 Southern countries, mainly former British and French colonies (Migani 2014). It encompassed the STABEX, an international fund designed to stabilize the export earnings of the basic products of the poorest countries. In the steel sector, from 1980 onwards, the EEC implemented a coordinated policy of steel restructuring. Even the West German government, who was extremely sceptical of the setting up of a European industrial policy based on neo-mercantilism, accepted it at the European level if it was strictly limited. Indeed, state aids were accepted by the Commission only if they fostered restructuring, and targeted protectionist measures were tolerated within the framework of the EEC trade policy only during the most serious international trade conflicts (in particular with the US), and only if they did not threaten to trigger trade wars.[6] The EEC also secured exemptions from international free trade in textiles, with the successive Multi-Fibre Agreements (MFAs), which allowed it to keep higher trade barriers for a transition period, and in automobiles, with voluntary export restraints granted by the Japanese (either on a bilateral basis or through the EEC) (Warlouzet 2018).

Third, EEC institutions managed to preserve a market-oriented institutional framework. Internally, the Commission was striving to fight against new barriers to trade. As early as May 1974, the Commission was unable to thwart Italian protectionist measures. It was forced to accept them, provided a close monitoring was implemented.[7] In 1976, the Commission faced a surge in protectionist measures and had to increase its staff to deal with more than 300 cases. The tide reversed in 1977 but was nevertheless worrying.[8]

In terms of macro-economic coordination, two systems of voluntary convergence were devised: the Snake in 1972 and then the European Monetary System (EMS) in 1979, which contained only slight improvements compared to the Snake (Mourlon-Druol 2012). The European Monetary System was an agreement, according to which all members maintained a relative stability in their currency's exchange rates with each other. It was a reaction against the growing monetary instability since the collapse of the Bretton Woods system in 1971 and the rise of volatile financial flows. It did not entail a major cession of sovereignty, so it was supported by all Member States, bar the United Kingdom, which did not participate in it. Lastly, it marked a convergence between French and German leaders in terms of macro-economic preferences. German officials, the Chancellor Helmut Schmidt but also the Bundesbank president Otmar Emminger, had confidence in the French Prime Minister Raymond Barre's determination to stick to a stability-oriented policy (Mourlon-Druol 2012). This was important to overcome the debate between the so-called 'monetarists' and 'economists' (Dyson and Maes 2016; McNamara 1998). The countries with weak currencies insisted on monetary solidarity, especially during financial crises, and were branded 'monetarists' in EEC debates (not to be mistaken with the heirs of Milton Friedman, also called 'monetarists'). In contrast, the countries with strong currencies favoured more discipline in macro-economic coordination and were dubbed 'economists'. In short, the German government did not want to be committed to support the French franc and the Italian lira if a monetary crisis were to erupt because those countries were less disciplined than they were. When Barre became French Prime Minister in 1976, Paris openly modelled its policy on its German neighbour, which was hailed in those days as '*Modell Deutschland*', such was its success in terms of trade balance despite the oil shocks.

A new idea emerged in the 1970s: to 'complete' the Common Market by targeting non-tariff barriers. It is often argued that this ambition originated in the jurisprudence of the European Court of Justice (ECJ) with two landmark cases, Dassonville (1974) and Cassis de Dijon (1979).[9] Both cases deal with restrictions to the selling of spirits, respectively Scottish whisky in Belgium and a French liquor in Germany. The Treaty of Rome established the principle of the prohibition of 'quantitative restrictions on importation and all measures with equivalent effect' (Article 30 EEC), but it also included exemptions (such as health issues, etc.), while at the same time indicating that those exceptions must not be used to disguise a protectionist measure (Article 36 EEC). In the Dassonville case, the Court limited the possibility of national administration to use non-tariff barriers as protectionist tools. In the Cassis de Dijon case, the Court established the principle of mutual recognition on national legislations with only four exemptions listed in ground 8: 'the effectiveness of fiscal supervision, the protection of public health, the fairness of commercial transactions, and the defence of the consumer'.

According to some authors, the combination of Dassonville and of Cassis de Dijon greatly facilitated the harmonization of all laws restricting intra-European trade (Dashwood 1983; Olivi and Giacone 2007: 196–7). The full approximation of the law was no longer necessary, as the harmonization process could be limited to the four exemptions listed in the Cassis de Dijon case. The diversity of products guaranteed by national laws was no longer incompatible with the freedom of circulation of goods. On the contrary, other authors have underlined that those ECJ rulings were indeed important, but not sufficient. For Karen Alter and Sophie Meunier, subsequent initiatives by the Commission were necessary to transform this case law into more general decisions, affecting not only those two spirits but a large variety of products (Alter and Meunier 1994: 540–3). For Andrew Moravcsik, it was the willingness of the Member States which provided the decisive impetus in 1985–86 (Moravcsik 1998: 354). Primary sources clearly support the second interpretation. Concerning the Dassonville case, the Commission tried to use this case to force Belgium to modify other parts of the legislation but the Court overturned its subsequent decisions.[10] Concerning Cassis de Dijon, Paolo Cecchini, in those days, Deputy Director General in charge of the internal market at the European Commission, and later on author of the well-known 1988 report on the Single Market, estimated in 1980 that the Court's decision was interesting but not revolutionary.[11] Others initiatives from the Commission were necessary to exploit this ruling. The Court cannot be considered a substitute for the Council and the Commission, nor was it always an ally of the latter. In 1984, for example, the Commission attempted to use the principle of mutual recognition against a French law, but the Court eventually dismissed the case and upheld the French provisions.[12]

This daunting task of harmonization was left to the new commissioner for the internal market appointed in 1981, Karl-Heinz Narjes. A German Christian Democrat and a former private secretary of Walter Hallstein, Narjes was a long-standing pro-European. For him, a large and unified internal market was a major asset in the international competition to attract foreign investment.[13] Narjes promoted the adoption of entire packages of harmonization directives. However, national governments remained reluctant to accept these. The use of unanimity within the Council proved to be an insurmountable barrier, which was eventually removed only in 1985.

The 'Single Market' period (1985–92)

After 1983–84, the economic situation improved in Western Europe but this did not signal a return to the economics of the Golden Years. The 1970s stagflation had condemned isolated Keynesian stimulus but neo-liberal economics ideas were not widespread, even if the British Prime minister Margaret Thatcher sought to implement them. In most countries, leaders still hesitated between Keynesianism and neo-liberalism. In the meantime, technical innovations disrupted certain sectors previously dominated by monopolies or stable oligopolies, such as telecommunications and air transportation. The cost of communication fell dramatically, thus fuelling globalization. The Organisation for European Economic Co-operation (OECC) adapted to these new trends.

From 1984 to 1986, a 'relaunch of Europe' unfolded. This term was coined by Western European leaders and even Margaret Thatcher used it (Warlouzet 2018: 188–97). It meant that the process of European integration was reinforced by a new Treaty, the first since the Treaty of Rome in 1957, the Single Act of 1986. It was largely based on the promotion of the Single Market, i.e. a market devoid of any non-tariff barriers (such as diverging technical standards). To implement this flagship project, a major institutional reform took place, the adoption of qualified majority voting for most issues related to this domain, with major exceptions for social and fiscal matters.

Six years later, the Maastricht Treaty (1992) completed this market-based dynamic with the setting up of Economic and Monetary Union (EMU), which eventually led to the adoption of a single currency, the euro, in 1999 (Dyson and Featherstone 1999). EMU clearly embodied a market-based idea of Europe and its incremental process of unification: after the Common Market (abolition of trade barriers) and the Single Market (abolition of technical barriers) came the Monetary Union (abolition of monetary barriers). Stringent criteria of convergence ensured that a stability-based approach was privileged. This development stems from the debate between 'monetarists' and 'economists' (see above): Germany, who was very reluctant to give up its much-loved D-Mark to team up with weaker currency countries, had demanded such commitment to stability-oriented policy. In addition, it fitted well with the preference of governments both in France and in Italy, who still wanted to emulate the Germans (ibid.; Howarth 2001; Varsori 2010). However, the EMU can also be associated with other dynamics than a univocal convergence towards stability-oriented policy. For some of its promoters – in particular, Jacques Delors, the President of the European Commission, and the French government – European monetary cooperation was an expression of European solidarity between strong-currency countries like Germany and weak-currency countries like France. For France, European monetary cooperation concretely meant assistance in case of financial crisis and lower interest rates, to the benefit of companies and of individual consumers alike (Abdelal 2007).

As a matter of fact, the neo-liberal dynamic appeared more clearly outside the Single Act and the Maastricht Treaty with competition policy. Through the regulation of state aid and the promotion of deregulation, the Commission targeted more directly the industrial part of the welfare state. The Single Act did not deal with competition policy, despite Thatcher's effort to promote the deregulation of air transport and of insurance.[14] However, the French government and to some extent its West German counterpart were hostile to this wave of neo-liberal reforms.[15] All in all, the development of EEC competition policy rested mainly on the initiative of bold commissioners for competition, like Peter Sutherland or Leon Brittan, rather than on the Single Act. Another neo-liberal dynamic was the financial crisis of the welfare state, itself linked to the economic crisis of the 1970s (O'Connor 1973; Rosanvallon 1981), but this momentum was also external to the EEC.

Social Europe evolved in terms of content, as the theme of the democratization of companies become much less prominent while the European social dialogue and regional policy, rebranded as cohesion policy, gained traction. Both elements were central to Delors' project of Europe. The Commission also secured an inclusion in the Single Act of an article ensuring that the approximation of laws concerning health, safety, environment and consumer protection would target 'a high level of protection', which meant concrete social progress. Moreover, in 1988, Delors secured a major overhaul of regional policy, the funding of which doubled (Jabko 2006). This enabled the Commission to use this tool to concretely promote solidarity throughout the EU by delivering a windfall of aid to the poorest countries (in those days, Greece, Ireland, Portugal and Spain), and to specific regions (Southern Italy, the rust belt of Britain, France, and Belgium, etc.).

Neo-mercantilism was declining but it was still present in some sectors. For example, the automobile market remained organized around the defence of 'European champions' until 1991 (Jullien *et al.* 2015). Thereafter, the end of Japanese voluntary export restraints and the Eastern enlargement signalled the end of a European neo-mercantilist approach specific to automobiles. The CAP maintained a strong neo-mercantilist streak until the 1992 and 2003 reforms. Even the EMU was defended by some actors as a tool to assert European interests against the US in international monetary negotiations. Neo-mercantilist approaches were certainly renewed. For example, Airbus was initially heavily influenced by the national governments' strategic priorities but it progressively transformed itself into a normal for-profit organization. More generally, the definition of industrial policy has changed, with a stronger emphasis on the need to encourage structural adjustment rather than prevent it. In some areas such as telecommunications, industrial and competition policy were considered complementary by some scholars (Sauter 1997). However, when competition policy was spearheaded by the neo-liberal Leon Brittan, it played a major role in eradicating neo-mercantilist practices. The British commissioner banned the purchase of a Canadian builder of aircraft by its Franco-Italian competitor, ATR, following a narrow interpretation of competition rules. This led to a clash within the Commission between the neo-liberal Brittan and the President Delors who defended the strengthening of the European high-technology sector (Ross 1995: 176–80). Subsequently, neo-mercantilism remained active at the national level through regular calls for 'economic patriotism' (Clift and Woll 2013). Sectors perceived as strategic – armament and aerospace, but also finance in the UK, or even the food industry in France – have been staunchly defended by national governments.

The 'end of history' (1992–2006)

After 1989, the context changed radically. The pressure of globalization became even more daunting, with new competitors outside Europe (China, etc.) and within Europe, with the ex-communist countries of Central and Eastern Europe eventually joining the EU in 2004 and 2007. The GATT Uruguay Round was concluded in 1994 and contributed to a global trend of liberalization of flows, not only for industrial goods, but also for capital and for some agricultural products and services. While the alternative of communism disappeared, the free movement of goods and capital was accepted as a norm by most moderate political parties from the centre-right to the centre-left (Abdelal 2007). Neo-liberal ideas based on the retrenchment of the welfare state, tax reductions, and deregulation gained momentum.[16] From a political point of view, liberal democracies seemed on the rise not only in former communist countries, but also in former authoritarian capitalist states such as South Korea. Francis Fukuyama famously coined the expression 'the end of history' to capture this mood of a seemingly irresistible victory of liberal values, both in the political and in the economic realms. He envisaged 'the end point of mankind's ideological evolution and the universalization of Western liberal democracy as the final form of human government' (Fukuyama 1992).

This evolution did not lead to a unique form of regulated globalization in Western Europe, because the three types of economic policies outlined above remained present. Certainly, the market-oriented side became prominent and neo-liberal policies of retrenchment of the welfare state and of pure deregulation sometimes gained the upper hand. This was visible mainly at the national level: in Great Britain, where the influence of the Thatcher revolution remained deeply ingrained; in ex-communist European countries, most of which embraced drastic liberalization packages (Ther 2016); and in other countries in a less drastic form. At the EU level, this move was clearly expressed by the centrality of the competitiveness paradigm, often promoted through the recourse to expertise (Jullien and Smith 2015). This legitimized a major strengthening of competition policy. The Commission attacked national industrial policies by fostering deregulation and privatization, as old national monopolies were perceived as chronically inefficient, even by some social democrats.[17] Deregulation brought competition to air transportation, telecommunications, postal services, energy, railways, and other sectors, while the EU Directive on Posted Workers adopted in 1996 increased intra-European competition for several types of jobs, notably in the construction industry. More generally, the Single Market became for some neo-liberals an occasion to retrench the state by removing national regulations without adding a European layer, rather than an instrument to ensure convergence towards a 'high level of protection' as stated in the Single Act (Article 100A-3).[18] Lastly, Economic and Monetary Union (EMU) contains clear ordoliberal features (Dyson 2016). The European Central Bank is both independent and focused on taming inflation, rather than on the dual aim of ensuring 'maximum employment' and 'stable prices' like the US Federal Reserve.[19] Arguably, ordoliberalism and neo-liberalism must not be confused (Mudge 2008). The ordoliberal influence is not neo-liberal per se since it was associated with the development of an extensive welfare state in West Germany. Many different strands of ordoliberalism have coexisted.[20] This ambiguity was captured by the notion of the 'Social Market Economy', coined by Alfred Müller-Armack, a prominent ordoliberal, and which was inserted in the Treaty of Lisbon (Article 3–3: 'a highly competitive social market economy'). Nevertheless, ordoliberal influence on the EMU had neo-liberal consequences since the European Central Bank (ECB) mandate was not counterbalanced by a strong framework of actors promoting other visions – unlike in the German national arena. Some Member States, notably the French socialist government of Lionel Jospin (1997–2002), tried to promote a more social orientation. Paris defended a reform of the EMU Stability Pact and of Article 90 EEC, which served as the basis for the deregulation of many sectors, but without clear success, bar the inclusion of the notion of 'service of general interest' in the Treaty of Amsterdam (1997) and the renaming of what became the 'Stability and Growth Pact'. The same ambiguous development occurred with regard to Article 117 EEC. In the Amsterdam Treaty, its scope was enlarged but a second paragraph urging 'the need to maintain the competitiveness of the Community economy' was imposed. This is now Article 151 TFEU. On the whole, this neo-liberal orientation fuelled the crisis of legitimacy of the European Union, which had been perceived as incapable of regulating globalization in some countries. Opposition to an EU perceived as too neo-liberal certainly played a role in the outcome of the 2015 French referendum on the Constitutional Treaty as well as in the 2016 British one on Brexit, even though it was not the only explanation for those voting decisions.

At the same time, some Western European leaders still successfully promoted a socially-oriented regulation of globalization through EEC/EU institutions. The Delors Commissions (1985–95) espoused an extensive interpretation of qualified majority voting for health and safety at work. Between 1989 and 1993, they managed to adopt major texts such as the Framework Directive on Health and Safety, the Pregnant Workers' Directive, and the Working Time Directive, the latter being unsuccessfully contested before the Court by the UK government (Giubboni 2006). Delors also managed to insert in the Treaty of Maastricht the Social Charter, with an opt-out for Britain. He also decisively strengthened regional policy in 1988 and in 1993 (Jabko 2006: 121–46). The poorer countries benefited from a windfall of European funds to develop their infrastructure. Some of them, such as Ireland, are now well above the European average in terms of wealth. Besides, the mere fact that the EU was enlarged to include Central and Eastern European countries despite a huge remaining gap in terms of GDP per capita is in itself a manifestation of solidarity: old EU members signalled their community of destiny with new EU members which had been cut off from Western European freedom and prosperity by the Cold War. Of course, Western European leaders also expected gains for their companies in terms of market access, but this opportunity could also have materialized outside the EU framework, either through a recourse to GATT/WTO rules or through an extension to them of the European Economic Area. Besides, the Maastricht Treaty also empowered the social partners to conclude collective agreements that could become legally binding after the Council's approval. This led to a string of decisions, for example, on parental leave or on part-time work in 1996–97 (Didry and Mias 2005). More generally, legislation concerning health and security, gender equality and environmental issues expanded at the EEC/EU level, sometimes by providing more social benefits than what national laws offered. However, this did not prevent a major shift from social policy to a focus on employment, and hence on the competitiveness paradigm. Major rows over social policy took place not only at the Council, but also within the Commission. Promoters of harmonization towards the lowest common denominator clashed with defenders of high standards for health and security and for the environment. Some ambitious pieces of legislation remained toothless. The representation of workers at the corporate board level revived earlier failed attempts, thanks to the Directive 94/45 of 1994 establishing European Works Council. It was upgraded in 2009, but it is still largely non-binding. Hence, it does not prevent intra-site competition within Europe. For example, Renault's European Works Council was not consulted on the closure of the Belgian factory of Vilvoorde in 1997 (Berthet *et al.* 2015: 205).

The crisis of Western globalization (2007–present)

The current economic crisis, lingering since 2007–08, is still visible either in poor macro-economic indicators (growth, unemployment, debt) and/or in rising inequalities (even in countries with good macro-economic indicators, such as Germany). Such a situation might alter the balance between the three types of economic policy, and more generally between competitiveness and solidarity. Certainly, the neo-liberal approach prevailed at first. During the Eurozone crisis, Southern European countries underwent a massive adjustment between 2009 and

2015, with current account deficits being transformed into surpluses thanks to a drop in domestic demand and a painful process of internal devaluation (i.e. a fall in relative wages) (Saadaoui 2016), much more than through solidarity. This adjustment was clearly neo-liberal as it led to a massive retrenchment of the welfare state.

On the other hand, whereas social Europe had been presented as a 'dead end' (Lechevalier and Wielgohs 2015), in reality, its form is constantly evolving. As a matter of fact, the crisis has led to the creation of a permanent instrument of financial solidarity among Europeans, the European Stability Mechanism (ESM), which materialized in earlier attempts at creating a European Monetary Fund. Billions in aid were transferred to the most indebted countries such as Greece, Ireland, Portugal, and Spain. Others, such as Italy and France, were indirectly supported by the European Central Bank's use of non-conventional instruments labelled 'quantitative easing'. In 2010, the ECB's head Jean-Claude Trichet launched the Securities Markets Programme (SMP), which allowed the Bank to purchase sovereign bonds in specific circumstances. Mario Draghi, the successor to Jean-Claude Trichet, was even bolder. He strengthened the ECB action, first, with its 26 July 2012 speech when he promised to do 'whatever it takes' to support the euro, and, second, with the 'outright monetary transactions' (OMT) programme a couple of weeks later, which allowed the ECB to buy sovereign bonds on the secondary markets. The ECB's determination has contributed to decrease interest rates and spreads all over the eurozone. More recently, the IMF, the OECD, and the European Commission have revived the idea of a concerted macro-economic policy of reflation for surplus countries, such as Germany, echoing the debates of 1978. Paradoxically, competition policy, which was a major lever to nurture a neo-liberal Europe, has recently been used in a much more socially-oriented way with recent cases over tax evasion, in particular, the 2016 Apple ruling.[21] Indeed, by targeting a massive Irish tax exemption made to a successful multinational, the Commissioner for Competition single-handedly revived the debate over the control of multinationals.

Neo-mercantilist tendencies have so far been checked by the resilience of the international trade system, in contrast to the post-1929 crisis. The conclusion of global international trade rounds remains as elusive as ever, but the emphasis is now put on bilateral agreements, which are still successfully concluded by the EU, recently with South Korea and with Canada. Protectionist tensions are managed by targeted sanctions, such as in the case of Chinese steel over-production, which had led to rising tariffs in the EU and mainly in the US. As a major exporter to China, the EU could not vehemently criticize Chinese's aggressive neo-mercantilism.

The recent UK possible Brexit decision and, most of all, the election of Donald Trump, present new challenges to this subtle balance between social, neo-mercantilist and market-oriented tendencies. Both events may be interpreted as a return of neo-mercantilist policies. The new US President has rejected both the Transatlantic Trade and Investment Partnership (TTIP), currently under negotiation between Europe and the US, and the Trans-Pacific Partnership

(TPP), which had already been signed. He has also put into question the North American Free Trade Agreement (NAFTA), in force since 1994. In Britain, Theresa May hinted at a 'hard Brexit' in her 8 January 2017 speech, where she clearly prioritized the restriction of immigration over access to the Single Market. It is not yet clear how she could square this clear retreat in terms of liberalization of trade with her claim to promote a 'global Britain' based on free trade deals.

Ironically, the defence of global free trade fell to the Chinese communist leader Xi Jinping, who released a staunch plea in favour of liberal multilateralism at the 2017 Davos summit, despite the strong neo-mercantilist flavour of Chinese economic policies. China and the Association of Southeast Asian Nations (ASEAN) countries established a free trade zone in 2010 and are currently negotiating the Regional Comprehensive Economic Partnership (RCEP) with ASEAN and other Pacific countries, such as South Korea and Australia. Similarly, the paradigm of free trade and international competitiveness remains at the core of the world economic order, even though it is no longer steered by a credible American leadership. Hence, the process of globalization has lost some of its liberal features.

Conclusion

Since 1957, the EEC/EU has always been founded on a shifting and dynamic balance between competitiveness and solidarity which has manifested itself in three types of socio-economic policies: social-oriented, neo-mercantilist, and market-oriented. The same dynamic compromises existed at national level.

The balance between those three types of socio-economic approaches, on the one hand, and between national and European actors, on the other hand, has evolved over time. During the 'embedded liberalism' era (1957–73), the welfare state was overwhelmingly national while the European institutions managed a controlled trade liberalization, with some targeted social elements. Social Europe really unfolded during the 'shock of the global' years (1973–84). The competitiveness paradigm was largely implemented through neo-mercantilist policies during those years, even if market-oriented policies were preserved and slightly strengthened through the EMS. Thereafter, the Single Market programme took centre stage in Western Europe (1985–92). With the Single Act and the Maastricht Treaty, the competitiveness impetus was decisively associated with a market-oriented paradigm. Neo-liberal policies aimed at dismantling the welfare state were on the rise. However, the yearning for a social Europe remained alive, with concrete results, such as the strengthening of regional policies and legislation on health and environmental issues. The 1990s and early 2000s were marked by the 'end of history' liberal utopia and the rise of neo-liberal policies, despite the preservation of ambitions of solidarity. Recently, the economic crisis lingering since 2007–08 has sparked a debate over the crisis of the Western liberal form of globalization, which eventually translated into the election of US President Trump. The three approaches, socially oriented, neo-mercantilist, and market-oriented, remain vital at the global level, but their equilibrium is constantly evolving.

Notes

1 This interpretation is present in many books as an underlying assumption. Among those who have developed it the most explicitly and with an historical approach are Denord and Schwartz (2009) and Gillingham (2003).
2 More details on this threefold classification, and on the distinction between market-oriented and neo-liberal policies, can be found in Warlouzet (2018), Chapter 1.
3 In addition to the author's two monographs (Warlouzet 2011a, 2018), the article draws on a blooming literature dealing with European integration history. For historiographical accounts, see Bossuat *et al.* (2010), Kaiser and Varsori (2010), Patel (2013), Mourlon-Druol (2015), and Warlouzet (2014).
4 The main primary sources consulted are the British national archives, the French national archives, the German national archives, and the EU Commission archive. Specific sub-funds include the French Foreign Affairs Ministry and the German Affairs Ministry. The published documents of the German Foreign Affairs Ministry (*Akten zur auswärtigen Politik der Bundesrepublik Deutschland*) were also consulted.
5 Jacob Viner (1947). 'Conflicts of principle in drafting a trade charter', *Foreign Affairs* 25: 613, quoted in Ruggie (1982: 397).
6 See state aid control and EEC-US trade conflicts in steel in Warlouzet (2018: 87–8).
7 Eighth Report of the Commission's activities, 1974, Brussels, EEC, 1975, point 102.
8 Tenth Report of the Commission's activities, 1976, Brussels, EEC, 1977, points 111–12; Eleventh Report of the Commission's activities, 1977, Brussels, EEC, 1978, points 122–3.
9 Judgment of the Court of 11 July 1974, case 8–74; Judgment of the Court of 20 February 1979, case 120/78.
10 Judgment of the Court of 16 May 1979, '*Commission of the European Communities* v. *Kingdom of Belgium*. – Certificates of authenticity', case 2/78.
11 AEU, BAC 91/94/56, note Cecchini, 23 January 1980.
12 Judgment of the Court of 28 January 1986, '*Commission of the European Communities* v. *French Republic*', case 188/84.
13 AEU, special minutes of the Commission meeting, 17 June 1981; Warlouzet (2018: 183–6).
14 AMAE-FR, DECE 2499, letter from Weston (British embassy in Paris) to Guigou, 21 November 1985.
15 AAPD, 1985, 129, note on a meeting of Kohl and Thatcher, 18 May 1985.
16 A vast array of literature exists, see in particular Burgin (2012) and Stedman Jones (2012).
17 Karel van Miert, who was Commissioner for Competition between 1995 and 1999, complained about the Belgium Postal Office, although he recognized that some state-owned monopolies in other countries, such as France, were more efficient (Van Miert 2000: 51).
18 See in particular the interviews of two Commission officials, Anne Houtman and Heinz Zourek, available on the European Union historical archives' website.
19 See www.federalreserve.gov
20 On ordoliberalism, a vast array of literature exists. Among the most useful books on the linkage between economic ideas and economic policies in Germany are Leaman (1987), Löffler (2002) and Nicholls (1994).
21 Commission's decision C(2016) 5605 final of 30 August 2016, addressed to Ireland, on State Aid case SA.38373 (2014/C).

References

Abdelal, Rawi (2007). *Capital rules: the construction of global finance*. Ithaca, NY: Cornell University Press.

Alter, Karen J. and Sophie Meunier-Aitsahalia (1994). 'Judicial politics in the European Community: European integration and the pathbreaking Cassis de Dijon decision', *Comparative Political Studies* 26(4): 535–61.

Berthet, Thierry, Bernard Conter, Tomasso Pardi, and Andy Smith (2015). 'Employment policy: desperately seeking a flexibility-security equilibrium', in Bernard Jullien and Andy Smith (eds). *The EU's government of industries: markets, institutions and politics*. London: Routledge, 190–215.

Bossuat, Gérard, Éric Bussière, Robert Frank, Wilfried Loth, and Antonio Varsori (eds) (2010). *L'expérience européenne. 50 ans de construction de l'Europe. 1957–2007. Des historiens en dialogue*. Brussels: Bruylant.

Boyce, Robert (2009). *The great interwar crisis and the collapse of globalization*. Basingstoke: Palgrave Macmillan.

Burgin, Angus (2012). *The Great Persuasion: reinventing free markets since the Depression*. Cambridge, MA: Harvard University Press.

Chélini, Michel-Pierre and Laurent Warlouzet (eds) (2016). *Slowing down prices: European inflation in the 1970s*. Paris: Presses de Sciences-Po.

Clift, Ben and Cornelia Woll (2013). *Economic patriotism in open economies*. London: Routledge.

Coppolaro, Lucia (2013). *The making of a world trading power: the European Economic Community (EEC) in the GATT Kennedy Round negotiations (1963–1967)*. Aldershot: Ashgate.

Dashwood, Alan (1983). 'Hastening slowly: the Communities' path towards harmonization', in Helen Wallace, William Wallace, and Carole Webb (eds). *Policy-making in the European Communities*. London: John Wiley & Sons, 177–208.

Denord, François and Antoine Schwartz (2009). *L'Europe sociale n'aura pas lieu*. Paris: Raisons d'agir.

Didry, Claude and Arnaud Mias (2005). *Le moment Delors: les syndicats au cœur de l'Europe sociale*. Brussels: Peter Lang.

Dyson, Kenneth (2016). 'Hans Tietmeyer, ethical Ordo-liberalism, and the architecture of EMU: getting the fundamentals right', in Kenneth Dyson and Ivo Maes (eds). *Architects of the Euro: intellectuals in the making of European Monetary Union*. Oxford: Oxford University Press, 138–69.

Dyson, Kenneth and Kevin Featherstone (1999). *The road to Maastricht: negotiating Economic and Monetary Union*. Oxford: Oxford University Press.

Dyson, Kenneth and Ivo Maes (eds) (2016). *Architects of the Euro: intellectuals in the making of European Monetary Union*. Oxford: Oxford University Press.

Ferguson, Niall, Charles Maier, Erez Manela, and Daniel Sargent (eds.) (2010). *The shock of the global: the 1970s in perspective*. Cambridge, MA: Harvard University Press.

Fukuyama, Francis (1992). *The end of history and the last man*. New York: The Free Press.

Garavini, Giuliano (2012). *After empires: European integration, decolonization, and the challenge from the Global South, 1957–1986*. Oxford: Oxford University Press.

Gillingham, John (2003). *European integration, 1950–2003: superstate or new market economy?* Cambridge: Cambridge University Press.

Giubboni, Stefano (2006). *Social rights and market freedom in the European Constitution: a labour law perspective*. Cambridge: Cambridge University Press.

Howarth, David (2001). *The French road to European monetary union*. Basingstoke: Palgrave.

Jabko, Nicolas (2006). *Playing the market: a political strategy for uniting Europe, 1985–2005*. Ithaca, NY: Cornell University Press.

Jullien, Bernard, Tomasso Pardi, and Sigfrido Ramírez Pérez (2015). 'The EU's government of automobiles: from "harmonization" to "deep incompleteness"', in Bernard Jullien and Andy Smith (eds). *The EU's government of industries: markets, institutions and politics*. London: Routledge, 57–83.

Jullien, Bernard and Andy Smith (eds) (2015). *The EU's government of industries: markets, institutions and politics*. London: Routledge.

Kaiser, Wolfram and Antonio Varsori (eds) (2010). *European Union history: themes and debates*. Basingstoke: Palgrave Macmillan.

Keynes, John Maynard (1919). *The economic consequences of the peace*. London: Macmillan.

Knudsen, Ann-Christina (2009). *Farmers on welfare: the making of Europe's Common Agricultural Policy*. Ithaca, NY: Cornell University Press.

Leaman, Jeremy (1987). *The political economy of West Germany, 1945–1985: an introduction*. New York: St Martin's Press.

Lechevalier, Arnaud and Jan Wielgohs (eds) (2015). *Social Europe: a dead end. What the eurozone crisis is doing to Europe's social dimension*. Copenhagen: Djoef.

Löffler, Bernhard (2002). *Soziale Marktwirtschaft und administrative Praxis: das Bundeswirtschaftsministerium unter Ludwig Erhard*. Stuttgart: Franz Steiner.

McNamara, Kathleen (1998). *The currency of ideas: monetary politics in the European Union*. Ithaca, NY: Cornell University Press.

Mechi, Lorenzo (2013). 'Du BIT à la politique sociale européenne: les origines d'un modèle', *Le Mouvement Social* 244: 17–30.

Migani, Guia (2014). 'Development aid: historic priorities and new dynamics', in Éric Bussière, Vincent Dujardin, Michel Dumoulin, Piers Ludlow, Pierre Tilly, and Jan Willem Brouwer (eds). *The European Commission, 1973–1986*. Luxembourg: EU Publications Office, 393–411.

Moravcsik, Andrew (1998). *The choice for Europe: social purpose and state power from Messina to Maastricht*. Ithaca, NY: Cornell University Press.

Mourlon-Druol, Emmanuel (2012). *A Europe made of money. the emergence of the European Monetary System*. Ithaca, NY: Cornell University Press.

Mourlon-Druol, Emmanuel (2015). 'Rich, vivid, and ignored: history in European studies', *Politique Européenne* 50: 9–21.

Mudge, Stephanie Lee (2008). 'What is neoliberalism?', *Socio-economic Review* 6(4): 703–31.

Nicholls, Anthony (1994). *Freedom with responsibility: the social market economy in Germany, 1918–1963*. Oxford: Clarendon Press.

O'Connor, James (1973). *The fiscal crisis of the state*. New York: St-Martin's Press.

Olivi, Bino and Alessandro Giacone (2007). *L'Europe difficile. La construction européenne*, Paris: Gallimard.

Palier, Bruno (2009). 'L'Europe et les États-providence', *Sociologie du Travail* 51(4): 518–35.

Parsons, Craig (2003). *A certain idea of Europe*. Ithaca, NY: Cornell University Press.

Patel, Kiran Klaus (2013). 'Provincialising European Union: co-operation and integration in Europe in a historical perspective', *Contemporary European History* 22(4): 649–73.

Petrini, Francesco (2013). 'Demanding democracy in the workplace: the European Trade Union Confederation and the struggle to regulate multinationals', in Wolfram Kaiser and Jan-Henrik Meyer (eds). *Societal actors in European integration: polity-building and policy-making, 1958–1992*. Basingstoke: Palgrave Macmillan, 151–72.

Rosanvallon, Pierre (1981). *La crise de l'État-Providence*. Paris: Seuil.

Ross, George (1995). *Jacques Delors and European integration*. Cambridge: Polity Press.

Ruggie, John Gerard (1982). 'International regimes, transactions, and change: embedded liberalism in the postwar economic order', *International Organization* 36(2): 379–415.

Saadaoui, Jamel (2016). 'Post-Brexit FEER', CEPN Working Paper No. 12. Paris: CEPN.

Sargent, Daniel (2010). 'The United States and globalization in the 1970s', in Niall Ferguson, Charles Maier, Erez Manela, and Daniel Sargent (eds). *The shock of the global: the 1970s in perspective*. Cambridge, MA: Harvard University Press, 49–64.

Sauter, Wolf (1997). *Competition law and industrial policy in the EU*. Oxford: Clarendon Press.

Stedman Jones, Daniel (2012). *Masters of the universe: Hayek, Friedman, and the birth of neoliberal politics*. Princeton, NJ: Princeton University Press.

Ther, Philipp (2016). *Europe since 1989: a history*. Princeton, NJ: Princeton University Press.

Van Miert, Karel (2000). *Le marché et le pouvoir: souvenirs d'un commissaire européen*. Brussels: Racine.

Varsori, Antonio (2010). *La cenerentola d'Europa? L'Italia e l'integrazione europea dal 1947 a oggi*. Soveria Mannelli: Rubbettino.

Warlouzet, Laurent (2011a). *Le choix de la CEE par la France. Les débats économiques de Pierre Mendès-France à Charles de Gaulle (1955–1969)*. Paris: Igpde/Cheff.

Warlouzet, Laurent (2011b). 'De Gaulle as a father of Europe: the unpredictability of the FTA's failure and the EEC's success (1956–1958)', *Contemporary European History* 20(4): 419–34.

Warlouzet, Laurent (2014). 'European integration history: beyond the crisis', *Politique Européenne* 44: 98–122.

Warlouzet, Laurent (2018). *Governing Europe in a globalizing world: neoliberalism and its alternatives following the 1973 oil crisis*. London: Routledge.

5 Competition, cooperation, and solidarity in EU law

A federal perspective

Sacha Garben

While being careful not to overstate the nature and degree of the EU's current problems, it seems fair to say that we are facing an increasingly volatile, tense, and complex social-political situation in Europe. Eurosceptic and Eurocritical political movements seem to be on the rise, culminating (for now) in the UK's possible decision to secede from the Union (FitzGibbon *et al.* 2017). There is a sense that, following a time where Eurosceptics' concerns were mostly directed at the perceived EU 'over-regulation' and generally stemmed from a limited group of Member States, they are now increasingly phrased in broader socio-economic terms appealing to citizens who may feel 'left behind' or wronged by globalization and Europeanization processes (Kuhn *et al.* 2016). These citizens tend to be wary of migration coming from both outside and within the EU. This plays into an East-West divide between 'old' and 'new' Member States, whereby the former are, first, suspicious of the internal labour mobility that for the latter is an intrinsic and important part of their political and constitutional settlement in the EU (Ferrera 2016), and, second, resentful of the latter's lack of cooperation in the intake of migrants from outside the EU. Furthermore, a North-South divide has opened up following the economic crisis, whereby both creditor and debtor states somehow feel short-changed by the Euro-crisis measures, directing their discontent at each other and at the EU (Della Porta *et al.* 2017; Hobolt and de Vries 2016). Almost all of these challenges can be usefully explored through the prism of the relationship between competition, cooperation, and solidarity in the European integration process, making it an apt choice for the subject of the present book.

The aim of this contribution is to provide some reflections that may aid in the establishment of a theoretical framework for the assessment of competition, cooperation, and solidarity in EU law. Federal theory may offer some insights in this respect. After all, the role of solidarity and competition, and their interrelation in federations, have been the subject of much global scholarship, and it could be interesting to apply it to the specific EU context. In doing so, we may cast some new light on the dynamics shaping the EU legal order, as well as on the current legal and political problems facing the Union.

The next section will define the notions of competition, cooperation, and solidarity for the purposes of this chapter. The following section will explore how these notions are conceived in the context of different federal models, and particularly the EU. It will look at the role of 'competitive federalism' and 'cooperative federalism' and will examine various legal mechanisms that are typically employed to ensure competition and solidarity in federal orders: the principle of federal loyalty, redistributive policies, constitutional requirements facilitating free movement and competition, and competences as regards property ownership and the organization and provision of welfare services. The final section will draw some tentative conclusions, considering if the EU legal order is geared more towards competition or solidarity, and will develop some proposals for establishing a degree of reciprocity-based solidarity as the normative and constitutional framework of the EU's constitutional settlement.

The notions of competition, cooperation, and solidarity

Of course, there are many different understandings of the key notions of competition, cooperation, and solidarity. While this contribution in no way seeks to provide an exhaustive discussion, it will nevertheless be necessary to establish some fundamental understanding of both terms and their interrelation, before applying them in the rest of the chapter.

Solidarity

On a theoretical level, there is a question of how solidarity is distinct from related 'other-regarding dispositions' that involve a measure of generosity, in that someone deliberately performs an action that is sub-optimal for him or her but for the benefit of another, such as altruism, sophisticated selfishness, team reasoning, and Kantian duty. It could be argued that while solidarity may very well co-exist with these other features, it motivates generosity independently (thus, even in the absence) of these other-regarding motivations, on the basis of 'an identification with the condition of a certain group of people' to whom one does not (directly) belong (Arnsperger and Varoufakis 2003). It would therefore be a self-standing notion. However, the lack of team spirit as motivation for the generous action in this narrow approach seems to be at odds with a more colloquial understanding of the term solidarity, in which it is, for instance, associated with collective action undertaken by workers against an employer where team reasoning is likely to play a key part (Sugden 1993). Indeed, the usefulness of the concept of solidarity to understand the functioning of (transnational) societies would be drastically limited if such a narrow definition were followed. Manifestations of genuine out-of-group non-reciprocal solidarity are very rare.[1]

For the purposes of this chapter, it does not seem necessary to take such a strict approach to solidarity that excludes the conceptual forms of 'other-regarding generosity' that somehow rely on team or group membership. Instead, the notion will be used more pragmatically, and its key features will be taken to lie in that a certain act is performed deliberately that is (perceived as) sub-optimal for the actor(s) at least in the short term, for the benefit of another or others, who may be members of the same group or may not. This includes actions that are expected to yield benefits for the actor(s) in the longer term, with the exception of guaranteed overall net benefits (which would simply make the action a rational investment). It will be taken as a gradual concept, in that something can reflect weaker or stronger solidarity. Thus, the smaller the role of reciprocity or expected returns, the higher the level of solidarity, but the fact that reciprocity or returns are expected does not eliminate solidarity as such.

This wider approach corresponds better to the conception of solidarity in the EU as defined by Sangiovanni (2013) in his landmark piece on the subject. He understands demands for social solidarity at all levels of governance as 'demands for a fair return in the mutual production of important collective goods' (ibid.: 217). The idea is that, in our societies,

> we depend on the joint contributions of myriad other citizens and residents for the ability not only to develop but also to act on a plan of life. Without the support those contributions provide for the political and legal authority of the state, we would lack the resources necessary to function as biological, social and political beings … [O]ur abilities to develop and make use of our talents, as well as our ability to profit from them, depend on the survival and maintenance of the scheme; without it, we would soon lose everything that we have gained. Therefore, those who are better able to gain from the scheme owe those less able, but who have made their gains possible, a fair return for what they have received.
>
> (Ibid.: 222)

This is clearly a reciprocity-based framework and includes team reasoning as an important basis for solidarity. I would argue that both (1) the participation in the survival and maintenance of the scheme of which one is not certain whether it will be to one's immediate benefit in addition to the expected common benefit, as well as (2) a measure of redistribution of the actual benefits yielded by it from the 'winners' to the 'losers', can – within this conception – be qualified as acts of solidarity. Such solidarity can be expected to be stronger when the common (societal) scheme is more developed and visible, and when participants feel more strongly attached to the identity of the underlying group, i.e. the 'team'. That clearly implies some challenges to the existence of such solidarity in a context that transcends one's primary community, which in the EU context is generally still the national level (Risse 2010).

Nevertheless, the fact that there are challenges does not mean such solidarity cannot be present in a transnational setting such as the EU as well (Gould 2007). It has already been shown that identity can, and in a majority of cases does, exist at several levels, including the national and EU level (Risse 2010). And, while it may be less developed and visible to citizens, it is clear that the EU provides a kind of common societal scheme from which all Member States are expected to benefit in the long run. For these purposes, Sangiovanni (2013: 221) distinguishes between (1) national solidarity, which defines obligations among citizens of Member States; (2) Member State solidarity, defining obligations among Member States; and (3) principles of transnational solidarity, defining obligations among EU citizens as such. At the national level, this means, for instance, paying taxes for the purpose of maintaining a generous welfare system. At the European level, Member State solidarity means, for instance, the participation in a policy allocating third-country migrants across the EU and the redistribution of wealth through the Structural Funds, and transnational solidarity means, for instance, the extension of social benefits to migrant EU citizens.

Competition

In a colloquial sense, competition refers to the activity or condition of striving to gain or win something by defeating or establishing superiority over others. This 'something to be won' can be a resource in limited supply, but also something more intangible such as prestige. Competition has many different manifestations. It can be a default state of affairs, when a certain good in scarce supply is pursued by a variety of actors in the absence of a regulatory framework, or instead a deliberate method to distribute a certain good among various actors on the basis of pre-defined criteria. In the latter sense, it can be used as a deliberate governance tool – as it is in most market economies. When competition leads to the attribution of a certain good, it is often considered 'fair' when this happens in compliance with the (implicitly) agreed criteria of the competition, for instance, when a company is successful on the market because it has developed an original, high-quality product. In contrast, such a result is considered 'unfair' when the implicit or explicit (social) rules framing the competition are not respected, such as when the company is successful on the market because it can operate low prices due to its products being produced by children in sweatshops. This illustrates the important normative dimension of the context in which the notion of competition operates, and while it is sometimes juxtaposed with regulation, it actually often has a close, dependent relationship to it.

Similar to the previously discussed notion of solidarity, competition can be applied in different contexts, in which case, it takes different forms. For the purposes of our discussion of the EU, competition can be taken to refer to: (1) a national context, in which it refers to the relationships between various national actors such as citizens and companies and the way in which the 'social market economy' is organized; (2) a Member State context, in which it refers to the relationships between the different European countries when they engage in some competition in an economic or a regulatory sense; and (3) a transnational context, referring to the relationship between individual citizens and economic actors in the EU as such. Introducing more competition on the national level can mean the privatization of public services, on the Member State level it can, for instance, refer to the lowering of tax rates to attract businesses from across the EU, and in a transnational setting it can, for instance, refer to economic competition between companies or workers from different Member States through the temporary posting of staff from a low-wage country to a high-wage one.

The foregoing examples show the tension that exists between competition, on the one hand, and solidarity, on the other. They can both be conceived as frameworks for the allocation of goods and the structuring of behaviour in society, but using very different methods and on the basis of different goals and values. However, it would be too simplistic to exclusively use them in opposition or mutual exclusion, as there is more nuanced conceptual interaction between the two than one would perhaps expect at face value. For one, competition can be a *governance tool used for* the pursuit of solidarity objectives. In the EU, for instance, the Social Open Method of Coordination places Member States in a comparative setting, competing for the best social performance (thus, for prestige in an international context and for the best policy outcomes in a national context), which encourages them to improve their national solidarity policies. More generally, policy competition such as that between constituent jurisdictions in federations, allows policy experimentation, which may yield important social benefits by developing best practices at the lowest risk/cost for the overall federation (Halberstam 2011: 16). In a different mutually reinforcing way, solidarity structures can make economies more resilient and stable, and as such more competitive in the long run. Competition can, to a certain extent, also be an *expression of* solidarity – when it constitutes the common system which is in the end expected to deliver common goods, but which does not guarantee immediate net benefits to all participants (for instance, participation in the internal market, where high-wage Member States may expect to lose some industry to lower-wage states). And, to constitute an overall successful governance tool, competition *may require to be complemented by* a degree of solidarity, for instance, in the redistribution of the yields of the common system of competition from the 'winners' to the 'losers'.

Cooperation

A final word on the notion of 'cooperation', understood as the action or process of working together towards the same end, which seems to be often used in contrast to competition and more closely aligned with solidarity. It is true that cooperation can be an alternative to competition, for instance, when the default state of competition to obtain a scarce good is replaced by a system of cooperation to obtain (and share) that good. Depending entirely on the context, replacing competition by cooperation may be considered societally desirable, such as when countries cooperate for the advance of technology rather than competing in isolation, or societally undesirable, such as when companies agree on setting common prices eliminating competition between them and overcharging the consumer. In other scenarios, however, competition and cooperation are not opposing alternatives and can indeed work together. Competition can be a precondition to, a form of, or an incentive for cooperation, and the other way around (Abell 1996). For instance, opening up one's markets to economic competition will usually lead to the establishment of some form of common regulatory framework with minimum rules of labour and environmental protection. Indeed, the expectation that economic integration through competition will lead to functional spill-over in the form of cooperation in many policy areas has often been mentioned as one of the main drivers of European integration.

Cooperation and solidarity are often regarded as having a mutually beneficial interaction, and they can indeed be conceived as going hand-in-hand in many situations, such as where workers collaborate through collective action to improve each other's working conditions, or where Member States cooperate on a common policy for the protection of a certain public interest. Cooperation can thus be an expression of solidarity, and solidarity an outcome of cooperation. Furthermore, it would seem that cooperation is more effective when there is a measure of solidarity among the participants, so as to avoid free-riding behaviour (Arnsperger and Varoufakis 2003; Weidlich and Helbing 1998). Nevertheless, cooperation can sometimes also have the result of challenging solidarity, especially in multi-level/transnational contexts such as the EU. Member States can cooperate to establish certain common policies which undermine solidarity structures on the national level, such as the freedom to provide services, which allows companies to undercut certain domestic social standards in certain situations. They can also cooperate to demand a measure of transnational solidarity, for instance, to extend national social benefits to migrant EU citizens, which may challenge national solidarity by expanding the group beyond the necessary level of identification and expected reciprocity (and, as such, lead to a lowering of social benefits for all).

Competition, cooperation, and solidarity in federations

Competitive and cooperative federalism

There is no single theory of federalism that explains in comprehensive terms the reasons why certain jurisdictions choose to coexist on the same territory and the different models in which they decide to organize their multi-level or polycentric polity. The sheer diversity of federal models currently in operation across the globe would seem to defy such comprehensive categorization and description. Indeed, the reasons why and the way in which authorities decide to give up part of their autonomy in order to cooperate with each other will be specific to each instance and depend on a range of historical, cultural, political, legal, economic, and other factors, the relative weight of each will be difficult to discern. The role played by competition, cooperation and solidarity will also depend on the actual circumstances and organization of the federal order in question, and hence differ from one system to another. Some general observations can nevertheless be made as to how the dynamics of a federal order and the way in which it is constitutionally designed (are generally conceived to) structurally influence these notions between the different constituent parts of the polity.

A major theoretical distinction between federal models is that between systems of 'cooperative federalism', on the one hand, and systems of 'competitive federalism', on the other (Watts 2006). While solidarity and cooperation are seen as the foundations of systems of cooperative federalism (Cyr 2014), competition is the hallmark of competitive federalism (Breton 1995). The former is characterized by intertwined executive and legislative powers and tasks between the various levels of government (Elazar 1962; Zimmerman 2001). There is furthermore a hypothesized tendency in this model to reduce differences between the constituent components of the federation through policy cooperation, 'harmonizing' legislation, and wealth redistribution. Competitive federalism, on the other hand, features separate sites of government, each autonomous in their separate spheres, with clearly divided legislative and executive competences. This largely coincides with the concept of 'dual federalism', which similarly stresses the independence of the different levels of government and their mutually exclusive powers. In this model, the differences between the members of the federation are guaranteed through their exclusive and autonomous powers, and this leads to competition, assuming that the federal settlement provides for mobility, mainly of economic factors and citizens (Halberstam 2011: 19). The different jurisdictions compete for the allegiance of companies and consumers/citizens through 'regulatory competition'. This may incite less competitive jurisdictions to adapt their systems, thereby potentially reducing intra-federal differences in the end, although it could also be that the other jurisdictions will again react to that adaptation, trying to maintain their competitive edge, and will make further adaptations to reassert the differences.

The idea of competitive federalism is not uncontested. First, many scholars have pointed out that the reality of effective policy-making in modern societies necessarily implies cooperation between the various sites of governance in a federal polity, making the ideal-type of dual or competitive federalism unrealistic (Resnik 2001; Schütze 2009). As Schütze (2009: 346) has noted in his work on EU federalism, the legislative reality within Europe 'is increasingly characterized by mutual interpenetration and interlocking laws', which is a natural consequence of the fact that 'an ever more interconnected social reality' cannot be divided into 'neat competence categories that mutually exclude each other'. As Schnabel (2014) similarly notes, 'complexity of the modern world increases interdependence in the interaction of governments in federal states', especially,

> if we distinguish between administrative and legislative interdependence, the assumption of watertight compartments attributed to dual federalism does not hold anymore: policy making is not the only point of reference when classifying federations, but one also needs to look at interdependence arising from policy administration or implementation.

Indeed, the EU clearly exhibits traits of both a competitive and a cooperative federal model. On the one hand, as Schütze (2009) has pointed out, the bulk of the EU's powers are shared with the Member States, it possesses a range of functional powers that cut through any policy area including those 'retained' by the Member States, exclusive EU powers are rare, exclusive Member State powers are illusory, and there is widespread administrative cooperation in a range of policy areas. On the other hand, the Lisbon Treaty has made a great effort to delineate more clearly the powers of the Member States and those of the EU, attempting to limit the latter through reiterations of the conferral principle, national autonomy and identity clauses, competence categories and prohibitions of harmonization, reflecting a 'dual federalist' approach (TFEU, Articles 2–6).

Resnik (2001) has criticized the approach of dual, or in her terms 'categorical', federalism as ineffective and ill-suited to deliver the common goods that citizens expect the government to guarantee. This ties in with the second common critique of competitive federalism. The deregulatory outcomes that are accepted in this model have been criticized by those who are in favour of high standards of public interest through governmental intervention, as they argue that a competitive model will lead to a 'race to the bottom' in terms of social, environmental, health and other non-economic objectives. Indeed, the fear is that competition in a federation will undermine solidarity structures within the jurisdictions, as national social rules will either be qualified as 'restrictions to trade' that are to be disapplied by order of the federal level or will simply be ignored through the economic forces of regulatory competition.

At the same time, the cooperative model has also been criticized for being inept at producing solidarity structures at the federal level. Scharpf (2006) has criticized joint decision-making from the viewpoint of its impact on the effectiveness of policy-making. As Watts (2006: 211) states, while 'cooperative federalism' may contribute to the reduction of conflict and enable coordination, when it becomes 'inter-locking federalism' to the extent experienced, for example, in Germany, it might lead to the 'joint decision trap' (Scharpf 2006), which undermines autonomous initiative and freedom of action of governments at both levels, producing inflexibility and lowest-common-denominator outcomes. This argument has had considerable impact in Germany (Hillgruber 2005), leading to calls for loosening up the interlocking character of intergovernmental relations and for the introduction of significant elements of 'competitive federalism' (Sturm 2000; Watts 2006). Indeed, to the extent that a federal model will usually require a higher threshold of consensus for the adoption of legislation, and include more veto-players, than a unitary political system, it would seem that there is a risk of under-regulation compared to a centralized state. However, it is questionable whether this risk is more pronounced under a cooperative model than a competitive model. Indeed, cooperative federalism is instead criticized by some for leading to *over*-regulation in comparison to competitive federations (Greve 2000), and competitive federalism for under-regulation, as seen above.

The two crucial differences between competitive and cooperative models of federalism seem to lie in the degree of (mutual) autonomy of the federal and constituent levels of government and in the degree of regulatory intervention on the part of the federal level. To the present author, however, it is not entirely clear that one model is inherently more suitable to produce competitive outcomes and the other to produce 'solidarity outcomes' or, in similar terms, that one is inherently biased to lead to deregulatory or neo-liberal outcomes and that the other instead fosters 'social' outcomes in the public interest. A system of cooperative federalism could be geared towards the adoption of common rules to liberalize public services, to entrench and foster free trade across the federal territory, and to maintain budgetary discipline. Such a system is, as such, unlikely to produce solidarity outcomes. In similar vein, a system of dual federalism could be envisaged where social and redistributive policies, as well as rules on property ownership, fall within the exclusive competence of the constituent jurisdictions, and where no federal-level intervention of any kind could negatively affect that competence, not even that based on the federal competences to foster intra-federal mobility and trade. Under such a system, constituent jurisdictions would be able to opt for systems of high solidarity, regardless of the choice of their fellow federates to do so or not. Autonomy of constituent members does not necessarily lead to competition, it would thus seem, nor does cooperation necessarily produce solidarity.

The picture emerges that the degree to which federations foster competition, cooperation and solidarity is much more complex than the mere question of whether the competences between the centre and the periphery are clearly drawn and respected or instead mixed. It would instead depend on the content of the competence and on who possesses/exercises it in a particular instance. So, apart from the fact that no federation in reality corresponds to either ideal-type of cooperative or competitive federalism, it seems that the conceptualization of the ideal-types themselves is flawed, at least to the extent that they attempt to explain the role of solidarity, cooperation, and competition or, roughly synonymously, the place of the public interest and the place of the market in the polity in question. Instead, the role of, and impact on, competition, cooperation, and solidarity would appear to depend on the *specific configuration of the federal constitution* and the conditions in which it operates, i.e. the objectives, tasks and procedures set for federal policy, the issues on which constituent members retain their autonomy, and the extent to which the overall polity is tied into a system of global economic competition.

Legal mechanisms to ensure competition

It is hard to imagine a federation that does not somehow guarantee the mobility of its citizens and companies, and their products and services, throughout the federal territory. This certainly does not have to be an unconditional mobility, but a baseline right to establish oneself freely in any of the constituent members and to pursue economic activities there seems to exist in virtually all federal systems. The way in which, and degree to which, this mobility is ensured are highly relevant for the purposes of our discussion. In general terms, it would seem that the more extensive the mobility rights, the more liable the system is to produce competition, and the more difficult it becomes to maintain or produce national solidarity outcomes. This first and foremost applies to the mobility rights of companies, which are generally considered to be more mobile than individual citizens. In Halberstam's (2011: 19) words:

> As soon as the incidents of regulation fall heavily on one entity, say a manufacturer (and its workers), while the benefits fall on another or on citizens more generally, [mobility of the objects of regulation] limits the exercise of public power. This is why, for example, redistributive policies are difficult to maintain at the level of local government, as the United States Supreme Court recognized in upholding federal unemployment laws.[2]

However, even if companies are indeed more mobile, such negative pressure on national solidarity could also be considered to derive from mobility rights for individual citizens, albeit more indirectly. While the mobility rights of individual citizens, and thus their freedom to choose the most attractive mix of taxes, services and social benefits across the federal territory, could, on the one hand, be portrayed as a social side of federalism (as it is often said to be in the context of the EU and the rights of non-economically active citizens), as it forces jurisdictions to extend a degree of solidarity to citizens of other jurisdictions, such mobility could also be hypothesized to lead to competition that undermines solidarity structures on the national level in the longer run. In Volden's (2002: 352) words, the idea is that

> competition may lead to the undersupply of welfare benefits. Some scholars portray this competition as a 'race to the bottom', with states cutting their benefits in response to their neighbours' cuts in order to avoid becoming 'welfare magnets' whose high payments attract potential recipients from surrounding states.

The requirement of transnational solidarity is thus liable to undermine national solidarity through the mechanisms of regulatory competition.

In the EU, the Court of Justice of the European Union (CJEU) has developed the principle of solidarity between the Member States in the context of the free movement of persons and specifically of EU citizenship. This has meant concretely that Member States cannot refuse access or deport non-national EU citizens simply because they have committed a crime or are not contributing to the economy. Furthermore, the fact that a non-national EU citizen does not contribute to the economy may not necessarily imply that they are not entitled to rely on national solidarity mechanisms, such as social benefits. The Court has held specifically that students are entitled to maintenance grants after fulfilling a certain prior-residence criterion and that work-seekers have the right to employment-related benefits on equal terms as nationals. But, indeed, this requirement of solidarity has proven politically controversial.[3] Concerns were raised in a number of Member States about 'welfare tourism', especially in the UK. EU scholars have thus pointed out the danger that such intra-European solidarity may well undermine national solidarity, ultimately lowering the level of social facilities for everyone (Hailbronner 2005; Menéndez 2010). Perhaps in response to these concerns, the CJEU has recently adjusted its stance in the much-debated Dano and Alimanovic cases.[4]

It is heavily contested whether mobility indeed empirically leads to a 'Delaware effect', where companies forum shop to find the lowest level of regulation,[5] or to welfare dumping (Volden 2002), but the potential is certainly there. For the purposes of our discussion, it would seem fair to say that mobility in all its capacities, including citizens' mobility, is due to foster all kinds of competition and to hamper national solidarity in particular. The extent to which a federal order enforces unconditional mobility is likely to influence the degree of regulatory competition and the remaining measure of local regulatory power. The effects of such competition can be mitigated through the adoption of federal-level solidarity structures and other regulation in the public interest, although it will be more difficult to do so than at the local level due to higher consensus thresholds and the increased scale and diversity that the federal level has to accommodate. Thus, mobility rights in a federal order are likely to lead to a certain loss of public regulatory capacity and make the adoption and maintenance of solidarity policies and structures less likely. Whether one considers this to be a good or a bad thing depends on one's political-economic views on the role of the state and the role of the market in our societies – as we have also seen in the above discussion on competitive vs cooperative federalism.

Federal systems operationalize this market mobility in different ways. In the US, the 'dormant commerce clause' serves a similar purpose as the prohibitions on free movement restrictions in the EU legal order (Eule 1982; Schütze 2014). In Australia, the 'rule of origin' entails that 'what is legally produced and sold in one State can automatically be produced and sold throughout the federation without regulatory impediments. This prohibits discrimination. This maxim … is also enshrined in the Constitution, though not always obeyed' (Kasper 2016). In the EU context, we have the free movement provisions, which, in addition to a non-discrimination requirement, have been interpreted by the CJEU to include an element of market access. In particular, the power of the freedom of establishment and of the freedom to provide services to overrule or undermine national solidarity mechanisms is, by now, well known (Garben 2017). High-profile cases like Centros, Viking, Laval, and Rüffert have brought this to the attention of not only academics but a much broader audience, but there are many others.[6] And, of course, this de-regulatory effect is not only measured by CJEU cases, as many such practices may simply go uncontested (and are in fact the very essence of these market freedoms) or dealt with in national courts.

The more sectors are opened up to the market, the more there can be economic integration into a single market. In the EU, Article 345 TFEU provides that 'the Treaties shall in no way prejudice the rules in Member States governing the system of property ownership'. Nevertheless, the EU has liberalized to a large extent a great number of public services, such as transport, energy, and telecommunications, through liberalization directives and through competition law. Indeed, a further legal mechanism to ensure both inter-company competition on an integrated market and inter-Member State economic competition is the adoption of anti-trust and state aid laws. Classic components of such rules are: (1) the regulation of mergers, in order to prevent competition from being eliminated by the creation of one single economic giant; (2) the regulation of anti-competitive behaviour towards other companies, in order to maintain a healthy pool of operators that can compete with each other, as well as of anti-competitive behaviour towards consumers, in order to ensure that the overall output objectives of competition, namely, low prices and wide choice for consumers, are guaranteed; and (3) the prohibition of regulatory intervention in the market by constituent jurisdictions to the benefit of their local economic operators (state aids), in order to maintain equal competition between companies throughout the federal territory as well as, indirectly, competition between the different jurisdictions themselves. As is well known, the EU possesses a broad competence in competition law that it uses ambitiously.

Legal mechanisms to ensure solidarity

Most federations feature a solidarity principle. According to Cyr (2014):

> The principle of federal solidarity … creates certain positive duties of assistance, and certain prohibitions against imposing certain negative externalities on other federal partners. Cooperative federalism is thus normatively justified by the need for each level of government to protect and promote the interests of a shared citizenry forming a common body politic.

This definition underlines the observation made in the previous section that a wide definition of solidarity encompasses both (1) the act of participating in a common system that does not guarantee immediate returns to each participant and (2) the redistribution of the general benefits generated by that system by the 'winners' to the 'losers'. Cooperation in itself can thus be an expression of solidarity, and therefore a requirement under a legal solidarity principle. The EU legal order does not know, in so many words, the principle of 'federal solidarity' or 'federal comity' as it exists, for instance, in German constitutional law (Schneider 1999: 64–5). Nevertheless, the Treaties do lay down the principle of sincere cooperation in Article 4(3) TEU.[7] While this may first and foremost refer to the duties of the Member States and the EU Institutions vis-à-vis each other, the principle also has an important horizontal dimension (Blanquet 1994; Klamert 2014; Vedder 2007), which could be explored more fully if one is to boost the EU's problem-solving capacity as well as Member State solidarity. The duty of sincere cooperation has not often been invoked in this context, but it would seem that it could be used whenever Member States are facing an essentially common problem (like an influx of third-country migration; see Vimont 2016), where the negative consequences fall more heavily on a single state or a limited group of states, to the potential 'benefit' of other states – in order to impose a duty on the 'free-riding' Member States to constructively seek a solution.

Indeed, such a positive duty of cooperation in terms of Member State solidarity has been further specified in the area of freedom, security and justice. Article 67(2) TFEU provides that the Union

> shall ensure the absence of internal border controls for persons and shall frame a common policy on asylum, immigration and external border control, based on solidarity between Member States, which is fair towards third-country nationals. For the purpose of this Title, stateless persons shall be treated as third-country nationals.

This is repeated in Article 80 TFEU, which states:

> the policies of the Union set out in this Chapter and their implementation shall be governed by the principle of solidarity and fair sharing of responsibility, including its financial implications, between the Member States. Whenever necessary, the Union acts adopted pursuant to this Chapter shall contain appropriate measures to give effect to this principle.

It could be argued that the obstructive behaviour of some Member States in the context of the migration crisis have infringed this duty of solidarity and have highlighted the risk of free-riding in the EU context.

Another context-specific reference to solidarity in the Treaties can be found in Article 122 TFEU:

> Without prejudice to any other procedures provided for in the Treaties, the Council, on a proposal from the Commission, may decide, in a spirit of solidarity between Member States, upon the measures appropriate to the economic situation, in particular if severe difficulties arise in the supply of certain products, notably in the area of energy. Where a Member State is in difficulties or is seriously threatened with severe difficulties caused by natural disasters or exceptional occurrences beyond its control, the Council, on a proposal from the Commission, may grant, under certain conditions, Union financial assistance to the Member State concerned. The President of the Council shall inform the European Parliament of the decision taken.

This is a rather different manifestation of the principle. On the one hand, it seems to call for a strong expression of solidarity, in that emergency assistance is provided without any expectation of benefits in return. On the other hand, if read in its context and particularly in conjunction with Article 125 TFEU,[8] the reciprocal nature of this provision becomes clear.

The fact that this gives rise to a limited form of conditional solidarity can clearly be seen in the context of the Euro-crisis, where the initial financial assistance was granted on the basis of Article 122 TFEU. In the case of Pringle, the CJEU held that this provision is concerned solely with ad hoc Union assistance to Member States and not inter-Member State assistance. The Court in that judgment also held that Article 125 TFEU

> prohibits the Union and the Member States from granting financial assistance as a result of which the incentive of the recipient Member State to

> conduct a sound budgetary policy is diminished.... However, Article 125 TFEU does not prohibit the granting of financial assistance by one or more Member States to a Member State which remains responsible for its commitments to its creditors provided that the conditions attached to such assistance are such as to prompt that Member State to implement a sound budgetary policy.

The Advocate General (AG) in the Pringle case had argued for such a balanced interpretation of Article 125 TFEU on the explicit basis of the principle of solidarity between Member States:

> Further, a broad interpretation of Article 125 TFEU would be incompatible with the concept of solidarity, as laid down at various points in the Treaties. For example the parties to the EU Treaty are, in accordance with the preamble to that Treaty, pursuing the desire 'to deepen the solidarity between their peoples'. Under the third subparagraph of Article 3(3) TEU the Union is to promote 'economic, social and territorial cohesion, and solidarity among Member States'. In the chapter on economic policy, Article 122(1) TFEU refers explicitly to solidarity between Member States.
>
> Admittedly, it cannot be inferred from the concept of solidarity that there exists a duty to provide financial assistance of the kind that is to be provided by the ESM. None the less, a broad teleological interpretation of Article 125 TFEU would also indeed prohibit the Member States, in a case of emergency, for example, to prevent the serious economic and social effects associated with a State bankruptcy, from *voluntarily* providing mutual assistance. Emergency assistance to any third State would be permitted, while emergency assistance within the Union would be banned. Such a prohibition, it appears to me, would call into question the very purpose and objective of a Union.
>
> Basic fundamental principles of the Treaties therefore militate against a broad interpretation of Article 125 TFEU.

The AG thus qualifies the principle of solidarity between Member States as a 'basic fundamental principle of the Treaties'[9] and, while not inferring (in this specific context of economic policy) a duty to provide assistance, argues that it must mean that the Treaty does allow the granting of such assistance, under conditions.

Of course, although the Treaties and the AG explicitly employ the language of solidarity, it may be asked to what extent these actions have involved a genuine measure of solidarity rather than rational self-interest by the creditor states. The term 'generosity', a requirement of solidarity, is indeed not easily used in this context. The money is to be paid back with interest, after all, and ensuring the stability of the euro area as well as preventing the bankruptcy of a Member State is certainly in the common interest. Still, under the wide definition of solidarity defined in the previous section, the fact that reciprocity is involved does not exclude solidarity, as long as the action in question does not have a guaranteed net benefit to the actor. As the 'bail-outs' involve a significant measure of risk and as such constitute a sub-optimal action for the assisting Member States, the necessary elements of a (weak) action of solidarity are indeed present. Ironically, however, the way that this transnational/Member State solidarity has been executed has infamously led to a grave erosion of national solidarity structures in the Member States affected (Garben 2017).

Beyond these provisions of relatively weak solidarity, the Treaties also feature some mechanisms of stronger solidarity, where the EU level is deployed to engage in large-scale redistribution and assistance. First, in recognition of the socially disruptive effects of the internal market mentioned in the previous section, the EU Treaties feature redistributive mechanisms, such as the European Social Fund (ESF). Article 162 TFEU provides that 'to improve employment opportunities for workers in the internal market and to contribute thereby to raising the standard of living', the ESF has been established, aiming to 'render the employment of workers easier and to increase their geographical and occupational mobility within the Union, and to facilitate their adaptation to industrial changes and to changes in production systems, in particular through vocational training and retraining'. More generally, Article 174 TFEU provides that 'to promote its overall harmonious development, the Union shall develop and pursue its actions leading to the strengthening of its economic, social and territorial cohesion'. These objectives are mainly pursued through the European Structural and Investment Funds, of which the ESF is part as well as the European Regional Development Fund (ERDF), the Cohesion Fund (CF), the European Agricultural Fund for Rural Development (EAFRD) and the European Maritime and Fisheries Fund (EMFF). These funds are governed by Common Provisions Regulation 1303/2013,[10] defining common principles, rules and standards for their implementation, and providing an overall budget of €454 billion for the period 2014–20. In addition, a separate Fund for European Aid to the Most Deprived disposes of €3.8 billion for the 2014–20 period to provide material assistance to the most deprived in the form of food, clothing, and other essential personal items.[11] Such redistributive measures can clearly be seen as an expression of federal solidarity (Follesdal 2006) and of the kind of reciprocity-based redistributive solidarity postulated by Sangiovanni (2013).

In addition, the EU's competence in civil protection should be mentioned (Article 196 TFEU). Council Decision 2001/792 established an EU Mechanism to facilitate cooperation in civil protection interventions.[12] The Mechanism was set up to enable coordinated assistance from the participating states to victims of natural and man-made disasters in Europe and elsewhere, and it currently includes all 28 EU Member States as well as Iceland, Norway, and Macedonia. The EU Civil Protection legislation was revised in 2013 by Decision 1313/2013/EU on a Union Civil Protection Mechanism,[13] placing greater emphasis on disaster prevention, risk management and disaster preparedness, including the organization of training, simulation exercises, and the exchange of experts, but also developing new elements, such as a voluntary pool of pre-committed response capacities by the Member States. The operational centre of the new EU Civil Protection Mechanism is the Emergency Response Coordination Centre (ERCC),[14] which continuously monitors emergencies around the world and coordinates the response of the participating countries in case of a crisis. The ERCC teams are ready to intervene at short notice both within and outside the EU. They undertake specialized tasks such as search and rescue, aerial forest fire fighting, advanced medical posts, and so forth. Since its launch in 2001, the EU Civil Protection Mechanism has monitored over 300 disasters and has received more than 180 requests for assistance.[15] The Mechanism also intends to help in marine pollution emergencies, where it works with the European Maritime Safety Agency. Furthermore, in the context of its youth policy, the EU has recently created a European Solidarity Corps. It comprises a volunteering strand, under which young people between 17 and 30 years of age receive a grant to carry out full-time voluntary service between two and 12 months, usually somewhere in the EU, and an occupational strand giving young people a traineeship or job in a wide range of sectors 'engaged in solidarity activities'.

Perhaps most importantly, the EU does possess hard legislative competence on a range of social policy issues. However, the objectives for which the Social Title permits the adoption of such EU legislation are generally not of a redistributive nature and, as such, do not arguably entail high levels of solidarity. The protection of workers' health and safety, the improvement of working conditions, protection in case of termination of employment, information and consultation of workers, gender equality as regards employment, and the other fields listed in Article 153(1) TFEU are social in nature, but can still be conceptualized as correcting (internal) market failures, particularly the risk of a race to the bottom, information and power asymmetries between workers and employers, and societal externalities.[16] By contrast, the more sensitive issues of combating social exclusion and modernizing social protection systems cannot be pursued through legislation on the EU level,[17] and the issues of wage setting, collective action, and the right to strike are excluded from any action under Article 153 TFEU.[18] For these issues, the Member States remain competent, to the extent that this competence is not undermined by the free movement provisions mentioned in the previous section.

Critical assessment and proposals for reform

The (im)balance between competition, cooperation, and solidarity in EU law

As we have seen, the real issue in trying to establish the role of competition, cooperation, and solidarity in any given federal model, including the EU, does not depend so much on an inevitably simplistic and rather superficial characterization of 'cooperative' or 'competitive', but rather on the specific constitutional configuration of the polity and the relative strength and weakness of the instruments to foster solidarity and competition. A certain perception exists that, in the

EU, the Union level provides for the conditions and ingredients of competition while the national level remains responsible for the provision of social solidarity (Streeck 1996: 64). This is reflected in the division of competences between the EU and the Member States, which endows the EU with far-reaching powers to integrate the European market (both 'negatively' through the Treaty provisions on free movement and 'positively' through the power to liberalize and fully harmonize in the internal market) and to guarantee competition within it, while it has only limited and generally non-redistributive competences in the area of social policy (Garben 2017). Various authors have pointed out the asymmetry between these powers and have claimed that this means not only that the EU can never be a social market economy, but that the EU inherently undermines national welfare policies as well (Scharpf 2010).

Indeed, looking at the various mechanisms of competition, cooperation, and solidarity in the EU, it seems fair to conclude that on balance, those that serve to foster competition are stronger than those fostering solidarity (either on the national or European level) in virtually all of the different meanings of these notions. The free movement provisions grant hard rights that can be enforced in national courts, for instance, by economic operators who can thereby seek to maximize their mobility in order to choose the regulatory system of their preference and operate throughout the EU from there. Through the principle of mutual recognition, the need for cooperative action is diminished and regulatory competition can do its work. When the EU does take cooperative action in this area, it tends to be to replace existing national impediments that are justified restrictions to trade; while the outcome is usually a common 'full' norm which removes regulatory differences and hence reduces regulatory competition, this does actually enhance inter-company competition in the EU and reduces the power of the national level to decide on the public (including social) interest. Furthermore, the EU has legislated to open up public sectors to the market, and strictly imposes competition on market actors through its competition law. In comparison, the EU's solidarity mechanisms are weak. Genuine redistributive social powers lie largely outside the scope of the EU's competence. Furthermore, the cooperative and solidarity mechanisms at the EU level that do exist have recently become instrumentalized to undermine solidarity structures at the national level, such as in the financial assistance granted in the context of the Euro-crisis, or to enhance competitiveness, such as making the grant of assistance through the Structural Funds conditional on meeting the country-specific recommendations in the context of the European Semester, Europe's overarching economic policy coordination framework.

It should once again be noted that competition and solidarity mechanisms are not always at odds with each other. For instance, while competition law is of course about fostering transnational competition between companies, this sometimes works out to actually limit regulatory competition between Member States, for instance, in corporate taxation, where the Commission has qualified 'Delaware-type' tax practices as state aid which will have to be repaid. Furthermore, as mentioned earlier, 'regulatory competition' can also be deployed in a different way, as a more benign mode of governance for social purposes, for instance, in the context of the Social Open Method of Coordination. Member States are here placed in a comparative context, are competing for the best social performance, and as such are encouraged to improve their national solidarity policies. Equally, it could be argued that strong solidarity mechanisms can make economies more competitive and resilient, showing that the two concepts do not always have to be traded off against each other but may be mutually reinforcing. This line of reasoning has been adopted by the European Commission recently when it launched the European Pillar of Social Rights, discussed in Chapter 13 of this book, which entails the 'socialization' of the European Semester through social benchmarking in view of Europe's overall economic stability. These synergies exist but should not be exaggerated. Very often there is a clear tension between competition and solidarity, and sides will have to be chosen. The EU legal order not only creates such conflicts (especially in the context of the internal market and economic governance) but also often decides them in favour of competition.

Towards a firmer institutionalization of solidarity mechanisms in EU law

The question can be raised whether integration primarily through competition rather than solidarity is a stable and sustainable course of action in the long run, and whether some of the political difficulties in which the EU finds itself at the moment cannot be taken as testimony that the expiry date on this approach has started to lapse. Following Habermas (2012), the stability of a federal union requires a degree of civil solidarity, which cannot develop if social inequalities between the Member States, or between certain groups of citizens within and between the Member States, become permanent structural features. In the second section of this chapter, we indicated that: (1) the participation in a common project (such as the EU as a whole or the internal market more specifically) without a guarantee of immediate net benefits, and (2) the subsequent redistribution of the yields of that common system from the winners to the losers, are both acts of solidarity. These two acts of reciprocity-based solidarity can furthermore be considered as interrelated. If the same actors (individuals, social groups, Member States) are consistently asked to perform the first act of solidarity, i.e. to participate in the scheme without guaranteed benefits, and it consistently turns out that the benefits that are generated do not fall to them, making them the 'losers' of the system, and if subsequently the 'winners' do not engage in the second act of solidarity, i.e. redistribution, then the losing group will at some point refuse to continue engaging in its first act of solidarity. Indeed, in such a situation, the 'losers' are not asked to participate in a common project where the individual yields will be uncertain, but instead in a framework where their personal loss is certain. Such sustained generosity can only be expected when group ties are so strong that the gains of another member of the group are vicariously felt, which is not likely in an EU context. It also works the other way around, as 'winners' are not likely to engage in the second act of redistributive solidarity if the 'losers' are not willing to fully cooperate in the common project that generated the benefits in the first place.

What can we make of this for the current EU? It would seem that, in order to ensure its stability and success as a federal system, the EU needs to better institutionalize the above mutually reinforcing two-step solidarity structure. It needs to ensure that: (1) everyone participates in the common project (largely defined) without expecting a guaranteed net benefit in the immediate term, and (2) that there are sufficiently robust redistributive mechanisms in place so that individuals, groups and Member States that (structurally) lose in the common system are duly compensated. EU law can play an important instrumental role here, as will be detailed in the tentative reform proposals below. Of course, in addition, it is also crucial that the EU's common scheme and the benefits it yields overall are clearly visible and understandable, which links to the much-debated problems of citizen alienation due to a lack of a direct communication link between the EU and its populace, and to the lack of a genuine European public sphere. The necessary changes on that front lie beyond the scope of this chapter, but do complete the overall picture.

It would seem that the principle of sincere cooperation as laid down in Article 4(3) TFEU, or the overarching general principle of EU law of inter-Member State solidarity, could be (re-)interpreted to impose some stronger positive duties of cooperation under EU law. Of course, there is a difficult balance between, on the one hand, the political freedom of the Member States to pursue their own interests, which may sometimes be precisely to the detriment of other Member States, and, on the other hand, a duty to cooperate in a spirit of solidarity to find common solutions to problems experienced disproportionally by another Member State. A case could be made that the duty to cooperate should be especially strong when: (1) the problem experienced by the Member State in need is linked to, or the consequence of, common policies, externalities, or Europeanization more generally, thus imparting a certain responsibility on some or all other Member States for the occurrence of this problem; (2) one or more Member States specifically benefit from the problem experienced by the Member State in need or from not solving it together (free-riding); and (3) the problem or situation experienced by the Member State in need is objectively considered undesirable, particularly in light of common EU objectives, such as high levels of social, health, and environmental protection or human rights. In such circumstances, the duty of federal solidarity could imply a strong procedural obligation for the Member States to negotiate in good faith towards a common solution.

Advocate General Sharpston has already provided some tentative reasoning in this regard, in respect of the Austrian-Belgian education saga (Garben 2010). Austria and Belgium found themselves in a similarly difficult situation where their universities (particularly medical courses) were overflooded by respectively German and French students, who under EU law have the right to study in other Member States under the same access (including tuition) conditions as nationals. This situation occurred because: (1) these two small countries share their language with a large neighbouring country; and (2) they operated a free and open-access higher education system, while their large neighbours operated a *numerus clausus* on medical studies. The situation was so extreme that: (1) it made it objectively difficult for Austria and Belgium to provide sufficient quality medical education (overcrowded classrooms, insufficient resources for practical training), and (2) it risked leaving Austria and Belgium without sufficient medical staff in the longer run, as most French and German students were expected to practise medicine 'back home' after their graduation. The CJEU in the Bressol case ultimately recognized that, under such extreme circumstances, it can be justified to limit the number of foreign students, but it attached very strict conditions to this possibility. What the Advocate General pointed out, in this regard, is:

> one of the objectives of the Community listed in Article 2 EC is to promote solidarity among the Member States, and that the Member States have a mutual duty of loyal cooperation on the basis of Article 10 EC. It seems to me that those provisions are very pertinent here. Where linguistic patterns and differing national policies on access to higher education encourage particularly high volumes of student mobility that cause real difficulties for the host Member State, it is surely incumbent on both the host Member State and the home Member State actively to seek a negotiated solution that complies with the Treaty.[19]

The free-riding behaviour of France and Germany in these cases could be considered contrary to the principle of federal loyalty and could therefore have been subject to infringement proceedings by the European Commission.

It may be possible to identify certain policy areas where the duty of federal loyalty should be especially strong, in line with what has been said above, namely, areas where there are externalities or spill-over effects from other common policies or Europeanization more generally, which are felt more strongly by some Member States than by others, and where these effects are considered undesirable in light of common EU objectives.

The area of migration is one of those, and it is therefore not coincidental that a specific formulation of solidarity already exists in the relevant Treaty provisions. This has, however, not been respected in the context of the migration crisis, or – if the obstructive behaviour of certain Member States is not considered to be contrary to the current provisions strictly interpreted – this duty has not been formulated in a sufficiently strong manner in the Treaties. Scope for enhancing the solidarity principle here would lie therefore with the Commission, which might take infringement action against uncooperative Member States, and with the CJEU, which might uphold such an interpretation of the Treaties. It would also be important to move away from intergovernmentalism in this area in order to facilitate cooperation instead of individualistic behaviour – a move which would require an amendment to the Treaties.

Another policy area in which the need for reciprocal solidarity is strong is the EMU, where again not coincidentally a specific manifestation of the principle of solidarity has already been formulated in the Treaties and the case law as discussed above. The problem with the status quo is perhaps not so much the requirement that financial assistance is to be conditional, since this still leaves sufficient scope for solidarity by creditors and may be necessary to prevent moral hazard and free-riding behaviour by debtors, but the concrete way in which the conditionality has been given shape. The conditionalities specified in the Memorandums of Understanding have clearly not been drafted in a spirit of transnational solidarity by the creditor states and with due regard to national solidarity structures, but instead carry a punitive flavour and have contributed to a grave social crisis in the debtor countries.[20] This has been made possible through a parallel framework that has been set out outside the EU's institutional and legal framework. While the CJEU had confirmed the validity of these practices in the Pringle case, they have proven highly problematic from a democratic, rule of law, and social perspective. The hard-core intergovernmental approach and its outcomes in the context of the Euro-crisis have gravely damaged the two-fold reciprocity-based solidarity fabric of the EU: citizens of debtor states feel that they have been made to sacrifice their social welfare in order to maintain the common economic system from which creditor states benefit too much, while citizens of the creditor states feel that they have been made to redistribute their hard-earned wealth to debtors who have not duly contributed to the common system that generated that wealth. There is certainly a problem of communication in how governments have sold Euro-crisis narratives to their constituents, but there is also a structural, institutional problem with the lack of a proper solidarity-based system of cooperation within the EU's constitutional settlement on the basis of which these problems could have been addressed.

Finally, the two-step solidarity framework outlined above should be improved in the internal market. As matters currently stand, the CJEU's wide interpretation of the free movement provisions and the regulatory gap that ensues from this (Garben 2017) lead to a situation where certain individuals, societal groups, and Member States are consistently being asked to engage in the first act of solidarity, namely, to participate in a market without guaranteed net benefits (and in some cases, guaranteed losses), but there is insufficient capacity for the EU to ensure the redistribution of the benefits from the winners to the losers. National solidarity policies risk being eroded without an equivalent replacement at the EU level (due to a lack of competence or political difficulties) and, while there are redistributive financial measures, it is not certain that these will sufficiently compensate for the losses incurred. I have set out some proposals to address this particular imbalance between 'the market' and 'the social' elsewhere (ibid.).

Conclusion

Solidarity may serve to provide a suitable normative framework for the federal entity that is the European Union. Within that framework, a reasonable degree of competition may be usefully accommodated as both a substantive (internal market, anti-trust, state aid) and procedural (regulatory competition) part of the overall common project within which all Member States are expected, or even legally required, to fully participate without a guarantee for immediate net benefits. This first act of solidarity should, however, be made possible by a sufficient redistribution of the yields of the common project to all Member States and, more generally, to all societal groups and individuals within the Member States. In addition, this second act of solidarity should be legally required as a fundamental part of the constitutional settlement of the EU. Care must be taken that, in the longer term, the costs of solidarity are not concentrated on the same groups or individuals without a reasonably equivalent return. For instance, workers who lose their jobs because of restructuring in the internal market but who are not compensated beyond being given some re-training sponsored by the Structural Funds, and who are being told that the EU is altogether beneficial because it means that they now live in peace and *other* people live in increased prosperity because of it, are not likely to continue to reproduce this first act of solidarity. Equally, tax-payers are not likely to agree to significant degrees of redistribution (or risk-sharing) under the second act of solidarity if they do not think that the recipients have equally contributed to the common system or have effectively worked towards the common benefit.

This chapter has tried to operationalize these considerations in the form of some concrete, albeit very tentative, reform proposals for the EU's constitutional order. It would be fruitful if further reflection on solutions to the EU's current predicament could take place along the lines that there should be a stronger legal obligation on Member States to fully commit to both acts of reciprocity-based solidarity (cooperation and redistribution). In addition, there is of course an important political side to the implementation of this normative framework for European integration, particularly in how it can be clearly communicated to EU citizens. If the case is coherently made that EU membership implies a degree of reciprocity-based solidarity entailing the full participation in the project for the common benefit, in which returns will not necessarily be immediate but eventually will be fairly distributed among all participants, and if the way in which all members participate and contribute, as well as the common benefit in its various manifestations, are clearly identified and communicated, this must help convince citizens to support European integration. If a specific group is not convinced on this basis, because levels of identification with the overall European community are too low to motivate even this limited degree of reciprocity-based solidarity, then it might be better for that group to secede from the Union. That outcome is to be preferred over a formula of differentiated integration, allowing states to be (quasi-)members without committing fully to the first (and perhaps second) act of solidarity and instead cherry-picking the parts of the project where immediate net-benefits are anticipated or even guaranteed; such an approach will ultimately unravel the very fabric of the Union. The foregoing discussion suggests that a Europe *à la carte* is not a sustainable federal model and would aggravate Europe's current crises instead of solving them. Indeed, as the tragic Brexit experience shows us, it would seem that a basic commitment to the twofold reciprocity-based solidarity as set out in this chapter is a de facto (and should be a *de iure*) sine qua non for EU membership. A forceful application of this core criterion may leave us with a smaller group, but one that is founded on the right kind of social contract.

Notes

1 One could think, for example, of the provision of humanitarian assistance to another group (country) in case of a natural disaster, when it is provided without any reasonable expectation of receiving such assistance when disaster strikes the assisting group (country) at a later point.

2 For a contribution contesting the existence of regulatory competition, see Kahan and Kamar (2002).

3 For a recent post-Brexit discussion, see Davies (2016).

4 Case C-333/13, *Elisabeta Dano and Florin Dano* v. *Jobcenter Leipzig*, EU:C:2014:2358; Case C-67/14, *Jobcenter Berlin Neukölln* v. *Nazifa Alimanovic and Others*, EU:C:2015:597.

5 For a recent critical assessment in the US, see Subramanian (2004). For an assessment in the EU, see McCahery and Vermeulen (2005).

6 Such as, e.g. C-576/13, *Commission* v. *Spain*, EU:C:2014:2430, Case C-201/15, AGET Iraklis, EU:C:2016:972.

7 Treaty on European Union, Article 4(3): 'Pursuant to the principle of sincere cooperation, the Union and the Member States shall, in full mutual respect, assist each other in carrying out tasks which flow from the Treaties.'

8 Treaty on the Functioning of the European Union, Article 125:

> The Union shall not be liable for or assume the commitments of central governments, regional, local or other public authorities, other bodies governed by public law, or public undertakings of any Member State, without prejudice to mutual financial guarantees for the joint execution of a specific project. A Member State shall not be liable for or assume the commitments of central governments, regional, local or other public authorities, other bodies governed by public law, or public undertakings of another Member State, without prejudice to mutual financial guarantees for the joint execution of a specific project.

9 See also in another context AG Wahl, in Case C-44/14, *Spain* v. *Parliament and Council*, EU:C:2015:320, para. 35:

> I am sensible of the need to avoid allowing Member States not participating in some of the Schengen acquis to cherry-pick such parts of the related Schengen-building measures as they see fit, and disregard the others. Not only would an unrestrained *à la carte* approach – even in this area of EU law in which some differentiation has been allowed – sit uneasily with the principles of solidarity between Member States, and of equality of Member States before the Treaties, which lie at the heart of the European project of integration, but that approach would also be inconsistent with the objective pursued by Article 4 of the Schengen Protocol which is, as the Court has stated, to seek to ensure the maximum participation of all Member States in the Schengen acquis.

10 O.J. 2013, L 347, at 320–469.

11 Regulation 223/2014, O.J. 2014, L 72, at 1–41.

12 O.J. 2001, L 297/7–11. It was adopted on the basis of the 'flexibility clause' of Art. 308 EC (now 352 TFEU).

13 O.J. 2013, L 347.924–947, adopted on the basis of Art. 196 TFEU.

14 Replacing and upgrading the functions of the previous Monitoring and Information Centre. See http://erccportal.jrc.ec.europa.eu/
15 It has intervened, for example, to offer aid in Hurricane Katrina in the USA (2005), the earthquake in Haiti (2010), the triple-disaster in Japan (2011), and the typhoon Haiyan that hit the Philippines (2013).
16 On the market-correcting rationale of labour law, see Collins (2003). For criticism on how the EU limits its social and employment policy to the existence of (internal) market failures, see Barnard (2000).
17 Article 153(1)(j) and (k), jo. (2)(b) TFEU.
18 Article 153(5) TFEU.
19 Opinion of AG Sharpston, Case C-73/08, *Nicolas Bressol and Others and Céline Chaverot and Others* v. *Gouvernement de la Communauté française*, EU:C:2009:396, para. 154.
20 For a comprehensive discussion, see Garben (2017).

References

Abell, Peter (1996). 'A model of the informal structure (culture) of organizations: help, trust, rivalry and team spirit', *Rationality and Society* 8(4): 433–52.

Arnsperger, Christian and Yanis Varoufakis (2003). 'Toward a theory of solidarity', *Erkenntnis* 59(2): 157–88.

Barnard, Catherine (2000). 'Regulating competitive federalism in the European Union? The case of EU social policy', in Joe Shaw (ed.). *Social law and policy in an evolving European Union*. Oxford: Hart, 49–70.

Blanquet, Marc (1994). *L'article 5 du Traité CEE: recherche sur les obligations de fidélité des États membres de la Communauté*. Paris: LGDJ.

Breton, Albert (1995). *Competitive governments*. New York: Cambridge University Press.

Collins, Hugh (2003). 'Justification and techniques of legal regulation of the employment relation', in Hugh Collins, Paul Davies, and Roger Rideout *Legal regulation and the employment relation*. Alphen an den Rijn: Kluwer Law International, 3–27.

Cyr, Hugo (2014). 'Autonomy, subsidiarity, solidarity: foundations of cooperative federalism', *Constitutional Forum* 23(4): 20–40.

Davies, Gareth (2016). 'Migrant Union citizens and social assistance: trying to be reasonable about self-sufficiency', College of Europe Research Paper. Bruges: College of Europe. Available at: www.coleurope.eu/sites/default/files/research-paper/research paper_2_2016_davies.pdf

Della Porta, Donatella, Hara Kouki, and Joseba Fernández (2017). 'Left's love and hate for Europe: Syriza, Podemos and critical visions of Europe during the crisis', in Manuela Caiani and Simona Guerra (eds) *Euroscepticism, democracy and the media*. London: Palgrave, 219–40.

Elazar, Daniel J. (1962). *The American partnership: intergovernmental cooperation in the nineteenth-century United States*. Chicago: University of Chicago Press.

Eule, Julian N. (1982). 'Laying the dormant commerce clause to rest', *The Yale Law Journal* 91(3): 425–85.

Ferrera, Maurizio (2016). 'The contentious politics of hospitality: intra-EU mobility and social rights', *European Law Journal* 22(6): 791–805.

FitzGibbon, John, Benjamin Leruth, and Nick Startin (eds) (2017). *Euroscepticism as a transnational and pan-European phenomenon: the emergence of a new sphere of opposition*. London: Routledge.

Follesdal, Andreas (2006). 'Justice, stability and toleration in a federation of well-ordered peoples', in Rex Martin and David A. Reidy (eds) *Rawls's law of peoples: a realistic utopia?* London: Wiley, 299–317.

Garben, Sacha (2010). 'Case C-73/08, Nicolas Bressol and Others, Céline Chaverot and Others v. Gouvernement de la Communauté française, Judgment of the Court (Grand Chamber) of 13 April 2010', *Common Market Law Review* 47(5): 1493–510.

Garben, Sacha (2017). 'The constitutional (im)balance between "the Market" and "the Social" in the European Union', *European Constitutional Law Review* 13(1): 23–61.

Gould, Carol C. (2007). 'Transnational solidarities', *Journal of Social Philosophy* 38(1): 148–64.

Greve, Michael S. (2000). 'Against cooperative federalism', *Mississippi Law Journal* 70(2): 557–624.

Habermas, Jürgen (2012). *The crisis of the European Union: a response*. Cambridge: Polity.

Hailbronner, Jay (2005). 'Union citizens and access to social benefits', *Common Market Law Review* 42: 1245–67.

Halberstam, Daniel (2011). 'Federalism: a critical guide', University of Michigan Public Law Working Paper No. 251. Ann Arbor, MI: University of Michigan Law School. Available at: https://papers.ssrn.com/sol3/Delivery.cfm/SSRN_ID1928794_code256592.pdf?abstractid=1924939&mirid=1&type=2

Hillgruber, Christian (2005). 'German federalism – an outdated relict?', *German Law Journal* 6: 1270–82.

Hobolt, Sara B. and Catherine de Vries (2016). 'Turning against the Union? The impact of the crisis on the Eurosceptic vote in the 2014 European Parliament elections', *Electoral Studies* 44: 504–14.

Kahan, Marcel and Ehud Kamar (2002). 'The myth of state competition in corporate law', *Stanford Law Journal* 55(3): 679–749.

Kasper, Wolfgang (2016). 'May the best-run state win', *Policy* 32(3): 37–40.

Klamert, Marcus (2014). *The principle of loyalty in EU law*. Oxford: Oxford University Press.

Kuhn, Theresa, Erika van Elsas, Armen Hakhverdian, and Wouter van der Brug (2016). 'An ever wider gap in an ever closer union: rising inequalities and euroscepticism in 12 West European democracies, 1975–2009', *Socio-economic Review* 14(1): 27–45.

McCahery, Joseph and Erik Vermeulen (2005). 'Does the European company prevent the "Delaware Effect"?', *European Law Journal* 11(6): 785–801.

Menéndez, Augustín José (2010). 'European citizenship after Martínez Sala and Baumbast: has European law become more human but less social?', in Miguel Poiares Maduro and Loïc Azoulai (eds) *The past and future of EU law: the classics of EU law revisited on the 50th anniversary of the Rome Treaty*. Oxford: Hart, 363–93.

Resnik, Judith (2001). 'Categorical federalism: jurisdiction, gender, and the globe', *The Yale Law Journal* 111(3): 619–80.

Risse, Thomas (2010). *A community of Europeans? Transnational identities and public spheres*. Ithaca, NY: Cornell University Press.

Sangiovanni, Andrea (2013). 'Solidarity in the European Union', *Oxford Journal of Legal Studies* 33(2): 213–41.

Scharpf, Fritz W. (2006). 'The joint-decision trap revisited', *Journal of Common Market Studies* 44(4): 845–64.

Scharpf, Fritz W. (2010). 'The socio-economic asymmetries of European integration: or why the EU cannot be a "social market economy"', *European Social Analysis* 10: 1–8.

Schnabel, Johanna (2014). 'Negotiating federalism's boundaries: intergovernmental relations as a federal safeguard', IPSA World Congress Paper. Available at: http://paper-room.ipsa.org/app/webroot/papers/paper_31810.pdf

Schneider, Hans-Peter (1999). 'German unification and the federal system: the challenge of reform', in Charlie Jeffery (ed.). *Recasting German federalism: legacies of unification*. London: Pinter, 58–84.

Schütze, Robert (2009). *From dual to cooperative federalism: the changing structure of European law*. Oxford: Oxford University Press.

Schütze, Robert (2014). 'Limits to the Union's 'internal market' competence(s): constitutional comparisons', in Loïc Azoulai (ed.). *The question of competence in the European Union*. Oxford: Oxford University Press.

Streeck, Wolfgang (1996). 'Neo-voluntarism: a new European social policy regime?', in Gary Marks, Fritz W. Scharpf, Philippe C. Schmitter, and Wolfgang Streeck (eds). *Governance in the European Union*. London: Sage, 31–59.

Sturm, Roland (2000). 'The federal system: breaking through the barriers of interlocking federalism?', in Ludger Helms (ed.). *Institutions and institutional change in the Federal Republic of Germany*. London: Palgrave, 105–23.

Subramanian, Guhan (2004). 'The disappearing Delaware effect', *The Journal of Law, Economics, and Organization* 20(1): 32–59.

Sugden, Robert (1993). 'Thinking as a team: towards an explanation of nonselfish behavior', *Social Philosophy and Policy* 10(1): 69–89.

Vedder, Christoph (2007). 'Art. I-5', in Christoph Vedder and Wolff Heintschel von Heinegg (eds). *Europäischer Verfassungsvertrag: Handkommentar*. Baden-Baden: Nomos.

Vimont, Pierre (2016). 'Migration in Europe: bridging the solidarity gap', Washington, DC: Carnegie Endowment for International Peace. Available at: http://carnegieendowment.org/files/Vimont_Migration_fulltext.pdf

Volden, Craig (2002). 'The politics of competitive federalism: a race to the bottom in welfare benefits?', *American Journal of Political Science* 46(2): 352–63.

Watts, Ronald L. (2006). 'Origins of cooperative and competitive federalism', in Scott L. Greer (ed.) *Territory, democracy and justice: regionalism and federalism in Western democracies*. London: Palgrave, 201–23.

Weidlich, Wolfgang and Dirk Helbing (1998). 'A mathematical model of group dynamics including the effects of solidarity', in Patrick Doreian and Thomas Fararo (eds). *The problem of solidarity: theories and models*. London: Routledge, 139–96.

Zimmerman, Joseph F. (2001). 'National-state relations: cooperative federalism in the twentieth century', *Publius* 31(2): 15–30.

6 Harnessing competitiveness for social and ecological goals

High-road competitiveness is necessary and feasible

Karl Aiginger

Competitiveness and ambitious social and environmental standards have often been assessed as conflicting goals. If politicians and the media declare that 'European competitiveness is challenged' or that 'America should bring industry back home', then politicians are implicitly or explicitly calling for an agenda of low wages, energy costs, and social standards. The Organisation for Economic Co-operation and Development (OECD) and the European Commission often summarize this approach under the request for 'structural reforms' focusing on the deregulation of labour markets.

This chapter emphasizes that there is, if any, only a short-run trade-off between social and ecological ambitions and economic performance. In the long run, firms and countries going for productivity, innovation, skills, and sophisticated markets are more successful than those which primarily focus on the cost side.

The chapter highlights (following Aiginger 2006, 2012) that a systemic industrial policy as well as a new definition of competitiveness are necessary to support social and ecological goals. Such a high-road approach is necessary and feasible for leading countries if they want to increase well-being. The acknowledgement that each country has to 'climb up' the quality ladder if welfare is to increase for all citizens is also important for catch-up economies and during periods of disequilibria (such as that experienced by Southern Europe after the financial crisis of 2008), even if the policy mix and the pressing problems may be different in the short run.

The next section discusses the term competitiveness, how it has changed from a 'dangerous obsession' (Krugman 1994) to a welfare-oriented concept. Three sections follow, which delineate high-road and low-road strategies, discriminate between the old failing concept of sectoral industrial policy and a new systemic approach, and finally introduce 'Beyond GDP goals' as a new performance measure for economies. A further section empirically compares the competitiveness of Europe and the US according to the new concepts and assesses whether European countries going for the high road are less successful than economies going for 'price competitiveness'. Next, the economic background of upcoming populist strategies is tentatively explored. Then, the economic strategy announced by the new US administration is analysed and the optimal response of Europe, given the empirical findings of this chapter, is identified. A further section discusses the merits and shortcomings of the current globalization policy and the alternative of a 'responsible globalization'. The final section summarizes the main findings of the analysis.

From cost competitiveness to outcome and performance

Competitiveness has been defined in many different ways over the past few decades (Aiginger 2006; Aiginger and Firgo 2016; Aiginger and Vogel 2015). We distinguish four approaches evolving over time (Figure 6.1), four different types of competitiveness.

Competitiveness 1.0: price competitiveness – primitive vs. enlightened

The economic debate on the 'competitiveness' of nations, regions, and firms started with a look at the cost side only (competitiveness 1.0). Economists soon added productivity as an important dimension, sometimes overemphasizing labour productivity as the only relevant indicator for competitiveness (Kohler 2006; Porter 1990). A cost compared to productivity is called a 'unit labour cost'. In Aiginger, Bärenthaler-Sieber, and Vogel (2013a), we label the costs-only approach the 'primitive' version and the cost-versus-productivity definition the 'enlightened' version of price competitiveness. If analysts and politicians claim that 'competitiveness is lost' (e.g. in the Southern European countries), the focus still lies on the cost side. The mistake of ignoring low productivity as a fact to be addressed by changes in economic policy or institutions was one of the reasons for the slow recovery of Southern Europe after the financial crisis (Aiginger 2011). The same holds if lobbyists claim that social costs or environmental regulations are 'too high', which is an unhappy generalization reinvented by the new US administration.

Competitiveness 2.0: quality competitiveness as measured by structure, capabilities, and ambitions

In the next stage, structural elements and drivers of competitiveness were added. Structural indicators comprise the market share of a country in specific sophisticated industries ('high tech') or price segments for production and exports. Drivers of competitiveness are those which come from standard growth theory, such as innovation and education, or from new growth theory, such as institutions and clusters. Welfare theory emphasizes that social capital is positive for the performance of firms and economies. Porter (1990) and Stern (2006) argue that sophisticated consumers and first movers provide competitive advantages; the concept of capabilities by Sen (1999) yields additional insights. In general, the factors analysed in competitiveness 2.0 are very heterogeneous; they are found in the middle between input and outcome competitiveness; current or future competitiveness is measured by high market shares of sectors in which

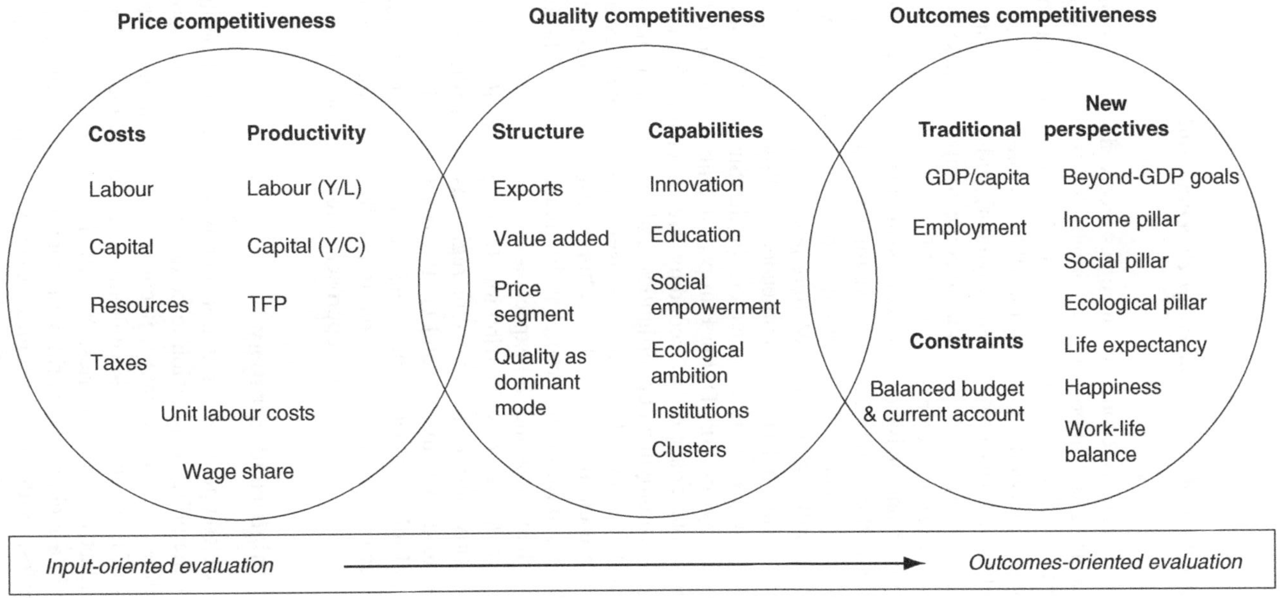

Figure 6.1 Towards a concept of competitiveness under new perspectives (competitiveness 4.0).

Source: Aiginger *et al.* (2013a).

sophisticated inputs are used, or by positions in the high end of markets. We summarize these different signals under the term quality competitiveness or competitiveness 2.0.

Competitiveness 3.0 and 4.0: outcome competitiveness under old and new perspectives

In the next stage of analysis, economic outcomes received greater attention. The view that results are more important than inputs led to measuring competitiveness by per capita GDP and employment (understanding these two goals as shorthand for measuring welfare) during the 1990s. More sophisticated analysis distinguished between goals (growth, employment) and concurrent conditions (balanced trade and budgets).[1] We call this outcome competitiveness under traditional perspectives, or simply competitiveness 3.0.

Today, economics has arrived at the consensus that neither the balance of trade nor a surplus in the current accounts is a final measure of performance, and that no single indicator such as GDP per capita or labour productivity is a sufficient measure of overall performance. Welfare has alternatively been defined by Beyond GDP goals, an approach recommended by Stiglitz *et al.* (2009), and operationalized by the Better Life indicators or the Sustainable Development Indicators (provided by the OECD, the European Commission, and the United Nations). The ultimate goals of an economy are to enable high and rising incomes, to provide employment opportunities, and to improve living conditions and ecological sustainability. These goals – weighted by countries differently according to their present position and to cultural differences – are presented in the Beyond GDP approach or in comprehensive indicators on well-being, such as life satisfaction, happiness and life expectancy.

Consequently, in a previous contribution (Aiginger *et al.* 2013: 67), we defined the competitiveness of a country or region as the 'ability of a country (region, location) to deliver the Beyond GDP goals for its citizens, today and tomorrow'. We call this 'competitiveness under a new perspective', namely, the perspective of a socio-ecological transition. In parallel to the upcoming industry 4.0 (or Internet of Things), we call this approach competitiveness 4.0.

The need for a 'high-road' strategy

The redefinition of competitiveness is not merely an analytical or theoretical detail. It changes the policy conclusion to be derived from the ever-present call for the 'competitiveness' of a country. It connects the term 'competitiveness' with the strategy of a country and, specifically, a strategy which is feasible and necessary for industrialized countries. It further gives guidance on how to increase welfare in a globalizing world with many new competitors and heterogeneous preferences. With rising incomes, basic wants are being satisfied and immaterial goods, such as quality of life, solidarity, and ecological sustainability, gain importance.

To emphasize this change in strategy needed for highly industrialized countries, we differentiate between a 'low-road' strategy and a 'high-road' strategy for countries based on five criteria (Table 6.1).

First, in a low-road strategy, countries look for low costs as *drivers of competitive advantage*, whether it is through low wages, low energy costs and taxes, or permissive social and ecological standards. In contrast, countries going for the high road try to boost productivity, whether it is through labour productivity or energy and resource efficiency. A high-road strategy focuses on quality upgrade, to avoid cost competition, and specializes in the high end of markets by product differentiation (smart specialization and smart diversification; see Reinstaller 2013).

Second, *growth drivers* on the low road are subsidies, specifically those attracting multinational firms looking for a low-wage location. Its supporters advocate the preservation of a low-wage segment in the labour market by preventing minimum wages and collective agreements. On the high road, in contrast, innovation, education, and excellent universities define the growth potential.

Third, the *ambitions* are different. Low-road strategies try to limit social standards and set no barriers to hiring and firing and demand-led labour flexibility. High-road strategies focus on social empowerment, skill upgrading, and ecological awareness as positive for long-run success. Stable employment leads to higher investment of firms and higher skills, while ecological awareness provides a first-mover advantage (Porter and Van der Linde 1995). In parallel, we should differentiate between structural policies calling for low costs and high flexibility of labour alone ('structural policy 1.0') and structural policies 'fostering broadly defined investment and labour productivity for inclusive growth' ('structural policy 2.0'; see Moscovici 2016).

Fourth, *instruments* are protective in low-road strategies and try to decelerate structural change: they comprise import restrictions, devaluation of currencies, and shielding from globalization and migration. High-road strategies are activating:

Table 6.1 Low-road vs. high-road strategies

	Low-road strategy	*High-road strategy*
Competitive advantage	Low costs (wages, energy, taxes)	Quality, sophisticated products, productivity
Growth drivers	Subsidies, dual labour market, inward FDI	Innovation, education, universities, cluster
Ambitions	Cost advantage, flexible labour	Social empowerment, ecological excellence, trust
Instruments	Import taxes, protectionism, devaluation (external, internal)	Business environment, entrepreneurship, dialogue
Objectives	Catching up in GDP per capita, employment	Beyond GDP goals, three pillars

Source: Aiginger (2016).

they provide capabilities for change and welcome open markets as drivers of competition, structural change, and mobility. Business start-ups and competition are welcomed as enablers of a dynamic discovery process.

Finally, the *objectives* in a low-road strategy are to prevent the loss of market shares, to eliminate disequilibria (unemployment, trade deficits) in sectors in which they are greatest, and to pursue rather conventional economic goals (increasing GDP, reducing GDP per capita gaps). The objectives of a high-road strategy are to deliver rising well-being, wider choices, ecological excellence, and lower unemployment and income differences.

Relevance to catching-up economies and the firm level

High-road strategies are important not only for high-income countries, even if the necessity to go for the highest quality and abilities is more pressing there. Even low-income countries have to consider the dynamic upgrading of productivity, skills, and innovation early on. If they are successful in catching up, the advantage of low wages will diminish and citizens will look for higher incomes as well as the quality of goods, thus boosting imports. Very labour-intensive goods face low income elasticity (low dynamism of demand). Therefore, specialization in labour-intensive industries in the lower quality segment, using imported technology and investment, will run into troubles sooner or later (a fact called the 'development trap'). Looking ahead towards the products and capabilities needed for medium-road and high-road countries are necessary in the long-run perspective of catching up.

Strategic management theory acknowledges implicitly the importance of high-road strategies and new concepts of competitiveness. Only in static models of perfect competition is productivity taken as a given and competitiveness (or better yet survival) depends on costs not being higher than the industry average; this model supports the concept of price competitiveness and going for a cost-cutting strategy in the case of problems. In dynamic models, with market power and product differentiation, either cost or productivity strategies are possible and product differentiation increases profits, opening space for skill upgrading and innovation. Strategic Management Theory posits that each firm has to look for a competitive advantage or, even better, a 'machine' which constantly produces innovations, so that the next becomes available if competitors have copied the last one. The final proof that this is not purely theory is given by firms on the stock market, which never tell potential buyers that they have cheap sources of labour or energy but rather that they possess a 'unique selling proposition'; they market their innovation potential and skills so as to fulfil the needs of customers or society in the future. The firms competing for buyers of their shares maintain that they can attract excellent staff and the best management and offer climate-friendly products.

To summarize, a low-road strategy (built on subsidies, tax exemptions, protection, and devaluation of currency) is not feasible for rich countries. The limits of low-road strategies should be understood by middle-income economies early on. And high-road strategies are well in line with firm strategies proposed in the industrial organization literature to generate long-run returns.

Essential for the high road: a systemic industrial policy[2]

The industrial policy needed for the high road has to be different from the past approach, which often preserved old structures and favoured big national champions. A new industrial policy should promote competition and be a discovery process generated by a cooperative climate between government and companies (Aghion *et al.* 2011; Rodrik 2004). It should align industrial policy with the long-term interests of the society; therefore, it has to be a systemic (Aiginger 2012), rather than a stand-alone policy in conflict with other strands of government policy. It should be based on a vision of socio-ecological transition.

Policy documents developed by international organizations (OECD 2011; Warwick 2013), the European Commission, and national governments have defined new goals for industrial policy that partially follow the ideas of academia. The OECD's New Perspectives Program (OECD 2014) promotes the inclusion of social and ecological goals into economic models and thinking. The European Commission puts sustainability at the centre stage of industrial policy. Its Energy Roadmap 2050 sets the goal of reducing greenhouse gas emissions by as much as '80–95%' (EC 2011).[3]

Yet, the new intentions on industrial policy are still on trial. Europe's fear of losing cost competitiveness relative to the US is weakening its determination to put sustainability at the centre stage.[4] Based on Juncker's ten priorities (EC 2014), the priority relevant to climate and energy reads 'making energy more secure, affordable and sustainable'. This is the complete opposite to setting a basic priority and putting sustainability at the top of a new agenda. Ecological issues are also lacking in Juncker's new White Paper (EC 2017), and none of the five 'reflection papers' published by the European Commission for preparing a new European strategy is about ecological issues.[5]

An unresolved problem in devising a sustainable industrial policy is that new energy sources are 'intermittent' and require complementary fossil fuels and investment in the power-grid infrastructure. Coal use in Europe increased after the collapse of the European emissions trading scheme. This led to coal replacing gas as 'reserve capacity' during the periods when renewable energy is not available. Increased US coal exports meant that coal was still cheaper in Europe than gas, and total emissions rose despite an increase in the share of renewables.[6]

The policy of the US administration under President Trump will bring the next, and an even larger, threat for a systemic industrial policy in Europe. Oil and gas lobbies have already started to persuade the European Commission to follow the US; countries with large supplies of coal will prevent a consistent sustainability strategy and call for an old industrial policy favouring capital- and energy-intensive large firms. In addition, Russia will provide financial and social media support for populist parties denying the climate problem and promoting fossil fuels, and this is already reflected in political statements by right-wing parties in France, Austria, Hungary, and Poland.

To summarize, a new systemic industrial policy should support the transition from traditional manufacturing to a sector producing greater consumer value and higher energy and resource efficiency, while furthering the economy's long-term goals. We therefore define an industrial policy for high-wage countries as a 'strategy to promote high-road competitiveness', where competitiveness is the ability of an economy to deliver 'Beyond GDP goals'.

A two-stage strategy with a new benchmark of success[7]

High-road competitiveness requires time and resources. It is best compatible with a two-stage strategy towards transition (Aiginger 2015a, 2016).

Reducing public debt, unemployment, and underemployment under the current trend of labour-saving technological progress will require economic growth, to boost employment and to provide resources for change. This holds for rich industrialized countries over the next one or two decades. If Europe plans to reduce inequality and allow a minimum of inward migration from countries with political unrest and ecological problems, such as Afghanistan, Syria, Libya, Egypt, or Sub-Saharan-Africa, growth rates should preferably be higher than in the years 2000s. In this 'first stage', tangible and intangible investment in the real economy has to be high and should be supported by an active systemic industrial policy.

On the other hand, it is essential to reduce the 'growth imperative', which is defined as the necessity of economies to grow in order to reach goals other than GDP growth (such as full employment, debt reduction, and the integration of migrants). This should not be done by reducing the overall rate of technical progress (total factor productivity), but by redirecting it from labour-saving to energy-saving. Furthermore, people who work longer than they prefer, or would like sabbaticals for education or other personal preferences, should be encouraged to partially or temporarily retreat from the labour market. The same holds if they wish to have more leisure, even at the cost of lower income. People should be encouraged to migrate from regions with oversupply of labour to those with labour shortages.

In 10 or 20 years, the growth trend of industrial countries will be lower for supply or demand reasons ('the new mediocre', see IMF 2015),[8] and people could enjoy this if some important changes were implemented. To make this probable, the benchmark of success for economies has to be changed now.

A new performance measure is needed

To guarantee that the first phase will not be business as usual and that countries will not have the same 'growth imperative' in the future, it is important to change the benchmark of success. We propose as the new performance measure 'high well-being in a sustainable environment'. Thus, GDP and GDP growth are replaced by high and increasing well-being. This is in line with the 'Beyond GDP' approach (Stiglitz *et al.* 2009), as underpinned by the broad economic literature.

The notion of 'well-being' calls for the simultaneous accomplishment of three strategic goals: economic dynamism, social inclusiveness, and environmental sustainability. Economic dynamism implies that an ever-increasing number of people benefit from the attainment of a broad set of economic achievements. Social inclusiveness implies that unemployment as well as income differences will decrease. Life chances, education, and capabilities are distributed more equitably; spreads in income and wealth are based on merit and limited to levels determined by democratically based political decisions. Environmental sustainability demands that planetary boundaries be respected. Technological, behavioural, and institutional changes lead to an absolute reduction of emissions and resource use. This gives poorer countries scope for economic development and poverty reduction and allows the next generation to make choices.

Empirical assessment of competitiveness: EU vs US

The concept of 'competitiveness as the ability to deliver Beyond GDP goals' (competitiveness 4.0) will now be used to assess the deficits and strengths of Europe relative to the US, and then to compare European countries to each other (Aiginger *et al.* 2013a; Aiginger and Vogel 2015).

Competitiveness 1.0

For the total economy, both wages and productivity in the EU-28 are on average about one-third lower than in the US, so that overall unit labour costs (and the absolute wage shares) are similar (Table 6.2). The productivity lead of the US is even larger for manufacturing, but so are wages. If the EU-15 is taken as a benchmark, the differences between the US and Europe are about 10 percentage points lower, and in some leading countries productivity and wages are even higher in Europe.

Competitiveness 2.0

Regarding technology-driven and skill-intensive exports, Europe no longer trails the US: Europe enjoys trade surpluses in all sophisticated sectors, while the US has trade deficits. Europe has a far larger export share in eco-industries and renewables (Table 6.3).

However, Europe lags behind the US in R&D expenditures and higher education. On the other hand, Europe invests more in early education, vocational training, and active labour market policies. As far as institutions are concerned, Europe has stricter rules for labour and business, lower regulatory quality, and a rule of law that is generally considered less stringent than in the US (tough goals,

Table 6.2 Labour costs and productivity of the EU relative to the US

	Compensation per employee		*Output per person employed*		*Unit labour costs*	
	Total economy	*Manufacturing*	*Total economy*	*Manufacturing*	*Total economy*	*Manufacturing*
	US = 100				*Levels (wage share)*	
EU-15	80.8	77.1	85.8	73.0	0.582	0.696
EU-17	79.2	74.7	84.6	69.8	0.573	0.667
EU-27	70.0	60.8	74.7	59.9	0.584	0.680
Switzerland	138.8	–	133.3	131.8	0.672	–
Japan	82.0	74.7	85.7	86.8	0.619	0.553
United States	100.0	100.0	100.0	100.0	0.593	0.544

Source: Aiginger *et al.* (2013a).

Table 6.3 Export structure and trade balance, EU vs US, 2011

	Exports				*Trade balance*			
	Technology-driven industries	*High-skill industries*	*Knowledge-based industries*	*High RQE*	*Technology-driven industries*	*High-skill industries*	*Knowledge-based industries*	*High RQE*
	Share (%)				*Billion €*			
EU-15	33.2	27.9	18.8	51.4	93,427	181,308	23,486	298,116
EU-17	33.0	26.3	17.8	50.9	108,276	169,473	22,296	304,991
EU-27	34.2	28.5	19.6	52.1	101,173	165,938	12,008	304,250
Switzerland	41.0	41.1	16.7	69.0	22,037	33,318	5,731	41,882
Japan	35.4	22.0	22.7	51.4	82,740	52,952	50,437	134,326
United States	32.0	23.2	22.3	45.0	−177,993	−79,886	−33,874	−192,297
China	30.4	19.9	19.9	35.4	128,877	92,350	13,079	158,774

Source: Aiginger *et al.* (2013a).

but looser adherence to legislated objectives). On the other hand, the quality of the parliamentary system is better in Europe. Environmental ambition is more pronounced, as shown in higher environmental taxes, more recycling, a higher share of environment-related technology patents, and a high share of organic farming.

We conclude that Europe lags behind the US in most capability groups and, specifically, in R&D and higher education – two of the most important indicators for frontier countries. However, Europe leads in indicators that are important for the transition to a more socially inclusive and ecologically sustainable economy.

Competitiveness 3.0

The traditional outcome indicators put the US in the lead: per capita GDP is higher (less in GDP per hour) and unemployment is lower than in Europe. The employment rate, however, is lower and declining in the US, in sharp contrast to Europe. Here, it is increasingly boosted by part-time work. In the US, workers have retreated from the labour market recently, disappointed by low wages offered at the low end of the labour market. Large public deficits and debts, as well as a negative current account balance, present limitations to the success of the US in traditional outcome competitiveness.

Competitiveness 4.0

For Beyond GDP goals, the picture is different. The US still leads in the income pillar (Table 6.4). As for the social pillar, the US trails in poverty prevention and equality but has lower youth and long-term unemployment, thus yielding mixed overall results. The US clearly lags behind Europe in the ecological pillar, with the exception that rules are monitored and adhered to more closely if legislated (e.g. emissions in diesel-driven cars).

Table 6.4 Outcome competitiveness under new perspectives: income pillar, EU vs. US, 2011

	GDP at PPS	*Net national income*	*Net disposible domestic income*	*Household final consumption expenditure*
	Per capita (US = 100)			
EU-15	72.7	70.2	58.9	58.6
EU-17	70.7	67.5	58.3	56.4
EU-27	65.5	63.1	53.5	52.9
Switzerland	92.9	88.8	74.9	76.1
Japan	72.2	66.3	59.4	60.3
United States	100.0	100.0	100.0	100.0

Source: Aiginger *et al.* (2013a).

Regarding comprehensive indicators, Europe does better in life expectancy, which is probably the best objective quantitative indicator. Self-reported life satisfaction, work-life balance, and happiness – all subjective indicators – are higher in the US.

Intra-European results

As far as individual countries are concerned, Denmark, Sweden, and Finland excel in capabilities, specifically in education and R&D expenditures. Germany and France receive a top position in innovation and social investment, but a less favourable one in education and institutions. Cost positions (price competitiveness 1.0) do not really determine performance, which is a warning to all analyses that overemphasize low costs as a strategy for medium- and high-income countries. The assessment is different for Southern European countries, whose labour-cost increases were higher than productivity in the years before the crisis and led to severe problems in current accounts and in public finance (Aiginger *et al.* 2012, 2013b). The results for Greece, Italy, Romania, and Bulgaria also show that outcomes could considerably improve if trust in governance and institutions was improved. If the role of upgrading productivity and governance had received more emphasis in the European reform programmes for the crisis countries from the beginning, the output and employment loss could have been smaller and opposition to European solutions, as well as the increase in poverty, could have been prevented.

Using the definition of competitiveness as the ability of a region or country to deliver Beyond GDP goals could be a way to forestall the critique that the term competitiveness is dangerous and misleading (Krugman 1994), as well as the critique that competitiveness is a concept only applicable at the firm level. Competitiveness 4.0 is now closely linked to the economic performance of a region and permits an analysis of how rich countries can successfully pursue a high-road strategy.

The empirical results show that countries going for a high road, such as the northern European countries but also Switzerland, can successfully compete by means of sophisticated capabilities. Social and ecological ambitions are not a burden; on the contrary, they can feed long-run success. Countries going for competitiveness 1.0, and specifically its primitive version of cost-cutting, do not perform well in the long run. Success can and should be measured by broader indicators (the Beyond GDP goals) instead of narrow economic ones, following the definition of competitiveness under new perspectives (competitiveness 4.0).

Populist movements in light of competitiveness 4.0

Populist movements are on rise in Europe and in the USA, pushing national goals up the agenda by demanding 'our country first' and a return to the past glory of the nation. A renationalization of policy and the closing of borders to people and goods are recommended. Populism exaggerates and reframes the existing problems of the economy and society, in an attempt to support ever more simplistic and drastic policy solutions. It accuses mainstream politics, but also the experts and the media, of supporting the elites, irregular migrants, and foreigners. It declares that common people ('us', 'the 99 per cent', 'Main Street') is being exploited by the privileged elite. Some authors distinguish between a right-wing populism, which glorifies the past and divides society, and a left-wing populism, which holds utopian ideas for a better society, pursues freedom from serfdom and imperialism, and calls for emancipation. Such a utopia might be a society without class division and with self-determination, leisure, and the capability to live a good life. There is an individualistic strand expecting 1,000 flowers to bloom (the new left of the 1968 movement) and an orthodox one calling for Big Brother to solve all problems through an ever larger public sector, nationalization of enterprises, and higher tax rates.

Real problems, wrong conclusions

Populism feeds on real, existing problems. The driving force of today's populism is the unholy trinity of unemployment, inequality, and inward migration.

Unemployment is in double digits in many European countries, higher than before the financial crisis. Long-term unemployment is spreading for less-skilled former factory workers and for young people without job experience. Employment in manufacturing is decreasing in all industrialized countries; its share is now less than 10 per cent of the total employment in many. This loss is compensated – in most countries overcompensated – by an increase in jobs in the service sector. However, these jobs require different qualifications, are sometimes paid less well, and are often only part-time. If factory workers lose their job due to the relocation of firms, they often find it very difficult to get a new one in the same region ('rust belts'). Moreover, even those who have not lost their job or income feel that this might be the case soon. Earnings are expected to decrease, and unemployment spells are becoming longer and more frequent. Most studies blame technological change for the job loss of low-skilled workers, and some blame globalization. Whatever the deeper cause is, it is evident that economic policy is not doing enough to compensate or – even better – requalify the losers of structural change. The upcoming problem of lower employment for less-skilled workers in industrialized countries was well predicted by economic theory.

Inequality is on the rise in practically all industrialized countries. Median wages have been stagnating or falling in the US for decades. Specifically, the income share of the top 1 per cent is exploding, along with incomes in the financial sector and among the top management. Inward migration, which tended to be welcomed in the ageing society and was fuelled by the integration of former socialist countries in the EU, is now viewed with more scepticism, since migrants tend to increase the labour supply in the low-skilled sector where there is already high unemployment. However, the inward migration of workers (even of unskilled workers) remains necessary to fill jobs in the housing, nursing, and tourism sectors.

As policy conclusions, populists advocate closing the borders to migrants as well as goods. They favour import tariffs on goods produced in low-income countries, exit from the EU, and the recalling of trade agreements. Stopping globalization and even re-erecting fences against neighbouring countries are part of their policy agenda.

Facts about well-being and competitiveness 4.0

If we look at the broad indicators for a better life and for competitiveness 4.0 (Figure 6.2, not all reported here), we see that unemployment and inequality are rising. However, the general picture for well-being is not so bleak.

GDP per capita in real terms is now about 85 per cent higher than in 1980 and has increased by about 20 per cent since 2000, both in the EU and in the US. The GDP surpassed the pre-crisis output in Europe in 2016 and is currently 10 per cent higher than at the start of the crisis in the US. Growth rates are decelerating over time in industrialized countries, a fact that opens up a discussion on whether this is demand-led (people giving increased income a lower preference) or supply-led (secular stagnation, lack of technical breakthroughs, rise of the market shares of low-income countries). Inflation is rather low; specifically, several consumer goods bought by low-income people have become absolutely cheaper.

Employment is higher in Europe than before the crisis, but employment rates decreased in the US. For unemployment the opposite occurred: it increased in

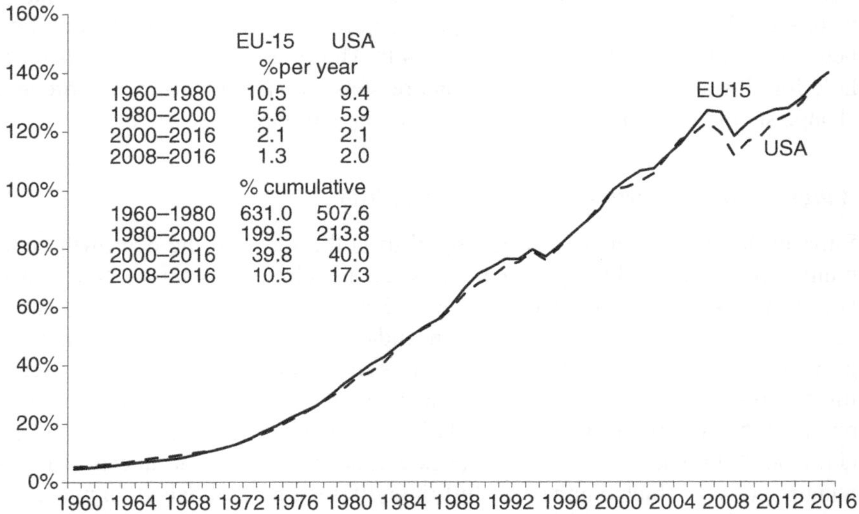

Figure 6.2 GDP per capita growth in Europe (EU-15) and the USA (2000 = 100).

Source: Eurostat (AMECO May 2016).

Europe (up to 2016) and decreased in the US towards rates normally considered to be 'full employment'.

Although inequality (relative incomes of rich vs. poor) is increasing in most countries, absolute poverty is decreasing. Life expectancy at birth – perhaps the most comprehensive and objective indicator of well-being – is increasing by about three months every year.[9] Life satisfaction is persistently high.

Social standards have not been reduced, but strains in the financing of pensions call for longer work and lower replacement rates. Ecological standards are rising, but not nearly as fast as it is necessary to combat climate change. Emissions and resource use are increasing in absolute terms but are falling relative to economic activity (relative decoupling). Signs of absolute decoupling are rare.

Open economies with high import and export shares, if anything, tend to grow more rapidly than closed economies, and even more so if they upgrade their social and ecological ambitions.

Populism, therefore, has some basis in reality, insofar as incomes are not rising as quickly as in the past and problems of inequality and losses of low-skilled jobs exist.[10] Between a condition of social insecurity partly fuelled by the financial crisis and a migration wave driven by political instability in the home countries instead of by demand in the countries of destination,[11] the fear arises that life incomes will not be higher in this generation than in the past. For some low-skilled workers more problems have arisen ('*Abstiegsangst*', the fear of downward social mobility): they fear becoming unemployed and dependent on social payments. In the long run, incomes and employment remain high, part-time employment is to a large extent voluntary, social nets exist, and poverty is low. Life expectancy, as well as healthy years of living, are rising. In general terms, recalling the glory of the past or the glory of a time in which countries were closed to goods, services, and people is thus absolutely not supported by better-life indicators or competitiveness 4.0. The problem is that this does not hold for all subgroups; social groups and regions who are the losers of structural change should therefore be a priority of economic policy.

A digression: degrowth vs. right-wing populism

Entirely different from right-wing populism is the focus of the degrowth community. It spread quickly, specifically in academic circles and among NGOs, and is to some extent concentrated in cities and subgroups with comfortable family incomes and property. At the top of its agenda is the claim that continued income growth is neither possible (due to the limits of the planet) nor desirable. Better life could be achieved through lower incomes than today. Formal work can be replaced by informal work, community relations, and empathy for others (Jackson 2009; Paech 2012). To some extent, degrowth is the antithesis of right-wing populism, which emphasizes full-time, lifelong jobs, above all in manufacturing. Right-wing populism is strongest among people striving for higher incomes and material consumption, even if this requires strenuous and dirty blue-collar jobs.

Right-wing populists give absolutely no priority to green goals, energy efficiency, and alternative energy. Climate change is considered exaggerated at best, or even declared an invention of the Chinese to endanger US competitiveness, as Donald Trump claims. And the newly appointed director of the US Environmental Protection Agency declares he would stop the 'war on coal'.

As far as migration is concerned, populists would like to stop it while the degrowth movement welcomes an open and heterogeneous society. The fact that openness – specifically for inward migration – is not only an economic problem in a stagnating or shrinking economy, but also a political issue favouring populism and xenophobia, is not addressed in the degrowth community.

This digression on the degrowth movement may seem far from the topic of competitiveness, but it is important. There are at least two types of 'populism' today. The first dominates in academia and in the rather wealthy segment of our society and it claims that 'we all have enough and should spend less'. The other one deplores that 'in the past we all had higher and rising incomes, and now we have less chances than our parents' and it is concentrated in the lower social stratum of our society. Since competitiveness 4.0 measures performance according to the objectives of society, we have to know whether we want to have more or less, whereby the more is not measured in incomes alone. This may provide a link between the losers of structural change and the goals of right-wing and green populism.

Industrial renaissance in the US and the best answer of Europe

Low-road policies in a high-tech country

'Remaking manufacturing in the US' had arrived on the agenda in the US before Trump, initiated by the high deficit in the trade balance and a dramatic loss of shares in output and employment.[12] The share of manufacturing is now lower in the US than in Europe (Table 6.5). The deeper reasons for the decline of US manufacturing are the lack of cooperation across US companies and their loss of learning capacity due to early offshoring (Berger 2013). However, policy proposals tend to start with cost issues.

The first hope was that the 'renaissance of manufacturing' could build on cheap energy prices due to offshore drilling, shale gas resources, or low-cost oil transported from Alaska via new pipelines. Indeed, the new energy sources, especially liquefied gas and gas extracted via fracking, have caused US energy prices to plummet; manufacturing output increased in the US to a somewhat greater extent than in Europe. However, the recovery was concentrated in energy-intensive sectors while the trade deficit in technology-intensive industries remained high; when the profitability of high-cost exploitation broke down – with the world-wide decline of oil and gas prices – the hope of revitalization of US manufacturing, specifically in the 'rust belt', faded away. Not having addressed the deeper problems fuelled populism.

Table 6.5 European and US sector balances and export shares, 1999 and 2011

	EU				*US*			
	1999	*2011*	*1999*	*2011*	*1999*	*2011*	*1999*	*2011*
	Trade in bn €		*Shares of exports*		*Trade in bn €*		*Shares of exports*	
Energy-intensive industries								
Exports	77.7	247.4	11.3	15.5	57.3	123.1	9.7	16.0
Imports	64.1	216.9	9.3	13.6	79.0	106.0	13.3	13.8
Trade balance	13.6	30.5	2.0	1.9	–21.7	17.1	–3.7	2.2
Technology-driven industries								
Exports	252.1	530.9	36.6	33.2	280.0	246.3	47.2	32.0
Imports	250.1	436.8	36.3	27.3	371.1	424.3	62.5	55.1
Trade balance	2.1	94.1	0.3	5.9	–91.1	–178.0	–15.3	–23.1
Resource-intensive industries								
Exports	76.1	192.2	11.1	12.0	50.2	76.0	8.5	9.9
Imports	72.0	198.1	10.5	12.4	121.6	116.2	20.5	15.1
Trade balance	4.1	–5.8	0.6	–0.4	–71.4	–40.1	–12.0	–5.2
Engineering industries								
Exports	365.1	767.8	53.1	48.1	379.7	367.9	64.0	47.7
Imports	328.5	580.8	47.7	36.3	490.7	576.3	82.7	74.8
Trade balance	36.6	187.0	5.3	11.7	–111.0	–208.5	–18.7	–27.1

Source: Eurostat (AMECO), WIFO database.

In reaction to this backlash in rebuilding manufacturing via low energy prices, Donald Trump found three culprits for the ongoing problems for US manufacturing: imports from China and ecological as well as social 'over-regulations'. Trump's assessment is in line with the primitive version of competitiveness 1.0, in which costs decide on outcomes and social and ecological norms are burdens. Consequently, his policy prescription also follows the concept of a low-road strategy (reduce wages and social standards) mixed with the old industrial policy approach of protecting against imports (via tariffs) and of micro-interventions, that is to influence the investment decisions of individual large firms (by bribing, persuading, and subsidizing). Giving permits for new oil pipelines should reduce energy costs and, more specifically, the costs of fossil energy.[13] Trade agreements with Asian partners will be cancelled; NAFTA should be at least renegotiated. Trump announced high tariffs for imports, more taxes for firms which invest abroad, and financial gifts to firms staying home. Energy prices should decrease by extending drilling and pipelines for fossil energy, while social standards including Obamacare are to be abandoned or at least made cheaper. Environmental standards, as well as the regulation of financial markets, will be lowered.

With this strategy, high-tech firms will be negatively affected, since they need qualified inward migration. Firms investing in energy efficiency, alternative energy production, and new power engine and construction models will enter the market later, as prices for fossil energy remain low. If we relate Trump's policy to the term competitiveness, he clearly has the view of the primitive version of competitiveness 1.0 combined with an old micro-interfering industrial policy. Increasing competitiveness by fostering innovation and skills or ecological ambitions is absent in the programme of the new administration.

The response of Europe, as recommended by competitiveness 4.0

In principle, European policy has two options to answer the low-road and high-intervention approach for industrial renaissance, either: (1) to imitate the new policy (perhaps a bit later, more moderately, and differently across countries), or (2) to develop a different strategy built on European strengths and capabilities.

Europe's potential for a strategic alternative can be highlighted by the following points:

- lower energy prices, specifically for fossil energy, can be answered by higher energy efficiency, a technological lead of Europe in renewables, a decarbonized infrastructure, and new power systems;
- lower social standards can be answered by improving skills and equality of opportunities. Shifting from ex-post protection to the so-called social investment approach (Leoni 2015) would reduce the probability of becoming unemployed. Symmetric labour flexibility, which allows firms to vary working hours according to demand in exchange for the right of workers to change their weekly working time according to preferences arising from

their work-life balance, could lower costs for firms as well as provide higher well-being for employees;

- import restrictions can be answered by upgrading skills and innovation and switching more quickly to new products and services, thus fulfilling the needs of individuals and of society;
- the 'America first policy' can be answered by closer cooperation of Europe with fast-growing economies and by investment in the neighbouring countries of Eastern and Southern Europe. Such neighbourhood programmes could mimic the US European Recovery Programme, which boosted investment in Europe and created a large and fast-growing market for the US. The cultural and educational exchange could be intensified by Fulbright or Schumpeter scholarships;
- lower corporate taxes for firms investing in the US can be answered by closing loopholes for US companies using tax shelters in individual European countries or tax-shifting from Europe into the US and by closely watching tax payments of firms with headquarters in Delaware.

This high-road policy response is not always easy; it requires cooperation between countries, it takes time, and some of the concepts have still to be developed. However, a high-road policy is sustainable, in the sense that it prepares Europe for the future and builds on activities which foster long-run competitiveness for countries with high incomes faced with competition from low-cost countries. It provides capabilities for tomorrow instead of short-run protection, and it allows people to increase well-being and the chances of long-run jobs without becoming dependent on idiosyncratic decisions or the financial support of government.

Confidence that the high-road approach works comes from the past performance of the European Union (which has no current account deficit, in contrast to the US) and of those European economies which did go for a broader set of goals and for capabilities as drivers of growth and competitiveness (like the Scandinavian countries, Switzerland, and Austria). These countries did not run into economic difficulties but became leaders in GDP per capita and Beyond GDP indicators. Many of these countries enjoy positive trade and investment balances. They prove that competitiveness 4.0 and a strategy of social ecological transition is viable, even in an open and globalizing world.

Reshaping globalization

One feature of populist policy in Europe and in the US is its opposition to globalization. However, the critique of globalization, its speed, and its current characteristics is not restricted to populists by any means (Bayer 2017; Rodrik 2016; Summers 2014). In this section we argue that globalization is in general positive, but it has to be monitored by economic policy; this has to a large extent not been the case (Aiginger and Handler 2017). Crucially, the use of new definitions for competitiveness and industrial policy will underscore the advantages of globalization. However, a new policy is needed to limit the losses for low-skilled workers in industrialized countries, and Europe should be more ambitious in shaping globalization. This is the essence of the current research of the Policy Crossover Center: Vienna-Europe (Aiginger and Handler 2017).

Most predictions have proved correct

Economic theory stresses the advantages of trade. It enables the deeper specialization of countries and a better use of abundant resources both in the 'North' and in the 'South'. However, theory has also predicted that there will be winners and losers. In the North, the winners will be capital and skilled labour and the losers will be the unskilled, whose labour is replaced by imports from the South. Since overall gains are larger than losses, the losers can – theoretically – be fully compensated. In the South, low-skilled labour will be utilized more intensively, and capital invested in sheltered, domestic-oriented industries is expected to lose. As technology disseminates, lower-income countries are expected to grow at a faster rate than rich countries.

During the wave of hyper-globalization ranging from the start of the 1990s to the financial crisis, output boomed, with average growth rates often higher than 3 per cent (implying a doubling of output in 25 years). Growth was even higher in developing countries, so that income inequality *across* countries declined.

In the North, multinational firms and profits boomed while wage rates declined. Income inequality *within* countries increased. At the same time, wages, in particular those of low-skilled workers, remained fairly constant (in Europe) or declined (in the US). Unemployment rose in the low-skilled segment. In the South, absolute poverty and child fatalities plummeted at a faster rate than envisaged by the UN Millennium Goals. Somewhat unexpectedly, however, income inequality within developing countries also rose, as a split occurred between workers able to cooperate with multinational firms and migrants from rural areas who could not.

The mood is turning against globalization, since policy ignored the losers

Despite the overall beneficial results for the North as well as for the South, opposition to globalization has increased. Anti-globalization movements and populist parties are booming, even in relatively prosperous European countries (e.g. the Netherlands, Belgium, and Austria), which have greatly profited from openness, integration, and globalization. Brexit and the US presidential elections have underlined the power of anti-globalization sentiments.

Economic policy has ignored the losers. They have neither been compensated for their losses nor provided with the capacity to take advantage of structural change. Instead, policy has often supported the winners by offering tax loopholes. Unemployment resulting from globalization has been amplified by a technological shift replacing low-skilled work and calling for higher qualifications. Unemployment has increased, also because of lower growth in the aftermath of the financial crisis and higher migration driven by political and ecological problems in the home countries. These four interacting causes of low-skilled unemployment can only be resolved through a similarly joint reaction of fiscal, industrial, and labour policy, including a policy to reduce income differences. 'Silo strategies' which pursue goals separately will not work, if unemployment originates from the interaction of four causes (Aiginger 2017).

Policy change towards 'responsible globalization' is needed

Globalization is not likely to continue, if policies do not change. A new policy for responsible globalization will need the following elements:

- economic policy retrains the losers, proactively and early, through skill upgrading, enabling them to switch into new jobs and industries;
- external costs, above all environmental damages, have to be internalized by pricing emissions and transportation costs; social standards will be monitored in international agreements; they cannot be challenged by court decisions;
- multinational firms have to use clean technologies developed for domestic plants for all investments abroad; country-by-country reporting of emissions for plants at the headquarter versus those in the subsidiary could be the initial step on this ambitious path;
- technical progress will be redirected from labour-saving to resource- and energy-saving through price changes, technological programmes, and tax policy;
- financial transactions will be taxed, so as to reduce the need for extreme dividends in the real economy; the revenues will be used to reduce taxes on labour and small corporations;
- labour market policy changes will be introduced, switching from paying primarily for unemployment if it occurs to preventing it *ex ante* through a social investment and activation policy.

All these changes can be supported by changes in policy concepts. Performance should not be measured by GDP but by Beyond GDP goals; industrial policy has to become systemic and integrate policy strands; finally, competitiveness should not be understood as price competitiveness, but as outcome competitiveness under the new social ecological perspectives (competitiveness 4.0).

Conclusion

Definitions can shape policies. Defining competitiveness in the narrow sense of price competition calls for reducing wages and non-wage costs. This is dangerous policy advice for medium- or high-income countries, because it further reduces incomes in the long run. In the short run, unemployment might temporarily decrease, as argued by both business-driven and populist parties. Even mainstream politicians, the quality newspapers, the European Commission, and the OECD often use this narrow approach.

Competitiveness 1.0, as we call it, comes in a primitive version, in which costs are the only important component, and in an enlightened one, in which costs are compared to productivity. Unit labour costs are still assessed independent of product quality, of the drivers of competitiveness, and of the social and ecological standards achieved. Innovation and skills, abilities and structures, are all part of an assessment according to competitiveness 2.0. Defining competitiveness by outcomes changes the perspective. Measuring competitiveness by rather traditional indicators like GDP, employment, and external balances (competitiveness 3.0) started in the 1990s in the documents of the European Commission, the OECD, and the US Congress. The consensus that the performance of an economy and a society should not be measured by narrow economic goals, but rather by broader societal goals, led to our proposal to define competitiveness as 'the ability to deliver Beyond GDP goals' (competitiveness 4.0).

However, changing definitions alone does not suffice, given the extent of political and societal problems in a globalizing world in the aftermath of the financial crisis. A decade will soon have passed since the crisis started, caused by excessive speculation in the financial sector. Economic dynamism is still low in Europe, and pre-crisis output was reached only in 2016. Unemployment and inequality have increased, and public debt has hit a limit – despite an interest burden lowered by an extremely expansive monetary policy.

In the long run, we know that economic growth for industrialized countries will be lower than in the past, and that this need not be a problem, if incentives and behaviour change. However, in the short run, Europe and the US require growth to eliminate inherited disequilibria and to reduce inequality, debt, and unemployment. This suggests a two-stage approach, with higher growth in the first stage but accepting and enjoying lower growth in the second (due to decreasing marginal utility of incomes and/or lower technical progress). Already in the first stage, however, incentives and behaviour have to change so as to reduce the 'growth imperative'. Technical progress has to be redirected from labour-saving to resource-saving and labour has to become more flexible, in a way dictated not by the fluctuations of demand but by the desire of citizens to reduce their working time (if their work-life balance requires it or their financial situation allows it). Taxes have to be shifted from labour to emissions, alcohol, tobacco, and inheritances. This transition should not be dictated by a top-down policy but supported by a two-tier policy in which (1) governments and international organizations take the lead in setting framework conditions (preventing tax evasion, stopping subsidies for fossil energy, pricing emissions); and (2) then, countries and regions decide how to implement the transition following national preferences, giving bottom-up initiatives and individuals more leeway than today (Aiginger 2017).

Globalization has tremendously improved welfare. It has reduced poverty and early child death more quickly than the UN Millennium Goals envisaged. It has also produced losers, as predicted by economic theory. In industrialized countries, low-skilled workers – often blue-collar workers in manufacturing – have lost their jobs. The mood has turned against globalization, and political movements and parties that support closing borders and erecting walls against goods and people are on the rise. Neither international organizations nor trade and investment agreements had the objective to raise social standards or to limit climate change. Ships, air traffic, and road transport are heavily undertaxed. A 'responsible globalization' that respects and develops standards, and incorporates societal goals, is needed. A new systemic industrial policy should not single out individual large firms or national champions for micro-interventions, persuasion, or bribing, but should rather empower firms and individuals to shift into new industries or segments that deliver consumer value and societal and environmental goals.

Appendix: The necessity of a two-stage approach

The best policy reaction to current legacies of the financial crisis and the uncertainty about future trends is a two-stage strategy (see Aiginger 2016).

Stage 1: Consolidation and reprogramming

In the first stage – the next 10–20 years – policies will still have to focus on preventing new crises and solving inherited disequilibria (unemployment, debt, inequality). This is the ideal time to start rebuilding the infrastructure, so as to prepare for decarbonization. Massive policy efforts and investments are required to redirect technologies and build a low-carbon infrastructure. It is the time for a green systemic industrial policy. These efforts will impact positively on economic dynamism and employment. Moreover, it is a good time to reduce unemployment by skill upgrading as well as to decrease inequality.

Crucially, this first stage should not be the continuation of established policies. Solving inherited problems has to be combined with massive investment in order to prepare for the second stage. Aiginger (2016) therefore labels stage one 'consolidation and reprogramming', with a strong emphasis on the latter.

Stage 2: Socio-ecological transition

Long-term forecasts for industrialized countries predict lower growth rates, declining even further along the time horizon. This may follow from the catching-up of emerging economies, the limits of the planet, the decreasing marginal utility of higher incomes, or secular stagnation tendencies. Therefore, in the second stage, the highest priority has to be given to achieving higher levels of well-being (employment, housing, health) based on – in a historical perspective – low growth rates. We call this second stage 'socio-ecological transition'.

Preconditions for increasing welfare in this second stage are a reduced gap between high and low incomes, a lower public debt, and a stable financial sector serving the needs of the real economy. These changes, as well as the decoupling of employment and emissions from output, have to be started by implementing new incentives, regulations, and behavioural change as soon as possible in the first stage. Countries can switch to stage two earlier if preconditions are given. The reasons for inward migration in Europe – economic and ecological problems in the neighbouring countries – have to be mitigated by a better neighbourhood policy.

Notes

1 Earlier, trade balances were seen as measures of competitiveness; now, they became not goals such as income or employment but 'side conditions', which only become relevant in the case of disequilibria.

2 This section closely follows Aiginger (2015b).

3 Radical innovation projects, e.g. on ultra-low carbon steel, have been started and proved feasible, but no existing firm intends to promote a pilot plant.

4 Recently, the European Commission set the goal to increase manufacturing's share of nominal Gross Value Added (GVA) to 20 per cent by 2020 (from currently 16 per cent), which is only realistic if the quality of production is significantly upgraded and service components are added (Peneder 2014). The goal is set without any reference to ecological goals or sustainability.

5 On the positive side, we can mention that the share of renewable energy has strongly increased, with some countries producing 50 per cent of electric energy from 'green' sources. Moreover, China is undertaking a deep transformation, boosting resource and energy efficiency – albeit from a very low initial level. It has set goals to increase R&D investment to 2 per cent of GDP (the current EU share) and is making advances in electric vehicles and alternative energies.

6 This unwarranted change arises from the low prices for emissions resulting from the breakdown of the emission trading and the oversupply of emission permits, due to the closure of inefficient firms in Eastern Europe and the opening of new reserves through fracking technology. A similar movement is predicted by Sinn (2015) in his 'green paradox': as demand is predicted to slow down, owners of resources will speed up extraction.

7 See also the Appendix.

8 While most projections predict rather low long-term growth for industrialized countries, some stress demand reasons (declining marginal utility of income), others the deceleration of technological progress ('all essential innovations are available now'). The debate about 'industry 4.0', on the contrary, predicts high labour-saving technological progress, again with the two possibilities that this might decrease labour input in total, or that product-specific labour productivity increases might stimulate output and provide rather stable employment. On the debate between 'secular stagnation' and 'industry 4.0', see Brynjolfsson and McAfee (2012), Gordon (2014), and Summers (2014).

9 This is not true for low-income people in the US.

10 For irrational routes of the debate, see Haidt (2012).

11 Immigration was welcomed, specifically in the UK, and helped solve labour shortages created by an ageing society.

12 In 2012, Jeff Immelt (General Electric's CEO) declared that 'outsourcing was quickly becoming mostly outdated as a business model' (Immelt 2012); US politicians praised Lenovo for restarting computer production in North Carolina and General Electric for returning washing machine manufacture to Kentucky.

13 Low-road features can also be seen in the UK, when tariffs for steel are called for or when it is deplored if low-skilled production leaves. The share of manufacturing in the UK and France has fallen to less than 10 per cent; one reason for this is the brain drain to the service sector in the UK and to the military or government sector in France.

References

Aghion, Philippe, Julian Boulanger, and Elie Cohen (2011). 'Rethinking industrial policy', Policy Brief 4. Brussels: Bruegel.

Aiginger, Karl (2006). 'Competitiveness: from a dangerous obsession to a welfare creating ability with positive externalities', *Journal of Industry, Competition and Trade* 6(2): 161–77.

Aiginger, Karl (2011). 'Why growth performance differed across countries in the recent crisis: the impact of pre-crisis conditions', *Review of Economics and Finance* 1(4): 35–52.

Aiginger, Karl (2012). 'A systemic industrial policy to pave a new growth path for Europe', Working Paper No. 421. Vienna: WIFO.

Aiginger, Karl (2015a). 'A two stage strategy for restarting growth', in Österreichische Nationalbank. *43rd economics conference 2015: long-term perspectives for economic growth*. Vienna: Österreichische Nationalbank, 30–40.

Aiginger, Karl (2015b). 'Industrial policy for a sustainable growth path', in David Bailey, Keith Cowling, and Philip Tomlinson (eds). *New perspectives on industrial policy*. Oxford: Oxford University Press, 365–94.

Aiginger, Karl (2016). 'New dynamics for Europe: reaping the benefits of socio-ecological transition', Synthesis Report Part I. Vienna, Brussels: WWWforEurope.

Aiginger, Karl (2017). 'How a strong Europe could create more national scope of action', Flash Paper 1. Vienna: Policy Crossover Center: Vienna-Europe.

Aiginger, Karl and Matthias Firgo (2016). 'Regional competitiveness', in Robert Huggins and Piers Thomson (eds). *Handbook of regions and competitiveness*. Cheltenham: Edward Elgar.

Aiginger, Karl and Heinz Handler (2017). 'Europe taking the lead in responsible globalization', Flash Paper 5. Vienna: Policy Crossover Center: Vienna-Europe.

Aiginger, Karl and Johanna Vogel (2015). 'Competitiveness: from a misleading concept to a strategy supporting Beyond GDP goals', *Competitiveness Review* 25(5): 497–523.

Aiginger, Karl, Matthias Firgo, and Peter Huber (2012). 'Policy options for the development of peripheral regions and countries of Europe', Policy Brief 2. Vienna: WWW forEurope.

Aiginger, Karl, Susanne Bärenthaler-Sieber, and Johanna Vogel (2013a). 'Competitiveness under new perspectives', Working Paper No. 44. Vienna: WWWforEurope.

Aiginger, Karl, Matthias Firgo, and Peter Huber (2013b). 'What can the EMU's peripheral countries learn from regional growth?', in Lubor Lacina, Petr Rozmahel, and Antonin Rusek (eds). *Political economy of Eurozone crisis: reforms and their limits*. Bučovice: Martin Stříž.

Bayer, Kurt (2017). 'Keine falschen Alternativen: Globalisierung muss gestaltet werden', Flash Paper 4. Vienna: Policy Crossover Center: Vienna-Europe.

Berger, Suzanne (2013). *Making in America: from innovation to market*. Cambridge, MA: MIT Press.

Brynjolfsson, Erik and Andrew McAfee (2012). *Race against the machine*. Lexington, MA: Digital Frontier Press.

EC (European Commission) (2011). 'Energy roadmap 2050'. COM(2011)885 final. Luxembourg: Publications Office of the European Union.

EC (European Commission) (2014). '10 Commission priorities for 2015–19'. Available at: https://ec.europa.eu/commission/priorities_en.

EC (European Commission) (2017). 'White Paper on the future of Europe'. COM(2017)2025. Luxembourg: Publications Office of the European Union.

Gordon, Robert .J. (2014). 'The demise of U.S. economic growth: restatement, rebuttal, and reflections', NBER Working Paper No. 19895. Cambridge, MA: NBER.

Haidt, Jonathan (2012). *The righteous mind: why good people are divided by politics and religion*. New York: Pantheon Books.

IMF (International Monetary Fund) (2015). 'Prevent "new mediocre" from becoming "new reality"'. Available at: www.imf.org/en/News/Articles/2015/09/28/04/53/sonew040915a

Immelt, Jeffrey R. (2012). 'The CEO of General Electric on sparking an American manufacturing renewal', *Harvard Business Review*, March.

Jackson, Tim (2009). *Prosperity without growth: economics for a finite planet*. London: Earthscan.

Kohler, Wilhelm (2006). 'The "Lisbon Goal" of the EU: rhetoric or substance?', *Journal of Industry, Competition and Trade* 6(2): 85–103.

Krugman, Paul (1994). 'Competitiveness: a dangerous obsession', *Foreign Affairs* 73(2): 28–44.

Leoni, Thomas (2015). 'Welfare state adjustments to new social risks in the post-crisis scenario: a review with focus on the social investment perspective', Working Paper No. 89. Vienna: WWWforEurope.

Moscovici, Pierre (2016). 'Structural reforms 2.0: for a stronger more inclusive recovery'. Available at: http://europa.eu/rapid/press-release_SPEECH-16-2124_en.htm

OECD (Organisation for Economic Co-operation and Development) (2011). *How's life? Measuring well-being*. Paris: OECD.

OECD (Organisation for Economic Co-operation and Development) (2014). *New approaches to economic challenges (NAEC): synthesis*. Paris: OECD.

Paech, Niko (2012). *Befreiung vom Überfluss*. München: oekom.

Peneder, Michael (2014). 'Warum die Neue Industriepolitik die Deindustrialisierung beschleunigen wird', Policy Brief 23. Vienna: FIW.

Porter, Michael E. (1990). *The competitive advantage of nations*. New York: The Free Press.

Porter, Michael E. and Claas van der Linde (1995). 'Toward a new conception of the environment-competitiveness relationship', *Journal of Economic Perspectives* 9(4): 97–118.

Reinstaller, Andreas (2013). 'An evolutionary view on social innovation and the process of economic change', Working Paper No. 43. Vienna: WWWforEurope.

Rodrik, Dani (2004). ''Industrial policy for the twenty-first century', Working Paper. Cambridge, MA: Harvard University. Available at: https://research.hks.harvard.edu/publications/getFile.aspx?Id=146

Rodrik, Dani (2016). 'There is no need to fret about deglobalisation', *Financial Times*, 4 October.

Sen, Amartya K. (1999). *Commodities and capabilities*. Oxford: Oxford University Press.

Sinn, Hans-Werner (2015). 'The green paradox: a supply-side view of the climate problem', *Review of Environmental Economics and Policy* 9(2): 239–45.

Stern, Nicholas (2006). *Stern Review: the economics of climate change*. London: HM Treasury.

Stiglitz, Joseph E., Amartya Sen, and Jean-Paul Fitoussi (2009). *Report by the Commission on the Measurement of Economic Performance and Social Progress*. Paris: the Commission on the Measurement of Economic Performance and Social Progress.

Summers, Larry H. (2014). 'US economic prospects: secular stagnation, hysteresis, and the zero lower bound', *Business Economics* 49(2): 65–73.

Warwick, Ken (2013). 'Beyond industrial policy – emerging issues and new trends', OECD Science, Technology and Industry Policy Papers 2. Paris: OECD.

7 The social and solidarity economy sector

A bottom-up alternative?

Jennifer Eschweiler and Lars Hulgård

Since the world economic crisis in 2008, the social and solidarity economy keeps gaining recognition as an alternative concept to address economic and state failure, not only among researchers but also among policy-makers and practitioners. Often used in conjunction with social economy, the solidarity economy (SE) has gained popularity in response to the failure of Western models of growth, industrialisation, and welfare redistribution to produce secure employment, wealth, and equality (Piketty 2014). SE is, on the one hand, part of a history of '30 years of privatization of social responsibility and on the other hand it is a history of experimentation with new and more responsive ways of enhancing the role of community, participation and the third sector in social policy' (Hulgård 2011: 202).

Where Streeck (1999) identified less redistributive solidarity within markets due to increased global competition and predicted the replacement of '*protective* and *redistributive* with *competitive* and *productive* solidarity', the solidarity economy identifies a scope for de-commodification of individuals and communities due to its civil society base. Accordingly, SE focuses on collective governance, self-organised production, and democratic reciprocity that open up the space for vulnerable people to become co-producers and co-owners (Laville 2015).

Social and solidarity economy encompasses cooperatives, associations, and mutuals (Defourny 2001: 5), but also third sector organisations providing health or social services and work integration social enterprises (Cooney *et al.* 2016) characterised by a social mission as guidance for economic action, participatory governance structures, and profit-redistribution constraint. It is difficult to draw clear boundaries between social and solidarity economy, but recent conceptual debates seem to suggest that solidarity economy adds a democratic layer to the former due to its combination of economic, social, and political empowerment, firmly rooted in social movements promoting self-help, self-responsibility, equality, and solidarity as well as in the third sector, with its associative tradition linking social action of free citizens to public spheres and common good (Habermas 1995). Furthermore, whereas the social economy is often identified through organisational entities such as cooperatives and social enterprises (Defourny 2001), solidarity economy is broadening the issue by relating the organisational analysis to the macro- level distribution of power (Laville 2015).

SE includes not only organisations operating in the area of social policy and social services but also a broad range of citizen-based activities ranging from fair trade, solidarity tourism, short supply chains, renewable energy, recycling, microfinance, and social currencies. SE is regarded as an alternative model in economic production and consumption (Laville 2015: 47) to counter 'gender inequality, environmental degradation, fiscal constraints on welfare spending, neoliberal deregulation and financial crisis' (Utting 2015: 8) by placing 'new actors into the workplace, in class strategies and citizenship struggles, in response to concerns over welfare, recognition and a meaningful life' (Gaiger *et al.* 2015: 5). Consequently, on an organisational level, the boundary is not between for-profit and non-profit organisations but between capitalist and social economy organisations.

This chapter will mainly focus on solidarity economy as a growing movement of initiatives combining elements of autonomy, equality, and democracy, summarising current academic conceptual work, evidence, and debates on the potential of democratising economy and society from the bottom up, particularly through reciprocity and democratic participation (Donati 2011; Donati and Martignani 2015; Hulgård 2014; Laville and Salmon 2015; Nyssens 2006; Pestoff 2014; Pestoff and Hulgård 2016). The aim is to address the question of whether the solidarity economy holds the potential to constitute a bottom-up alternative to market domination over democratic participation and social inclusion that can reintegrate economic activity into a sphere of democratic redistribution and reciprocity for the common interest.

Thus, solidarity in this case constitutes a 'constructed solidarity' (Laville and Cattani 2006) or solidarity as free choice, as opposed to solidarity rooted in family, religion, neighbourhood, or village. It furthermore refers to a variety of practices rather than to a concept (Ould Ahmed 2015), linked to features like the rejection of competitive individualism, placing the service to members or the community ahead of profit, and the promotion of self-management. It focuses on the inclusion of disadvantaged or weaker groups in society and on equality of rights, which correlates to political equality and democratic decision-making. Accordingly, the solidarity economy relates to the issue of competitiveness in indirect manners, since it contributes to sustain the long-term base of sustainability and prosperity of a society by building platforms and bridges of integration and social capital for potentially socially marginalised citizens (Putnam 2000). Furthermore, solidarity generated in the arenas of the SE are forms of co-production that, for scholars like Ostrom (1990), are able to govern economic and democratic institutions as efficiently as market-based enterprises or public agencies. Similar to the notion of associations as schools for democracy, 'solidarity encourages broader reciprocity practices, where practical experience in managing the common good lends new value to the notions of justice and public interest' (Gaiger *et al.* 2015: 5). Such characteristics of individual action are structured by the normative principles of reciprocity and democratic participation, which will both be explored in more detail below (Laville and Cattani 2006).

While some thinkers regard SE as complementary to the market economy, others see a potential 'towards a new economic paradigm' (Sahakian and Dunand 2015: 404) through a counter-discourse to the state and market dualism which tends to distinguish democracy and economic production. With its emphasis on the common good in economic activity, SE rethinks economic practice in terms of democratic self-management and active citizenship (Dacheux and Goujon 2011; Gibson-Graham 2006). Thus, it has the potential to breach the subordination of citizen activity under market logics (Zimmer and Pahl 2016) while emphasising redistributive justice through voluntary and intersubjective action by individuals to benefit the community.

While indications for transforming the economy itself are missing, as such initiatives are rarely considered as important contributions to a new socio-economic paradigm (Laville and Hulgård 2017), there are nevertheless signs that SE is becoming more and more a global movement, albeit with multiple expressions, each arising in specific historical, geographical, social, and political contexts: certainly in Europe and the Americas (Gaiger *et al.* 2015; Hillenkamp 2011) and tentatively in Africa and Asia (Sahakian and Dunand 2015; Satgar 2014). SE initiatives are producing and selling products and services on the market, while the spirit of profit maximisation is only oriented towards supporting their social mission. Arguably, they do contribute not only to local, regional, or national economies through job, goods, and service production, but also to social cohesion and the democratic fabric of the country they operate in, as they collaborate with the public sector, innovate and develop goods and services, and thus contribute to institutional diversity (Evers *et al.* 2014; Klein 2000; Moulaert and Ailenai 2005; Salamon and Sokolowski 2016).

As initiatives and researchers in the field are starting to connect across Europe and between some European and Latin American countries (e.g. research networks, RIPESS, EMES, RILESS, or CRISES), we will point to some examples that show how SE is conceptualised and practised differently around the world while sharing two important features of reciprocity and democratic participation: 'A solidarity economy can be defined as a set of economic activities governed by a will to act democratically, and in which social relationships of solidarity are preferred to those based on individual interest and material profit' (Eme and Laville 2006: 303), thus referring to non-economic principles in economic practice that meet the needs of consumers, the welfare of the workers, or of a fair society.

After outlining the origins of the concept of SE and filtering the key theoretical contributions, we will turn our attention to the relevance of framework conditions for SE to blossom. Even though mostly operating at the local level, researchers draw attention to the need of broader recognition of SE by political institutions, i.e. by adjusting the relationship between institutions of the welfare state (Hulgård 2015; Laville and Hulgård 2017; Nyssens and Petrella 2015). If supported by the right public policies, researchers argue that the solidarity economy can contribute to the common good via the participation of multiple stakeholders in a variety of economic activities, provided its principles of autonomy, equal rights, and democracy are enshrined in policies at the micro-, meso-, and macro-levels of society.

A brief history of the solidarity economy

Laville traces the different stages of the solidarity economy, dependent on relations between state, market, and society, starting with forms of democratic solidarity in the early nineteenth century via associations that emphasised both economic and political empowerment through collective action in the wake of democratic revolutions and the emergence of a public sphere inhabited by citizens (Habermas 1989), aiming 'to reinforce political democracy through economic and social democracy' (Laville 2015: 41–2). A modern solidarity unfolded that focused on mutual aid as much as on protest actions such as the self-organisation of workers or movements demanding equal rights.

According to Laville, the late nineteenth century saw the emergence of a 'philanthropic solidarity' that focused on micro-level poverty reduction through individual giving; replacing equality with private benevolence and paternalism. Ongoing threats to peace made the philanthropic solution untenable, leading to the resurgence of democratic solidarity in the early and mid-twentieth century, when public authorities took control over social protection and market regulation, driven by concerns for social cohesion, introducing a public dimension of solidarity distributed by the welfare state:

> The divides caused by the market economy had to be corrected through policy and legal interventions – hence the concept of social rights that combined workers' rights within the enterprise with social protection aiming to protect workers against specific risks, leading to a separation of the economic and the social.
>
> (Ibid.: 43–4)

The newly created welfare states in some countries reduced associative activity to service provision rather than to collective action, until the new social movements arisen in the 1970s paved the way for a resurgence of 'a strong version of solidarity', questioning the clash between capital and labour as well as consumption and ways of life, leading to experiments with 'alternative ways of organising production and exchange' (ibid.: 45). The civil base of solidarity economy becomes visible in this short chronology, as much as the context dependence of collective action. As social movements dispersed, the market, state, and non-profit sector separated conceptually, sidelining the democratic and societal integration functions of non-profit activity until a revival of social and solidarity economy in the 1980s and 1990s in Europe and Latin America, in response to the perceived failure of capitalism, that started to see growing economic inequalities and environmental ails (Laville and Cattani 2006).

Clearly, risks and shocks related to economic liberalisation and multiple crises, reconfiguring power relations, public policies, and identities, are a driving force for solidarity economy. Recurring crises linked to finance, the environment, food, and energy call conventional wisdom about growth and industrialisation models into question (Utting 2015). Processes of deregulation, state retrenchment, financialisation, and commodification have produced new relations of domination and subordination (Vail 2010). Emancipatory movements have reconfigured the subjective preferences of individuals and groups, fuelling activist and practitioner networks and new social movements (Agyeman, 2013; della Porta 2005; Fraser 2013), leading to discursive shifts that 'have elevated notions of equality, rights, empowerment and participation in framings of what ("inclusive", "sustainable" and "rights-based") development means' (Utting 2015: 6), giving rise to a plethora of mostly local bottom-up pluralist economic initiatives promoting democratic principles of autonomy, participation, and social equality. However, despite frequent collaboration of such initiatives with other actors from state and market sectors, only a few countries, and mostly in the Global South, reflect on their multiple contributions and support them systematically.

We will now dig deeper into the conceptual origins of solidarity to detail the connection between economy and democracy und underline the transformative potential of SE through a conceptual re-embedding of the economy as a means to serve human goals.

Conceptual development

We present a conceptual framework that is heavily influenced by the writings of Karl Polanyi and particularly his 1944 book *The Great Transformation.* SE insists on the plurality of the economy, the principle of reciprocity and the democratising effect of the solidarity economy, taking further inspiration from Elinor Ostrom's (1990) work on *Governing the Commons* and Jürgen Habermas' (1996) *Between Facts and Norms*.

Writing in the 1930s, economist Karl Polanyi identified a relentless push to extend and deregulate markets, destroying livelihoods, weakening communities, and seeking to commodify work and money, leading to 'wholesale destabilization of the economic system on the one hand, and of nature and society on the other' (Fraser 2013: 119). While Polanyi acknowledged the profit motive of capitalist economy, he regarded the market as the aggregate of human behaviours and thus referred to a 'fictitious commodification' of labour, social, and private spheres by drawing attention to economic practices like redistribution, reciprocity, and household administration, safeguarded by a double movement of political elites and commercial interests, on the one hand, and cross-class social movements leading to an understanding that regulation – and redistribution – are needed in order to save society, on the other.

In Polanyi's substantive and pluralist approach to the economy, the first system is the market, which allows supply of and demand for goods and services. Exchange happens on the basis of price setting and contracts informed by calculation of interest. It is a historically new system, where production is entirely for market exchange and profit. According to Polanyi, this approach to societal integration used to be peripheral, but is now dominant (Laville 2010; Laville and Hulgård 2017).

Redistribution, or the second system, allows central authorities to be responsible for allocating what is produced, according to political priorities and interests in re-allocating and redistributing both values and consequences (Titmuss 1974) of social change. It happens through central taxation or philanthropic giving, spending according to political priorities, or steering by local, regional, national, and international associations and governments (Gardin 2015: 115).

Reciprocity, or the non-monetary third system, refers to the production of use values to satisfy family and community needs. It allows relations to be established between groups or persons, referring to giving, receiving and giving in return, binding people in solidarity (Laville and Cattani 2006: 18), turning vulnerable people into co-producers and co-owners.

This plural understanding of the economy sees the market as culturally and politically embedded, rather than autonomous and dominating political and private spheres, manifested in the structure of government redistribution, but also in 'social rights and legislative and regulatory mechanisms, such as collective bargaining' (Laville *et al*. 2006: 278). In other words:

> To treat markets as if they are (or can be) somehow 'disembedded' – set apart and elevated above socio-political forces, is simply to misunderstand how markets work: markets are part of society and cannot operate properly without the legitimation and structures that states provide.
>
> (Roy 2015: 35)

Underlining the role of social movements, Fraser suggests re-phrasing Polanyi's research programme. She argues that in order to be able to capture the possibility for emancipation it is necessary to think of a triple, rather than a double movement in relation to Polanyi's account of fictitious commodification, since she observes an increasing commodification process in the sphere of social reproduction through the entry of market logics in childcare and householding (Fraser 2014: 554). She refers to the emancipatory movements that started to emerge post-war and that rally around status like gender, ethnicity, sexuality, religion, or nationality, struggling for freedom from domination, including the suppressive factors of welfare and redistribution dependence. This infrastructure of a solidarity economy is 'aware that a wage could serve as a resource against domination premised on status … they claimed the freedom of contract not as an end in itself, but rather as a means to emancipation' (Fraser 2013: 128), converting the social dimension into economic leverage or specific productive strength.

Solidarity-based initiatives within a Polanyian framework of economy can help to decommodify the three economic factors that Polanyi does not deem commodities: land, labour, and money, as none of them are produced for sale, while being substantive for the two other economic systems. 'The substantive meaning of economic derives from man's dependence for his living upon nature and his fellows. It refers to the interchange with his natural and social environment' (Polanyi 1957: 243), which are essential to satisfy his material needs. The notion of economy as a substantive concept is based on Weber's distinction between *Zweckrationalität* and *Wertrationalität*, the latter referring to principles other than maximising utility or profit, and 'the institutionalized process of interaction between man and his environment' (Laville and Salmon 2015: 155). This hybrid view of different types of economic exchanges complementing each other rather than working in isolation (Nyssens 2006: 318) shows the potential impact of solidarity economy initiatives and organisations, as they combine different economic principles in the mission and realisation of their projects.

As mentioned above, Polanyi's hybrid conceptualisation of the economy leads to a twofold movement: on the one hand, the priority given to market exchange in institutionalist processes of the economy (Polanyi 1957: 5–17); on the other hand, the invention of modern solidarity in the form of law enshrined in the constitution that manifests a deliberative process and a resource for legitimate emancipatory social action. This is similar to what Habermas (1996) described as the socially integrating force of solidarity to counter the power of money and administrative power. Thus, personal autonomy is guaranteed through legal provisions and democratic society, which constitute each other: citizens can make use of their legal rights to decide on the rules of their intercourse (Eriksen and Weigård 2003: 9).

Habermas moved on from classical sociology and its distinction in spheres of enterprise and government on the one hand and community and participation on the other as separate principles (Laville and Salmon 2015). Engagement in communication in the public sphere is a legitimate source of power, providing the normative foundations of democracy (Habermas 1996), thus leading to the political dimension of SE. While solidarity-based public redistribution 'saw its rules enacted through representative democracy, reciprocity could unfold on the basis of voluntary commitments, in the public space, of free and equal citizens' (Laville 2015: 50–1). The Habermasian framework of communicative power understands civil society as an emancipatory force if admitted access to the public sphere, the same emancipatory power that Fraser (2013) identified as important counter- or third movement to prevent commodification. 'Strictly speaking, this power springs from the interactions among legally institutionalised will-formation and culturally mobilized publics. The latter, for their part, find a basis in the associations of a civil society quite distinct from both state and economy alike' (Habermas 1996: 301).

In the centre of Habermas' argument stands the application of a sluice model of problem-solving that is a crucial part of his version of deliberative democracy, which in principle also allows minority interests to enter public discourse (Eschweiler 2013; Hulgård 2015). The legitimacy of political decisions is secured only by 'communication flows that start at the periphery and pass through the sluices of democratic and constitutional procedures' (Habermas 1996: 356). Deliberative is opposed to either strategic or instrumental; a process is deliberatively rational to the extent that its interactions are egalitarian, uncoerced, competent, and free from delusion, deception, power, and strategy. Deliberative democracy puts focus on a context in which preferences can be altered by taking different and informed views into account. What matters most is that 'public opinion be formed on the basis of adequate information and relevant reasons and that those whose interests are involved have an equal and effective opportunity to make their own interests (and the reasons for them) known' (Baynes 2002: 127).

The ideal of a public sphere as a normative concept 'symbolically constitutes the matrix of the political community' (Laville and Salmon 2015: 153), whereas Habermas' notion of pluralist public spheres free from domination allows concrete forms of expression on issues related to recognition, empowerment, and equality (1996: 330). They are the key for social integration and bottom-up democratisation, realised by the interplay of institutionalised procedures of political will-formation and civil society, where SE is located in form of citizen-driven initiatives, associations, non-profit organisations, etc. However, Habermas does not claim that civil society discourse in the public sphere forms a new base of political and economic life. Civil society actors can only gain influence, not political power. Accordingly, this is a place where the solidarity economy framework departs most radically from the Habermasian theory of deliberation and communicative action. 'Public influence is transformed into communicative power only after it passes through the filters of the institutionalised procedures of democratic opinion-and will-formation and enters through parliamentary debates into legitimate law making' (ibid.: 371). Civil society cannot replace the state, but it can mobilise counter-knowledge and offer new interpretations based on lifeworld forms of expertise (ibid.: 372).

Habermas clearly locates civil society between the state, market, and private spheres and focuses only on associations that are neither economic nor linked to the state. Laville and Salmon (2015: 155), however, argue that such a separation of spheres is unsustainable in practice, since many associations are striving for autonomy, on the one hand, but often must give in to isomorphic pressures in their search for resources, influence, and thus modes for survival: 'It is preferable to accept that the oppositions between systems and lifeworlds run through each sphere with varying intensity.' They furthermore state that civil society is not limited to the formation of opinions but depending on situational context can be involved in decision-making, leading us to Elinor Ostrom and the 'governing of the commons'.

Ostrom states that there is a specific space for commons in the gaps left by the market and the state throughout the world. Referring to systems of production, fisheries, pastures, forests, or irrigation systems as commons, she maintains that their management must be governed by collective rules to prevent individual exploitation and finally exhaustion of the resources by depletion (Laville and Salmon 2015: 151). She insists on the importance of instituted collective rules that characterise the governance of commons, assuming that 'institutions affect what people think and what they value' (Ostrom 1990). Laville and Salmon (2015: 152) argue that the commons principle can be extended to a number of collective actions that put the right to use the service or product over ownership and profit accumulation and do so in a participatory governed way.

Comparing the features, differences, and commonalities between social and solidarity economy organisations and the commons, Nyssens and Petrella (2015) highlight Ostrom's contribution to underscore the importance of an 'eco-diversity' of institutional forms other than state and market, as well as the importance of participatory and collective governance, bringing us to the meso-level of civil society and collective action where SE is situated. Referring to products and services produced by SE organisations as 'quasi-collective goods', they elaborate on property regimes and the institutions established to govern natural resources.

First of all, SE and commons do not have owners but are collectively or quasi-collectively governed. Departing from a legal understanding of SE firmly based in the third sector, and thus in institutional forms neither belonging to the market nor to the state, combined with the ethical demand of delivering a service to the members of a community rather than generating profits, self-managed and democratically governed SE organisations are oriented towards 'economic democracy', moving away from a state–market dichotomy (Nyssens and Petrella 2015: 179). The same is true for Ostrom's conceptualisation of the commons: 'neither the state nor the market is uniformly successful in enabling individuals to sustain long-term, productive use of natural resource systems' (Ostrom 1990: 1), leading to new institutional forms in which plural actors self-organise and set up their own rules, dependent on local context and anchored in social practice to manage common natural resources in a sustainable way. 'It is these practices that can point to the pathways for reinserting the economy in democratic norms' (Laville and Cattani 2006: 257), detached from traditional conceptions of ownership, which entail both the right to control and the right to surplus earnings.

In SE, investors do not own the organisation, multiple stakeholders are involved in its governance, and profit distribution is forbidden or significantly constrained. In non-profit organisations, the net financial surplus is reinvested in the social mission, while in cooperatives profits are partly distributed by feeding into the collective fund, partly given to shareholders. While producing services through economic activity, they create benefits for the users (who might also be the producers) and the collectivity through the creation of jobs, local development, public health, etc. (ibid.: 183).

In the case of the commons, the 'appropriators', consumers and producers who draw on the natural resource (herders, fishermen, or irrigators, using the resource for their own consumptions or for further production), are also not owners (Nyssens and Petrella 2015: 181). Ostrom identifies a plurality of property regimes, depending on a 'bundle of rights' which varies according to context: who has the right of access, of appropriation, the right of management, of determination of who has access and who can transfer the right of access (Schlager and Ostrom 1992), deriving principles adopted by institutions managing common resources that usually strengthen local communities (Poteete *et al*. 2010: 47). The main challenge is to avoid over-exploitation of the resource, which requires a degree of self-limitation by individuals.

The main difference between the commons and the social and solidarity economy identified by Nyssens and Petrella in the context of property regimes and profit lies in the composition of management structures. While the commons are managed by a more or less homogeneous group, in the sense that they are all beneficiaries of the resource which is their main interest, SE initiatives have social benefits at the core of their objective (lower cost for public bodies, fight against inequality, environmental protection, to name a few), hence the products and services they produce are termed quasi-collective (Nyssens and Petrella 2015: 183).

Both the commons and SE depend on trust relations in the face of imperfect information, once more underlining their local character. 'Actors are very often in situations of profoundly imperfect information characterized by great uncertainty' (Kiser and Ostrom 2000: 61), but based on extensive case study work Ostrom was able to show general principles for effective and sustainable management of natural resources, fostering trust and reciprocity in the context of local conditions, including collectively agreed operational, collective choice and constitutional choice rules, which also determine sanctions and conflict resolution mechanisms, thus 'involving the actors in the institutional arrangement they have created' (Nyssens and Petrella 2015: 185–6).

In SE organisations, governance is usually shared by multiple stakeholders such as professionals or volunteers, represented on the board of directors together with other stakeholders, including users or public authorities, and a general assembly, who must find compromises between multiple perspectives and interests in order to serve the common interest. Often SE organisations must work closely together with state institutions, who provide funding by 'ordering' services, provide the legal structures, or even have a place on the board. In the governance of the commons, the group of governors is not only more homogeneous, there is also less state involvement, which mostly provides institutional legitimacy by accepting the rules set up to manage the resource (ibid.: 184).

According to Ostrom, SE can learn about the importance of collectively developed rules and norms to ensure durability, linked to governance structures and internal democracy, constrained but not entirely determined by external institutional arrangements or the political embeddedness of SE. SE organisations have to co-construct the rules and norms by trying to impact social policy, i.e. through institutional entrepreneurship (Lawrence and Suddaby 2006).

The solidarity economy: reciprocity and democratic participation

The solidarity economy, in the tradition of democracy found in associationalism, contains an element of democratising society through self-organisation and varying degrees of collective governance, participation, and deliberation. It is also based on the recognition that economic principles are plural, and that by including all people in a self-managed and self-organised way in some form of economic life, SE is considered to have a democratising effect on the economy and society as a whole (Defourny and Develtere 1999; Fraisse *et al.* 2007; Laville 2003). Hence, the solidarity economy opens up the broader question of the initiatives' relationship to both the *economy* and *democracy* as they push for systemic change and social transformation.

Laville and others consider the solidarity economy framework a new epistemological perspective, coupling economic and political approaches for a comprehensive understanding of citizen initiatives, highlighting the common good, pluralism in democracy, the capacity to mobilize pluralism in economy and re-embedding of the economy 'as a means to serve human goals' (Laville and Salmon 2015: 158).

The public space as a sphere of democracy expressed in citizen and civil society action is combined with a pluralist notion of the economy: the market economy, the non-market economy, and the non-monetary economy, the latter two describing: (1) the redistribution of produced goods and services by foundations or public institutions as part of the welfare state, providing citizens with individual rights, subject to democratic control; and (2) a redistribution of goods based on reciprocity, turning vulnerable people into co-producers and co-owners, in contrast to markets because they are inextricably linked to human relationships (ibid.: 148–51). Key factors are reciprocity and democratic participation.

As outlined above, reciprocity is a key concept in the solidarity economy. Polanyi (1957) referred to economic activity as reciprocity when production is for family or community use which nowadays shows itself in multiple forms, both in terms of the heterogeneity of the actors involved and in the degree of symmetry between different actors. Actors are consumers or users, workers, and volunteers, but also representatives of public authorities or providers of capital.

While reciprocity suggests a social expectation of giving, taking, and giving back in return in value or in kind, as described in Marcel Mauss' theory of *The Gift* (2011), it is not necessarily a source of equality, nor triggered by altruistic motives, as one might associate with SE. Critics in anthropology, psychology, and sociology see an economy of exchange hidden in the concept of reciprocity that is linked to domination and self-interest (Malinowski 1978), hence some authors try to distinguish weak and strong reciprocity. While weak reciprocity describes situations in which actors expect a profitable result, strong reciprocity refers to long-term cooperation in which the social mission is more important than self-interest (Guala 2012). It is this latter notion of reciprocity, identified by Polanyi as the condition for markets and state redistribution, that SE is linked to, a sphere under threat through the conditions of neo-liberalism, benefitting a few while limiting the free choices of people to lead a 'dignified social life' (Sumiala and Valaskivi 2014).

Scholars of the solidarity economy underline the fact that also in SE there is a continuum of reciprocity, linked to conditions of context, resources, and governance, that determine the degree of reciprocity as the integrating principle of SE, due to the 'tensions and compromises that emerge among reciprocity, the market and redistribution' (Gardin 2015: 115). First of all, Gardin distinguishes three types of reciprocity in Europe:

- *Unequal reciprocity*: the group in charge of the initiative (volunteers, professionals, public authorities) differs from the users/consumers of a service or product (i.e. workers in a work integration social enterprise), but who might move from vertical to horizontal reciprocity through the introduction of participatory governance after inception.

- *Reciprocity among peers*: a homogeneous and self-organised group who will provide the future workers of an initiative, e.g. in production cooperatives (Bataille-Chedotel and Huntzinger 2004), or its users, e.g. in consumer cooperatives (Linden 2008), or both, e.g. in local exchange trading systems (Healy 2008; Pacione 1998).
- *Multilateral reciprocity*: a variety of actors in different relationships with the initiative (as workers, volunteers, or users) come together in a symmetrical position, either from the start or over time, e.g. in solidarity-based finance (Glémain 2009; Lovera 2015), in fair trade (Nicholls and Huybrechts 2016), small farmer associations, or on neighbourhood management boards (Gardin 2015: 118).

The first two types refer to vertical and horizontal forms of reciprocity. The first can transform into multilateral reciprocity 'provided the beneficiary group is given consideration and able to *dictate its terms*' (ibid.: 115). In other words, 'the gift does not appear simply as a moral obligation; it must meet the requirements of others, who dictate their conditions' (Temple and Chabal 1995: 190–1), thus linking reciprocity to equal rights.

Based on the analysis and review of hundreds of solidarity-based initiatives in France and Europe, Gardin furthermore concludes that reciprocity is often examined at an individual level only, lacking a political dimension of reciprocity that takes into account its relationships with the market, redistribution, and the level of democratic process in the way redistributing intermediaries are chosen and distribute resources based on which rights and notions of equality (Gardin 2015: 126). However, it is this careful analysis that eventually determines how a solidarity economy initiative is truly different from market and public economies.

In other words, reciprocity produced in SE is politically and economically embedded in a system based on public redistribution and market exchange logic, which can all be used as resources for SE, but can also be a barrier for common good production. Different types of resource allocation can be combined by the solidarity economy, as they might sell products and services on the market, receive state subsidies and funding or private donations, as well as benefit from the time and expertise of volunteers. The question is whether reciprocity as the founding logic of an initiative actually integrates market and state logics (ibid.: 116; Laville and Salmon 2015), or whether it is simply a side effect of the economic consolidation of an initiative (through government funding or income earned).

This can be assessed by studying both the budgets and the non-monetary resources of an organisation, including the motivations and characteristics of participants to understand their dominant economic behaviour, and the impact of negotiations between public bodies and the solidarity economy organisations concerning resources and regulations (Gardin 2015: 120). Are working criteria set unilaterally by public bodies, i.e. are the institutions of the welfare state funding organisations to tackle social exclusion (termed tutelary regulation by Gardin)? Is there a dominant logic of quasi-market regulation or a 'relationship of substitution' in the form of public procurement practices that put non-profit associations in competition with for-profit private companies, facilitating the withdrawal of the state without recognising the reciprocity dimension of SE (ibid.: 124)? Or are the modes of working the result of SE advocacy or negotiated regulation, even 'solidarity-based' which envisages partnership relations in which 'associations have their say on the rules concerning them' (Vaillancourt and Laville 1998: 131)?

Such analysis can provide insights into the nature of an SE initiative and the type of reciprocity at play in relation to state and market (Table 7.1). Furthermore, and from a democracy perspective, it allows conclusions about the co-production of services and collaboration in the production of public goods between SE and the public sector and the distribution of roles for non-state actors, a field that to date lacks comparative work. We will revisit the role of the state at the macro- and meso-levels later, but at this point it is fair to conclude that the actual type of reciprocity in relation to the state and the market determines if SE can maintain what it promises on a broader societal level.

Reciprocity in SE is linked to democracy. Democracy is attractive as a concept because its normative foundation is the promise of a good life for each individual living in society. From this derives the 'norm of moral equality in collective rule: because each individual's life is an end in itself, collective decisions ought to recognize, respect, and benefit individuals' interests and values equally, insofar as possible' (Castiglione and Warren 2006: 4). Within the framework of SE there is a democratic dimension both at the meso-level of initiatives, in terms of democratic governance or collective rules inspired by Ostrom, and at the macro-level, by embedding SE initiatives in a broader democratic framework of political decision-making and the power of citizens to use institutionalised procedures enshrining solidarity to strive for autonomy, equality, and participation.

The link between reciprocity and democracy situated on a continuum is reflected in Laville's argument that there is confusion between democratic solidarity and philanthropic giving or redistribution. Although philanthropic solidarity is also an expression of private or public solidarity, he criticises it for bringing 'a mechanism of social hierarchy and support for the inequality that is built into the social fabric of the community' (Laville 2015: 106), if it does not entail a resource for empowerment. The new forms of 'venture philanthropy' funding social businesses, corporate social responsibility, and social entrepreneurs often function as a potential extension of capitalism along philanthropic lines (ibid.: 53). This puts further pressure on third sector organisations to demonstrate impact, thus reducing the social and democratic value that non-profit organisations create to measurable outputs in economic terms (Enjolras 2015), subordinating them to market logics through impact bonds and competition for funding.

On the contrary, the concept of democratic solidarity is built on redistribution to 'reinforce social cohesion and to redress inequality' and an egalitarian understanding

Table 7.1 Distinctive characteristics of the different types of economic behaviour

	Market decisional exchange	*Redistribution*	*Reciprocity*
Relations among actors/goals of the exchanges	Symmetrical relation of equivalence between the goods	Hierarchical relation with a central authority	Relations among symmetrical individuals and groups
Time	Immediacy of the exchange	Lasting relation	Long-term strengthening of networks of social relations
Typical institutions	Capitalist enterprises	State, regional and local governments; para-public organisations	Solidarity economy organisations
Types of resource allocation	Purchase of goods and services	Public funding, subsidies, etc.	Gifts, volunteering, grants, etc.
Dominant principle	Individual interest – profit	General interest – commitment	Give-and-take

Source: author's elaboration based on Gardin (2015: 116).

of reciprocity as a way to enhance 'voluntary social relations between free and equal citizens' (Laville 2015: 107), inspired by the concept of communicative rationality, equal rights, and self-organisation in relation to state and market (Laville and Salmon 2015). This relation between redistribution and reciprocity is the foundation of democratic solidarity in which 'it is not a question of replacing the state with civil society but rather one of combining redistributive solidarity with a more reciprocal version of the latter in order to rebuild society's capacity for self-organisation' (Laville 2015: 107–8), potentially by moving towards the evolution of an institutional-reciprocal welfare state (Hulgård 2015). Solidarity is produced in such a way that the recipient can become the giver. Democratic solidarity aims to allow the recipient to reciprocate, so as to avoid the 'permanent position of inferiority' (Laville 2015: 106).

A local phenomenon or transformative potential?

Whether SE is a counter-discourse that will change the solidarity-eroding logic of market competition or whether this is merely a fantasy of researchers (Gardin 2015) is a subject of debate. SE theorists would agree that the market economy has failed to live up to its promise of social equality, as stated by Fraser (2013: 119): 'Free-market fundamentalists have sought to commodify all the necessary preconditions of commodity production, turning labour, nature and money into objects for sale on *self-regulating* markets.'

Today, we can observe an increase in popularity of the social and solidarity economy among policy-makers, facilitated by a gradual transition of especially European and North American welfare states from institutional and redistributive orientations towards enabling and work-oriented welfare policies, with social responsibility shifting from being a public concern to an individual and private concern (Gilbert 2002; Hulgård 2011; Hulgård and Andersen 2012). Evidence suggests that it is the hand-in-hand of public actors and SE initiatives that promotes multilateral reciprocity, but legal frameworks and political will to support such collaboration often remain limited to certain groups and to the local level (Eschweiler and Hulgård 2018).

However, SE organisations such as social enterprises 'are supposed to combine social purpose activities in poor constituencies with capital, knowhow and managerial structures developed in the for-profit market sphere of society' (Hulgård 2015: 207), moving from a half-movement, half-government character of civil society towards a half-charity, half-business logic (Wijkström 2011: 46), which is diametrically opposed to Laville's concept of democratic solidarity based on reciprocity. Due to the context dependence and the individual straits important for the development of solidarity initiatives at the local level, broader results could only be achieved if political and economic contexts stimulate such practice. Providing institutional arrangements that strike the right balance between the welfare state and SE, i.e. in the form of a 'welfare mix' made up of shared responsibilities among various types of actors – state, private for-profit companies, and communities (Evers 1995; Evers and Laville,

2004; Laville and Hulgård 2017; Pestoff 2005) – is the task for an enabling public sector.

The general-interest dimension of SE means that the state plays an important role in its production of goods and services. Governments would have to abandon the neo-liberal course, or at least counter its detrimental effects by providing an institutional infrastructure that facilitates and promotes SE (Defourny *et al.* 2014: 10; Mair 2010: 26). As Nyssens and Petrella remind us, SE organisations usually have to integrate diverse stakeholders, embedded in legal frameworks, institutional support mechanisms, as well as political culture and history in terms of accommodating transformative movements, traditions of welfare, and co-production of public services. This 'hybridization of commercial, public and voluntary resources' (Nyssens and Petrella 2015: 185) raises the question of how consciously principles of reciprocity and democracy lead to action (Gardin 2015). And could these principles, 'inevitably limited in number, be institutionalised and applied throughout an entire society' (Ould Ahmed 2015: 431)?

The procedure for institutionalising SE through legal and administrative reforms is highly context-dependent. Empirical evidence shows different degrees of institutionalisation and intentions across contexts. Sahakian and Dunand (2015), who studied SE in Manila and Geneva, demonstrate different development processes. While organisations in Geneva were trying to implement SE principles in existing initiatives engaged in different product and service development, supported by network and institutional structures, SE organisations in Manila were more oriented towards incubating solidarity across agricultural supply chains throughout the country, oriented towards transformation. The authors conclude that, in Manila, SE 'has the potential to become an economy of sustainability, working towards more sustainable community development' (Sahakian and Dunand 2015: 403).

Corragio (2015) observes a shift in some South American countries from policies centred on social assistance to what might be called productive social policy, which is sometimes a response to bottom-up forces and new societal practices and politics, and sometimes a top-down process to shape economic behaviour. Brazil, for example, where the concept of SE typically refers to economic initiatives generating employment, income, and social benefits for their members, such as quality of life and citizen participation, has seen the emergence of a 'popular economy' characterised by informality, 'inseparable from the mesh of social relations of small-scale economic agents' (Gaiger *et al.* 2015: 10). During the 1990s, SE became part of the political programme of the government, with the majority of ministries referring to it in their programmes, particularly the National Solidarity Economy Department that provides public funding (ibid.: 12). According to Gaiger, SE organisations rarely replace existing forms of popular economy. As demonstrated throughout this chapter, their main purpose is to reorganise 'the productive, material and human factors of the popular economy through progressive changes' (ibid.: 5).

Corragio (2015) insists that policies supporting SE cannot merely be social policy, but require multiple policies (macro-economic, industrial, labour market, etc.). This is visible in France, where a Ministry for Social and Solidarity Economy was created in 2012, but, according to national SE advocates, sufficient policies were neither formulated nor implemented.[1] At the macro-level, the state is responsible for facilitating voluntary commitment, must promise an idea of solidarity focused on individual rights and redistribution, and must 'promote common goods and social relations based on respect for the principles of freedom and equality' (Laville 2015: 55). At the local level, Bateman (2015) recommends institutional arrangements that de-commercialise local service provisioning and micro-finance and support cooperatives. Gardin (2015: 125) reminds us that it is not only important to negotiate relationships with public authorities at the local level: 'It requires a legitimization of networks, and initiatives of the solidarity economy to ensure that the dialogue with public authorities goes beyond the mere involvement of solidarity-based initiatives in the definition of public policies.'

Hence institutionalising SE as a bottom-up infrastructure requires thinking in terms of partnerships. After all, SE organisations can be capable partners in designing and implementing policies. Laville and Hulgård (2017) argue that the welfare states of Northern and Western Europe seem fragile if they are not able to link positively the institutional capacity of the welfare state to these new citizen-driven initiatives and hybrid entities that are emerging at an increasing speed. They fear that

> if the withdrawal of the universal welfare state is happening without a simultaneous investment in the institutionalization of new links between the redistributive capacity of the state and the reciprocal capacity of civil society, citizens will intensify their competition and fight over scarce resources between themselves.

This can drive apart today's pluralist, highly functionally differentiated societies that no longer share a homogeneous national or cultural identity (Imbusch and Rucht 2005: 13).

Laville (2015: 55) argues that 'the democratic state will regain legitimacy only if it integrates possibilities for increased participation by salaried workers and users and if it is supported by forms of associative activity influenced by democratic solidarity' and maintains that SE can integrate initiatives of civil society into the public space of modern democratic societies, as it is linked to politics in two ways: (1) to 'non-institutional politics, centred on the potential for active citizenship which supposes that citizens make use of the positive freedom to which they are formally entitled' and (2) to 'institutional politics, centred on the exercise of power. The interactions between public authorities and civil society initiatives translate into mutual effects' (ibid.: 51). In other words, ensuring the institutionalisation of SE rather than reducing it to 'fragmentary forms of self-management' (Utting 2015: 18) requires not only an enabling environment but also pressures from below.

Utting concludes that the field of SE needs to be more analytically prepared, in terms of understanding the complexities and contradictions of change and building the evidence base needed to be convincing in its arguments about why policy-makers, activists, scholars, and others should be taking SE seriously (ibid.: 5). Laville and Hulgård (2017) add the urgency to understand if and how systematic investments in programmes supporting SE, co-production, and 'relational types of welfare provision' can build a new type of welfare state that they call the 'institutional reciprocal model of welfare'.

While some scholars may see the potential for the SE to be an alternative to the current market economy, it is urgent to critically evaluate situations where marginalised communities are fed with nothing but their own networks, while being victims of a situation pointed out by Margaret Somers in one sentence: 'Let them eat social capital' (Somers 2008). Countering the marketisation or instrumentalisation of SE would first of all require an institutional framework that leaves room for several logics of economic action. At the same time, it needs a new relationship between citizen-based initiatives and organisations oriented towards the common good, the state, and the economy.

Note

1 Hugues Sibille at TSI Final Event on 9 November 2016. Available at: http://thirdsectorimpact.eu/news/giving-third-sector-visibility-deserves/

References

Agyeman, Julian (2013). *Just sustainabilities: policy, planning and practice*. London: Zed Books.

Bataille-Chedotel, Frédérique and France Huntzinger (2004). 'Faces of governance of production cooperatives: an exploratory study of ten French cooperatives', *Annals of Public and Cooperative Economics* 75(1): 89–111.

Bateman, Milford (2015). 'Rebuilding solidarity-driven economies after neoliberalism: the role of cooperatives and local developmental states in Latin America', in Peter Utting (ed.). *Social and solidarity economy: beyond the fringe*. London: Zed Books.

Baynes, Kenneth (2002). 'A critical theory perspective on civil society and the state', in Nancy Rosenblum and Robert Post (eds). *Civil society and government*. Princeton, NJ: Princeton University Press.

Castiglione Dario and Mark E. Warren (2006). 'Rethinking democratic representation. eight theoretical issues', paper presented at Centre for the Study of Democratic Institutions, University of British Columbia, 18–19 May.

Cooney, Kate, Marthe Nyssens, Mary O'Shaughnessy, and Jacques Defourny (2016). 'Public policies and work integration social enterprises: the challenge of institutionalization in a neoliberal era', *Non-profit Policy Forum* 7(4): 415–33.

Coraggio, José Luis (2015). 'Institutionalising the social and solidarity economy in Latin America', in Peter Utting (ed.). *Social and solidarity economy: beyond the fringe*. London: Zed Books.

Dacheux, Eric and Daniel Goujon (2011). 'The solidarity economy: an alternative development strategy?' *International Social Science Journal* 62(203–4): 205–15.

Defourny, Jacques (2001). 'From third sector to social enterprise', in Carlo Borzaga and Jacques Defourny (eds). *The emergence of social enterprise*. London: Routledge, 1–28.

Defourny, Jacques and Patrick Develtere (1999). 'Origines et contours de l'économie sociale au Nord et au Sud', in Jacques Defourny, Patrick Develtere, and Bénédicte Fonteneau (eds). *L'économie sociale au Nord et au Sud*. Brussels: De Boeck, 25–50.
Defourny, Jacques, Lars Hulgård, and Victor Pestoff (eds) (2014). *Social enterprise and the third sector: changing European landscapes in a comparative perspective*. London: Routledge.
Della Porta, Donatella (2005) 'The social bases of the global justice movement: some theoretical reflections and empirical evidence from the first European social forum', Civil Society and Social Movements Programme Paper 21. Geneva: United Nations Research Institute for Social Development.
Donati, Pierpaolo (2011). *Relational sociology: a new paradigm for the social sciences*. London: Routledge.
Donati, Pierpaolo and Luca Martignani (2015). *Towards a new local welfare: best practices and networks of social inclusion*. Bologna: Bononia University Press.
Eme, Bernard and Jean-Louis Laville (2006). 'Economie solidaire (2)', in Jean-Louis Laville and Antonio David Cattani (eds). *Dictionnaire de l'autre économie*, Paris: Gallimard, 303–12.
Enjolras, Bernard (2015). 'Measuring the impact of the third sector: from concept to metrics', TSI Working Paper No. 5. Brussels: Third Sector Impact.
Eriksen, Erik Oddvar and Jarle Weigård (2003). *Understanding Habermas: communicative action and deliberative democracy*. London: Continuum.
Eschweiler, Jennifer (2013) *Towards a voice in the public sphere? Deliberation with Muslim civil society in Berlin*. Berlin: De Gruyter.
Eschweiler, Jennifer and Lars Hulgård (2012). ''Social innovation and deliberative democracy, MES Working Papers no. 12/04. Liège: EMES European Research Network asbl.
Eschweiler, Jennifer and Lars Hulgård (2018). 'Channelling solidarity: inputs from third sector, social innovation and co-creation of public goods', Solidus Project Report. Available at: http://solidush2020.eu/wp-content/uploads/2018/04/Deliverable-Report-5.2.pdf
Evers, Adalbert (1995). 'Part of the welfare mix: the third sector as an intermediate area', *Voluntas* 6(2): 159–82.
Evers, Adalbert, Benjamin Ewert, and Taco Brandsen (eds) (2014). *Social innovations for social cohesion: transnational patterns and approaches from 20 European cities*. Liège: EMES European Research Network asbl.
Evers, Adalbert and Jean-Louis Laville (eds) (2004). *The third sector in Europe*. Cheltenham: Edward Elgar.
Fraisse, Laurent, Isabelle Guérin, and Jean-Louis Laville (2007). 'Economie solidaire: des initiatives locales à l'action publique. Introduction', *Revue Tiers Monde* 190(2): 245–53.
Fraser, Nancy (1992). 'Rethinking the public sphere: a contribution to the critique of actually existing democracy', in Craig Calhoun (ed.). *Habermas and the public sphere*. Cambridge, MA: MIT Press.
Fraser, Nancy (2013). 'A triple movement? Parsing the politics of crisis after Polanyi', *New Left Review* 81, May–June.
Fraser, Nancy (2014). 'Can society be commodities all the way down? Post-Polanyian reflections on capitalist crisis', *Economy and Society* 43(4): 541–58.
Gaiger, Luiz Inácio, Adriane Ferrarini, and Marília Veronese (2015). 'Social enterprise in Brazil: an overview of solidarity economy enterprises', ICSEM Working Paper Series No. 10. Liège: ICSEM.

Gardin, Laurent (2015) 'Solidarity-based initiatives: field realities and analysis', in Jacques Defourny, Lars Hulgård, and Victor Pestoff (eds). *Social enterprise and the third sector: changing European landscapes in a comparative perspective*. London: Routledge, 114–29.

Gibson-Graham, J. K. (2006). *A postcapitalist politics*. Minneapolis, MN: University of Minnesota Press.

Gilbert, Neil (2002). *Transformation of the welfare state: the silent surrender of public responsibility*. Oxford: Oxford University Press.

Glémain, Pascal (2009). 'The French context of microfinance: a socioeconomic approach of short financial relationships through modern "solidarity-based" financial structures and actors', *International Journal of Social Economics* 36(12): 1118–32.

Guala, Francesco (2012). 'Reciprocity: weak or strong? What punishment experiments do (and do not) demonstrate', *Behavioral and Brain Sciences* 35(1): 1–59.

Habermas, Jürgen (1989). *The structural transformation of the public sphere*. Cambridge, MA: MIT Press.

Habermas, Jürgen (1995). *Theorie des kommunikativen Handelns*. Vols 1 and 2. Frankfurt am Main: Suhrkamp Verlag.

Habermas, Jürgen (1996). *Between facts and norms: contributions to a discourse theory of law and democracy*. Cambridge, MA: MIT Press.

Hart, Keith, Jean-Louis Laville, and Antonio David Cattani (2010). *The human economy*. Cambridge: Polity Press.

Healy, Stephen (2008). 'Alternative economies', in Rob Kitchin and Nigel Thrift (eds). *International encyclopedia of human geography*. Vol. 3. Oxford: Elsevier, 338–44.

Hillenkamp, Isabelle (2011). 'Solidarités, marché et démocratie: éclairages boliviens', *Finance & Bien Commun* 37–8: 76–95.

Hulgård, Lars (2011). 'Social economy and social enterprise: an emerging alternative to mainstream market economy?', *China Journal of Social Work* 4(3): 201–15.

Hulgård, Lars (2014). 'El futuro de la socialdemocracia', in José Luis Coraggio and Jean-Louis Laville (eds). *Reinventar la izquierda en el siglo XXI*. Buenos Aires: Clasco.

Hulgård, Lars (2015). 'Differing perspectives on civil society and the state', in Jean-Louis Laville, Denis Young, and Philippe Eynaud (eds). *Civil society, the third sector and social enterprise: governance and democracy*. London: Routledge, 204–22.

Hulgård, Lars and Linda L. Andersen (2012). 'Socialt entreprenørskab – velfærdsafvikling eller arenaer for solidaritet', *Dansk Sociologi* 23(4): 11–28.

Imbusch, Peter und Dieter Rucht (2005). 'Integration und Desintegration in modernen Gesellschaften', in Wilhelm Heitmeyer and Peter Imbusch (eds). *Integrationspotentiale einer modernen Gesellschaft*. Wiesbaden: VS Verlag, 13–71.

Kawano, Emily, Thomas N. Masterson, and Jonathan Teller-Elsberg (2009). *Solidarity economy I: building alternatives for people and planet*. Amherst, MA: Center for Popular Economics.

Kiser, Larry and Elinor Ostrom (2000). 'The three worlds of action: a metatheoretical synthesis of institutional approaches', in Michael McGinnis (ed.). *Polycentric games and institutions*. Ann Arbor, MI: University of Michigan Press, 56–88.

Klein, Ansgar (2000). *Der Diskurs der Zivilgesellschaft*. Münster: Arbeitsstelle Aktive Bürgerschaft.

Laville, Jean-Louis (2003). 'A new European socioeconomic perspective', *Review of Social Economy* 61(3): 389–405.

Laville, Jean-Louis (2010). 'Plural economy', in Keith Hart, Jean-Louis Laville, and Antonio David Cattani (eds). *The human economy*. Cambridge: Polity Press.

Laville, Jean-Louis (2015). 'Social and solidarity economy in historical perspective', in Peter Utting (ed.). *Social and solidarity economy: beyond the fringe*. London: Zed Books.
Laville, Jean-Louis and Antonio David Cattani (eds) (2006). *Dictionnaire de l'autre économie*. Paris: Gallimard.
Laville, Jean-Louis and Lars Hulgård (2017). 'Solidarity economy, reciprocity and social innovation', paper presented at EMES Conference, Louvain-la-Neuve, 3–6 July 2017.
Laville, Jean-Louis, Andreia Lemaître, and Marthe Nyssens (2006). 'Public policies and social enterprises in Europe: the challenge of institutionalization', in Marthe Nyssens (ed.). *Social enterprise: at the crossroads of market, public policies and civil society*. London: Routledge, 272–95.
Laville, Jean-Louis and Anne Salmon (2015). 'Rethinking the relationship between governance and democracy: the theoretical framework of the solidarity economy', in Jean-Louis Laville, Denis Young, and Philippe Eynaud (eds). *Civil society, the third sector and social enterprise: governance and democracy*. London: Routledge, 145–62.
Lawrence, Thomas B. and Roy Suddaby (2006). 'Institutions and institutional work', in Stewart R. Clegg, Cynthia Hardy, Thomas B. Lawrence, and Walter R. Nord (eds). *SAGE handbook of organization studies*. London: SAGE, 215–54.
Lovera, Arianna (2015). 'Debts, differently: alternative finance organizations in Italy and France', *Partecipazione & Conflitto* 8(2): 585–608.
Mair, Johanna (2010). 'Social entrepreneurship: taking stock and looking ahead', in Alain Fayolle and Harry Matlay (eds). *Handbook of research on social entrepreneurship*. Cheltenham: Edward Elgar.
Malinowski, Bronislaw (1978). *Argonauts of the Western Pacific*. London: Routledge.
Mauss, Marcel (2011). *The gift: forms and functions of exchange in archaic societies*. Eastford, CT: Martino Fine Books.
Moulaert, Frank and Oana Ailenai (2005). 'Social economy, third sector and solidarity relations: a conceptual synthesis from history to present', *Urban Studies* 42(11): 2037–53.
Nicholls, Alex and Benjamin Huybrechts (2016). 'Sustaining inter-organizational relationships across institutional logics and power asymmetries: the case of fair trade', *Journal of Business Ethics* 135(4): 699–714.
Nyssens, Marthe (2006). *Social enterprise: at the crossroads of market, public policies and civil society*. London: Routledge.
Nyssens, Marthe and Francesca Petrella (2015). 'The social and solidarity economy and Ostrom's approach to common pool resources: towards a better understanding of institutional diversity?' in Jean-Louis Laville, Denis Young, and Philippe Eynaud (eds). *Civil society, the third sector and social enterprise: governance and democracy*. London: Routledge, 178–90.
Ostrom, Elinor (1990). *Governing the commons: the evolution of institutions for collective action*. Cambridge: Cambridge University Press.
Ould Ahmed, Pepita (2010). 'Can a community currency be independent of the state currency?' *Environment and Planning A* 42(6): 1346–464.
Ould Ahmed, Pepita (2015). 'What does "solidarity economy" mean? Contours and feasibility of a theoretical and political project', *Business Ethics: A European Review* 24(4): 425–35.
Pacione, Michael (1998). 'Toward a community economy: an examination of local exchange trading systems in West Glasgow', *Urban Geography* 19(3): 211–31.
Pestoff, Victor (2005). 'Democratizing the welfare state', paper prepared for the EGPA Third Sector Study Group Conference, Bern, Switzerland.

Pestoff, Victor (2014). 'Hybridity, innovation and the third sector: the co-production of public services', in Jacques Defourny, Lars Hulgård, and Victor Pestoff (eds). *Social enterprise and the third sector: changing European landscapes in a comparative perspective.* London: Routledge, 250–69.

Pestoff, Victor and Lars Hulgård (2016). 'Participatory governance in social enterprise', *Voluntas* 27(4): 1742–59.

Piketty, Thomas (2014). *Capital in the twenty-first century.* Cambridge, MA: Harvard University Press.

Polanyi, Karl (1944). *The great transformation: the political and economic origins of our time.* Boston: Beacon Press.

Polanyi, Karl (1957). 'The economy as instituted process', in Karl Polanyi, Conrad Arensberg, and Harry Pearson (eds). *Trade and market in the early empires: economies in history and theory.* Glencoe, IL: The Free Press, 243–70.

Poteete, Amy R., Marco A. Janssen, and Elinor Ostrom (2010). *Working together: collective action, the commons and multiple methods in practice.* Princeton, NJ: Princeton University Press.

Putnam, Robert (2000). *Bowling alone: the collapse and revival of American community.* New York: Simon & Schuster.

Roy, Michael (2015). 'Conceptualizing social enterprise as a health and well-being "intervention"', PhD thesis, Glasgow Caledonian University.

Sahakian, Marlyne D. and Christope Dunand (2015). 'The social and solidarity economy towards greater "sustainability": learning across contexts and cultures, from Geneva to Manila', *Community Development Journal* 50(3): 403–17.

Salamon, Lester M. and Wojciech Sokolowski (2016). 'The size and scope of the European third sector', TSI Working Paper No. 12. Brussels: Third Sector Impact.

Satgar, Vishwas (2014). *The solidarity economy alternative: emerging theory and practice.* Pietermaritzburg: University of KwaZulu-Natal Press.

Schlager, Edella and Elinor Ostrom (1992). 'Property rights regimes and natural resources: a conceptual analysis', *Land Economics* 68(3): 249–62.

Somers, Margaret (2008). *Genealogies of citizenship: markets, statelessness, and the right to have rights.* Cambridge: Cambridge University Press.

Streeck, Wolfgang (1999). Competitive solidarity: rethinking the "European Social Model"', MPIfG Working Paper No. 99/8. Köln: Max-Planck-Institut für Gesellschaftsforschung.

Sumiala, Johanna and Katja Valaskivi (2014). 'Circulation, reciprocity and activism: an interview with Professor Michael Herzfeld', *European Journal of Cultural Studies* 17(3): 275–81.

Temple, Dominique and Mireille Chabal (1995). *La réciprocité et la naissance des valeurs humaines.* Paris: L'Harmattan.

Titmuss, Richard M. (1974). *Social policy.* London: Allen and Unwin.

Utting, Peter (ed.) (2015). *Social and solidarity economy: beyond the fringe.* London: Zed Books.

Vail, John (2010). 'Decommodification and egalitarian political economy', *Politics and Society* 38(3): 310–46.

Vaillancourt, Yves and Jean-Louis Laville (1998). 'Les rapports entre associations et État: un enjeu politique', *Revue du MAUSS* 11: 119–35.

van der Linden, Marcel (2008). 'Consumer cooperatives', in Marcel van der Linden. *Workers of the world.* Leiden: Brill, 133–50.

Wijkström, Filip (2011). '"Charity speak and business talk": the on-going (re)hybridization of civil society', in Filip Wijkström and Annette Zimmer (eds). *Nordic civil society at a cross-roads*. Baden-Baden: Nomos.

Zimmer, Annette and Benedikt Pahl (2016). 'Learning from Europe: report on third sector enabling and disabling factors', TSI Comparative Report No. 1. Brussels: Third Sector Impact.

8 Social capitalism is a thing of the past

Competition-driven *Landnahme* and the metamorphosis of the German Model

Klaus Dörre

I assume we all remember how we felt in 2009, during what seemed like an unimaginably deep crisis. The global financial crash affected the German export sector with full force and, for a brief moment, it appeared as if Germany would enter a phase of de-industrialisation similar to that already seen in Great Britain, albeit in a less radical form. This, however, did not occur. Despite levels of negative growth unprecedented in the post-war era, a disastrous wave of layoffs was ultimately averted. The combination of swiftly recovering demand from the larger emerging economies and China in particular, the subsidised employment of core workforces (long-term short-time work), and a bastardised form of Keynesianism that boosted the sales of new cars through a premium (*Abwrack-prämie*) paid for scrapping used automobiles facilitated a relatively smooth landing for the German economy. Ever since, we have seen record levels of employment across the country. The German job miracle, currently employing 43 million economically active people, is now hailed as the model for Europe in elite discourse. According to Italian philosopher Angelo Bolaffi, Germany plays 'a hegemonial role' and is 'the better social model' (Bolaffi 2014b). In his view, this has been accomplished through a partnership between capital and labour that is not only intact but has successfully adapted, through the policies of the 'Agenda 2010' and labour market reforms, to the framework conditions of a globalised economy (Bolaffi 2014a: 130). Such enthusiasm and praise make criticism of the 'German Model' seem out of place. Whoever nevertheless dares to point out the downside of the German job miracle is quickly accused of fear-mongering or even populism (Jacobi and Müller-Jentsch 2017).

That being said, polemical interventions should not prevent social scientists and the interested public from acknowledging and interpreting social realities. Talking heads who loudly proclaim the Canticles of the Social Market Economy and even celebrate it as a model for Europe and the rest of the world fail to take the metamorphoses of German social capitalism caused by the market-driven *Landnahme*[1] into account. I, for my part, claim that the old Fordist social capitalism is a thing of the past in Germany, as it is in the rest of the world. Modern capitalism rests on a form of competitive solidarity which combines domestic selective social inclusion with half-hegemonic economic dominance in Europe. Whoever speaks of the German Model today is thus referring to something very different from the successful social capitalism of the past. He or she would instead be referring to the advantages of an export-oriented variety of capitalism that has contributed significantly to the ongoing crisis in the EU. This chapter will flesh out this argument in several steps. To begin with, the chapter outlines the basics of German social capitalism, before presenting an assessment of the transition to competitive solidarity as a process of capitalist *Landnahme*. Next, the chapter analyses the German job miracle as the emergence of a precarious full-employment and de-mobilised class society. To conclude, some of the changes still ongoing are discussed. For pragmatic reasons, I will largely confine my deliberations to the labour market and labour relations, although I am fully aware that the political economy of German capitalism in Europe deserves a more thorough analysis.

(West) German social capitalism

Let us start with the specific characteristics of the old 'German Model'. What exactly does this label entail? How has this model of capitalism changed since the early 1990s? Is it still possible to speak of *the* German Model today? The neo-institutionalist literature (Berghahn and Vitols 2006; Beyer 2003; Crouch and Streeck 1997; Hall and Soskice 2001) depicts West German *social* capitalism as an example of a capitalist society in which corporate actors can orient the pursuit of profits towards the long term, thus balancing profit-seeking with the interests of organised labour (Albert 1992; Shonfield 1964). Key to this balance was diversified high-quality production in market niches that could support relatively high wages. Production occurred in the context of key institutions, including central banks, dual vocational education and training,[2] and a distinct system of German labour relations – company-wide collective bargaining agreements, sector-specific wages for different regions, and flexible adjustment at the shop floor level (Abelshauser 2005; Hassel 2006; Streeck 1997). The class struggle was fought at the industry-wide level, while individual companies faced a more or less vigorous representation of interests that ensured cooperative and flexible adjustment of wage standards to the respective local conditions (Kotthoff 1994; Müller-Jentsch 2008: 51–78; Thelen 2014). It was accepted that wage norms took priority over in-house agreements, leading to a 'convoy' effect. Militant workforces at large companies could push through agreements in exemplary labour conflicts, which would then also go into effect for less well-organised workers (Dörre 2010: 873–912). The state only provided negotiating parties with a legal framework, while labour and management could draw on a comprehensive set of labour laws.

Questions arose during the 1990s whether this dual system of interest representation by works councils at the enterprise level and wage regulation at the industry-wide level could survive in a globalised world. Social capitalism had to fight for its survival, being pressured by problems resulting from German reunification and economic globalisation. It was widely held that, ultimately, traditionalist German economic culture with all of its collectivist traditions would be unable to resist the temptations of the American individualist model. For instance, Wolfgang Streeck (1997: 33–54) claimed that the 'deregulating tendency of globalization' was threatening to produce the 'perverse outcome' in which the 'less productive Anglo-American model of capitalism may replace the more efficient "Rhenish model" '.

From this perspective, it must seem only natural that German social capitalism was fundamentally reformed post-2000. The Social Democratic and Green government (1998–2005), in particular, oversaw several reforms introducing elements of competition into the social security systems, partially privatising social protection against social risks, liberalising access to financial markets, weakening labour market protections, and promoting atypical and often precarious forms of employment (Gumbrell-McCormick 2011: 293–310; Holst and Dörre 2013: 132–49; Lehndorff 2012; Streeck 2009). The hope that corporatist regulation of interests could adapt to the reconfigured framework by building social compromise based on a supply side orientation, i.e. the shared concern for enterprise competitiveness, was abandoned following the failure of the tripartite Alliance for Jobs, Training and Competitiveness (Heinze 2006). Changes in the system of collective bargaining, which at least for a while could have been interpreted as a kind of 'coordinated decentralisation' embedded in corporatist arrangements (Rehder 2003), in reality meant a weakening of labour unions (Brinkmann *et al.* 2008; Gumbrell-McCormick and Hyman 2013; Urban 2013). At the same time, the capacity for tripartite deals that mobilised support from trade unions for government projects was severely reduced after the politics of the 'Agenda 2010'[3] had alienated the trade unions and their membership. Social Democracy lost influence among white- and blue-collar workers, and has not recovered it to this day. A parallel development to the introduction of the 'Hartz Reforms' was the rise of the Left Party (*Die Linke*), which managed to establish itself at the national level during this period. A substantial segment of working-class voters as well as of trade union members, however, does not lean to the left but rather votes conservative or even for the right-populist *Alternative für Deutschland* (AfD, 'Alternative for Germany'). The outcome of all this is that the traditionally close ties between the trade unions united under the umbrella of the DGB (German Federation of Trade Unions) and the SPD have loosened noticeably (Brenke and Kritikos 2017; Rennwald 2015).

Capitalist *Landnahme*

We call these changes '*Landnahme*', a selective expropriation of wage earners' social assets (Dörre 2009, 2011a). There is no adequate English translation of the German term *Landnahme* and thus, when Michael Burawoy spoke of 'the *Landnahme*' in his address to the International Sociological Association (Burawoy 2015), this was obviously a small triumph for Germanists around the world – a tiny spot that has avoided conquest by English, the world's *lingua franca*. *Landnahme* is a socio-economic concept, a category central to theories which seek to analyse and criticise industrial capitalism as an expansive system. These theories are united in their assumption that capitalist societies cannot reproduce themselves exclusively from within. Capitalist development always occurs as a complex internal-external movement. It commonly involves the internalisation of some form of the external, the conquest of a not (yet) fully commodified Other. In contrast to what the term might suggest, *Landnahmen* (plural) do not exhaust themselves in a socio-spatial or physico-material dimension. The expansion of capitalism occurs within space and time. It unfolds both within and outside of national societies. It proceeds sectorally as well as in a field-specific way, encompassing distinct modes of production, social groups, life forms and even personality structures (Dörre 2009, 2015).

The nub of the matter is that the 'primitive accumulation' Marx describes in the first volume of *Capital* (Marx 1973) is periodically repeated. Capitalist *Landnahme* requires the use and exploitation of non-capitalist milieux, which it encounters outside and within certain not (yet) commercialised sectors of capitalist societies. Each time the accumulation of capital encounters obstacles which cannot be surmounted within existing forms, a special intervention is needed to get the process back on track. In such periods, political disciplining, repression, violence, over-exploitation, and breaches of social norms are common. However, in contrast to Rosa Luxemburg's assumption, these continuous *Landnahmen* do not lead to the collapse of capitalism (Luxemburg 1975). Instead, a non-capitalist Other can be actively created (Harvey 2005: 140). The chain of *Landnahmen* is thus potentially endless. The 'blasting apart of purely economic regularities through political action' (Arendt 2006: 335) can and must repeat itself constantly on an ever-expanding scale to allow for new *Landnahmen* that help capitalism reproduce itself.[4]

The welfare state represents a functional non-capitalist Other to capital. This is the point from which a contemporary analysis of a *Landnahme* of the social proceeds. The new *Landnahme* strengthens private-capitalist ownership rights, driving re-commodification of areas of life previously withdrawn and thereby protected from the market. It rests on the subordination of economic activities to the rules of liberalised financial markets and restrictive fiscal policies. At its centre lies the weakening of wage earners' power. Moreover, it amounts to restrictions on or even selective dispossession of publicly owned goods.

The financialised *Landnahme* which has engulfed major capitalist economies since the 1980s creates an *exterior* through re-commodification and social exclusion (de-commodification). Employees are released from the protections of the welfare state and in some cases driven out of the production process altogether, only to be reintegrated under precarious conditions, which eliminate some of the social and participatory rights of a 'social citizen' in German capitalism (Castel 2005). The *modus operandi* of financial capitalist *Landnahmen* includes institutions, forms of social organisation, and social rules. The co-determined, negotiated enterprise and organised labour relations thus become targets. Policies of (re-)commodification in business and throughout society lead to fewer social assets and a more selective distribution of the remaining goods. Social assets refer to 'assets to maintain one's existence', which the welfare state provides to those who previously had no such assets. These are the equivalent of social security provisions: eligibility for pensions, health care, wage norms, etc. (ibid.: 41). *Landnahme* then means that the protective shield of the welfare state is peeled away layer by layer, resulting in a rising number of precariously employed workers (low-wage workers, temporary workers, special order contractors, fixed-term and marginally employed, single self-employed, involuntary part-timers, 'multi-jobbers' and zero-hour contracts). They are exposed to an above-average risk of poverty and unemployment and disadvantaged in terms of participatory rights, occupational safety, health insurance, and pension benefits (Brinkmann *et al.* 2006; Castel and Dörre 2009).

The competition-driven *Landnahme*, however, occurs at different speeds as it is modified and influenced by field-specific and sector-specific counter-movements. Trade unions, for example, still have their strongholds in manufacturing. Moreover, Germany relies more heavily on its manufacturing sector than other countries. With a share of 22.4 per cent of total gross value added (GVA) in Germany in 2012, the country's industrial base is still relatively broad (Deutsche Bank 2013: 1–5) and has remained stable since the onset of the global economic crisis. Moreover, with a share of 30.5 per cent of the EU's GVA, Germany is by far the most important European industrial nation. Mechanical engineering and automotive industries are the heart of German manufacturing, with each accounting for about 16 per cent of industrial GVA in 2011. Both sectors are characterised by their high export ratios, respectively 62 per cent and 64 per cent of the goods produced in 2012. These industries are deeply anchored in German society. Many companies look back on long traditions and cooperate closely with established suppliers, equipment dealers, and research institutions. The technology-intensive sectors employ about 40 per cent of all industrial workers (Deutsche Bank 2013). These firms enjoy good international standing, even though they are often medium-sized and family-owned (Amable 2003; Berghahn 1986; Quack 2006: 63–85). German manufacturing has adapted to growing demand from Asia, particularly from China. German-made products are often necessary for these economies to catch up economically and highly desired by an emerging Chinese middle class, making it possible 'to increase industrial value creation in Germany, although it remains a high-wage location' (Deutsche Bank 2013: 7).

Furthermore, the trend towards shifting production abroad waned despite relatively high labour costs, with an average of almost €37 per hour as compared to €10 in the Czech Republic and €6.65 in Poland (ibid.: 6). Approximately 25 per cent of firms reported shifting production abroad between the mid-1990s and the early 2000s, but only about 15 per cent of firms in 2006 indicated that they had shifted production abroad over the preceding two years, while the figure dropped to only 11 per cent by 2010–11 (Fraunhofer ISI 2013). In 2003, 87 per cent of companies relocating production stated that the main reason for this move was lower wage costs abroad; by 2012, this figure had dropped to 71 per cent. Generally, the labour cost share in manufacturing has decreased and eventually fallen below 20 per cent (Deutsche Bank 2013: 13). Manufacturing's stability and export capacity allow for co-determination and labour relations to remain comparatively stable within the organisational sector of the metalworkers' union, IG Metall. While employees in other sectors accept above-average losses, those in the manufacturing export economy have managed to maintain their actual earnings or even increase them (Hauptmann and Schmerer 2012). Industry 4.0 represents an ambitious project conducted by both the private economy and the state, aiming to improve Germany's competitive advantages over the course of the digitalisation of its production model. At least in the productive sector, Germany appears to be continuing to pursue a path of rationalisation which many businesses had already embarked on during the lean production debate of the 1990s (Butollo *et al.* 2017). The future effects of this rationalisation path remain unknown for the time being; thus far, however, digitalisation has not led to any significant job losses in Germany industry.

Expansion of the industrial export sector and the relative stability of corresponding labour relations, however, should not blind us to the fact that this economic success rests on a competitive solidarity accompanied by a significant weakening of wage earners' institutional and organisational power, as well as selective dispossession of social goods. A complex blend of factors has driven and continues to drive the metamorphosis of erstwhile social capitalism forward.

(1) *Altered ownership relations.* The old network of Germany, Inc. ('*Deutschland AG*'), in which credit institutions and market leaders supported each other by promoting common industrial policies, has been destroyed by the internationalisation strategies of export-oriented companies and the market for corporate control. In contrast to the 1990s, when internationalisation primarily meant capital exports, today Germany has become a popular market for foreign direct investment (FDI). This capital inflow has also triggered a shift in the ownership relations of many major corporations. While the share of stocks held by foreigners in 24 DAX (*Deutscher Aktienindex*) companies was at 45 per cent in 2005, it rose to about 57 per cent by 2012. As a result of this altered ownership structure, the old network of Germany, Inc. has been replaced by international corporate management networks. Here, financial market actors have greater influence over operations even when owning relatively few shares in a company, avoiding costly control practices.

(2) *Capital market-oriented corporate governance.* Altered ownership relations have facilitated a transition to capital market-oriented forms of corporate management and the financialisation of corporate organisation as a whole. German corporations once guided by stable, negotiated relations between capital and labour are now subjected to a system of strict profit control. In export-oriented companies, profit targets are broken down by company headquarters and transmitted to the various facilities and decentralised units via benchmark schemes. As a consequence, branches and profit centres for financial controlling may operate at a loss even when generating profits, in that they may nevertheless fail to meet specified targets. The precise instruments for implementing tight profit management differ from company to company. These include equity

returns (economic value added, EVA) or operative earnings before interests and taxes (EBIT). The main aim, however, is always to secure a minimum return for the company. Less profitable departments are restructured or their functions outsourced, which in turn represents an important impetus for the emergence of transnational value chains and production networks. The pursuit of relatively stable profit margins in volatile markets is conducted via long-established instruments which, however, take on new meaning in the value-based mode of corporate governance. Thus, human resource planning is guided by the 'median' of an average workload. Sales fluctuations, both upwards and downwards, are to be buffered by flexible staff. From the perspective of financialised corporate governance, permanently employing a worker becomes an investment that absorbs capital for decades to come. Such investments are to be made with as little risk as possible in volatile markets. Headcounts (specific targets for employment equivalents) and the strict budgeting of business activities are the levers with which to limit such investments. If decentralised management cannot meet targets with their specified full-time equivalents, the only plausible options become outsourcing, temporary labour, special-order contracts, or other forms of flexible employment which can then even be – as is particularly the case for temporary work – written off as material expenses. This leads to a lasting division of workforces.

Take the automobile industry around Leipzig, for example, which accounts for about 18,000 jobs. Only 8,300 of these jobs are permanent positions at Porsche and BMW, while the rest are with supplier companies, special-order contractors, or temporary work. Almost 30 per cent of surveyed wage earners have a gross monthly income of less than €1,750, even with all possible overtime and bonuses. Almost 44 per cent have no money left to go on holiday, despite the fact that 90 per cent also work at weekends and national holidays (Dörre *et al.* 2013a; IG Metall 2015).[5] Temporary workers are hired in addition to permanent employees by the same company: in our case study, this was the BMW plant in Leipzig. We also find permanent de facto temporary workers employed by subcontractors whose services are purchased through special-order contracts, and in turn differ from the temporary workers hired by that same subcontracting company. As a result, a peculiar kind of stability through unstable employment emerges. Grouped around the core workforces of end-producers almost like concentric circles, we find varying precarious forms of employment – the wages, standards of security, and work quality of which decrease, the greater the distance from the core workforce.

(3) *Fragmented labour relations.* This development is accompanied by drastic changes in the German labour relations system. Of particular note here is the decline in trade unions' organisational power. The unionisation rate in the former West Germany was at roughly 35 per cent of all workers in 1980 but declined to 18 per cent for all of Germany by 2015. As a result of this erosion of trade union organisational power, the incentive for corporations to organise in employers' associations has also waned. Responding to losses in membership or to a simple refusal on the part of corporations to become members in the first place, many

employers' associations introduced a new form of membership that no longer ties members to collective bargaining agreements. As a result, trade unions have lost their traditional negotiating counterpart in some sectors. In general, compliance with collective bargaining agreements has been declining. However, we have not seen an all-out assault on trade unions, the collective bargaining system, or the structures of co-determination in Germany. Rather, the erosion of organised industrial relations has taken place through incremental reforms (Dörre 2011b: 8–48). These nevertheless amount to severe changes in the system of German labour relations, even though they are obscured by the existence of formally intact institutions.

The number of wage earners paid according to collective agreements is disproportionately lower in the 'new' states of eastern Germany than in the West (Figure 8.1).

The share of companies committed to industry-wide bargaining agreements in West Germany was still 31 per cent in 2014 (in 2000: 45 per cent), but true for only 17 per cent of companies in the East (in 2000: 23 per cent). We find a similar picture with regard to wage earners paid according to collective bargaining agreements. In 2000, 60 per cent of wage earners in the West and 39 per cent in the East were paid according to industry-wide wage agreements. By 2014, this number had declined to 47 per cent in the West and 28 per cent in the East. This decline was not compensated by company-level agreements, however. As had already been the case by the year 2000, in-house and internal company-level labour agreements accounted for only 7 per cent of West German and 11 per cent of East German wage earners (Ellguth and Kohaut 2015: 290–7; Kohaut 2007). However, these numbers also underscore the fact that decentralised company-level and in-house agreements played a role in the East earlier than in the West. The proportion of

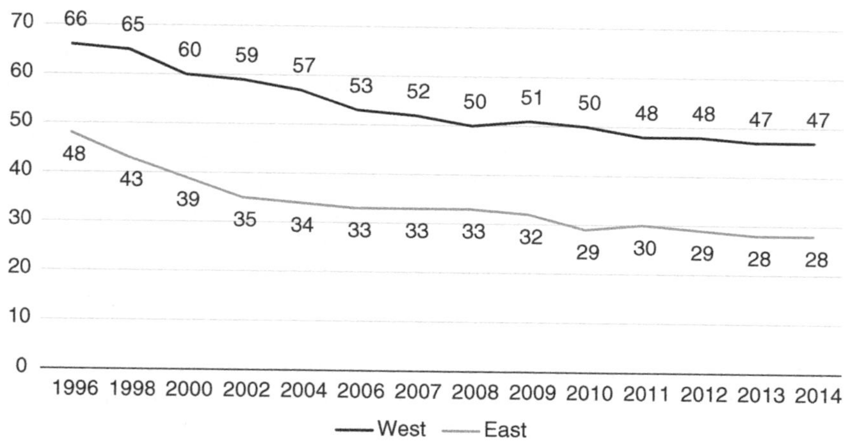

Figure 8.1 Collective agreement coverage in the private sector, share of employees (%).
Source: author's elaboration based on Ellguth and Kohaut (2015).

companies in industry-related support services committed to collective bargaining agreements lies at only about 14 per cent in West Germany and 18 per cent in East Germany (Ellguth and Kohaut 2011; Helfen 2011).

This erosion of collective bargaining fosters low-wage competition and a fragmentation of collective bargaining, characterised by under-cutting and out-bidding. Small trade unions in certain professional branches where occupational groups possess high primary power (pilots, doctors, engine drivers, air traffic controllers, etc.) may manage to realise demands that the conglomerate trade unions (Ver.di, IG Metall, IG BCE) can barely dream of. On the other hand, small splinter unions in poorly organised sectors such as temporary labour have long accepted labour contracts that involve low wages of less than €5 an hour. In sum, the lack of compliance with collective bargaining agreements has contributed to the erosion of the organisational and institutional power of wage earners.[6]

Indications of the erosion of institutional wage earners' power can also be seen in the second pillar of German industrial relations: the prevalence of works councils. At first glance, there hardly seems to be any difference between West and East Germany in this regard, as there were works councils in 9 per cent of the companies in both halves of the country in 2014. Once we consider the numbers of employees represented by a works council, however, the differences become quite clear indeed: in 2014, 33 per cent of employees in the East and around 43 per cent in the West (Ellguth and Kohaut 2015: 294). In manufacturing industry, which the main body of companies we surveyed are part of, works councils were more prevalent. In 2013, there were works councils in 16 per cent of the West German businesses and in 11 per cent in the East, representing a total of 69 per cent (West) and 48 per cent (East) of the workforce respectively (Ellguth and Kohaut 2014: 292, 2015).

(4) *Labour market reforms.* This transformation necessarily required market-centred political reforms. The most important of these measures is the so-called 'Hartz Reforms', whose protagonists viewed the long-term unemployed as a passive 'Lazarus layer' of the working class, lacking initiative and unwilling to advance socially. In order to change this 'passive mentality', conditions for the long-term unemployed were to be made as uncomfortable as possible. In the form of a special body of laws (the 'Hartz laws'), the standard rates of unemployment benefits were to be lowered to the level of basic security benefits after one year of unemployment. The labour authorities, namely, the 'job centres', now enjoy extensive authority to encroach upon and control the private lives of benefit seekers and intervene in their residential and financial situations. Adding to this is the fact that the recipients' entitlement is subject to continuous review. Assets, savings, and income, of the so-called 'benefit community' are monitored and calculated into benefit entitlements. Such a 'benefit community' includes all the members of a household. Because of the abolition of individual benefits eligibility, it is becoming increasingly difficult for entitlement claims to be recognised altogether. Moreover, employability itself has been redefined. Anyone able to pursue gainful employment for more than three hours per day is considered fit

for employment. These measures, which also include the revaluation of non-standardised forms of employment, such as temporary labour, are tied to strict rules concerning what work claimants can be reasonably expected to do, as well as the corresponding sanctions should they refuse. Benefit recipients must be prepared to resettle in order to take up a position and are expected to work far below their previous income and qualification level. Any type of work that unemployed people are physically, intellectually, and emotionally capable of performing is deemed reasonable. As turning down potential job offers may lead to further sanctioning, those affected are often forced to lower their standards concerning remuneration and quality of work.

In addition to tight profit control, corporate financialisation, and the aforementioned labour market reforms, market-centred policies in the areas of social security, health, education and care work have gradually extended the principle of competition into spheres of society beyond the export economy. In orchestrated, organisation-internal 'quasi-markets', bureaucratic instruments, such as budgeting, rankings, ratings, or target specifications, are applied in hospitals, universities, public administration, but also in elderly care as well as in youth and social work, so as to universalise the logic of competition (Schimank and Volkmann 2017). However, competition inevitably produces winners and losers. As neo-liberal pioneer Friedrich von Hayek once put it: comparatively more rational individuals can thus 'make it necessary' for the rest 'to emulate them, in order to prevail'. This 'competification' of society, which we call the *Landnahme* of the social, is based on a selective dispossession of 'social property' or the commons. Targets include institutions, forms of social organisation, and social rules designed to limit the effects of market-based coordination mechanisms. *Landnahme*, in this case, means that the protective shield of the welfare state, which ascribed to wage labour a recognised social status and transformed it into a central medium of social integration, is gradually being cut down, bit by bit. In Germany, this process has received a tremendous boost from the labour market reforms. The reforms, which initially appeared incremental and gradual, in sum, constitute a change of the model as such. The old social capitalism is a thing of the past, and whoever praises its ongoing vitality and adaptability has most likely been taken in by a myth.

Precarious full-employment society

This assessment absolutely applies to the labour market as well. Pressured by labour market reforms, the precarisation of work and employment has progressed even further, while the Hartz reforms have been crucial in the emergence of a precarious full-employment society (Dörre *et al.* 2013b).[7] Unemployment has consistently declined since 2005 – except for a brief increase in 2009. Between 1995 and 2014, the unemployment rate, which reached its peak of 11.7 per cent in 2005, dropped from 9.5 to 6.7 per cent. At the same time, the rate of gainful employment has increased considerably. Compared to 1991, the number of economically active people rose by roughly 3.7 million by 2014. Particularly striking, however, is that the volume of paid working hours is still below the figure for 1991 – despite the aforementioned record number of economically active people in 2014. While in 1991 a total of 63.3 billion hours worked were counted, only 58.3 billion hours worked are registered for 2014 (in 2005: 55.5 billion hours). This tendency is even more pronounced when considering the average number of paid hours worked per wage earner. In 1991, each economically active person still worked some 1,554 hours a month, but worked only 1,366 hours by 2014 – a decline of 12 per cent. The total volume of labour reached its lowest point in 2013 (1,362 hours). Ongoing growth aside, the volume of paid hours worked in 2016 remained below that of 1991, accompanied by a record number of economically active people. In sum, then, we can say that a shrinking volume of work, albeit rising again ever so slightly since 2005, is shared between ever more economically active people – and in a strongly asymmetrical manner. While the highly qualified tend to work excessive hours of over 50 hours per week or more, those in atypical or precarious employment are often underemployed against their will. Many of them work less than 12 hours per week. The actual average working hours of wage earners are significantly above the 40-hour mark once again, even in the relatively well-organised metal and electronics industries. The 35-hour week as stipulated by a fair number of collective bargaining agreements often exists only on paper.

It is worth noting that job creation occurs to a large extent via the integration of female workers, particularly in the service sector and mainly in atypical forms of employment.[8] Non-standardised forms of employment relations as a share of total employment rose to 38 per cent in the East and 39 per cent in the West in 2013. In 2014, about one in five economically active people (21 per cent, or 7.5 million in absolute numbers; in 2004: 19 per cent) worked in an 'atypical' job, meaning in part-time, marginal, or temporary employment or as part of a hired labour force. Indeed, not every atypical form of employment is precarious, but neither is precarity limited to these forms of work. Germany today has one of the largest low-wage sectors of all OECD countries, regularly accounting for 22–24 per cent of economically active people as a whole (Bosch 2014). More than 10 per cent of people working full-time are employed in the low-wage sector. Adding to them are the increasing numbers of solo freelancers, also largely precarious. About 5 per cent of wage earners are multi-jobbers who pursue several jobs as the only way to make ends meet for their families. These figures suffice to illustrate that precarity has by no means disappeared from the German job market. On the contrary, unemployment and long-term unemployment are being reduced via the expansion of precarious work and employment relations. Despite favourable economic and demographic developments, atypical forms of employment have receded only slightly since 2010; the hidden labour reserve, by contrast, remained at six million in 2014 (2.1 million unemployed, 2.9 million underemployed, one million hidden reserve).

Hardly any less significant than the emergence of a precarious full-employment society is the tendency towards class formation at, or slightly below, the threshold of social respectability. Crucial factors here were activating labour market policies as well as the Hartz IV reforms. The main effect of Hartz IV has been to shift the threshold of social respectability closer to the 'zone of normality' in socio-spatial terms. Anyone remaining unemployed for more than a year risks descending to Hartz IV status and thus slipping below the threshold of social respectability. Although the number of long-term unemployed declined by about 40 per cent between 2006 and 2011, stalling at that level ever since, there is an entrenched core of roughly one million people who have never left the benefit system over an entire decade. In 2014, a total 4.4 million people depended on social benefits, 3.1 million of whom were long-term recipients. That said, only half of all benefit recipients were actually unemployed, and only 770,000 people were both long-term unemployed and long-term benefit recipients.

What are the specific measures of the Hartz reforms that were implemented during the second term of the Schröder government? Initially, the reforms were a reaction to the fact that the number of long-term unemployed in Germany was doubling during each economic cycle. From the viewpoint of the reformers, the long-term unemployed represented a passive Lazarus-like social layer, lacking self-initiative and the will to advance. In order to change this, the status of long-term unemployed people was to be made as uncomfortable as possible. To this end, several packages of measures were introduced in the shape of the laws on Modern Services on the Labour Market, of which I will name only a few.

First, the former unemployment benefits and social assistance (*Sozialhilfe*), were merged into the new social system of *Arbeitslosengeld II* (Hartz IV). The standard benefit rates in this new system were established at the level of the former social assistance (*Sozialhilfe*). These standard benefit rates were set in 2017 at €409 a month for single adults and at €374 for members of a 'benefit community' (*Bedarfsgemeinschaft*). There is an additional payment for each child, depending on the child's age. So today, if you lose a well-paid job and become unemployed, you will be paid full unemployment benefits for one year; after 12 months, you end up with welfare status and will receive Hartz IV only. Irrespective of their occupational biography, those affected are then likely to slip below what Bourdieu has called the 'threshold of social respectability'.

Second, these changes granted extended powers to the labour administration. The authorities have the right to monitor the personal lives of benefit recipients and to intervene in their residential and financial situations. This means, for example, housing is only funded if living space and rent costs do not exceed a certain limit. If they do, benefit recipients face the choice of either moving to appropriate, which means cheaper, accommodation in line with the requirements within six months, or of privately paying the difference.

Third, another change concerns the permanent means testing. There is a special focus on potential private and family-related resources or funding capacities. All personal assets as well as savings and income within the benefit community are set off against a potential benefit entitlement. The benefit community includes all members of a household. Those on benefits have to enter an integration agreement with the employment agency's case managers. This is an agreement between a job seeker and the authorities that establishes in written form the specific steps to be taken to put the individual to work, that is to say, to (re-)integrate him or her into the labour market. These agreements specify the number of applications to be submitted; agreements also define the frequency with which recipients must report to the labour authorities. The benefit recipient's failure to live up to the agreement authorises the labour administration to impose sanctions – such as a reduction of benefit payments.

Fourth, the definition of earning capacity has been completely reworked. In contrast to what is common in other European countries, earning capacity in Germany is defined in an extremely broad sense nowadays. That is, anyone who is fit enough to engage in any kind of work for at least three hours per day is considered able to earn a living. This has noticeably reduced the number of recipients of social assistance. The majority of those who were previously eligible for social assistance today receive payments as provided for by Hartz IV. Therefore, the labour administrations now find themselves confronted with the task of having to consult and put these 'clients' to work, some of whom have severe health impairments. Moreover, they are treated in exactly the same way as those benefit recipients who have been economically active for decades.

Fifth, strict rules on what can be reasonably expected from benefit recipients, as well as corresponding sanctions, were introduced. These rules pertain to the reasonable acceptability of jobs, the participation in (unpaid) schemes, the attendance of meetings with case managers, and so forth. Benefit recipients are expected to change their place of residence in order to take up a job and also to work below the income level corresponding to their qualification. Any work that the unemployed person is physically, mentally, and psychologically capable of doing is deemed reasonably acceptable. Moreover, since the refusal of job offers may result in sanctions, those affected are forced to lower their standards – with respect to income level and quality of work – to a minimum. Misconduct that is commonly sanctioned includes the failure to report, the refusal to take up or continue a job, the refusal to enter an integration agreement or to meet the obligations stated in such an agreement, and also the lack of visible efforts. These are just some of the most important reform measures. Further elements of activating labour market policies include the reorganisation of labour administration and the (legal) facilitation of atypical employment, especially subcontracted labour and agency work.

Contrary to a widespread misperception, benefit recipients are not primarily low qualified. Of individuals entering basic security benefits for the first time in 2012, 70 per cent had completed vocational training or *Abitur* (German school-leaving degree, permitting access to tertiary education), and only one quarter had not completed any form of job training. Nevertheless, almost two-thirds had performed only low-qualified work before receiving benefits. Roughly three-quarters of new entrants had previously worked full-time, 70 per cent of them in the low-wage sector. Whoever had been employed in the low-wage sector before entering into benefit receipt hardly stands any chance of finding work outside this sector while on benefits (Hofmann and Stephan 2016). Only one-quarter of benefit recipients actually manage to exit the benefit status relatively quickly through taking up an unsubsidised job; all others take longer. The 'cluster' of 'transition into employment' is dominated by full-time wage earners requiring a wage supplement on top of their income (34–41 per cent of the cluster) and part-time work (39–43 per cent of the cluster). Adding to this are the transition into subsidised jobs or continuation of unemployment (Bruckmeier *et al.* 2017). One aspect worth noting is that only one-third of benefit recipients are actually unemployed.

These data signal profound changes in Germany's social structure. Receiving benefits constitutes a social condition that has produced a new or at least a reconfigured social underclass (Dörre *et al.* 2013b).[9] The data suggest a consolidation of life conditions in which social mobility is limited to moving between precarious job, socially subsidised activity, and unemployment. This may be characterised by constant positional shifts, but social mobility remains circular, rarely leading out of precarious life conditions as such. Over the course of seven years, only very few of our respondents managed to enter into employment conditions which permanently liberated them from the status of benefit recipient. The rest passed through two, four, six, or even more jobs. First, most move from unemployment to an *Ein-Euro-Job* (a 'one-euro job', a low-paying job supplementing welfare payments). After that, they might move into temporary employment, after which they enter a training scheme, and so forth, only to end up claiming benefits again.

The longer one receives benefits, the greater the pressure to develop a habitus of social survival becomes. This survival habitus in turn sets the implicated individual apart from the rest of society, although this 'survival' only rarely denotes actual physical survival. As benefits status persists, recipients are forced to adapt themselves to a situation of material scarcity, low social recognition, and tight-knit bureaucratic surveillance and control of their everyday life. Precisely because benefit recipients adapt to adverse conditions, they then become the target of negative classifications by the so-called 'mainstream society'. As a consequence, the benefit recipients we interviewed see themselves as members of a 'stigmatised minority', forced to do whatever they can to establish or maintain a connection to social normality. Whoever remains on benefits for a longer period of time is considered discreditable. Once ascribed, the stigma of Hartz IV becomes very difficult to shake off. This produces a cycle of veritable powerlessness. The logic of Hartz IV ('Any work is better than no work at all!') dictates abandoning certain aspirations concerning quality of work and life – aspirations which in fact motivate increased proactivity. When circular mobility produces strain, standards and norms are lowered – feeding further resignation and passivity. In this sense, an activating labour market policy that grasps unemployment not as a structural problem, but rather as one's individual shortcoming, fosters class-formation through debasement, that is to say, social depreciation. Receiving benefits for a longer stretch of time means assuming a position below the invisible 'threshold of respectability'. Hartz IV thus acts as a deterrent. It raises the willingness of those still in stable employment to accept sub-standard, precarious jobs simply to avoid social contempt, precisely at a moment when slipping below the threshold of respectability becomes more likely.

Demobilised class society and exclusive solidarity

What the labour market reforms have not created is actual additional paid work. Instead, unemployment is hidden, or at least significantly reduced, through an expansion of insecure, poorly paid, and undervalued jobs. This was possible because the forces and institutions which could have worked towards a distribution of social wealth in favour of wage earners had been weakened beforehand, resulting in the emergence not only of a precarious full-employment society, but also a class society resting on demobilisation and collective debasement. Even liberal economists admit that Germany is one of the 'most unequal countries in the industrialised world' today (Fratzscher 2016: 9, 43). According to recent studies, the top thousandth of the German population owns 17 per cent of overall wealth, while the richest tenth owns more than 64 per cent (Bach *et al.* 2015: 11). Not only has the gap between rich and poor widened; income differentials among wage earners have increased as well. Half of all wage earners make less today than they did 15 years ago. That said, the bottom four income deciles have lost out disproportionately (Fratzscher 2016: 64), as these groups experienced losses in real income over the period from 1995 to 2015. Moderate wage increases in the recent past have failed to compensate for this income inequality (BMAS 2017).

The more pronounced class-specific inequalities correspond to an undeniable weakening of all forms of wage earners' power. Class relations take effect even if movements and political organisations fail to pool experiences in a way that leads to collective action for the improvement of a shared life situation. After all – according to Didier Eribon, in his brilliant book, *Returning to Reims* – if you 'simply remove "classes" and class relations as categories of thought and comprehension, and therefore from political discourse, there is certainly no guarantee that those denoted by those terms will not feel collectively abandoned' (Eribon 2013). In the absence of intellectual orientations potentially engendered by mobilised classes, class relations manifest in the form of competition as a result of the permanent distinction between winners and losers, as well as through collective debasement and appreciation. The state, which in modern capitalism directly distributes between 40 and 60 per cent of a country's GDP, assumes a central role here. Through the allocation or withdrawal of social goods – i.e. social assets for subsistence purposes which in turn render wage earners social citizens – state activities have a major impact on the class structure in a given society. Political demarcations linked to the allocation of social goods cause class formation via collective debasement and stigmatisation of large social groups. Owing to debasement by the so-called mainstream of society, new 'dangerous classes' emerge, whose mere existence justifies an increasingly authoritarian form of state interventionism.

This is precisely what has happened in Germany, as demonstrated by our research across German enterprises over the last decade.[10] In a demobilised class society, even the retention of one's permanent position becomes an ongoing challenge. Those confronted with such challenges easily grow intolerant of people or groups perceived as less able or willing to work hard, fostering a tendency towards exclusive solidarity which, as we were able to demonstrate, is most strongly present among core workforces in the industrial export sector (Dörre *et al.* 2013a). Correspondingly, the statement that 'a society that takes care of everybody is not viable over the long term' resonates strongest among workers and production-related staff; the lowest approval rating of this statement is given by clerks. Superficially, this appears to contradict the notion that respondents working in production or production-related areas reject the labour market reforms most forcefully and consider Hartz IV to be above all a means of disciplining wage earners – and yet majorities in the same groups of workers and production-related staff are the most inclined to approve of treating the unemployed more harshly (Figure 8.2 and Figure 8.3).

What seems contradictory at first glance, however, can be accounted for when considering the disciplining effects of precarity and the Hartz IV regime. Whoever feels relatively secure in their job is still aware of the fact that, should they become unemployed, the social safety net has been weakened. Almost every permanent employee we interviewed knows of someone among their immediate social surrounding who depends or used to depend on basic security benefits. A worker who loses a relatively well-paid position in the export sector

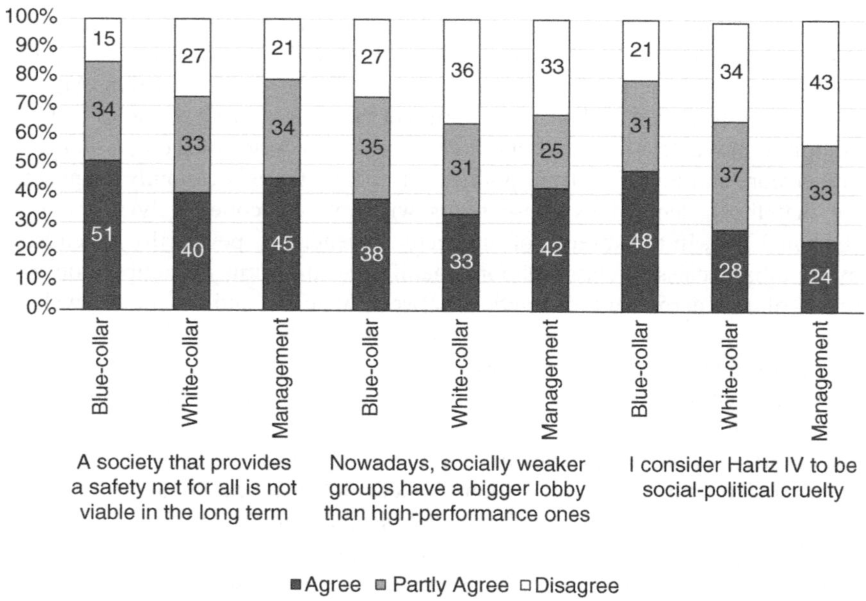

Figure 8.2 Indicators for exclusive solidarity I.

Source: author's elaboration based on Dörre *et al.* (2013a: 158).

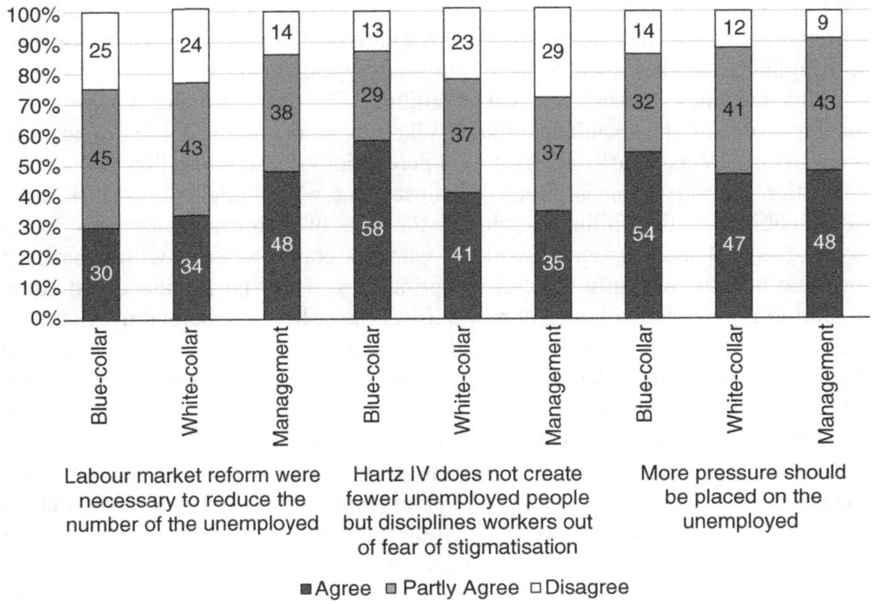

Figure 8.3 Indicators for exclusive solidarity II.

Source: author's elaboration based on Dörre *et al.* (2013a: 158).

is unlikely to find a similar job of an equal standard, even in the more prosperous regions. In the worst case, should this continue over a longer period, one may even become eligible for Hartz IV and thus fall below the threshold of social respectability. The vague fear of this possibility alone leads to growing insecurity which – particularly in the area of production, so it seems – is accompanied by the tendency to dissociate oneself not only from 'above' and 'the Other', but also from 'below'.

Such dissociations occur within competition between companies or regional industries, but also with regard to competitors inside of one's own workplace. It would be inaccurate to insinuate an actively fought competitive struggle on the part of wage earners, waged consciously against one's colleagues on the basis of social resentment. At the same time, however, it would be just as misleading to trivialise such conflicts and reduce exclusive solidarity to a case of false consciousness. Instead, we find reason to believe that the tendency towards exclusive solidarity can in fact be reinforced through the strategic use of in-house flexibilisation. Although empathy, political declarations against the *AÜG* (*Arbeitnehmerüberlassungsgesetz* – the law regulating the leasing of labour forces), and the demand for equal pay for temporary workers do form part of a widespread basic solidary mindset even among core workforces, most respondents ultimately put themselves first in times of crisis. The fact that many temporary workers were laid off during the 2008–09 crisis was perceived by many permanent employees as a protective measure on their behalf. All understanding and sympathy for their colleagues aside, their own employment security took priority.

This tendency towards exclusive solidarity is even stronger vis-à-vis the unemployed and the socially excluded. Whoever works and is willing to perform views Hartz IV as an affront, creating a perception of unfairness that often seeks an outlet. Pent-up anger is directed against those who – allegedly – shirk these responsibilities while failing to abide by the rules of performance fairness. In the eyes of skilled and production workers, whoever comes to terms with depending on state benefits not only violates the principles of fair performance and equal opportunity, but also voluntarily relinquishes his or her own autonomy; that is to say, from their perspective, benefit recipients act in a veritably anti-emancipatory manner because they allegedly resign themselves to a constellation of extreme alienation. Alienation in this context means 'that one's identity and action [are] determined entirely by others, to the point' at which one 'begins to perceive oneself only through the action and the perspective of the dominant subject' (Dubet 2008: 170). Many workers and permanently employed staff view such an arrangement with disgust, as a situation of complete powerlessness. These workers often make quite an effort to preserve as much autonomy within heteronomous conditions as possible, so as to lead an at least somewhat self-determined life. It is therefore not just the accusation of 'social parasitism' that drives a desire for distinction. The sense that a complete subjection to external command and permanent dependence on others are actually possible, could even exist as a way of life – that subjective sacrifice of the entire ensemble of activities that could mitigate alienation and exploitation – can manifest itself as collective debasement and stigmatisation of those classified in this way. People and groups who subject themselves this way entirely, who succumb to a situation of total alienation without resistance, represent a latent or even manifest threat to any kind of solidarity among wage earners, particularly in the eyes of organised workers and employees. This attitude helps explain why even active trade unionists we surveyed openly identify and attack alleged 'benefits scrounging' committed by the long-term unemployed.

It must be noted, however, that the tendency towards exclusive solidarity rejecting precarised and excluded groups is not all-pervasive: it is also intrinsically contradictory and liable to provoke unambiguous rejections. The different opinions present among the workforce and the contradictoriness inherent in individuals tending towards exclusive solidarity underscore that there is no inevitability or automatism in the assertion of mechanisms of de-solidarisation. It seems a modicum of leeway exists for strategies aiming at inclusive solidarity with the precariously employed and unemployed; yet, the danger of a sectional politics custom-tailored to serve particular stakeholders among core workforces is hardly reversed by this fact.

To a certain degree, this danger is rooted precisely in the positive identification with one's own workplace or one's own company, as such identification conceals (among other things) veritably competitive logics which explode from time to time, for example, in the form of competition between production sites. One's identity as a member of a core workforce (instead of the working class or of any other major social group of wage earners) denotes a social relation in which the workplace at least temporarily appears as experienceable beyond otherwise common boundaries of status and class, which in turn means it must be jointly defended within capitalist competition by workers and managers alike. Correspondingly, exclusive solidarity may be directed against rival production sites and workforces even inside the same company. It may also find expression in harsh conditions for supplier companies and their employees, who contribute to the prosperity of a focal company at the head of a value chain composed of differently situated companies. This threat is quite clear to thinking practitioners in both business and the trade unions, although they generally do not comment on these ideas publicly. Thus, a high annual premium may heighten workers' and employees' sense of belonging as well. The mere question of whether the workforces of foreign subsidiaries who contribute a high share of the company's overall success ought to participate in the company's prosperity to the same degree suffices to provoke an uproar. After all, such a proposition touches on an issue of injustice present within many companies, the resolution of which could provide fuel for further conflict.[11]

The new conflict formation

Reviewing the changes described above, there is little reason to believe that the old West German social capitalism can be revived. That said, a partial return to forms of regulation can be observed since the 2008–09 crisis, arguably reminiscent of some characteristics of that system.

The fact that it was possible to preserve Germany's industrial sector during the 2008–9 crisis is largely due to a crisis management which – through extensive participation by the industrial trade unions – essentially signified an abandonment of the neo-liberal 'Agenda policies' (referring to the 'Agenda 2010') of the Schröder government and a return to the job creation policies of the 1980s and 1990s. The state protected long-term employment through subsidised short-time work, while the scrapping of older passenger vehicles ensured that unemployment did not nosedive during the crisis. Having said that, works councils and trade unions capable of acting and dealing with conflict were crucial in ensuring that job-securing measures were actually implemented at the company level. This successful crisis management has earned the trade unions renewed prestige but does not signify a return to the old social capitalism. There are two reasons for this.

First, crisis management mainly benefitted the *core workforces in the export sector*. In the less-organised service sector with its high share of female workers, nothing of the sort was achieved. Successful crisis management has thus failed to fundamentally rectify the power asymmetries on the labour market in favour of 'weak interests' and the precariously employed. In this context, a central weakness of the German economic model becomes evident: namely, that support for the export-oriented industrial sector has traditionally been linked to a modicum of social contempt for and depreciation of person-related care services and reproductive labour in Germany.

Powerful export-driven sectors with a high share of skilled employees in the high-tech field are matched by an expanding sector of low-paid, unstable, and often lowly-regarded service activities, the labour productivity of which, at least when measured by conventional standards, lags behind that of the industrial sector. Simultaneously, we can observe a shift in the relative weight of the two sectors in terms of employment relations. In the rapidly expanding social economy alone (whose share of total employment has risen from 4.5 to 6.2 per cent in the last decade), there are about 1.7 million employees in employment, subject to social security contributions, just as many as are employed in mechanical and automotive production, the heart of the German economy. This shows that in relation to the highly productive export-oriented sectors, the supposedly less productive yet labour-intensive sector of paid care work (including all those activities aiding in the 'production of labour power') is increasingly important. Because professional care work is largely funded by state transfers, this appears primarily as a cost problematic from the microeconomic perspective of export-oriented industry. State policy has structured the exchange between the export sector and care work as a 'metabolism' of valued internal and devalued external markets. A competition-oriented tax policy designed to ensure the inflow of liquid capital encourages governments to implement tax breaks for the wealthy and for corporations, thus creating problems for state revenues and preventing generous transfers in favour of person-oriented services or paid care work. One consequence is that the reproductive responsibilities of the state gradually come to require financing via the privatisation of public goods and public borrowing. While private assets expand and become increasingly concentrated, public assets are being 'melted down', so to speak. As a result, the state is unable to fund increased demand for care services. In this way, the production of care as a public good comes under additional pressure, lacking state-funded solvent demand. Political decision-makers react with a mix of commodification, 'competification', precarisation of working conditions, and a re-channelling of care work into private households.

The German export model rests, this much we can establish, on a capitalist *Landnahme* of both person-related services and care work. In the German case, *Landnahme* means increasing the competitiveness of the export sector via an intensified depreciation and precarisation of (paid) care work. However, the two sectors by no means face off as homogeneous blocs with antagonistic interests in this process. The export sector is also witnessing the erosion of a citizenship status founded on the notion of 'social property', for here as well we find precarious employment and the disciplining of core workforces. In the case of care work, however, the status of social citizen was never institutionalised, or only to a very minor extent. Traditionally regarded as women's work, continuously reproduced gender-specific mechanisms of discrimination can be drawn upon in order to preserve the social depreciation of this sector in order to lower costs of reproduction.

Second, the Merkel government, the European half-hegemon, is prescribing a *recipe for the southern European periphery* it has long ceased to apply domestically, at least in this form.

The German government bears significant responsibility for the institutional consolidation – over the course of its crisis management – of a supra-national disciplinary regime in the EU and the eurozone which accentuates and exacerbates inequalities within as well as between the eurozone member states, which is why the periphery's compliance must increasingly be ensured through authoritarian means. The institutionalisation of this authoritarian mode of regulation has a longer prehistory which, via a sequence of ultimately constitutionally relevant reforms, amounts to a continuation and institutional consolidation of an authoritative, radical free-market transformation (crisis constitutionalism). The objectives of this 'new constitutionalism' include all that which I have termed the *Landnahme* of the social:

- the strengthening of private-capitalist ownership rights;
- the expropriation of public goods;
- the re-commodification of sectors and spaces of life previously protected from the market;
- the subordination of economic activities to the rules of liberalised financial markets and restrictive fiscal policies.

This new constitutionalism was further boosted during the crisis of 2008–09, when it became both detached from its technocratic shell and simultaneously politicised, as that which had remained latent throughout the years of the debt-driven Euro boom now began to emerge. The EU states, and in particular the members of European Monetary Union (EMU), continue to drift apart both economically and socially. This is the result of a European Stability Mechanism (ESM), which seeks to achieve social stabilisation through austerity programmes, whose enforcement and execution are largely divorced from the democratic decision-making processes of individual nation states. It was clear from the outset that the ESM and its pro-cyclical financial policy would create barriers to economic growth while exposing the weaker economies in particular to an interest-risk spiral, as the latter are less able to raise the necessary funds to refinance budget deficits and other debts. Regardless of this fact, authoritarian austerity policies were further elaborated in a bundle of measures and agreements (the European Fiscal Compact, the European Semester, the Two-pack, Sixpack, etc.) and institutionally grounded. As a result, we now find strongly asymmetrical patterns of interrelations, conflicts of interest between Member Sstates as well as increasing conflicts overall, articulated in equally strongly asymmetrical debtor-creditor-relationships.

As the Greek case in particular illustrates, the imposed austerity entails devastating consequences. In order to regain competitiveness and service the public debt, the European institutions and the German government forcefully imposed harsh austerity measures, including wage and pension cuts, the elimination of public sector jobs, tax hikes, and the privatisation of public enterprises and land holdings. The outcomes of this policy have been economically and socially dramatic: the Greek GDP has continuously contracted from 2008 to 2016; more than 180,000 businesses went bankrupt or were threatened by insolvency; the statistically established unemployment rate rose from 7.7 per cent in 2008 to 27.1 per cent in 2013, declining only slightly since (25 per cent in 2017); roughly one-third of the officially employed work irregular hours; and so forth. Despite all the sacrifices the population has made, Greece's public debt has risen from 120 per cent of GDP in 2010 to about 180 per cent of GDP in 2017, and even the IMF is now dubbing it 'unsustainable' and calling for debt-relief measures. The German government, however, refuses to accept any retreat from this new form of interest slavery.

In other words: German financial capitalism is a political capitalism in the Weberian sense and has little to do with the rational capitalism depicted by Marx in the pages of *Capital* (Jessop 2013, 2017). To put it bluntly: confronted with dwindling growth rates, capitalism becomes cannibalistic. We can already see indications of this within the eurozone. Here, the rule is: bad news from Greece is good news for the German revenues office. The worse the crisis in Greece gets, the more attractive German government bonds become, as they appear a safe haven to investors. Because the European Central Bank (ECB) is flooding the market with cheap money, Germany is able to replace expiring government bonds with titles at lower interest rates. As a result, the German treasury has managed to save at least €100 billion over the past four and a half years. This is significantly more than the roughly €90 billion that Greece owes Germany for the so-called 'rescue packages' from the ECB, the ESM, and the IMF (IWH 2015).[12] Germany will continue to profit from the crisis, even in the case of a total Greek default. I would describe such a situation as capitalist cannibalism, in that the hegemonic countries stabilise their economies by destroying those of weaker states. The scenario of political cannibalism implies that such phenomena will become increasingly dominant. Equally true of such a scenario, however, is that it is highly fragile and crisis-prone. This is precisely what we are seeing in Europe today. Integration – what was once conceived as a response to the deregulating tendencies of globalisation (common European market) and a safeguard against German dominance (a transnational European currency) – has itself become a trouble spot and a driver of deregulation. Instead of using access to the massive European common market as a tool to enforce social standards across the world economy, a supra-national disciplinary regime has emerged which reinforces the inequalities within and between member states of the eurozone and increasingly relies on authoritarian means to ensure compliance (Blyth 2013; Galbraith 2016; Streeck 2016).

European constitutionalism and its core projects have effectively withdrawn this aspect of European politics from the democratic decision-making process. They have driven forward a transformation that firmly implants market radicalism into the institutions of the EU empire. The degree to which this political trajectory has tied the EU and especially the eurozone states to the global financial economy was revealed during the crisis. One truth that continues to apply is: institutions matter! Yet institutional divergence, at least in the Atlantic countries, manifests itself as a variation of – rather than protection from – the results of the crisis. Austerity, firmly institutionalised through the Fiscal Compact, the European Semester, the Two-pack, Sixpack, etc., has had devastating effects – particularly in the crisis-ridden states of southern Europe. Unemployment, poverty, and precarity have skyrocketed, but public debt – particularly damaging in the Greek case – has continued to rise nonetheless. As it targets collective security systems, collective wage agreements, dismissal protection, and co-determination structures, austerity weakens the very institutions that have proven the most reliable protections against the crisis for at least certain parts of the labour force.

The fundamental economic problematic of Western Europe in the 1970s has therefore, as it were, been reversed. Triggered by elite perceptions of a profit squeeze crisis, the *Landnahme* of the social diminished the power resources of the trade unions and their political allies to a degree that the new-found structural weakness in demand has engendered a new, utterly differently configured barrier to capital accumulation. As a result of a weakening of the trade unions and the decline of the Social Democratic and Socialist parties, the 'political economy of the labour force' (Negt und Kluge 1993: 83) was pushed onto the defensive to the point where even system-stabilising redistributive measures lacked the necessary political support in many countries.

But there are counter-tendencies as well. In Germany, we are currently witnessing a trade union comeback. The membership figures of important unions are growing and the willingness to engage in labour conflicts is on the rise as well. What could be interpreted as a revitalisation of the 'social market economy' at first glimpse is actually a reaction to (financial) market-driven capitalism with fragmented labour relations, a capitalism that resembles the social capitalism of the past only in its – crumbling – institutional façade. This capitalism's regulation of labour relations takes place in two separate worlds. The first world includes whole industries and large or medium-sized corporations in which industry-wide collective bargaining or company-level agreements further the interests of wage earners by regulating wages, salaries, and working conditions. The institutionalisation of the class conflict appears unchanged in this world. The second world is one of outsourcing, circumvention of social and wage norms, low-wage competition, eroding collective bargaining agreements, and the abandonment of even company-wide agreements. It is a world of over-exploitation and insecure, lowly regarded, and therefore precarious gainful employment. These two worlds are not, if you will, worlds apart. The boundaries between them are fluid, while conflict-ridden movements can lead a company from one world to the other (Dörre *et al.* 2017).

And that is the real novelty: what is left of co-determination structures, trade union organisational power, and redistributive effects of the welfare state has become the point of departure for a conflict dynamic around restraining the new finance capitalism. The steady rise in labour conflicts, and the strike year of 2015 in particular, bear witness to a new-found confidence among trade unionists. Some two million strike days (2014: 392,000) involving the participation of about 1.1 million wage earners (2014: 345,000 on strike) stand in stark contrast to the general decline of labour conflicts in many OECD countries (WSI 2016). Trade unions obviously have the greatest scope of action in the first world of collective agreement-based regulation, in which industry-wide agreements still represent the norm. In the world of deregulated work, trade unions have to conduct painstaking fights, company by company, or even go on strike in order to win even a modicum of such scope for action. The 'border regime' between the two worlds is structurally conflict-prone, producing countless small-scale conflicts related to company-level and in-house wage agreements that follow their own logic. Only the most spectacular cases make headlines, and thus often go unregistered in official strike statistics. According to the available figures, labour conflicts involving strike action have almost tripled in less than a decade, from 82 (2007) to 214 (2014) (ibid.). More than half of these conflicts take place in the service sector and commonly involve only small numbers of workers, but they also occur in core industrial areas, albeit less frequently.

Five phenomena stand out (Table 8.1). First, the new conflict formation results from the fragmentation of both labour relations as well as labour conflicts. This in turn requires the trade unions to return to their social movement role. Quite surprisingly, movement elements also influence conflicts fought by and for individual occupational groups. This is true, for instance, of the German engine drivers, who are often characterised as a section of highly privileged, corporatist workers. Occupational pride and faith in one's own professional capabilities clash with the market- and competition-driven depreciation of entire occupational groups' labour. If used correctly, what appears as a strictly occupational consciousness can become a source of recalcitrance, protest, and collective action. A similar phenomenon can be observed in education and social services. Here, professional identity – long considered an obstacle to trade union organisation – has instilled a form of collective consciousness similar to that of other skilled labourers, which has now become the subjective driving force of an intense labour conflict.

Second, the constellation illustrates how wage earners' obstinacy and activists' convictions can become an important trade union power resource. This dimension of class-based union action is neglected not only in the concept of conflict partnership, but in institutionalist approaches more generally. Collective action of wage earners cannot be adequately grasped as mere rationalisations of an intermediary conflict logic, nor as the result of individual cost-benefit calculations. Measured by labour conflict outcomes, the strikes in the postal service, in social and educational services (kindergartens, etc.) and at Amazon must appear utterly irrational from the perspective of Mancur Olson's logics of collective action. This is very different from the perspective of the strike activists themselves, however. Although there is certainly no political consciousness among wage earners resembling that of a socialist workers' movement, key active groups do

Table 8.1 The new conflict formation as seen in labour conflicts in 2015

Conflict	*Pacemaker*	*Object of dispute*	*Strike function*	*Role of the state*
Postal service, DHL	Company, top-level management	Outsourcing, wages, working conditions	Economic pressure, defence, organisation	Indirect, privatiser, co-owner
German rail company	Train drivers' union (GDL)	Wages, working hours, working conditions, right to organise	Unlimited strike, powerful position within the logistics chain, social movement	Direct/indirect, co-owner/ legislator
Social and childcare services	Occupational/wage earner groups, trade unions	Recognition and revaluation of profession	Political demonstration, refusal to provide public services, social movement, organisation	Direct, employer/ bargaining counterpart
Metal and electronics industry	IG Metall trade union	Wages, advanced training	Token strike, economic and political pressure	Indirect, legitimation of wage demands
Amazon	Trade union, company	Regimes of work and supervision	Demonstration strike, militant minority, organisation	Indirect (location policies)
Workplace organisational conflicts	Management or staff, trade union	Wages as signifier of the quality of life	Economic pressure, organisation	Indirect, political support

Source: author's elaboration based on Dörre *et al.* (2017: 246).

exhibit some nuclei of identity and motivations which feed efforts towards an obstinate, independent assertion of trade union interest-driven politics. Subjective gains in the eyes of strike activists can include the experience of standing up to their employer, which becomes particularly important when a labour conflict does not – as was the case with the postal service and the childcare workers – end with demands being (fully) met. The question as to how those involved in a strike deal with a negative outcome depends not least on how core activists interpret and collectively understand it.

Third, labour conflicts and trade union organisation drives are an expression of a Polanyian wage earners' reaction to unjust market-driven distribution. Wage demands often act as a trigger, which ostensibly corresponds to the operating principle of intermediary trade unions mainly addressing quantitative demands (wages). In these new labour conflicts, however, we see a different configuration: wage issues represent a mere catalyst for more qualitative demands. Wage conflicts often see the development and articulation of a critique of excessive working hours, pressure to perform, a lack of time sovereignty, and authoritarian internal regimes. Incremental wage demands can only mobilise skilled workers and qualified staff precisely because of this accumulation of experiences of injustice. Even seemingly conventional wage conflicts are thus never 'only' about the money, although the latter is of course very important. What wage earners demand is more justice, more recognition, more time for friends and family, more co-determination as well as self-determination. It is a question of 'living wages', that is wages informed by the standard of industry-wide collective bargaining agreements and regional average wage levels. Wages sufficient for living become synonymous with quality of life, while major differences in wages and income are obviously perceived as limitations on a self-determined life. Highly skilled workers in particular complain about the treadmill of a constant 'always more, but never enough', which they perceive as an intensifying burden at the workplace, but also in other areas of life. This suggests that the contents of social conflict are likewise subject to change. Class conflicts become conflicts over quality of life and part of a greater socio-ecological conflict throughout society.

Fourth, this differentiation of labour conflicts has been accompanied by a gradual functional transformation of strike action. Labour conflicts continue to offer the possibility of implementing, through economic pressure, exemplary wage agreements for entire industries. That said, they are increasingly becoming a – primarily symbolic-political – form of mobilisation which is only deployed as a last resort to strengthen trade union organisational power and thereby create the necessary conditions for negotiated conflict regulation. The functional transformation of labour conflict is not always obvious. It is more readily apparent in the world of deregulated labour, but its impact is nevertheless severe. The trade unions are less and less able to rely on their institutional power resources and depend on their capacity to engage in conflict, which in turn rests on organisational power. The capacity for collective action and strike activity must be rebuilt anew, company by company. This urgently requires organising new groups of wage earners. Labour conflicts are becoming increasingly women-dominated as they move into the precarious sector and are particularly fierce in the new service industries. They are based in part on conditioned forms of membership and workforce participation which in turn shape strike forms and other demands and objectives. Condition-bound trade union work renders the attainment of a certain level of workplace organisation the precondition for conflict activity. As a result, conflicts become less predictable. Moreover, their outcome is made uncertain by the unpredictability of the conflict parties' action strategies.

Finally, whether this will lead to a sustained development of social movement elements within the trade unions or to an increase in their organisational power and willingness to strike as such, we cannot say. The compulsion to engage in trade union renewal while in conflict complicates interest politics. The state appears as a conflict actor in diverse contexts and with surprising frequency. Indeed, the state has itself become a conflict party. As an agent of privatisation and owner, it exerts at least a partial influence at the Deutsche Post (the postal service) as well as the Bahn AG (the railway operator), thereby acting as the ultimate instance in terms of a redefinition of the rules governing labour conflict and adjusting them to structural changes in labour relations. The crucial aspect, however, is not whether the state intervenes – nor that it actually does so – but the way in which it does. Wherever the state, and with it organised labour relations, is on the retreat, standardised, regulated contestations are replaced by other forms of conflict – riots, youth unrest, spontaneous revolts, or, as in the French suburbs, religiously veiled violence. In those places where left-popular forces such as Syriza, Podemos or the Portuguese Left Bloc unfold a democratic form of representation, this often occurs in deliberate dissociation from the old Left and partly also from established trade unions. Their right-populist counterparts, by contrast, practise a *völkisch*, that is an ethnic-nationalist, form of exclusive solidarity. Their reinterpretation of the distributional struggle as a fight for the 'people's wealth' not between the top and the bottom of society but instead between an inside and an outside, between the 'German people' and the supposed migrant 'invaders', resonates alarmingly well with some sections of the unionised labour force. This is a further reason why the new conflict formation brings with it challenges for trade unions to exert targeted influence on the balance of power within the state apparatus in order to mobilise institutional support, without which the future of organised labour relations is likely to be rather grim.

Conclusion

To summarise: (West) German social capitalism is a thing of the past. Although the institutions and action strategies of the old form of conflict partnership still exist in the first world of collective agreement-based wage regulation, in the bigger picture, a new game with different rules is emerging. The fact that we have witnessed a return – albeit with little substance – to mechanisms of the social-capitalist era during the financial crisis does not contradict this assertion.

Successful crisis management has consolidated Germany's – primarily economic, and therefore at best half-hegemonic – position in Europe. Nevertheless, relevant actors would be unable to universalise the German system of dual interest representation on a European scale, the strength of which emanates from its core within the industrial export sector, even if they wanted to. And, besides, the political will to do anything of the sort is nowhere to be found in the current constellation.

The austerity therapy which the EU empire, under considerable pressure from the Merkel government, imposes not only on its Southern European periphery further weakens organised labour relations. The abolition of the favourability principle, which allows for deviations from industry-wide collective bargaining agreements only in the case of improvements in the agreed conditions (Spain, Greece); the prioritisation of company- and workplace-based collective agreements over industry-wide agreements; the elimination or limitation of the universal applicability of collective agreement-related regulations (Greece, Hungary, Portugal, Romania); legally sanctioned downward deviations from labour agreements; strong declines in coverage rates of industry-wide regulations (Spain, Greece, Portugal); the dilution of dismissal protection and the lowering of the legal minimum wage; these represent the standard arsenal of wage-political interventionism in Europe today. Even if trade union organisation drives were to continue, co-determination were consolidated, and the applicability of labour agreements were once again increased, the old social-capitalist conditions cannot and will not be restored. The very function of labour relations is changing fundamentally. In the future, they will deal, regardless at which level of regulation, with only a fraction of the problems that, taken as a whole, represent the social question of the twenty-first century.

Conflicts which typically develop along the fault lines between the two worlds can no longer be adequately grasped with a conceptual framework which ascribes to the trade unions a pragmatic role of intermediary between systemic interests and their members' interests. The new transnational conflict formation can no longer be explained with concepts of intermediarity or conflict partnership, nor can organised labour relations be fully understood from the perspective of proving their contribution to economic efficiency. As Max Weber would say, contemporary financial capitalism is of a thoroughly political nature and is thus unresponsive to such demonstrations of rationality. Wherever capitalism and economic-industrial democracy develop an antagonistic relationship, trade unions will have no choice but to reshape their dual character in the fight *within* as well as *against* the wage system. Research exploring the possibilities of a corresponding strategic choice by the unions should preferably be designed in the spirit of a public sociology – as an organic public sociology founded on the closest possible interaction and exchange with the subalterns and their forms of self-organisation, so as to take into account innovative practices of trade union renewal. Whether or not such research can establish itself in the academic landscape in a lasting way remains to be seen.

Acknowledgements

I would like to thank Jan-Peter Herrmann and Loren Balhorn for translating this article.

Notes

1 Translators' note: literally translated, *Landnahme* means land grabbing, land appropriation, or territorial gain. It refers to internal as well as external capitalist expansion. The concept of *Landnahme* argues that, in the long run, capitalist societies cannot reproduce themselves on their own foundations. In order to reproduce themselves, they continuously have to occupy and commodify a non-capitalist 'other' (i.e. regions, milieux, groups, activities) in, so to speak, ceaseless repetition of the act of primitive accumulation. Due to the difficulty of finding a conclusive exact translation in English, the term *Landnahme* will be used throughout the text.

2 This system of professional training in Germany combines on-the-job training and vocational education.

3 The Agenda 2010 was a comprehensive reform agenda drawn up by the government of Gerhard Schröder in 2003.

4 The *Landnahme* theorem resembles Polanyi's concept of a market-driven double movement (Polanyi 1978), although they are not identical. The *Landnahme* of the social is not only pushed forward by markets. It rather appears more appropriate to speak of a self-negating market economy starkly characterised by the formation of oligopolies and the transformation of economic into political power (Jessop 2013, 2017).

5 Full-time employees in the manufacturing industry and service sector earned on average about €3,527 in gross monthly wages in Germany in 2014. In the former West Germany, gross monthly income was €3,652, while it was only €2,760 in the former East Germany. The average gross hourly wage in the manufacturing industry was €22.61 in 2014, while gross monthly income in this sector was €3,785 (Destatis 2016: 141).

6 We distinguish between wage earners' structural power, which may result from a certain position in the labour market or the production process, organisational power, which is based on a formal association in unions and political organisations, and institutionally constituted power, in the form of law, wage standards, co-determination, etc. (Dörre 2011b: 33–67; Silver 2003; Wright 2000).

7 Unless stated otherwise, the labour market figures presented in the following are taken from Destatis (2016: 125–49).

8 The term 'atypical' is somewhat misleading, given that atypical employment has become the standard in a significant number of industries.

9 The empirical sample consists of regional labour market analyses, panel surveys of those officials in charge of implementing the reforms, as well as a panel survey of benefit recipients (2006–12), totalling 188 interviews. That is to say, it is a qualitative study without any claim to statistical representativity. It is a study, however, that captures the everyday life of benefit recipients in a lot of detail.

10 Unless stated otherwise, our claims are based on a series of studies of the workforce of German enterprises through standardised quantitative surveys, personal interviews, and expert interviews (Dörre *et al.* 2013a, 2017). These include in particular an in-depth case study of a southern car manufacturer (2001: 2009–12) and qualitative and quantitative surveys in more than 60 western and eastern industrial enterprises and service providers (2010–17). Further empirical data originate from interviews with trade union secretaries, works councils, and staff conducted in the framework of an on-going sub-project of the eLabour association.

11 Correspondingly, we often encounter a kind of double talk when interviewing shop stewards and trade union practitioners. Officially and outwardly, they harshly criticise our findings of exclusive solidarity; informally, however, they often present examples very much underscoring the potential explosiveness of the issue.

12 This calculation was met with criticism, as it operates with a fictitious interest rate and ignores the losses suffered by German savers. Yet savings account holders do not shape European policy. Furthermore, some consider the 100-billion figure to be a rather conservative estimate.

References

Abelshauser, Werner (2005). *The dynamics of German industry: Germany's path toward the new economy and the American challenge*. New York: Berghahn Books.

Albert, Michel (1992). *Kapitalismus kontra Kapitalismus*. Frankfurt am Main: Campus.

Amable, Bruno (2003). *The diversity of modern capitalism*. Oxford: Oxford University Press.

Arendt, Hannah (2006). *Elemente und Ursprünge totaler Herrschaft: Antisemitismus, Imperialismus, totale Herrschaft*. München: Piper.

Bach, Stefan, Andreas Thiemann, and Aline Zucco (2015). 'The top tail of the wealth distribution in Germany, France & Spain', DIW Discussion Paper No. 1502. Berlin: DIW.

Berghahn, Volker R. (1986). *The Americanisation of West German industry, 1945–73*. New York: Berg Publishers.

Berghahn, Volker R. and Sigurt Vitols (2006). *Gibt es einen deutschen Kapitalismus? Tradition und globale Perspektiven der sozialen Marktwirtschaft*. Frankfurt am Main: Campus.

Beyer, Jürgen (2003). 'Deutschland AG a.d.: Deutsche Bank, Allianz und das Verflechtungszentrum des deutschen Kapitalismus', in Wolfgang Streeck and Martin Höppner (eds). *Alle Macht dem Markt? Fallstudien zur Abwicklung der Deutschland AG*. Frankfurt am Main: Campus, 11–59.

Blyth, Mark (2013). *Wie Europa sich kaputtspart: Die gescheiterte Idee der Austeritätspolitik*. Bonn: J. H. W. Dietz.

BMAS (Bundesministerium für Arbeit und Soziales) (2017). 'Lebenslagen in Deutschland. Der fünfte Armuts- und Reichtumsbericht der Bundesregierung'. Available at: www.armuts-und-reichtumsbericht.de/SharedDocs/Downloads/Berichte/5-arb-langfassung.html

Bolaffi, Angelo (2014a). *Deutsches Herz: Das Modell Deutschland und die europäische Krise*. Stuttgart: Klett-Cotta.

Bolaffi, Angelo (2014b). 'Interview', *Frankfurter Rundschau*, 23 February, 26–7.

Bosch, Gerhard (2014). 'Neuordnung des deutschen Arbeitsmarkts', in Klaus Dörre, Kerstin Jürgens, and Ingo Matuschek (eds). *Arbeiten in Europa: Marktfundamentalismus als Zerreißprobe*. Frankfurt am Main: Campus, 91–106.

Brenke, Karl and Alexander S. Kritikos (2017). 'Wählerstruktur im Wandel', *DIW-Wochenbericht* 29: 595–606.

Brinkmann, Ulrich, Hae-Lin Choi, Richard Detje, *et al.* (2008). *Strategic Unionism: Aus der Krise zur Erneuerung?* Wiesbaden: VS Verlag für Sozialwissenschaften.

Brinkmann, Ulrich, Klaus Dörre, Silke Röbenack, *et al.* (2006). *Prekäre Arbeit: Ursachen, Ausmaß, soziale Folgen und subjektive Verarbeitungsformen unsicherer Beschäftigungsverhältnisse*. Bonn: Friedrich-Ebert-Stiftung.

Bruckmeier, Kerstin, Tobias Graf, Torsten Lietzmann, *et al.* (2017). 'Typische Verlaufsformen beim Grundsicherungsbezug: für einige Dauerzustand, für andere nur eine Episode', *IAB Kurzbericht* 4.

Burawoy, Michael (2015). *Public Sociology: Öffentliche Soziologie gegen Marktfundamentalismus und globale Ungleichheit*. Weinheim: Beltz Juventa.

Butollo, Florian, Martin Ehrlich, and Thomas Engel (2017). 'Amazonisierung der Industriearbeit?', *Arbeit* 26(1): 33–59.

Castel, Robert (2005). *Die Stärkung des Sozialen: Leben im neuen Wohlfahrtsstaat*. Hamburg: Hamburger Edition.

Castel, Robert and Klaus Dörre (2009). *Prekarität, Abstieg, Ausgrenzung: Die soziale Frage am Beginn des 21. Jahrhunderts*. Frankfurt am Main: Campus.

Crouch, Colin and Wolfgang Streeck (1997). *Political economy of modern capitalism: mapping convergence and diversity*. London: Sage.

Destatis – Statistisches Bundesamt (2016). *Datenreport 2016: Ein Sozialbericht für die Bundesrepublik Deutschland*. Wiesbaden: Destatis.

Deutsche Bank (2013). *Re-Industrialisierung Europas: Anspruch und Wirklichkeit*. Frankfurt am Main: EU Monitor Integration.

Dörre, Klaus (2009). 'Die neue Landnahme', in Klaus Dörre, Stephan Lessenich, and Hartmut Rosa. *Soziologie – Kapitalismus – Kritik. Eine Debatte*. Frankfurt am Main: Suhrkamp, 21–86.

Dörre, Klaus (2010). 'Überbetriebliche Regulierung von Arbeitsbeziehungen', in Fritz Böhle, Gerd-Günther Voß, and Günther Wachtler (eds). *Handbuch Arbeitssoziologie*. Wiesbaden: Springer VS, 873–912.

Dörre, Klaus (2011a). 'Landnahme und die Grenzen kapitalistischer Dynamik: eine Ideenskizze', *Berliner Debatte Initial* 22(4): 56–72.

Dörre, Klaus (2011b). 'Functional changes in the trade unions: from intermediary to fractal organization?', *International Journal of Action Research* 7(1): 8–48.

Dörre, Klaus (2015). 'The new *Landnahme*: dynamics and limits of financial market capitalism', in Klaus Dörre, Stephan Lessenich, and Hartmut Rosa. *Sociology – Capitalism – Critique*. London: Verso, 11–66.

Dörre, Klaus, Thomas Goes, Stefan Schmalz, and Marcel Thiel (2017). *Streikrepublik Deutschland? Die Erneuerung der Gewerkschaften in Ost und West*. 2nd edn. Frankfurt am Main: Campus.

Dörre, Klaus, Anja Happ, and Ingo Matuschek (eds) (2013a). *Das Gesellschaftsbild der LohnarbeiterInnen: Soziologische Untersuchungen in ost- und westdeutschen Industriebetrieben*. Hamburg: VSA Verlag.

Dörre, Klaus, Karin Scherschel, Melanie Booth, *et al.* (2013b). *Bewährungsproben für die Unterschicht? Soziale Folgen aktivierender Arbeitsmarktpolitik*. Frankfurt am Main: Campus.

Dubet, François (2008). *Ungerechtigkeiten: zum subjektiven Ungerechtigkeitsempfinden am Arbeitsplatz*. Hamburg: Hamburger Edition.

Ellguth, Peter and Susanne Kohaut (2011). 'Tarifbindung und betriebliche Interessenvertretung: aktuelle Ergebnisse aus dem IAB-Betriebspanel 2010', *WSI-Mitteilungen* 64(4): 242–7.

Ellguth, Peter and Susanne Kohaut (2014). 'Tarifbindung und betriebliche Interessenvertretung: aktuelle Ergebnisse aus dem IAB-Betriebspanel 2013', *WSI-Mitteilungen* 67(4): 286–95.

Ellguth, Peter and Susanne Kohaut (2015). 'Tarifbindung und betriebliche Interessenvertretung: aktuelle Ergebnisse aus dem IAB-Betriebspanel 2014', *WSI-Mitteilungen* 68(4): 290–7.

Eribon, Didier (2013). *Returning to Reims*. Cambridge, MA: MIT Press.

Fratzscher, Marcel (2016). *Verteilungskampf: Warum Deutschland immer ungleicher wird*. München: Carl Hanser.

Fraunhofer ISI (2013). *Globale Produktion von einer starken Heimatbasis aus: Modernisierung der Produktion*. Karlsruhe: Fraunhofer ISI.

Galbraith, James (2016). *Wachstum neu denken: was die Wirtschaft aus der Krise lernen muss*. Zürich: Rotpunktverlag.

Gumbrell-McCormick, Rebecca (2011). 'European trade unions and "atypical" workers', *Industrial Relations Journal* 42(3): 293–310.

Gumbrell-McCormick, Rebecca and Richard Hyman (2013). *Trade unions in Western Europe: hard times, hard choices*. Oxford: Oxford University Press.

Hall, Peter A. and David Soskice (2001). *Varieties of capitalism: the institutional foundations of comparative advantage*. Oxford: Oxford University Press.

Harvey, David (2005). *A brief history of neoliberalism*. Oxford: Oxford University Press.

Hassel, Anke (2006). 'Erosion gewerkschaftlicher Lobbymacht', in Thomas Leif and Rudolf Speht (eds). *Die fünfte Gewalt: Lobbyismus in Deutschland*. Wiesbaden: Springer VS, 188–98.

Hauptmann, Andreas and Hans-Jörg Schmerer (2012). 'Lohnentwicklung im verarbeitenden Gewerbe. Wer profitiert vom deutschen Exportboom?', IAB Kurzbericht 20. Nürnberg: Institut für Arbeitsmarkt- und Berufsforschung.

Heinze, Rolf-G. (2006). *Wandel wider Willen: Deutschland auf der Suche nach neuer Prosperität*. Wiesbaden: Springer VS.

Helfen, Markus (2011). 'Tarifpolitische Parallelwelten', *Mitbestimmung* 67(7–8).

Hofmann, Barbara and Christoph Stephan (2016). 'Arbeitslose Neuzugänge in den ALG-II-Bezug: Ausgewählte Befunde nach Herkunfts- und Zielbranchen', IAB Aktuelle Berichte 18. Nürnberg: Institut für Arbeitsmarkt- und Berufsforschung.

Holst, Hajo and Klaus Dörre (2013). 'The revival of the German Model? Destandardization of employment and work and the new labour market regime', in Max Koch and Martin Fritz (eds). *Non-standard employment in Europe: paradigms, prevalence and policy responses*. Basingstoke: Palgrave Macmillan, 132–49.

IG Metall (2015). *Sozialreport Automobilcluster Leipzig. Zur Lage der Beschäftigten bei industriellen Dienstleistern*. Frankfurt am Main: IG Metall.

IWH (Institut für Wirtschaftsforschung Halle) (2015). 'Germany's benefit from the Greek crisis', IWH Online 7. Halle: Institut für Wirtschaftsforschung Halle.

Jacobi, Otto and Walther Müller-Jentsch (2017). 'Sozialer Kapitalismus: Gegen die Schwarzmaler'. Available at: www.magazin-mitbestimmung.de/artikel/Sozialer+Kapitalismus%3A+Gegen+die+Schwarzmaler@efDDqagARKiYiU1XXD7OYg

Jessop, Bob (2013). 'Finance-dominated accumulation and post-democratic capitalism', in Sebastian Fadda and Pasquale Tridico (eds). *Institutions and economic development after the financial crisis*. London: Routledge, 83–105.

Jessop, Bob (2017). 'Finance-dominated accumulation and enduring austerity', in Roland Sturm, Tim Griebel, and Thorsten Winkelmann (eds). *Austerity and its social and political consequences*. Baden-Baden: Nomos Verlag, 29–49.

Kohaut, Susanne (2007). 'Tarifbindung und tarifliche Öffnungsklauseln: Ergebnisse aus dem IAB-Betriebspanel 2005', *WSI-Mitteilungen* 60(2): 94–7.

Kotthoff, Hermann (1994). 'Betriebsräte und Kontinuität betrieblicher Mitbestimmung', in Walther Müller-Jentsch (ed.). *Schriftenreihe industrielle Beziehungen*. Vol. 8. München: Rainer Hampp.

Lehndorff, Steffen (2012). *A triumph of failed ideas: European models of capitalism in the crisis*. Brussels: ETUI.

Luxemburg, Rosa (1975). *Die Akkumulation des Kapitals*, in *Gesammelte Werke*. Vol 5. Berlin: Dietz, 5–411.

Marx, Karl (1973). *Das Kapital. Kritik der politischen Ökonomie*. Vol 1*: Der Produktionsprozess des Kapitals*, in *Marx-Engels-Werke (MEW)*. Vol. 23. Berlin: Dietz.

Müller-Jentsch, Walther (2008). *Arbeit und Bürgerstatus: Studien zur sozialen und industriellen Demokratie*. Wiesbaden: Springer VS.

Negt, Oskar and Alexander Kluge (1993). *Geschichte und Eigensinn*. Vol. 1. *Entstehung der industriellen Disziplin aus Trennung und Enteignung*. Frankfurt am Main: Suhrkamp.

Polanyi, Karl (1978). *The great transformation: Politische und ökonomische Ursprünge von Gesellschaften und Wirtschaftssystemen*. Frankfurt am Main: Suhrkamp.

Quack, Sigrid (2006). 'Die transnationalen Ursprünge des "deutschen Kapitalismus" ', in Volker R. Berghahn and Sigurt Vitols (eds). *Tradition und globale Perspektiven der sozialen Marktwirtschaft*. Frankfurt am Main: Campus, 63–85.

Rehder, Britta (2003). *Betriebliche Bündnisse für Arbeit in Deutschland. Mitbestimmung und Flächentarif im Wandel*. Frankfurt am Main: Campus.

Rennwald, Line (2015). *Partis socialistes et classe ouvrière: ruptures et continuités du lien électoral en Suisse, en Autriche, en Allemagne, en Grande-Bretagne et en France (1970–2008)*. Neuchâtel: Editions Alphil.

Schimank, Uwe and Ute Volkmann (2017). *Das Regime der Konkurrenz: Gesellschaftliche Ökonomisierungsdynamik heute*. Weinheim: Beltz.

Shonfield, Andrew (1964). *Geplanter Kapitalismus: Wirtschaftspolitik in Westeuropa und USA*. Berlin: Kiepenheuer & Witsch.

Silver, Beverly J. (2003). *Forces of labor: workers movements and globalization since 1870*. Cambridge: Cambridge University Press.

Streeck, Wolfgang (1997). 'German capitalism: does it exist? Can it survive?', in Colin Crouch and Wolfgang Streeck (eds). *Political economy of modern capitalism: mapping convergence and diversity*. London: Sage, 33–54.

Streeck, Wolfgang (2009). *Re-forming capitalism: institutional change in the German political economy*. Oxford: Oxford University Press.

Streeck, Wolfgang (2016). *How will capitalism end?* London: Verso.

Thelen, Kathleen (2014). *Varieties of liberalization and the new politics of social solidarity*. Cambridge: Cambridge University Press.

Urban, Hans-Jürgen (2013). *Der Tiger und seine Dompteure: Gewerkschaften und Wohlfahrtsstaat unter dem Druck der Finanzmärkte*. Hamburg: VSA-Verlag.

Wright, Erik Olin (2000). 'Working class power, capitalist class interests, and class compromise', *American Journal of Sociology* 105(4): 957–1002.

WSI (Wirtschafts- und Sozialwissenschaftliches Institut der Hans Böckler Stiftung) (2016). WSI-Arbeitskampfbilanz 2015. Ein außergewöhnliches Streikjahr – Zwei Millionen Streiktage, ganz unterschiedliche Arbeitskämpfe fielen zusammen. Available at: www.boeckler.de/pdf/pm_ta_2016_03_03.pdf.

9 Competitiveness in public hospitals

The case of France

Hicham Rassafi-Guibal

Examining the question of public hospitals from the perspective of competitiveness involves breaking an inherent taboo about the economic realities of health care. The reluctance to do so is highlighted by the fact that the term *competitiveness* never appears in reports, publications, studies, papers, and analyses about hospitals. While we often encounter the term *productivity* (IGAS 2013) or the more discreet concept of *efficiency* (Bras and Duhamel 2008: 35), we fail to look at hospitals from the angle of the competition they inevitably face.[1]

The notion of competitiveness refers to the ability of an active entity to 'perform', in economic terms, better than others in the same sector. As the harshly pragmatic saying goes, 'even if good health has no price, we cannot deny that it has a cost'. The cost of public health care weighs heavily on national budgets. But public health services also represent a vital expression of national solidarity: 'Health has become one of the most sensitive matters of social concern' (Truchet 2009: 5). Analysing public hospitals from the perspective of competitiveness is a highly challenging task, but there is no denying the clear links between health care spending and competitiveness. It must be recognised that there are

> considerable differences … among the various national situations. They reveal differences in performance in terms of the quality of services provided and production costs ... these differences can help us understand not only certain disparities in the general economic attractiveness of countries but also geographical mobility observed in patients' use of health care.
>
> (André 2014)

Any analysis of the subject, however, must take account of the specific dynamics of public services. Under Article L.6112-1 of the French Public Health Code, public health undertakings are involved in public service missions in the area of health. In France, the theory of public services is based on the idea that they satisfy the needs of the community as a whole. Without wishing to return to well-worn and as yet unresolved debates, we can assume that public services contribute to the notion of national solidarity in a broad sense.

The tensions between competitiveness, on the one hand, and solidarity, public service and health care, on the other, prompt a broader reflection on the tensions between pragmatism/realism/necessity and idealism/values. Neither extreme can claim to have supremacy over the other. This chapter therefore sets out to investigate the mechanisms designed to reconcile competitiveness and solidarity. This involves identifying the areas in which public hospitals face competition, so as to pinpoint the strategies, tools, and legal procedures developed to address it.

The areas in which public hospitals face competition

Public hospitals are no longer sidelined from debates about competition. The notion of health economy is now analysed in the same way as that of the market economy. Public hospitals interact closely with their mediate and immediate environment. It is therefore important to determine the areas which exert competitive pressure on this specific public service. These areas may be identified primarily within the national framework, but international dynamics should also be taken into consideration.

Domestic competition within the national framework

In essence, hospitals are faced with two areas of competition within the national framework. The first is related to their primary activity, namely, competition in terms of health care provision. The second concerns tensions in the realm of medical demographics, which further heighten the effects of this activity-based competition.

As far as competition in terms of health care provision is concerned, the organisation of health care is fragmented and underpinned by competing dynamics. There is no public monopoly over health care. Alongside public establishments, private entities may be involved in providing public hospital services.[2] The activities of the hospital sector in a broad sense may be performed by public health establishments[3] or private establishments, the latter being divided into two sub-categories, namely, private for-profit and private not-for-profit hospitals (hospitals 'in the general interest').[4] Even more generally, health care may be provided via a private practice system known as 'community' medicine (*médecine de ville*). This may be carried out by local physicians or within *centres de santé*[5] (health care centres) or *maisons de santé*[6] (care homes). Both provide primary or secondary health care without patient admission. The main difference between the two is the status of the owners: health care centres are set up and managed by non-profit organisations, local authorities and their various groupings, or health care establishments. They represent an extension or separate branch of their governing body. They are created by means of a centripetal approach. Care homes, on the other hand, are legal entities set up by medical practitioners, other health care workers and pharmacists via a centrifugal approach. They are the result of an association of independent professionals.

Competition between these different structures arises because patients' freedom of choice is enshrined as a 'fundamental principle'.[7] In light of this principle, the French Competition Authority includes public hospitals in its studies on the competitive environment in terms of concentrations of private establishments.[8] Competition is only attenuated by the health needs of patients. In economic terms, one might say that the available offering is an imperfect substitute. Some conditions require treatments, drugs, processes, techniques or instruments that have only limited availability. Competition arises when an identical offering is available within a geographically realistic area for the patient. This is why the Technical Agency for Hospital Admissions Information (ATIH)[9] indicates the 'market share' for each hospital both at the regional level and also in terms of an 'area of attractiveness', in other words the geographical area within which patients are willing to travel.[10] The Competition Authority emphasises that

> the national decision-making process, which takes account of the regulatory instruments used by Regional Health Agencies, sees health care markets as having a local, departmental or regional dimension, whose external limits depend on the specialisation concerned by the market … in question.[11]

It adds that the size and facilities of different hospitals result in significant variations in the geographical limits of a given market and that 'coverage by health insurance of the transport costs borne by some patients tends to increase their willingness to travel', thereby generally extending the area to a journey time of one hour.

As far as competition on the hospital employment market is concerned, France is characterised by a rigid training system for its doctors. Higher education in the area of health care is subject to a strict *numerus clausus* system. But there are currently major difficulties in adjusting this *numerus* to meet demographic needs, especially as comprehensive medical training can take more than 10 years. A report by the IGAS (French General Inspectorate for Social Affairs) notes that, 'The shortage of medical professionals is having a major impact on some disciplines and in some regions', although it adds that 'At the current time, it is not so much the number of specialists as their geographical distribution across the country that is a problem' (IGAS 2013). In the run-up to the 2017 presidential election, the French National Medical Council (CNOM) called on the presidential candidates to change the method for calculating the *numerus clausus* by adopting a regional approach (CNOM 2017). These difficulties are having a detrimental effect on hospital recruitment. To address the staff shortages caused by the *numerus clausus*, hospitals are encouraging the development of alternative options, by recruiting either French staff who trained at universities in other EU Member States or third country nationals who trained outside the EU (Huguier and Romestaing 2014). But these palliative strategies appear to be more of a desperate attempt to salvage the situation than an effective HR management technique. While doctors with a non-EU qualification cannot be recruited as 'doctors' but only as 'acting interns', which automatically results in a lower level of remuneration,[12] conversely, a parliamentary report points to abuses in the recruitment of temporary doctors, which cost on average three times more each day than permanent doctors (Véran 2013).

Tensions in the medical employment market have prompted regulatory powers to develop several corrective mechanisms. Under Article D.6152-23 of the French Public Health Code, the remuneration of hospital practitioners is composed of two parts: a fixed part, determined on the basis of the hospital practitioner pay scale, and a variable part. Details of the variable part can be found in Article D.6152-23-1 of the Public Health Code. Incentive measures are mostly converted into variable remuneration. With reference to Article R.6152-5 of the Public Health Code on recruitment to positions where there are 'particular difficulties in recruitment and performance', paragraph 3 of the article provides the possibility for a lump-sum payment to be made to doctors who agree to work at the recruiting establishment, 'by the signing of an agreement', for five years. Alongside this recruitment mechanism for priority positions, paragraph 6 of Article R.6152-23 of the Public Health Code also provides for the possibility of agreeing to a 'recruitment bonus for exclusive public service' for practitioners who undertake to work exclusively for the establishment for a renewable period of three years, with no possibility of working simultaneously on an independent basis.[13]

Conversely, under certain conditions, hospital practitioners may also be required to comply with a non-competition obligation for a period of two years after resigning. Article L.6152-5-1 of the Public Health Code provides that a non-competition obligation may be applied in conditions where practitioners 'may enter into direct competition with the public establishment from which they have resigned'.

External international competition

There is no direct international competition on hospitals per se. International competition affects public hospitals as one aspect of a broader dynamic. Hospitals are a variable in the general competitiveness of the French health care system. They are also part of the movement to develop a European market for health care.

On the one hand, hospitals may be considered as an adjustment variable for the competitiveness of the French health care system. The requirement for sustainability of social security is linked with the ongoing competitiveness of the French social model of health insurance. It also helps to establish a link between budget balance and national competitiveness. Hospital activities are caught up in this dynamic, as an institutional component of the health insurance system in a broad sense. A report by the Institute Montaigne think tank emphasises that 'in terms of value creation in France, health represents a key sector in the country's competitiveness at international level', adding that 'Health products are the country's third leading sector in terms of exports' (Institut Montaigne 2016: 6). Competition in the health care system can be considered in two ways. First, we need to assess the importance of indicators of health care systems in the overall measure of a country's competitiveness. We then have to identify how the organisation of the health care system influences specific economic sectors.

National Reform Programmes (NRPs), developed by EU Member States as part of attempts to coordinate economic policies at the EU level,[14] take full account of the issue of social expenditure in general, and health care spending in particular. The French NRP for 2016 proposes 'the continued rollout of the national healthcare strategy and the savings plan built on four pillars', which include 'improving the efficiency of hospital expenditure through a national programme with adaptations at the regional level' and 'developing outpatient care and ensuring appropriate inpatient care' (Prime Minister of France 2016: 33). The European Commission is particularly attentive to the development of reforms in the area of public hospitals and is careful to emphasise 'progress in reforming healthcare systems, with the aim of ensuring cost-effectiveness' (EC 2017: 15–18). In terms of French public hospitals, it notes that although good results have been obtained in terms of health care, costs remain high (IGAS 2013). The management and funding of public hospitals, as well as the developments under consideration, undoubtedly have an important part to play in broader reflections on the competitiveness of the French economy. That is why public hospitals, like other public services, represent an adjustment variable.

The public funding system for social security influences those economic sectors with which it is closely linked, such as the pharmaceutical industry. Investment in research and development is close to €5 billion and has an impact on approximately 100,000 direct jobs. A joint report by the IGF (French General Inspectorate for Finance) and IGAS emphasises the need to maintain health expenditure so that the sector can remain competitive in terms of innovation (IGF/IGAS 2012). It believes that '[t]he effort on prices should remain consistent with the competitiveness of the industry'. This effort is all the more important given that the pharmaceutical industry showed a positive trade balance of €3.9 billion for 2016, an upward trend, with exports totalling nearly €30 billion, despite the fact that French exports overall fell by 0.6 per cent (DGDDI 2017). The costs of drugs reimbursed in France are set by an administrative body, the Economic Committee for Health Products (CEPS). Article L.162-17-3 of the French Social Security Code provides for this committee to 'contribute to the development of the economic policy on drugs'. It is responsible for making sure the interests of all stakeholders are taken into consideration. When determining drug costs, it particularly takes into account the French health insurance expenditure target (ONDAM), which has a specific section for the hospital sector. The committee's 2015 Annual Report clearly shows that the cost-cutting efforts of public hospitals also partly depend on the decisions taken by this committee.[15]

On the other hand, public hospitals are part of the development of a European health care market. The European Union has a considerable impact on the health care market – despite the fact that EU law contains seemingly contradictory objectives that need to be reconciled. First, the government share of health care expenditure, which in Europe represents the majority of health spending (Lunt *et al.* 2011), is a major factor in government debt. This means that the rules developed to consolidate public sector finances are closely linked with issues related to the competitiveness of the health care system in general, and public hospitals in particular. Second, the fundamental rights of EU citizens and workers have had the effect of facilitating 'patient mobility'. While in practice this mobility remains limited in quantitative terms, the possible effects are huge. When the Court of Justice ruled that

> Union citizenship is destined to be the fundamental status of nationals of the Member States, enabling those who find themselves in the same situation to enjoy the same treatment in law irrespective of their nationality, subject to such exceptions as are expressly provided for,[16]

it made patient mobility possible. In the same way, the Court may invoke the freedom to provide services as a basis for this very right to patient mobility. The *Kohll*[17] judgment gave precedence to the logic and aims of the freedom to provide services, including in the medical sector, which it qualified as an economic sector on the basis of Regulation 1408/71. By controversially ruling out the application of Article 22 of the Regulation to the case at hand, the Court based its reasoning on the fundamental right to the freedom to provide services.[18] Since then, secondary law has intervened to clarify the arrangements for patient mobility. Regulation 883/2004 on the coordination of social security systems replaces Regulation 148/771, and Directive 2011/24 on the application of patients' rights in cross-border health care completes the picture.

'Health tourism' remains a rare occurrence within the EU. The question of financial sustainability does not seem to be a particular cause for concern, inasmuch as the Member State in which the health care is provided will be reimbursed, either by the social security system of the patient's Member State or by the patient him- or herself. On the other hand, public establishments based near borders may see patient mobility from the perspective of competitiveness. The real impact is hard to determine, especially because of a shortage of systematic data. But an OECD study comes to the conclusion that medical tourism may potentially improve cost competitiveness (Lunt *et al.* 2011).[19]

The wide range of legal instruments used is worth noting. France is party to several ad hoc agreements or agreements based on the application of EU regulations on the coordination of health care systems. Two examples provide a clear illustration of some of the parallel cooperation arrangements that are being developed, mainly in border regions. The first concerns two health care establishments, one public – the Centre hospitalier de Calais (Calais Hospital) – and the other private and non-profit – the Institut Calot in Berck-sur-Mer. Since April 2016, these two establishments have been fully integrated into the network of the UK National Health Service (Albert and Moniez 2016). They have both received NHS accreditation in the same way as UK-based hospitals, and in practice they are fully affiliated with the NHS system. This is the first time that accreditations of this nature have been issued. British patients have access to the treatment offered by these two establishments, in a national context that is under significant pressure. This mechanism perfectly reflects how public hospitals may experience the effects of competitiveness (in this case non-price competitiveness), especially in a European context.

The cooperation agreement concluded between France and Germany on 22 July 2005 in Weil am Rhein for the French regions of Alsace and Lorraine and the German regions of the Saar, Rhineland-Palatinate, and Baden-Württemberg is based on a different approach. The aim is not to integrate hospitals from one Member State into the health care system of another Member State, but to facilitate administrative relations. Other instruments of international law strengthen these cooperation mechanisms, without resulting in significant extensions to hospital markets.

Mechanisms to address the demands of competitiveness

To meet the demands of competitiveness, public hospitals have had to adapt. National legislators and regulatory authorities can draw on two categories of mechanism: budgetary and non-budgetary. While budgetary mechanisms have been largely adopted to align the funding framework of public hospitals with that of private establishments, the results have been mixed. Non-budgetary mechanisms have long remained outside the scope of discussions on the competitiveness of public hospitals, but they are nevertheless undergoing continuous development.

Mixed results for budgetary mechanisms

Public hospital funding has been subject to major reforms ever since costs began to weigh more heavily on health care budgets (Gay 2011).[20] In 1996, the legislator took a first major step by setting a budgetary framework with a target cap on health spending, in which public hospitals play an important part. But it was the 2003 law[21] that provided for a new hospital funding mechanism. Despite the fact that results are mixed after 10 years of application,[22] this law addresses the imperatives of competitiveness – albeit with several limits.

Initially, France sought to optimise the overall budgetary performance through the ONDAM system. The French Decree of 24 April 1996 set up a national health insurance expenditure target (ONDAM). Article L.174-1-1 of the French Social Security Code outlines the structure of this target for medical spending that should not be exceeded. The target is annexed to the law on social security funding and is therefore adopted by a vote in Parliament.[23] To avoid exceeding the limits, an 'Alert Committee' was set up.[24] The ONDAM provides for an overall budget divided into specific items. It is the primary mechanism for controlling health care expenditure.

The ONDAM does not lay down specific measures to be taken by public hospitals to make savings or increase their competitiveness, but it is a central consideration for all supervisory and regulatory activities. Regional Health Agencies (ARSs) are therefore required to 'contribute to compliance'[25] with the ONDAM by implementing national best practices at local level and by adopting new practices that meet local needs in the region for which they are responsible. Managing Directors of ARSs have considerable power. Article L.6145-4 of the French Public Health Code outlines their room for manoeuvre in the event of exceeding their budget or cost overrun. The assessments made by Managing Directors of ARSs are primarily based on the need to comply with the ONDAM. If there is no hospital manager, the Managing Director has power of substitution. Taking this logic one step further, it is the French government that determines reimbursement rates.[26] If the Alert Committee on health care expenditure issues an opinion that the ONDAM may be exceeded, the government may reduce the rates of services related to hospital care.[27] The ONDAM is also taken into account by the Economic Committee for Health Products (CEPS), one of whose main tasks is to ensure the effectiveness of this target.[28]

Controls on health care expenditure are further strengthened by contract-based incentive mechanisms. At local level, planning for health care expenditure has revealed the importance of establishing contractual relations between the government, represented by the ARS, and the public establishment. This is achieved by multi-year contracts for targets and resources, provided for in Articles L.6114-1ff. of the Public Health Code. According to Article L.6114-3, these contracts should 'incorporate targets for more effective medical use [*maîtrise médicalisée*] of expenditure'. The contracts serve as a basis for an incentive fund linked to best practices,[29] which in theory should lead to an increase in competitiveness. They are also associated with a sanction mechanism,[30] capped at 5 per cent of the revenue received by the establishment.

The competitiveness of public hospitals, especially in terms of costs, is an induced competitiveness. The underlying idea of this system is that hospitals are incapable of adjusting to the demands and requirements of competition by themselves. They need to be guided towards a new, 'healthier' approach.

Later on, France sought to reform hospital funding through a new incentive mechanism. The French system of activity-based payment (*tarification à l'activité*, or T2A) is based on the idea that there needs to be a level playing field between public health care establishments and private clinics.[31] This public-private convergence is reflected in an emphasis on competitiveness:

> The aim of the T2A system is to introduce transparency in terms of costs so that all health care establishments can be compared on equal terms, to base their funding on their real activity and therefore to incentivise them to make quantitative and qualitative improvements, to align their costs with those of the best-performing establishments, and to gradually achieve price convergence between the public and private sector.
>
> (Truchet 2009: 181)

This activity-based payment system therefore places public and private establishments in direct competition for the majority of their activities. Somewhat ironically, this levelling out of the conditions governing competition was designed to force hospitals out of their supposed 'comfort zone', in which there was no performance-based incentive. The new situation therefore introduces competition as a means of responding more effectively to the demands of competitiveness.

Despite the impression given by the name of this new funding system, in practice, pricing is not actually adjusted to the specific medical treatment provided. Instead, each patient is classified according to a *Groupe homogène des malades* (GHM), or diagnosis-related group (DRG), whose cost is determined by a 'stay-related group' (*Groupe homogène de séjour*, or GHS). So there are different funding allowances depending on the type of ailment treated. There may be variations depending on the medical capabilities of each hospital. A given GHM may therefore be associated with several GHSs.[32]

Several years after the T2A system was implemented, results have been mixed. The French Court of Auditors points out that, 'The implementation of the T2A, which revealed frequent situations of under-performance or insufficient efficiency, has led some establishments to reconsider internal hospital organisational structures and, to a lesser extent, hospital capacity so as to increase productivity', while emphasising that 'the T2A has had virtually no restrictive effect on medical expenditure' (Cour des Comptes 2016: 302). This situation is partly caused by the fact that it has 'proved to be an inflationary income mechanism, prompting other [establishments] to increase rather than rationalise activities' (Court des Comptes 2015: 185–216). While some studies indicate a significant correlation between the level of specialisation and budgetary performance (Evain and Yilmaz 2012), it remains true that in certain cases, especially in former local hospitals, low-paying mono-specialisation can lead to a budgetary shortfall that is difficult to sustain.[33]

Furthermore, some activities have been deliberately removed from the activity-based payment system, suggesting an attempt to find a balance between competitiveness and solidarity. Activities in the area of hospital care that are hard to cost are still funded on a flat-rate basis. These activities have been enumerated for the purposes of clarifying the scope of application of the T2A system. An exhaustive list can be found in Article D.162-6 of the Social Security Code, in application of Article L.162-23-1 of that code. These activities, which are mostly related to teaching, health crisis management, organisation of the regional framework for available health care and public health activities, are funded by a national allowance designed 'to fund missions of general interest and contracting assistance' (known by the French abbreviation MIGAC), set up as part of the ONDAM.[34] A Senate report refers to them as 'missions that are not quantifiable treatment activities' (Jégou 2011: 11). But these activities should not be seen as being entirely excluded from incentive mechanisms for competitiveness. Article L.6131-5 of the Public Health Code provides that Directors of Regional Health Agencies can draw on the MIGAC allowance as a means of engaging stakeholders for restructuring purposes.

Other health care fields continue to be funded by fixed allowances. This is the case for psychiatry,[35] health care provided in long-term treatment units,[36] and follow-up and rehabilitation care.[37] The most expensive and lengthy activities and, generally, those whose results require a sizeable investment of time but are not visible immediately have been removed from the T2A system. In other words, long-term activities whose results cannot immediately be felt in terms of patient flows and which are relatively inflexible in terms of response times fall outside the scope of competitive funding.

Identifying these activities limits the strict scope for competition among public hospitals. Hospitals are working towards the achievement of missions that are largely the same as those pursued by private for-profit establishments and private establishments in the public interest.[38] The Public Health Code, in its version issued after the entry into force of the 2016 law,[39] makes a clear separation between hospital public service missions and those categories of people authorised to perform them.

This method of funding should be understood in terms of the specific constraints of missions that run alongside health care activities per se and contribute to their effectiveness. These activities are divided into two broad groups: MERRIs (teaching, research, reference and innovation missions) and MIGs (missions in the general interest). They are performed in the general interest; they are more difficult to exploit on an economic market than health care activities. Taking this observation as a starting point, MIGAC funding should be seen as a means of compensating specific public service obligations. This approach is very similar to that applied by EU law to the funding of services of general economic interest.[40] But the fact that MIGACs are hard to assess in monetary terms distances them from this category, despite the attractive nature of the notion of enterprise in EU law,[41] which encourages a more thorough examination of how these missions should be qualified. Regardless of this question, it is clear that in French law, these missions are separated from those which represent the 'core activity' of hospitals, and they are not subject to the same activity-based funding system.

The reluctance of the legislator when it comes to 'market-based' funding of public hospitals is evident. As one author remarks, 'Reforms swing between two models: the growing intervention of public authorities in the management of health care establishments, and the market as the only means of coordinating stakeholders'; he adds that 'The complex movement that emerges … therefore oscillates between state control and commodification. Rather ironically, the process of increasing state control results in the growth of commodification' (Domin 2014: 306). The same observation can be applied to non-budgetary mechanisms.

The growing role of non-budgetary mechanisms

In addition to budgetary mechanisms, the legislator has turned to other instruments aimed at improving hospital competitiveness. Some are institution-based, such as local hospital clusters (GHTs), and others are contract-based.

The first group of mechanisms aims at strengthening cooperation and economies of scale. Public hospitals are torn between the conflicting priorities of making budgetary savings while maintaining a high level of public service. When savings are made by pooling services to create economies of scale, they may endanger the level of access to health care. Local hospital clusters (*groupements hospitaliers territoriaux*, or GHTs)[42] are the successor to local hospital communities,[43] which themselves had their origins in the former 'interhospital unions'. Under Article L.6132-1 of the French Public Health Code, all public establishments (unless they have a justified exemption) are required to be part of a GHT, whereas membership of the previous incarnations was optional. But only public hospitals must fulfil this obligation; private establishments are merely given the possibility of joining.[44] GHTs are based on a shared medical plan for the local area and on a pooling of some functions or resources.[45] The aim is to guarantee a high level of health care while achieving economic optimisation through economies of scale.

The presentation of GHTs in the 2016 French National Reform Programme explains that '[l]ocal hospital clusters should enable healthcare institutions to create joint medical projects to improve the medical services provided to the public and to pool a number of support functions (purchasing, information systems, etc.)' (Prime Minister of France 2016), based around pivot institutions. This was the basis for the drafting of Article 50 of the Healthcare Modernisation Bill.[46] According to the impact study,

> [c]ooperation between hospitals is a decisive factor in controlling health care spending by improving efficiency with the potential pooling of investment costs, structural costs and fixed charges, operating expenses and operational strategies of the members of a GCS [health cooperation cluster].[47]

The Social Security Funding Bill for 2017 provided for savings of €845 million over one year because of the GHT cluster system.[48] But this is qualified by the GHT heads of mission: In their May 2015 interim report, they warned against focusing on the wrong objective: the justification for GHTs should be the 'optimisation of territorial coverage and the scaling of hospital treatment' rather than the 'generation of efficiency margins' (Hubert and Martineau 2015: 42) – which should be a consequence rather than a cause.

The effect of pooling services at local level as a result of the new GHTs could in fact be to reduce the availability of competing health care options within a given geographical area. In economic terms, depending on the accessibility of different public hospitals, GHTs could lead to the monopolisation of a local cluster. This effect of concentration also applies to private competitors (Paillé 2016). Authors note that '[t]his objective of optimising the range of available health care [pursued by Regional Health Agencies] leads them to promote *complementarity* among establishments at the expense of competition, seen as a source of inefficiency at local level' (Pascal *et al.* 2011).

The second group of mechanisms is contract-based. It is worth noting the extent to which the 'contractual turn' that has characterised the French administration in the early twenty-first century can also be seen in hospitals. The most striking example is once again the introduction of GHTs. While they reflect a tendency towards institutionalisation, GHTs remain governed by agreements whose substance is circumscribed by laws and regulations. This is indicative of the particularities involved in rationalising the activities of public hospitals: agreements, which underpin the existence of freedom of contract, are nonetheless compulsory; they must comply with regional health care plans and are approved by the Managing Director of the local ARS.[49] Establishments that do not wish to join a GHT may see their MIGAC allowances withdrawn.[50] It should also be noted that support establishments for GHTs necessarily perform a number of vital tasks such as organising the strategy and management of medical information, carrying out procurement tasks and coordinating training institutes.[51]

Contract-based processes can also be seen at the individual level. Some contractual mechanisms are very clearly designed to improve the competitiveness and productivity of staff. The contract-based approach used to determine relationships and incentives between the state and health care establishments is therefore also echoed at the staff level. Ideally, the similarity between these two types of contract-based relationship should result in a degree of consistency, with the latter ultimately improving the efficiency of the former. This is especially the case for doctors. The variable share in the salary of hospital practitioners, as detailed in Article D.6152-23-1 of the Public Health Code, provides (in point number 5) that

> An allowance corresponding to a variable complementary share of the remuneration mentioned in point 1 of Article R.6152-23 and subject to compliance with a strong contractual commitment [and] to the quality and activity targets measured by indicators determined by official decisions

may complement a doctor's salary. The Decision of 28 March 2007[52] sets the fixed share of remuneration at 15 per cent. It also lays down the procedures for measuring the quality and activity criteria taken into account for the award of this bonus. Productivity is linked to efforts to improve quality, especially by the award of certifications. We can therefore note that, for the four medical procedures taken into consideration, activity is measured by a ratio between the 'total number of interventions' and the 'total number of surgeons'. For each of these four procedures that are taken as a reference, the percentage performed in outpatient care is also measured. The level of hospital-acquired infections, the average length of stay, the readmission rate and other criteria are assessed on the basis of a contractually established reference value. But the calculation of the variable part of the remuneration should be carried out in compliance with Article R.4127-97, which provides that

> A salaried doctor may in no case accept payment based on standards of productivity, hourly output or any other provision whose consequence would be to restrict or remove his/her independence or to have a negative effect on the quality of the care provided.

Conclusion

The inherent tension between the quest for competitiveness and the maintenance of a level of quality in health care that upholds the general principles of social rights is clearly evident in the health care sector, especially in public hospitals. At the same time, it is also possible to claim that, as the term 'competitiveness' has gained currency in public governance, hospitals may have actually contributed the development of this concept towards a more inclusive logic. The competitiveness sought by hospitals is not price competitiveness – or not exclusively, at any rate. The authors of the forward-looking report on performance-based remuneration for doctors emphasised the equivocal and multidimensional nature of 'performance':

> The notion of performance contains several dimensions. It can be applied to clinical performance and to the quality of health care, to the quality of patient relationships and their level of satisfaction, and finally to the efficiency of hospital practice, to the ability to minimise costs for a given level of quality.
>
> (Bras and Duhamel 2008: 35)

They note that 'given that the introduction of efficiency indicators runs the risk of discrediting any performance-based payment mechanism, such indicators should only be applied in the absence of an alternative' (ibid.: 36). In methodological terms, while the 'regulatory' approach adopted by Regional Health Agencies[53] demonstrates a desire for liberalisation in the field, it seems unable to fully dispense with planning tools (Blanc 2017). It may ultimately be this intermediate path that leads to a balance between the requirements of competitiveness and solidarity.

Acknowledgements

Many thanks to Sarah Cooper for the translation of this chapter from French.

Notes

1 For an exception, see Serré (2001).
2 Art. L.6112-3 French Public Health Code.
3 Including military hospitals, mentioned in Art. L.6147-7 French Public Health Code.
4 Art. L.6111-1 French Public Health Code.
5 Art. L.6323-1 French Public Health Code.
6 Art. L.6323-3 French Public Health Code.
7 Art. L.1110-8 French Public Health Code.
8 ADLC, Déc., *relative à la prise de contrôle exclusif des sociétés Clinique Esquirol Saint Hilaire et Ware Système par Médipôle Partenaires*, no 16-DCC-125, par. 5:

> When it comes to markets for diagnostics and hospital treatment in France, the national and European decision-making practice is based on the premise that it is not relevant to distinguish between services from private and public establishments.

Indeed, in France, patients are free to choose their health care establishment, public or private, without economic considerations, since the reimbursement of health care does not depend on the status of the establishment in which the treatment was provided.

9 The Agency is a public undertaking (Art. R.6113-34 of the Public Health Code) which is responsible for the task of classifying conditions treated in hospitals, thereby contributing to the *Programme de médicalisation des systèmes d'information* (PMSI), a model based on the concept of 'diagnosis related groups' that forms the backbone of the T2A system (see below). It is also involved in the statistical and analytical processing of these data (Art. R.6113-33 French Public Health Code).

10 All public data are available at: www.hospidiag.atih.santé.fr. The 'recruitment area' of a hospital is an indicator that is calculated as follows:

> The recruitment area around a hospital is calculated by ranking the geographical codes of patients treated at the hospital by decreasing number of stays, and only considering those that collectively make up 80% of the hospital's activities. The market share of a hospital in a given area for a given activity is calculated by taking the number of stays by residents of the area in the given hospital as a share of the total number of hospital stays of residents in the area for the selected activity.
>
> (ATIH 2012)

11 ADLC, Déc., relative à la prise de contrôle exclusif des sociétés Clinique Esquirol Saint Hilaire et Ware Système par Médipôle Partenaires, no 16-DCC-125.

12 Art. 60 of Act 99-641 of 27 July 1999 for the introduction of universal health coverage. See also Oral question 1302 in the Senate by Michel Boutant on 21 April 2011.

13 As things currently stand, in application of the Decision of 20 December 2016, amending the Decision of 8 June 2000 on the recruitment bonus for exclusive public service, the bonus broadly represents 10 per cent of the gross basic salary of hospital practitioners.

14 Art. 126 TFEU. These programmes are fully integrated into the systematic surveillance conducted as part of the European Semester (Art. 2-a of Regulation 1466/97).

15 For 2015, the drop in medical spending billed in addition to the T2A (the activity-based payment system – see below) represented savings of €73 million. Since 2010, total savings have reached €341 million, roughly equivalent to a major non-teaching hospital like the hospital in Valenciennes (€365 million in 2015) or a small teaching hospital.

16 CJEC, 20 September 2001, *Grzelczyk*, Case C-184/99.

17 CJEC, 28 April 1998, Case C-158/96.

18 For a general overview on this question, see Hennion (2014).

19 According to Lunt *et al.*:

> A development such as medical tourism can potentially exert competitive pressure on systems importing healthcare and help drive down the costs and prices offered in domestic systems.... Medical tourism may encourage economies to maximize their comparative advantage in labour costs, technology and/or capacity.
>
> (2011: 32)

20 Act of 19 January 1983 concerning various measures relating to social security, and Decree of 11 August 1983 on the management and funding of public and private hospital establishments providing public hospital services.

21 Act 2003-1199 of 18 December 2003 on social security funding for 2004.

22 The reform has been fully applicable since 2007.

23 Art. LO.111-3 French Social Security Code.

24 The 'Alert Committee on Health Insurance' (CADAM) was set up by Law no. 2004-811 of 13 August 2004 on the modernisation of health insurance.
25 Art. L.1431-1 French Public Health Code.
26 Art. L.162-22-9 ff. French Social Security Code.
27 Art. L.162-22-10 French Social Security Code.
28 See above. See also Art. L.162–17–3 French Social Security Code.
29 Art. L.6114-2 par. 3 French Public Health Code.
30 Art. L.6114-1, last paragraph, French Public Health Code.
31 François Hollande, then a candidate for the presidential election, stated at a conference at Robert Debré Hospital on 2 February 2012: 'I will bring an end to the level playing field between public and private health care, since it is a factor that creates unfair and inappropriate competition. Hospitals should be considered as a public service and not as companies' (Favereau 2012).
32 The nuances of these variations cannot be further elucidated here. It should merely be noted that they represent corrective mechanisms designed to cover treatment that does not fit in with the model of competitiveness provided in the funding scheme.
33 Former local hospitals were only subject to the T2A system gradually from 2015 onwards (Art. 52 of Act XXX of December 2014 on social security funding for 2015). In its report on the social security accounts for 2013, the French Court of Auditors noted this risk for these structures (Cour des Comptes 2013: 307–32).
34 Art. L.162-22-13 French Social Security Code.
35 Art. R.162-31ff. French Social Security Code.
36 Art. L.174-5 French Social Security Code.
37 Art. L.162-23-1 French Social Security Code.
38 Art. L.6111-1 French Public Health Code. *Centres de santé* and *maisons de santé* only compete with hospitals to a limited degree. Under Article L.6112-2 of the French Public Health Code, they are required to carry out some public hospital services. But their tasks cannot go beyond those provided in Articles L.6323-1 and 3 of the Public Health Code, in other words, primary health care as provided under Article L.1411-1 of the Public Health Code.
39 Art. L.6112-1 French Public Health Code as modified by Law no. 2016-41 of 26 January 2016 *de modernisation de notre système de santé.*
40 Truchet (2009: 182) also notes that

> [t]his approach is in compliance with the view of services of general interest that is now being promoted by EU law: identifying missions in detail to compensate their exact cost without any distortion of competition to the benefit or detriment of the operators performing them.

41 CJEC, *Höfner and Esler*, 23 April 1991, case C-41/90.
42 Introduced by Act 2016-41 of 26 January 2016 for the modernisation of our health care system.
43 Derived from Act 2009-879 of 21 July 2009 on hospital reform and concerning patients, health and regions.
44 Art. L.6132-1 VIII French Public Health Code.
45 Art. L.6132-1 French Public Health Code.
46 Adopted, Act 2016-41 of 16 January 2016.
47 Impact study on the Health Bill, 14 October 2014, NOR: AFSX1418355L/Bleue-1, p. 208.
48 Bill for social security funding, Annex 7, ONDAM and health care spending, p. 14.
49 Art. L.6132-2 French Public Health Code.
50 Art. L.6132-5 II French Public Health Code.
51 Art. L.6132-3 French Public Health Code.
52 Decision of 28 March 2007 on the additional variable share of remuneration provided in point 5 of Articles D.6152-23-1 and D.6152-220-1 of the French Public Health Code.
53 Art. L.1431-1 ff. French Public Health Code.

References

Albert, Éric and Laurie Moniez (2016). 'L'hôpital de Calais au secours du système de santé anglais', *Le Monde*, 15 April.

André, Jean-Marie (2014). 'La place des dépenses de santé dans l'économie européenne', in Sylvie Hennion and Otto Kaufmann (eds). *Citoyenneté européenne et libre circulation des patients*. Berlin: Springer, 127–43.

ATIH (Agence technique de l'information sur l'hospitalisation) (2012). 'Parts de marché par zone de recrutement pour un FINESS ou par territoire de santé'. Available at: www.scansante.fr/sites/default/files/content/51/notice_part_de_marche.pdf

Blanc, François (2017). 'Libéralisation ou planification?', *Revue française de droit administratif* 179(1): 76–84.

Bras, Pierre-Louis and Gilles Duhamel (2008). *Rapport sur rémunérer les médecins selon leurs performances: les enseignements des expériences étrangères*. Paris: IGAS/La Documentation française. Available at: www.ladocumentationfrancaise.fr/docfra/rapport_telechargement/var/storage/rapports-publics/084000596.pdf

CNOM (Conseil National de l'Ordre des Médecins) (2017). 'Construire l'avenir à partir des territoires: la réforme voulue par les médecins'. Available at: www.conseil-national.medecin.fr/sites/default/files/reformevoulueparlesmedecins.pdf

Cour des Comptes (2013). *La sécurité sociale: rapport sur l'application des lois de financement de la sécurité sociale*. Paris: La Documentation française.

Cour des Comptes (2015). *La sécurité sociale: rapport sur l'application des lois de financement de la sécurité sociale*. Paris: La Documentation française.

Cour des Comptes (2016). *La sécurité sociale: rapport sur l'application des lois de financement de la sécurité sociale*. Paris: La Documentation française.

DGDDI (Direction Générale des Douanes et Droits Indirects) (2017). 'Le Chiffre du commerce extérieur, année 2016'. Available at: http://lekiosque.finances.gouv.fr/fichiers/etudes/thematiques/a2016.pdf

Domin, Jean-Paul (2014). *Une histoire économique de l'hôpital (XIXe–XXe siècles): une analyse rétrospective du développement hospitalier*. Vol. II *(1946–2009)*. Paris: La Documentation française.

EC (European Commission) (2017). 'Communication: 2017 European Semester: assessment of progress on structural reforms, prevention and correction of macroeconomic imbalances, and results of in-depth reviews under Regulation (EU) No 1176/2011'. COM(2017) 90 final, 22 February. Brussels: European Commission.

Evain, Franck and Engin Yilmaz (2012). 'Les déterminants de la rentabilité économique des établissements de santé', *Économie publique* 28–9(1–2): 305–16.

Favereau, Éric (2012). 'Hollande, tant qu'on a la santé…', *Libération*, 3 February. Available at: www.liberation.fr/france/2012/02/03/hollande-tant-qu-on-a-la-sante_793279

Gay, Renaud (2011). 'Les reformes hospitalières au début des années 1980: une bifurcation du système hospitalier? Politisation de l'action publique et capacités réformatrices limitées'. Available at: https://halshs.archives-ouvertes.fr/halshs-00687835

Hennion, Sylvie (2014). 'Maîtrise des dépenses de santé et libertés de circulation', in Sylvie Hennion and Otto Kaufmann (eds). *Citoyenneté européenne et libre circulation des patients*. Berlin: Springer, 31–48.

Hubert, Jacqueline and Frédéric Martineau (2015). *Mission Groupements Hospitaliers de Territoire – Rapport intermédiaire*. Paris: Ministère des Affaires Sociales, de la Santé et des Droits des Femmes. Available at: www.sante.gouv.fr/IMG/pdf/Rapport_intermediaire_Mission_GHT_definitif.pdf

Huguier, Michel and Patrick Romestaing (2014). 'Numerus clausus et démographie médicale en France', *Bulletin de l'Académie Nationale de Médecine* 198(7): 1367–78.

IGAS (Inspection Générale des Affaires Sociales) (2013). *L'hôpital: rapport 2012*. Paris: La Documentation française. Available at: www.ladocumentationfrancaise.fr/docfra/rapport_telechargement/var/storage/rapports-publics/134000107.pdf

IGF/IGAS (Inspection Générale des Finances/Inspéction Générale des Affaires Sociales) (2012). *Rapport. Propositions pour la maîtrise de l'ONDAM 2013–2017*. Paris: La Documentation française. Available at: www.ladocumentationfrancaise.fr/docfra/rapport_telechargement/var/storage/rapports-publics/124000347.pdf

Institut Montaigne (2016). 'Réanimer le système de santé: propositions pour 2017'. Available at: www.institutmontaigne.org/ressources/pdfs/publications/reanimer_systeme_de_sante.pdf

Jégou, Jean-Jacques (2011). *Rapport d'information fait au nom de la Commission des finances sur les missions d'intérêt général et d'aide à la contractualisation*. No. 686. Paris: Sénat. Available at: www.senat.fr/rap/r10-686/r10-6861.pdf

Lunt, Neil, Richard Smith, Mark Exworthy, Stephen Green, Daniel Horsfall, and Russell Mannion (2011). *Medical tourism: treatments, markets and health system implications: a scoping review*. Paris: OECD.

Paillé, Jean-Yves (2016). 'Cliniques: "Le secteur va continuer à animer le marché des fusions et acquisitions"', *La Tribune*, 26 June. Available at: www.latribune.fr/economie/france/cliniques-le-secteur-va-continuer-a-animer-le-marche-des-fusions-et-acquisition-580944.html

Pascal, Christophe, Jean-Baptiste Capgras, Nicholas Guilhot, and Jean-Pierre Claveranne (2011). 'L'information médico-économique entre décision stratégique et action publique: tout savoir pour peu pouvoir!', *Politiques et management public* 28(1).

Prime Minister of France (2016). 'National Reform Programme 2016'. Available at: www.economie.gouv.fr/files/files/PDF/PNR2016-integral-anglais.pdf

Serré, Marina (2001). 'Le "tournant néo-libéral" de la santé? Les réformes de la protection maladie en France dans les années 1990 ou l'acclimatation d'un référentiel de marché', PhD thesis, Université Paris I, Paris.

Truchet, Didier (2009). *Droit de la santé publique*. 7th edn. Paris: Dalloz.

Véran, Olivier (2013). 'Hôpital cherche médecins, coûte que coûte: essor et dérives du marché de l'emploi médical temporaire à l'hôpital public'. Available at: www.apmnews.com/Documents/rapportemploimdicaltemporairelhpital.pdf

10 Competitive solidarity and regional development

The case of Italy

Laura Polverari

Regional development policies embody the concept of 'competitive solidarity' probably more so than any other public policy. They aim to raise the levels of socio-economic development and quality of life in lagging regions. To do so, they mobilise additional public investments in these territories. As such, regional policies epitomise the concept of solidarity between regions. At the same time, based on an increasing recognition that the sustained development of lagging regions and their resiliency require a step change in their ability to compete in international markets, regional policies have been reframed over the past decades. Emphasis has tended to shift from generalised infrastructure and business aids to: R&D and innovation; investments in infrastructure and skills more closely linked to the development of productive activities; and the enhancement of administrative capacity to create a more suitable context for endogenous development. In other words, regional policies put the concept of competitive solidarity in action and to the test.[1]

Italy is one of the countries in Europe that has one of the longest-standing experiences of regional development policy. However, success has been mixed and contested (Polverari 2013), and over the past 10 years the economic crisis has eroded the progress that had been made during the late 1990s and early 2000s (SVIMEZ 2017).

This chapter discusses Italian regional policy as a case of concrete application of the concept of competitive solidarity. More precisely, it discusses the degree to which Italian regional policy can be viewed as having been successful, as well as the factors that might explain this. The next section reviews the evolution of regional disparities in Italy. The following section describes the evolution of regional policy over time and the key elements of the current policy approach. Then, the institutional framework for policy implementation is illustrated, followed by an assessment of the policy's success. Summary conclusions are presented at the end.

The evolution of regional disparities in Italy

From a medium-term perspective – with the exception of the years 1998–2001, when 'the gap between North and South went down by two/three decimals per year' (La Spina 2016: 997), and the slight convergence during 2002–08 (largely linked to a slowing-down of the Centre-North's economy and to demographic trends) – not only have regional disparities persisted but, in the last decade, they have actually widened. Between 2008 and 2014, gross domestic produce (GDP) shrank by 7.9 per cent in the Centre-North and by 12.7 per cent in the South (MEF 2016: 9). Looking further back in time, a process of real GDP convergence was realised only until the mid-1970s (Franco 2010), arguably as a result of the massive investment programmes realised under the Special Intervention.

There have been some signs of recovery from the crisis in the last couple of years. Since 2014, the Centre-North regions have started to grow (Banca d'Italia 2015) and 2015 marked the end of the seven-year-long recession for the *Mezzogiorno* too: not only did the *Mezzogiorno* start to grow again, but it also grew at a higher rate than the rest of the country (1 per cent versus 0.7 per cent in the Centre-North). This growth, however, was primarily due to the positive performance of the agriculture, tourism, and construction sectors: thus, largely linked to conjunctural factors, rather than to regaining competitiveness (SVIMEZ 2016). The acceleration of investments under the EU Cohesion Policy, in the spending rush for the closure of the 2007–13 programming cycle, arguably played a role too, partly compensating for the reduction of public capital spending that followed the crisis. Employment and unemployment data also became positive in 2015, with stronger improvements in the *Mezzogiorno* than the Centre-North. However, as it was the *Mezzogiorno* that bore the most significant job losses during the recession, the employment rate there continues to remain significantly lower than in the rest of the country. In-work poverty and youth poverty are also highly regionally differentiated and concentrated predominantly in the Southern regions (Ciccarone *et al.* 2016; Gallo and Forte 2016). As underlined by SVIMEZ in their last annual report:

> If the consolidation of the South's recovery suggests that the crisis has not undermined the ability of Southern regions to remain hooked onto the development of the rest of the country and of Europe, nevertheless the rhythm of the conjuncture appears fully insufficient to tackle the social emergencies of the area, which remain alarming.
>
> (SVIMEZ 2017: 5, author's translation from Italian)

If we take a wider perspective – EU-wide rather than country-wide – we can see that the relative positioning of the laggard Italian regions has deteriorated also when compared to the rest of the EU. Sardinia and Basilicata, that had escaped the status of less developed/Art. 107(3)(a) regions[2] in the 2007–13 programming cycle, are once again below this threshold, and analyses based on more recent (2012–14) GDP data at NUTS 2 level[3] confirm that they would continue to be so also post-2020.[4]

In short, the hopes for a continued upward catching-up of the Italian South were crushed by the economic crisis and by the austerity measures that were introduced to curb it. However, a key question lies with the reasons for this.

The policy response

The evolution of regional policy in Italy: a long-term perspective

As is well known, the North-South divide in Italy is a long-standing question that has accompanied the life of the Italian State since its birth as a putative unitary country in 1861. The first policy action to address the socio-economic backwardness of this part of country dates back to the Giolitti age, when the first special laws to this purpose were approved (Carabba 2011).[5] But it is really after the Second World War, in parallel with similar developments in other European countries (for example, the UK and France), that a systematic and substantial policy response to regional disparities was formulated with the creation of the Special Intervention and the institution of the Cassa per il Mezzogiorno. Since then, and strong in Constitutional recognition (Art. 119), the need for a policy response to the 'Mezzogiorno question' – *la questione meridionale* – has been a constant feature of Italian political debates. Policy responses, however, have fluctuated over time, both in terms of rationale and intensity. We can identify a number of distinct policy phases.

The *first period of Special Intervention* lasted from the post-war reconstruction effort (the 1947 Marshall Plan) and the institution of the Cassa (in 1950) until the mid/late 1960s (Gualini 2004; La Spina 2003, 2016). This is a period that was inspired by Keynesian approaches to development and that is considered to have been, on the whole, successful in improving economic indicators, albeit from a top-down (and thus not self-sustaining) perspective (Trigilia 1992).

The *second period of Special Intervention* started in the late 1960s/early 1970s and ended with its abolition in 1992. This is a period when the policy is largely viewed to have been unsuccessful. This was partly linked to the reform of the policy's operation – e.g. the substitution of the Cassa with the Agency for the Mezzogiorno with Law 64/1986, which has been interpreted as leading to increased politicisation and 'particularistic' resource allocation (Trigilia 1992) – and partly connected to factors external to the policy, such as: the oil crisis; labour reform and abolition of the so-called *gabbie salariali*; and the creation of regional authorities and their quest for autonomy in economic development programming (Gualini 2004; La Spina 2003).

The '*nuova programmazione*' (new programming) was inaugurated in the late 1990s, after a few years of stalemate represented by the interim period between the abolition of the Special Intervention and the approval, in 1996, of the implementation decrees for the new, major industrial incentive scheme for laggard regions (known as Law 488/1992). This period entails a radical overhaul of the policy, Europeanisation of the policy response and implementation arrangements, and acceleration of devolution of responsibilities in certain policy areas to the regional authorities (Graziano 2013; Gualini 2004; Polverari and Tagle 2013). The new policy adopted an endogenous growth model and provided a highly coordinated policy response through the 2000–06 Community Support Framework (CSF), which provided a common structure and strategy applicable to all Regional and National Operational Programmes (ROPs and NOPs) implemented in the *Mezzogiorno* regions under the banner of the EU Cohesion Policy. A mix of instruments was used, ranging from more traditional (e.g. construction or upgrading of infrastructure of different sorts) to more innovative in fields such as support to business (e.g. the Integrated Support Packages in the NOP local development) and local development (the new Integrated Territorial Projects) (Polverari and Tagle 2013). This phase led to mixed results, with achievements well below initial targets both in macro- and micro-economic terms (Barca 2006; Scalera and Zazzaro 2010; Viesti 2009).

The period of the failed '*unitary programming*' largely coincided with the 2007–13 programming period of the European Cohesion Policy (Polverari 2013). Conceptually, the strategies implemented in this period represented a continuation of the endogenous growth model introduced in 2000–06, but with the major innovation of the declared integration of the co-funded strand of regional policy (the EU Cohesion Policy programmes) with the domestic strand of Italian regional policy (then called FAS, Fund for the Underutilised Areas), under a so-called 'unitary policy' (*politica unitaria*). Under the new framework, represented by a National Strategic Reference Framework (NSRF, although country-wide rather than applicable to the *Mezzogiorno* regions only, a number of parallel regional and multi-regional programmes were established to work in synergy and in coherence and complementarity with the Structural Funds co-funded ones. As already observed elsewhere (Polverari 2013; Polverari and Tagle 2013), after the approval of the NSRF, the change in national government in 2008 brought in a drastic reduction of the financial resources for the domestic regional development policy. This resulted in a substantial, de facto alteration of the strategies that regions could implement, given the specialisation previously sought between domestic and co-funded programmes. Central coordination activities also decreased (Polverari 2013). The onset of the crisis, and the absorption and co-financing challenges it caused, led to a further weakening of the policy framework, with consequences that will be discussed in the next section.

Lastly, the *current policy phase* (2014–20) was characterised by institutional change, with the creation of new institutions and partial recentralisation of policy competences, abandonment of the unitary programming approach, and policy reorientation. These latest developments are the focus of the next section.

The current policy framework

The main focus of regional policy support are the *eight Mezzogiorno regions*. The 2014–20 regional aid map, approved in September 2014, included five regions (Apulia, Basilicata, Calabria, Campania, and Sicily) encompassing 29.04 per cent of the Italian population as eligible under Article 107(3)(a), just as in 2007–13 (EC 2014a).[6] In addition, 25 zones covering 5.03 per cent of the national population were eligible for support as non-predefined areas under Article 107(3)(c). Following the European Commission's amendment of the Regional Aid Guidelines in June 2016, Sardinia also became eligible to change status to an Article 107(3)(a) area (EC 2016c). Thus, at present, the group of Less Developed regions is wider compared to 2007–13. This group now includes not only Apulia, Campania, Calabria and Sicily (as in 2007–13), but also Basilicata (which was a Phasing-Out region in 2007–13) and, since the end of June 2016, Sardinia. Moreover, the regions Abruzzo and Molise (both more developed regions in 2007–13) are now Transition regions (Sardinia, which was Phasing-In in 2007–13, was also originally classified as Transition region, but re-classified as a Less Developed region in June 2016). This essentially re-confirms the traditional *Mezzogiorno* macro-area, comprising the eight Southern regions, in contrast to the more developed 13 regions and autonomous provinces (Trento and Bolzano) of the Centre-North. The focus on the *Mezzogiorno* regions is also confirmed by the government's commitment to concentrate at least 80 per cent of expenditure under the domestic fund for regional development (so-called FSC, *Fondo Sviluppo e Coesione*) and at least 34 per cent[7] of the ordinary capital expenditure of national administrations in these regions. It should be noted that similar thresholds had been in place in the past but were never achieved in practice.

The strategic framework of current regional policy is represented by the 2014–20 Partnership Agreement, required by the Common Provisions Regulations of the European Structural and Investment Funds (ESI Funds or ESIF).[8] The overarching objective of regional policy is, however, set out in the *Italian Constitution* (Art. 3 and Art. 119), which includes a commitment to state intervention to promote socio-economic development across the territory geared at ensuring that all citizens, irrespective of where they live, have equal economic and social rights. Thus, regional policy is conceived as an additional intervention to support investment and public services, which aims to stimulate more spatially equal economic growth and social opportunities (DPS 2012: 175–6; Ministro per la Coesione Territoriale 2014: 3).

The *Partnership Agreement* (PA) translates these objectives into specific goals relating to the allocation of 'additional' capital funding for structurally weaker regions, with the aim of facilitating the accumulation of capital and capacities. It places this macro-objective in the context of the economic crisis, which had made it necessary to make considerable adjustments to the 2007–13 programmes. In the Centre-North, the focus is on the competitive relaunch of the economy, particularly via modernisation of the 'Made in Italy' project and the development of high-technology sectors. In the South, the emphasis is on supporting existing firms and new competitive, high-value sectors, as well as human capital, social inclusion, employment, and the capacities necessary for more effective implementation. A special focus is on internal areas and cities, viewed as underexploited drivers of economic and social development (DPS 2014: 117–21). Cities, in particular, are now supported through a National Operational Programme which delegates implementation responsibilities to the 13 metropolitan cities covered (across the entire country, but with higher resource allocations for the cities in the South). The PA broadly follows on from 2007–13: (1) it views, in principle at least, regional policy as a unitary policy that integrates domestic and EU funding; (2) it considers regional policy as an 'additional' policy aimed at overcoming territorial disparities (compared to 'ordinary' public capital spending and current expenditure); and (3) it largely focuses on endogenous growth based on the exploitation of local assets and opportunities. In addition to EU-driven changes (e.g. Thematic Objectives, results-orientation, territorial dimension via new instruments[9]), the PA also shifts the weight on social interventions; it increases the number of national (as opposed to regional) Operational Programmes and emphasises institutional/administrative strengthening (on this issue, see Nifo and Vecchione 2015; Terracciano and Graziano 2016). One further important aspect of the regional development policy framework entailed by the PA for the 2014–20 period is industrial development in line with the national and regional smart specialisation strategies and support of the productive system through capitalisation-enhancing measures for firms in the *Mezzogiorno*.

The PA is implemented through regional and multi-regional/national programmes (abbreviated as ROPs and NOPs respectively), the latter with varying territorial coverage, as illustrated in Table 10.1.

Table 10.1 Structural Funds co-funded programmes in Italy and their territorial coverage, 2014–20

	ERDF	*ESF*	*Multi Fund ERDF ESF*
National territory		NOP Active Employment Policies Systems NOP Inclusion NOP YEI	NOP Education NOP Metropolitan Cities NOP Governance
Less Developed & Transition Regions	NOP Enterprises and Competitiveness SME Initiative NOP (also applies to Abruzzo)		NOP Research and Innovation
Less Developed Regions	NOP Infrastructure and Networks NOP Culture and Development		NOP Legality
Regional territory	A ROP for each region/ autonomous province, except for Calabria, Molise and Apulia	A ROP for each region / autonomous province, except for Calabria, Molise and Apulia	ROP Calabria, Molise and Apulia

Source: Rusca (2015), plus information on the SME Initiative Programme (approved 30 November 2015).

The strategy outlined in the Partnership Agreement was supplemented, after the issuance of this document, by a '*Masterplan for the Mezzogiorno*' and the ensuing '*Pacts*' (eight regional, seven for the metropolitan cities of the Mezzogiorno,[10] plus one for Taranto, linked to an institutional development contract). These represent the domestic side of regional policy, financed by the Fondo Sviluppo e Coesione (FSC).[11] Except for the special Pact for Taranto, the Pacts were all signed between April and November 2016. The 15 regional and metropolitan pacts together mobilise about €13.4 million from the FSC, for a total investment of about €39.2 million.[12]

The Masterplan has been described as complementary to the Partnership Agreement. For example, the eight city Pacts complement interventions in the National Operational Programme for the Metropolitan Cities (NOP Metro). The Pacts were intended to realise a middle way between the fragmentation and delays of the decentralised '*nuova programmazione*' and the top-down approach of the Special Intervention. Guiding principles for the Pacts include their synergy and complementarity with the programmes funded by the EU Cohesion Policy (i.e. the PA and the related OPs), the strategic nature of the interventions, the integration between funds, and the implementation readiness of projects (MEF 2017: 48). However, in practice, the Pacts place emphasis on ready-to-start projects (primarily infrastructure projects), stringent implementation timetables, and integration/synergy with other funding sources beyond the FSC (PCM 2016). The approach is thus quite opposite to the programming approach of the Partnership Agreement: while this applies the multi-annual programming approach that is typical of the EU Cohesion Policy, the Pacts essentially comprise lists of interventions (projects), selected from existing plans and programmes based on implementation speed and, arguably, political preference.

Notwithstanding the fact that they represent an improvement compared to the long period of standstill in domestic regional policy that preceded the Masterplan,[13] the Masterplan and the Pacts have been criticised by regional policy experts for their 'modest scope', limited financial relevance, lack of strategic vision, lack of additional impetus, and absence of any programming and monitoring mechanisms to ensure that the foreseen territorial earmarking of the domestic regional development fund (80 per cent to be spent in the *Mezzogiorno* regions, as mentioned) is achieved in practice (Viesti 2016).

An overview of the financial resources deployed to support this composite strategic framework is provided in Table 10.2. This includes both EU funds (headings A, B and C) and domestic resources (co-financing to EU programmes and FSC) (headings D and E).

The institutional framework of regional policy

In keeping with the multilevel territorial governance of Italy more widely, the design and implementation of *regional policy involve both national and regional levels*. National authorities are responsible for key strategic and coordination tasks and for implementing sectoral Cohesion Policy OPs and sectoral programmes

Table 10.2 Regional policy resources in Italy in 2014–20 (million euro)

	EU resources				*National resources (National Cofinancing to EU programmes, FSC, Piano Azione Coesione)*				*Total resources*			
	Mezzogiorno	*Centre-North*	*Not pre-allocated*	*Total*	*Mezzogiorno*	*Centre-North*	*Not pre-allocated*	*Total*	*Mezzogiorno*	*Centre-North*	*Not pre-allocated*	*Total*
A) Structural and Investment Funds	29,275.7	11,832.3	1,559.9	42,667.9	16,582.7	12,700.9	1,672.9	30,956.5	45,858.4	24,533.2	3,232.9	73,624.4
ERDF	17,243.4	3,407.0	–	20,650.4	8,592.2	3,407.0	–	1,999.2	25,835.6	6,814.0	–	32,649.5
ESF	6,307.3	4,161.1	–	10,468.4	4,024.8	4,061.4	–	8,086.2	10,332.1	8,222.4	–	18,554.6
EAFRD	5,456.5	3,965.2	1,022.7	10,444.4	3,965.8	5,232.5	1,232.1	10,430.4	9,422.3	9,197.7	2,254.8	20,874.7
EMFF	–	–	537.3	537.3	–	–	440.8	440.8	–	–	978.1	978.1
YEI	268.4	299.1	–	567.5	–	–	–	–	268.4	299.1	–	567.5
B) European Territorial Cooperation Programmes (ETCP)	–	–	1,136.8	1,136.8	–	–	200.6	200.6	–	–	1,337.4	1,337.4
C) FEAD (Fund for European Aid to the Most Deprived)	–	–	670.6	670.6	–	–	118.3	118.3	–	–	788.9	788.9
D) Complementary programmes–Cohesion Action Plans 2014–20	–	–	–	–	7,425.3	–	–	7,425.3	7,425.3	–	–	7,425.3
E) Development and Cohesion Fund (FSC 2014–20)	–	–	–	–	40,069.2	9,608.9	–	49,678.1	40,069.2	9,608.9	–	49,678.1
TOTAL	29,275.7	11,832.3	3,367.3	44,475.3	64,077.3	22,309.8	1,991.9	88,378.9	93,352.9	34,142.1	5,359.2	132,854.2

Source: reproduced from /www.opencoesione.gov.it/risorse_2014_2020/ (data at 9 March 2017; accessed 1 February 2018).

financed by the domestic Fund for Development and Cohesion (FSC, formerly FAS – *Fondo Aree Sottoutilizzate*), while regional authorities design and implement regional programmes funded by the EU Cohesion Policy and also by the FSC. In addition to bilateral interactions between state authorities and individual regions, cooperation between the state and sub-national authorities has been facilitated for many years by the State-Region and Unified Conferences (*Conferenze Stato-Regioni e Unificata*), which bring together state, regional, and local authorities. An Inter-ministerial Committee for Economic Programming (*Comitato Interministeriale per la Programmazione Economica*, CIPE), chaired by the President of the Council of Ministers and made up of ministers with responsibilities related to economic policy, takes key decisions on economic and financial policy, including Cohesion Policy and the FSC; while a General Inspectorate for the Management of Financial Relations with the EU (IGRUE) is in charge of the financial flows of the EU Cohesion Policy programmes through two dedicated funds (EU resources and national co-financing).

Since 2014, there have been significant changes in the national attribution of tasks (Boscariol 2015). First, political responsibility for regional policy, co-financed by both ESIF and domestic funds, lies in the hands of the President of the Council of Ministers, who can also delegate tasks to a Minister or Under-secretary (as at the time of writing, following the appointment by Paolo Gentiloni of Claudio De Vincenti as Minister for Territorial Cohesion and the Mezzogiorno). Recent legislation strengthened the role of the President of the Council of Ministers, who now monitors the EU Cohesion Policy and the FSC programmes to ensure that they are on track. If programmes do not progress as anticipated, the Presidency can propose the reprogramming of funds (even across administrations) and even exert 'substitution powers', taking on managing authority tasks.

Second, a new *Agency for Territorial Cohesion* has been launched. Responsibility for national coordination of regional policy previously lay with the Department for Economic Development and Cohesion (Dipartimento per lo Sviluppo e la Coesione Economica, DPS) which had been under the Ministry for Economic Development since the mid-2000s. The Department's tasks and personnel have now been reassigned partly to the Presidency of the Council of Ministers (in a new and streamlined Department for Cohesion Policies) but mainly to the new Agency for Territorial Cohesion.[14] The Agency was expected in 2012, but was only formally instituted with Legislative Decree 101/2013 (converted into Law 125/2013 of 30 October 2013, the 'Stability Law') and then required the approval of a statute by the President of the Council of Ministers (on 9 July 2014, OJ General Series, no. 191 of 19 August 2014) and three decrees of the President of the Council of Ministers to effectively start operation (issued on 15 December 2014). These decrees: (1) integrated the 'Department for Development and Cohesion Policies' into the Presidency of the Council of Ministers; (2) defined the Agency's new tasks; and (3) transferred financial, human, and operational resources to both the Department and the Agency.

The Agency is in charge of the following tasks:

- systematic and on-going monitoring of the EU Cohesion Policy Operational Programmes and interventions, including through dedicated evaluations and analyses;
- support and technical assistance to the administrations in charge of managing teh EU Cohesion Policy and the FSC programmes, including through dedicated training and hands-on support;
- supervising the implementation of the EU Cohesion Policy and the FSC programmes and projects, including institutional development contracts and negotiated programming agreements;
- promotion of the quality, timeliness, efficacy, and transparency of programming and implementation relating to the EU Cohesion Policy and the FSC fund;
- undertaking management of authority functions for experimental projects or substituting for an underperforming managing authority;
- undertaking management of authority functions for two ERDF NOPs: Governance and institutional capacity and Metropolitan Cities.

Even after the approval of all the necessary legislation and decrees, it took the Agency quite some time to become fully operational, however. For example, the appointment of two managing authorities for the two aforementioned NOPs was delayed quite significantly. To illustrate, the Monitoring Committee of the NOP Metro met for the first time only in December 2015, effectively two years after the start of the 2014–20 programming period.

In parallel with the launch of the Agency for Cohesion, a Decree of the President of the Council of Ministers (19 November 2014) reorganised the national Evaluation and Verification Units (UVAL and UVER) which had been in place since the 1980s, under the aegis of the Department for Development and Cohesion (DPS). After some delay, a new *Evaluation and Analysis for Programming Unit* (NUVAP, *Nucleo di valutazione e analisi per la programmazione*) now supports the Presidency of the Council of Ministers, and a new *Verification and Control Unit* (NUVEC, *Nucleo di verifica e controllo*) supports the Agency for Territorial Cohesion.

A further important recent change is the institution of a new committee or *Cabina di Regia* for the domestic FSC side of regional policy in 2014–20.[15] Led by the Minister or Undersecretary for Cohesion and the Department for Cohesion Policies, the Cabina is made up of a few representatives from the regional authorities and autonomous provinces as well as the relevant sectoral ministries (first and foremost the Ministry of Infrastructures and Transport). It is charged with defining and monitoring implementation of the 'Masterplan for the *Mezzogiorno*' and the various Pacts funded by the FSC under its aegis.[16]

The main thrust of these institutional changes has been the desire to *increase national-level coordination and oversight*, particularly in the light of the implementation problems and delays experienced in the programmes for some

Southern regions during 2007–13: a goal that had already been anticipated by Fabrizio Barca, when he was Minister for Territorial Cohesion during the Monti Government (November 2011–April 2013; see Barca 2012). However, the increased fragmentation of regional policy responsibilities – entailed by the operational separation between the EU co-funded and the domestic side of regional policy, the institution of new bodies to coordinate the latter (not only the *Cabina di Regia* but also Pact-specific coordination committees dedicated to monitoring the progress of the Pacts), and the delegation of some policy responsibilities to the metropolitan cities – present the risk, in the absence of a single strategic document bringing all the policy strands and instruments into a coherent whole, of generating operational inefficiencies.

Assessment: is Italian regional policy a good example of competitive solidarity?

Against the strategic, financial, and operational background described above, a key question is whether the policy is delivering its goals: has regional policy in Italy been effective? Has it realised its ultimate goal of overcoming the development gap between Centre-North and South? The data discussed in the first section, as well as available statistical and evaluative evidence, suggest that regional policy in Italy has not achieved its objectives. After a detailed analysis of the long-term achievements of the EU Cohesion Policy in Campania, for example, a recent evaluation formulated the 'sobering judgement … that the region continued to have the same problems of poverty, unemployment, worklessness, hidden employment and organised crime as it had two decades previously', and featured as the worst performer among the 15 regions considered by the study, trapped in a 'vicious circle' of relative decline (Bachtler *et al.* 2016: 85, 103).

Public policy, however, does not operate in a vacuum and the picture is more nuanced. Although the development gap, as illustrated in the introduction to this chapter, remains, some important achievements have nevertheless been realised. That said, the results have been disappointing and require an appraisal of the reasons for this performance so significantly below expectations.

An important contribution both in the short and in the long term

Starting with the positive achievements realised so far, two important issues need to be mentioned.

First, over the shorter term, the policy, particularly the EU co-funded side of it, has been fundamental to *protect public investments during the period of austerity which followed the economic crisis*. Both current and capital expenditure have contracted since 2010 across Italy, but more strongly in the *Mezzogiorno*, and the *Mezzogiorno* has also disproportionately paid for the effect of the fiscal consolidation measures introduced by the Italian government, as demonstrated by recent analyses by Francesco Prota and Gianfranco Viesti (Prota 2016; Viesti

2015a, 2015b). In this framework in Italy, as in other Southern European countries that were also severely affected by the economic crisis, the policy has 'protected' public investment budgets from cuts that would have been deeper in its absence. Financial allocations have supported regions in dealing with their declining fiscal capacity and reductions in central transfers (Bubbico and Catalina Rubianes 2015). This support to investment has been particularly crucial in the short term for Italy which, due to its scarce fiscal margins, could not implement substantial fiscal stimulus programmes like the other EU Member States in the years immediately after 2008 (ibid.). According to the European Commission, during 2011–13, Cohesion Policy expenditure represented 8.6 per cent of total public investment in Italy – a figure that is considerably lower than the equivalent values for Greece, Portugal, and Spain (respectively a staggering 62.4 per cent, 23.0 per cent, and 11.2 per cent) but significant nevertheless (EC 2014b). This funding has arguably *prevented the further aggravation of regional disparities* (ibid.; see also Merler 2016). Further, it could be argued that the policy may have played a *redistributive function*, given the constraints to public spending which continue to limit 'any room for redistributive policies' (Ciccarone *et al.* 2016: 5). For example, 'the inadequate supply and quality of public welfare services (especially a widespread system of early childhood care) further obstruct female participation in the labour market' (ibid.: 5): this is an area in which regional policy has invested and thus the situation would have been worse off in its absence.

Second, from a longer-term perspective, regional policy has contributed to the *realisation of essential investments in the Southern regions*, notably in relation to essential and transport infrastructure, which did improve the quality of life of residents in the Southern regions and these regions' development potential.[17] In illustration, research on the long-term achievements of the EU Cohesion Policy in the region of Campania (1989–12) found that, thanks to the investments realised:

> The region saw dramatic improvements in public rail networks with the completion of the regional integrated network including the Naples underground, local surface lines and the connection to the high-speed rail network from Rome to Salerno. Journey times to Rome were cut by 38 percent to sixty-five minutes, and local commuting has also become much easier, thereby increasing access to employment. Most of the 139 million passengers per year using the metro network are due to the new facilities built with ERDF support. The consequences for local mobility have been huge – but they are difficult to quantify, despite anecdotal evidence.
>
> (Bachtler *et al.* 2016: 64–5)

Similar observations can be made for other types of investments – environmental and social infrastructure, urban regeneration, and support to firms, which was crucial to maintain jobs despite not proving capable of raising the game in terms of the competitiveness of the economic fabric (ibid.). Research on the region of

Basilicata reached similar conclusions: major improvements realised in the availability of public services allowed the development of certain economic sectors, albeit 'without solving the fundamental isolation of the region and altering the overall economic model based largely on agriculture and (increasingly, thanks to the programmes) tourism' (ibid.: 105).

In summary, while regional policy has not reached its objectives, the situation of the *Mezzogiorno* regions would probably have been worse off in its absence, both in the short and in the long term.

The lack of a comprehensive and sustained policy approach

When considering the stubborn nature of North-South disparities in Italy and the severity of the impact of the crisis on the *Mezzogiorno* regions especially, one ought to recognise that the performance of the Italian economic system overall has been weak for many years, and that it was already so pre-crisis. *National economic growth has been consistently below the eurozone average since the mid-1990s*, a period during which 'the differences in terms of productivity with other European countries have increased' (SVIMEZ 2013: 8). In 2000, the average per capita GDP for Italy was 120 per cent of the EU-15 average; this value has deteriorated steadily ever since, reaching 96 per cent of the EU-28 average in 2015 (Eurostat data). The difficulties experienced by the *Mezzogiorno* are part and parcel of the wider difficulties that have affected Italy as a whole, which are long-term and linked to a *loss of competitiveness of the country in its entirety*. A number of indicators show this, for example: the decline of FDI by 58 per cent since 2007 (CENSIS 2014); the country's below-par performance in terms of innovation, 22nd out of 28 countries. Almost all Italian regions are classified as 'moderate innovators' (EC 2016a, 2016b) and thus lag behind the most advanced regions of Scandinavia, Central Europe, France, the UK, and Ireland. Italy has also been struggling in relation to the social dimensions of development. In the latest Social Justice Index ranking of EU Member States by the Bertelsmann Stiftung, the country ranks in the bottom third group (19th and below) in all the main variables considered – poverty prevention (21st), equitable education (22nd), labour market access (23rd), social cohesion and non-discrimination (19th), health (19th), intergenerational justice (27th) – and is 24th overall, followed only by Spain, Bulgaria, Romania, and Greece (Schraad-Tischler and Schiller 2016). It features last for family policies, old-age dependency ratio (over-65 as a percentage of the working-age population), and NEET rate (the share of youth who are not in education, training, or employment) and second to last for government debt as a proportion of GDP, followed only by Greece (ibid.). Almost one-third of the Italian population is at risk of poverty and social exclusion (Ciccarone *et al.* 2016). This, *the country as a whole has been retrenching for a number of years.*

Beyond this, there have been also specific weaknesses on the policy side that explain the lack of progress in regional catching-up. First, as masterfully demonstrated by Viesti (2009), *regional policy in the Mezzogiorno has not been (and continues not to be) additional.* The financial thresholds earmarked for the *Mezzogiorno* under both domestic regional policy and ordinary public capital expenditure were never met (Viesti 2009, see also Polverari 2013).

Second, and related, *regional policy would require a wider set of domestic policies* (e.g. industrial policy, innovation policy, infrastructure policies) *and reforms* (e.g. in fields such as labour market, welfare, taxation, and administrative procedures) in order to 'work'. Over the past few years, the national government has set in motion wider reforms that affect regional development, including: legislation to reorganise local authorities; public sector reform; a new industrial policy (Industria 4.0); labour market reforms; and employment incentives, such as tax credits. For these reforms to reinforce, rather than undermine, regional policy, effective coordination and monitoring mechanisms will have to be put in place.[18]

Third, *regional policy itself has been fragmented in its operation.* On the domestic side, there has been an unsystematic approach based on CIPE deliberations rather than multi-annual programmes (based on the assumption that the attempt, during 2007–13, to introduce multi-annual programmes also for the domestic side of policy failed). On the EU co-funded side, there has been 'a dispersion of the policy effort across too many themes and funding streams, which hindered the achievement of critical mass' (Polverari and Tagle 2013). Poor coordination between national and regional programmes (Bachtler *et al.* 2016: 99) and significant use of retrospective projects (and strategic reorientation of the programmes *in itinere* in some cases) were also factors that contributed to a lack of overall coherence.

Fourth, *political instability and a bipartisan lack of sustained political commitment to regional policy* have caused delays in implementation and lack of continuity in the policy choices pursued, damaging the prospect of policy effectiveness. Related to this, *institutional fragmentation, unresolved centre-periphery tensions, and low levels of institutional and administrative capacities* at all levels but certainly more prominently in the Southern regions (Charron *et al.* 2014), compounded by a tendency to add on new institutions, rules, and procedures without first rationalising the existing ones, have meant that considerable attempts have been made over the years in programming and procedural processes that are subsequently not implemented (see also Polverari and Tagle 2013). These factors raise important concerns about the real potential of the administrative strengthening efforts foreseen in the current EU Cohesion Policy programmes. The ambitions are laudable. However, tackling the problemss through the lever of EU Cohesion Policy the deficiencies in the Italian public administration that go beyond the specific confines of this policy may prove unrealistic.

One last factor is the persistent lack of a *culture of evidence-based policy-making.* Largely thanks to the impetus of the EU Cohesion Policy, the evaluation of regional development programmes has become common practice across Italy. Institutional innovations introduced since the 1980s, such as the creation of national and, subsequently, regional evaluation units, aimed to strengthen evaluation culture and capacities. As a result, the evaluation market grew and the number of evaluations produced on programmes and instruments has steadily increased.[19] Despite this, the linkage between evaluation and decision-making remains weak (La Spina 2016) and evaluation results are not debated within political spheres but only 'in restricted circles and primarily on technical and conceptual-methodological dimensions' (Marra 2016, author's translation from Italian).

Conclusion

Despite having played a very important role during the crisis, and despite having realised important achievements over the longer term, regional policy in Italy has not been able to affect the long-term factors that continue to condition the development of laggard regions. This chapter has highlighted some of the key factors in this. With limited resources, without support from other policies, with narrow political buy-in, and caught between the dual ambition of improving the competitiveness of the economic fabric while at the same time delivering social equity, regional policy has achieved neither. Thinking prospectively, the fluid political landscape and looming general elections make it difficult to predict future developments. There are nevertheless areas of concern. The problems that have marred regional policy implementation in the past persist in the current programming period: the 2014–20 programmes were launched with significant delays, implementation progress is slow, funding is still assigned to retrospective projects, and there is still a strong focus on financial absorption. While the domestic side of policy was relaunched under the Renzi and Gentiloni governments, the political uncertainty that may follow the election, on 4 March 2018, may undermine this. Furthermore, the two strands of policy – domestic and EU co-funded – are fundamentally different in their principles and approach. The debate on the EU Multi-Annual Financial Framework for the post-2020 period is already indicating that the financial resources dedicated to the EU Cohesion Policy are likely to be reduced, perhaps substantially (Bachtler and Polverari 2017). Despite its administrative complexity, EU regional policy has been of the utmost importance for Italy, providing continuity, predictability, a stimulus to institutional and policy innovation, and an all-important 'external constraint'. Its demise, in the absence of an at least equivalent domestic policy effort (which, given Italy's constrained public finances, seems highly unlikely), could well prove fatal to the Italian *Mezzogiorno* – and, with it, to Italy as a whole. The Italian regional policy case shows that while competitive (territorial) solidarity as a concept may appear straightforward in principle, its practical achievement is neither easy nor uncontested.

Acknowledgements

Part of this research was realised under the aegis of the European Regional Policy Research Consortium (EoRPA), managed by the European Research

Centre at the University of Strathclyde (Glasgow). The financial contribution of EoRPA partners is gratefully acknowledged.

Notes

1 Not all EU Member States have a domestic regional development policy. At the same time, the European Union has its own regional policy, funded by the EU budget. It is commonly referred to as 'EU Cohesion Policy'. This means that some countries, like Italy, have both an EU and a domestic regional development policy. In other countries, regional policy is essentially subsumed under the EU Cohesion Policy. The latter supports all regions across the entire EU in growing and achieving the targets of the Europe 2020 Strategy. At the same time, in keeping with the policy's mission defined by Art. 174 of the Treaty of Lisbon (Consolidated version of the Treaty on the Functioning of the European Union, TFEU), while territorial coverage is universal, the focus is especially on regions with a GDP lower than 75 per cent of the EU average, the so-called less developed regions. It is for these regions that the majority of the resources is earmarked. For a review of the goals, principles, outcomes, and theoretical and empirical implications of EU Cohesion Policy, the reader is referred to Piattoni and Polverari (2016). The present chapter discusses Italian regional policy in its entirety, i.e. both domestic and EU co-funded strands.

2 The two terminologies indicate the same concept, i.e. regions with a per capita GDP lower than 75 per cent of the EU average. The first is the terminology used in the EU Cohesion Policy, the second is the terminology used in the context of regional aid control/EU Competition Policy. Art. 107(3) TFEU lists the type of aid considered compatible with the internal market (which includes regional aid).

3 NUTS, or nomenclature of territorial units for statistics, is a classification by Eurostat of the European territory according to standardised criteria: NUTS 1 corresponds to major socio-economic regions (i.e. with a population between three and seven million; 98 regions); NUTS 2 to basic regions for the application of regional policies (with a population between 800,000 and three million); and NUTS 3 to small regions for specific diagnoses (regions with between 150,000 and 300,000 inhabitants). The classification tends to mirror the administrative territorial organisation of Member States, so there can be significant variations in the definition of NUTS units across countries. For more detail, see http://ec.europa.eu/eurostat/web/nuts/overview

4 Both regions received transitional support in 2007–13. Basilicata became a less developed region already at the beginning of the 2014–20 programming period, while Sardinia was downgraded in 2016 (EC 2016c).

5 Those passed for the Basilicata region in 1904, following a visit by Minister Zanardelli to the region in 1902; that for the industrialisation of Naples, also of 1904; and those for Calabria, Sicily, and Sardinia, which were passed in the years 1906–7 (Carabba 2011: 9).

6 The total population coverage of the regional aid map for 2014–20 amounts to 34.07 per cent of the Italian population.

7 Law Decree 243/2016, 29 December 2016, converted into law as Law No. 18, 27 February 2017 (GU 28/02/2017, No. 49). See, for a recent contribution, Giannola and Prezioso (2017).

8 These funds are the European Regional Development Fund (ERDF), the European Social Fund (ESF), the Cohesion Fund, the European Maritime and Fishery Fund (EMFF), and the European Agricultural Fund for Rural Development (EAFRD).

9 Namely the Community-Led Local Development (CLLD) and Integrated Territorial Instruments (ITIs).

10 Bari, Cagliari, Catania, Messina, Naples, Palermo, and Reggio Calabria.

11 Guidelines for the Masterplan were issued by the Presidency of the Council of Ministers in November 2015, the financial resources for the Pacts were officially deliberated by CIPE in August 2016 (CIPE deliberation no. 26, 10 August 2016) and recorded by the Italian Corte dei Conti in November 2016.

12 Of this overall amount, about 35 per cent is for infrastructure projects, 29 per cent for environmental projects, 18 per cent for economic and productive development interventions, and about 7 per cent for tourism, culture, and natural resources. About 3 and 1 per cent of the total amount, respectively, are allocated to social inclusion and training measures and to administrative strengthening.

13 For example, the 'Piano Sud' announced by Berlusconi in 2009 in parallel with the progressive emptying of the domestic side of the 2007–13 NSRF, remained a dead letter. I describe these developments in detail in Polverari (2013).

14 A similar agency, ANPAL – Agenzia Nazionale per le Politiche Attive del Lavoro (National Agency for Active Labour Market Policies) was also recently established with responsibility for the coordination, monitoring, and oversight of all bodies in charge of labour market policies and the management of national ESF programmes.

15 Law 190/2014, the so-called Stability Law 2015. The Cabina was instituted by the Decree of the President of the Council of Ministers dated 25 February 2016, published in OJ No. 67 of 21 March 2016. Law 190/2014 also restated the commitment to concentrating FSC expenditure in the South for at least 80 per cent (lower than the previous, but never achieved, threshold of 85 per cent).

16 There are also other bodies involved in the delivery of regional policy, the most important of which is the national agency Invitalia, responsible for business investment attraction and development, for the implementation of a number of national schemes, and for the provision of technical assistance to the Ministry of Economic Development.

17 With the major caveat represented by the lack of availability of resources for maintenance and running costs; see Bachtler *et al.* (2016) for more detail.

18 For example, the recent 'Jobs Act' has been deemed to strengthen job insecurity and may thus hinder, rather than favour, social (and with it territorial) equity (Tridico 2017). On the other hand, Industria 4.0 includes elements of coordination and synergy with regional policy (for example, coherence with Industria 4.0 is a criterion for the new 'Development agreements for large strategic projects' introduced in 2016 and the NOP Competitiveness contributes resources to certain schemes of the plan); however, given the competitive allocation, the plan's resources may end up predominantly in the strongest regions.

19 This is an issue that could also be viewed as a weakness rather than a strength. A recent paper by Perotti and Teoldi (2014), focused on the evaluations realised under the European Social Fund in Italy, asserts that these evaluations were largely useless and only instrumental to sustain the large number of companies that provide such evaluation services.

References

Bachtler, John, Iain Begg, David Charles, and Laura Polverari (2016). *EU Cohesion Policy in practice: what does it achieve?* London: Rowman & Littlefield.

Bachtler, John and Polverari Laura (2017). *Building blocks for a future cohesion policy – first reflections*. Brussels: European Parliament.

Banca d'Italia (2015). *Economie regionali: l'economia delle regioni italiane nel 2014 (21/2015)*. Rome: Banca d'Italia.

Barca, Fabrizio (2006). *Italia frenata: paradossi della politica per lo sviluppo*. Rome: Donzelli.

Barca, Fabrizio (2012). *Metodi e obiettivi per un uso efficace dei fondi comunitari 2014–2020*. Rome: Ministro per la Coesione Territoriale.

Boscariol, Gian Paolo (2015). 'Politiche di coesione 2014–2020 e governance', *Rivista Giuridica del Mezzogiorno* 29(1–2): 193–220.

Bubbico, Rocco L. and Angel Catalina Rubianes (2015). 'L'impatto della crisi sugli investimenti pubblici in Europa. Il ruolo dei Fondi Strutturali nel sostegno dei potenziali di crescita regionali', *Rivista Giuridica del Mezzogiorno* 29(1–2): 37–64.

Carabba, Manin (2011). 'Introduzione', *Rivista Giuridica del Mezzogiorno* 25(1–2): 7–13.

CENSIS (2014). 'Cattiva reputazione per l'Italia: −58% di investimenti esteri dall'inizio della crisi'. Available at: www.censis.it/7?shadow_comunicato_stampa=120963

Charron, Nicholas, Lewis Dijkstra, and Victor Lapuente (2014). 'Regional governance matters: quality of government within European Union member states', *Regional Studies* 48(1): 68–90.

Ciccarone, Giuseppe, Giancarlo Dente, and Simone Rosini (2016). *Labour market and social policy in Italy: challenges and changes*. Policy Brief No. 02. Rome: Fondazione Brodolini.

DPS (Dipartimento per lo Sviluppo e la Coesione Economica) (2012). *Rapporto Annuale 2011 DPS sugli interventi nelle aree sottoutilizzate*. Rome: DPS.

DPS (Dipartimento per lo Sviluppo e la Coesione Economica) (2014). *Accordo di Partenariato 2014–2020 Italia*. Rome: DPS.

EC (European Commission) (2014a). 'State aid: Commission approves Italy's regional aid map 2014–2020'. Press release IP/14/1009. Available at: http://europa.eu/rapid/press-release_IP-14-1009_en.htm

EC (European Commission) (2014b). *Investments for jobs and growth: promoting development and good governance in EU regions and cities. Sixth report on economic, social and territorial cohesion*. Luxembourg: Publications Office of the European Union.

EC (European Commission) (2016a). *European innovation scoreboard 2016 main report and database*. Luxembourg: Publications Office of the European Union.

EC (European Commission) (2016b). *Regional innovation scoreboard main report*. Luxembourg: Publications Office of the European Union.

EC (European Commission) (2016c). 'Communication from the Commission amending Annex I to the Guidelines on regional aid for 2014–2020'. C/2016/3514.

Franco, Daniele (2010). 'L'economia del Mezzogiorno', in Luigi Cannari e Daniele Franco (eds). *Il Mezzogiorno e la politica economica dell'Italia.* Roma (Seminari e Convegni 4). Rome: Banca d'Italia, 1–13.

Gallo, Giovanni and Giuseppe Forte (2016). 'Le persone maggiormente a rischio di esclusione sociale in Italia', in Giancarlo Dente and Giuseppe Fioriani (eds). *Povertà ed inclusione sociale in Italia: sfide e cambiamenti all'inizio della nuova programmazione dei Fondi Strutturali*. Quaderni Fondazione G. Brodolini 54). Rome: Fondazione Brodolini, 67–88.

Giannola, Adriano and Stefano Prezioso (2017). 'La clausola del "34%" delle risorse ordinarie a favore del Sud: una valutazione relativa al periodo 2009–2015', *Rivista Economica del Mezzogiorno* 28(1–2): 5–18.

Graziano, Paolo R. (2013). *Europeanization and domestic policy change: the case of Italy*. London: Routledge.

Gualini, Enrico (2004). *Multi-level governance and institutional change: the Europeanization of regional policy in Italy*. Aldershot: Ashgate.

La Spina, Antonio (2003). *La politica per il Mezzogiorno*. Bologna: Il Mulino.

La Spina, Antonio (2016). 'La valutazione delle politiche meridionaliste', *Rivista Giuridica del Mezzogiorno* 4: 989–1003.

Marra, Mita (2016). 'Ruolo, criticità e potenziale della valutazione per la politica di sviluppo regionale in Italia', in Manin Carabba, Riccardo Padovani, and Laura Polverari (eds). *Le politiche di coesione in Europa tra austerità e nuove sfide*. Quaderni SVIMEZ 47. Rome: SVIMEZ, 135–42.

Merler, Silvia (2016). 'Income convergence during the crisis: did EU funds provide a buffer?' Bruegel Working Paper No. 6. Brussels: Bruegel.

MEF (Ministero dell'Economia e delle Finanze) (2016). 'Documento di Economia e Finanza 2016, Allegato: Relazione sugli interventi delle aree sottoutilizzate. L. 196/2009, art. 10 integrata dal D. LGs 88/2011 art. 7'. Rome: MEF.

MEF (Ministero dell'Economia e delle Finanze) (2017). 'Documento di economia e finanza 2017. Allegato: Relazione sugli interventi nelle aree sottoutilizzate. L. 196/2009, art. 10, integrata dal D. Lgs. 88/2011, art.7'. Rome: MEF.

Ministro per la Coesione Territoriale (2014). *Relazione sull'attività svolta e sulle azioni in corso*. Roma: Ministro per la Coesione Territoriale.

Nifo, Annamaria and Gaetano Vecchione (2015). 'Measuring institutional quality in Italy', *Rivista Economica del Mezzogiorno* 29(1–2): 157–81.

Perotti, Roberto and Filippo Teoldi (2014) 'Il disastro dei fondi strutturali europei'. Available at: www.lavoce.info/wp-content/uploads/2014/07/fondi-strutturali-europei.pdf

Piattoni, Simona and Laura Polverari (eds) (2016). *Handbook on cohesion policy in the EU*. Cheltenham: Edward Elgar.

Polverari, Laura (2013). 'Policy rhetoric versus political reality: has the Italian state given up on the Mezzogiorno?', *Regional & Federal Studies* 23(5): 571–90.

Polverari, Laura (2016). 'Cohesion policy in the southern periphery', in Simona Piattoni and Laura Polverari (eds). *Handbook on cohesion policy in the EU*. Cheltenham: Edward Elgar, 231–49.

Polverari, Laura and Laura Tagle (2013). 'Evaluation of the main achievements of cohesion policy programmes and projects over the longer term in 15 selected regions. Case Study Campania (Report to the European Commission, DG Regio, September 2013)'. Glasgow: University of Strathclyde.

Prota, Francesco (2016). 'L'effetto dell'austerity sulle politiche di sviluppo nei Paesi dell'Unione Europea', in Manin Carabba, Riccardo Padovani, and Laura Polverari (eds). *Le politiche di coesione in Europa tra austerità e nuove sfide*, Quaderni SVIMEZ 47. Rome: SVIMEZ, 57–69.

PCM (Presidenza del Consiglio dei Ministri, Dipartimento per la programmazione e il coordinamento della politica economica) (2016). *Ricognizione e aggiornamento sull'andamento dei Patti per il Sud stipulati dal Governo con le Regioni del Mezzogiorno e col le città metropolitane*. Rome: DIPE.

Rusca, Rossella (2015). 'Il negoziato per la politica di coesione 2014–2020 e le prospettive per il futuro: Questioni chiave, battaglie, alleanze, obiettivi e sfide visti da un insider', *Rivista Giuridica del Mezzogiorno* 29(1–2): 137–92.

Scalera, Domenico and Alberto Zazzaro (2010). 'L'economia del Mezzogiorno: nuova politica regionale, crisi globale e federalismo fiscale', in Maria Cecilia Guerra and Alberto Zanardi (eds). *La finanza pubblica italiana. Rapporto 2010*. Bologna: Il Mulino.

Schraad-Tischler, Daniel and Christof Schiller (2016). *Social justice in the EU – index report 2016*. Social inclusion monitor Europe. Gütersloh: Bertelsmann Stiftung.

SVIMEZ (2013). *Rapporto SVIMEZ 2013 sull'economia del Mezzogiorno*. Bologna: il Mulino.

SVIMEZ (2016). *Rapporto SVIMEZ 2016 sull'economia del Mezzogiorno*. Bologna: il Mulino.

SVIMEZ (2017). *Rapporto SVIMEZ 2017 sull'economia del Mezzogiorno*. Bologna: il Mulino.

Terracciano, Brian and Paolo R. Graziano (2016). 'EU cohesion policy implementation and administrative capacities: insights from Italian regions', *Regional & Federal Studies* 26(3): 293–320.

Tridico, Pasquale (2017). 'Jobs Act tra evidenze empiriche e false verità'. Available at: www.eticaeconomia.it/jobs-act-tra-evidenze-empiriche-e-false-verita/

Trigilia, Carlo (1992). *Sviluppo senza autonomia: effetti perversi delle politiche nel Mezzogiorno*. Bologna: Il Mulino.

Viesti, Gianfranco (2009). *Mezzogiorno a tradimento: il Nord, il Sud e la politica che non c'è*. Bari: Laterza.

Viesti, Gianfranco (2015a). 'Le conseguenze territoriali dell'austerità disuguale'. Available at: www.eticaeconomia.it/le-conseguenze-territoriali-dellausterita-disuguale/

Viesti, Gianfranco (2015b). 'Why Europe is in a trap', *Stato e Mercato* 35(1): 53–83.

Viesti, Gianfranco (2016). 'Masterplan per il Mezzogiorno: spunti critici sui contenuti', *StrumentiRes* 8(2). Available at: www.strumentires.com/attachments/article/646/Viesti_SRes_2_16.pdf

11 Competitive solidarity and regional development

The case of Poland

Bolesław Domański

The relationship between competitiveness and solidarity is especially interesting in Central-Eastern European countries, which experienced the transition from state socialism to capitalism. This is particularly true of Poland, where post-socialist transformation was largely brought about by the Solidarity trade union.

Until 1989, the country was part of the Soviet bloc characterized by the system of centralized power, which attempted to control all political, economic, and social activity. There was state ownership of the means of production and economic activity was carried out by state-owned enterprises rather than private firms. Market relationships were broadly replaced by non-market administrative mechanisms of the distribution of goods and the national economy was relatively isolated from the global economy.

The opening of the Polish economy to international competition, market liberalization, and privatization took place together with political democratization and technological modernization. This meant multiple transformations in the political, social, economic, and technological spheres happening at the same time (Sztompka 2004). During the shock phase between 1989 and 1991 the gross domestic product (GDP) of Poland declined by 18 per cent. This was the result of the difficult adjustment processes of enterprises to the entirely new economic conditions and institutional context, the rise of the competition of imported goods, and the loss of the Soviet market. In 1992, economic growth began, facilitated by local entrepreneurship and, gradually, by foreign direct investment as well. In 2004 Poland and several other post-socialist countries joined the European Union. This meant the adoption of the social, economic, and environmental regulations of the EU, as well as access to EU Structural Funds within the EU Cohesion Policy.

The rate of economic growth of Poland was higher than in other Member States. The recession of the late 2000s slowed down, but did not interrupt, this growth. As a result, the country reduced the gap vis-à-vis the Western European economies in terms of GDP per capita. In 1990, Poland's GDP represented a mere 26 per cent of the average GDP per capita of the EU (at purchasing power standards), whereas it reached 70 per cent in 2016.[1] The productivity in manufacturing measured by value added per employee has increased five-fold. The share of the country in world exports has tripled and Poland is showing a growing surplus in its trade with the largest Western European economies: Germany, France, and the United Kingdom.

However, the radical restructuring of the economy with the decline of some traditional industries, such as coal mining and textiles, technological modernization, and increased productivity has brought about serious unemployment. The unemployment rate was 16 per cent in 1993; after decreasing in the late 1990s, it reached its peak of 20 per cent in 2002. Then it began to fall very rapidly until 2008, increased again during the period of recession, and remains at a record low now: 5.5 per cent. This illustrates the social costs of economic transformation as well as the impact of demographic structures: a large number of young people entered the labour market between 2000 and 2003, but their numbers shrank afterwards while migration to Western Europe in the aftermath of the accession to the EU grew. There was a general increase in income inequalities in Polish society. The income Gini coefficient grew in Poland from the 1990s till 2008, then it began to fall and it is now below the average of the EU. The percentage of people living in absolute poverty in Poland has decreased from 12 per cent in 2005 to 6 per cent in 2015, the share of people below the legal poverty line in the country (entitlement to social welfare) is 12 per cent.

The vast improvement in the quality of life can be seen, among other things, in health indicators. In 2014, life expectancy in Poland was 77.8 years in comparison to 82.3 in France and 81.4 in the United Kingdom, while infant mortality was 4.0 per 1,000 live births in comparison to 3.5 in France and 3.9 in the United Kingdom. The progress in non-material aspects of social well-being has generally been greater than in material ones. This finds expression in the fact that the position of Poland in international rankings is markedly higher in the Human Development Index (HDI) of the United Nations (36th place), the Sustainable Economic Development Assessment (SEDA) of the Boston Consulting Group (BCG) (30th place), and the Better Life Index (BLI) of OECD (27th place) than in terms of GDP per capita (45th place). The SEDA and BLI indicators take into account up to ten dimensions of well-being including health, education, and environmental situation.

All in all, at the national level, there are many arguments to see the post-socialist development of Poland as a general success manifesting itself in a gradual convergence with Western European countries in economic, social, and environmental terms. However, the perspective taken in this chapter is a regional, not a national one.

The chapter explores how the enhanced competitiveness of the national economy and the higher quality of life in the country affect economic and social conditions at the regional level. It shows what types of areas are winners and losers in the development of the capitalist economy of Poland since 1989. The effects for metropolitan areas, industrial regions, and towns, as well as rural non-metropolitan areas, are analysed, including high-road versus low-road types of development. Special focus is on trends in the historically under-privileged peripheral regions – to what extent they have benefited from the positive changes in Poland as a whole. Spatial polarization of the country in both social and economic dimensions is also taken into consideration when answering the question whether regional convergence or divergence in competitiveness and social well-being has taken place. In addition, the impact of various public and private agents, including European institutions, national government and local authorities, transnational corporations, and domestic firms, is discussed.

The analysis of the economic performance and social well-being of various areas in the country is preceded by an outline of the debate on the relationships between economic efficiency and social justice from a regional perspective. This is followed by the interpretation of the processes of regional change in Poland since the 1990s, their social and economic effects, along with their underlying mechanisms and determinants.

The debate on economic efficiency and social justice from a regional perspective: approaches and concepts

Academic discourse on the relationships between economic efficiency and social justice from the perspective of regional development and policy (Pike *et al.* 2007; Smith and Lee 2004) has developed in recent years. Three fundamental issues have to be addressed here.

For a long time, redistribution towards weaker regions was perceived as contradictory to the rapid economic growth of a country. In other words, the governmental support for the disadvantaged areas (commonly defined as the search for greater regional equality) could only take place at the expense of the competitiveness of the national economy. This was often presented as a dilemma of (economic) efficiency versus (territorial) equality.

In this conceptual framework, the priority given to the growth of the national economy was based on the assumption that the government was primarily responsible for the development of the country as a whole. This could be strengthened by the argument that weaker regions also benefit from the economic growth of the country and by the belief that regional disparities are inevitable 'natural' effects of fast economic growth. The latter idea can be accounted for by several theories of regional development, for example, Vernon's theory of product life cycle (Vernon 1966) and the theory of cumulative causation with backwash effects weakening the development of the disadvantaged regions (Myrdal 1957). Regions appear in this perspective as structures of long duration, and public interventions attempting to change the core-periphery structures are doomed to failure (Fagerberg and Verspagen 1996; Fischer and Nijkamp 1999). Public policy oriented towards stimulating the development of laggard regions was also questioned on totally different grounds. Various theories based upon neo-classical equilibrium approach argue that, in the long run, the development of the country will lead to diminishing regional inequalities. Thus, regional disparities are a temporary phenomenon and will be reduced over time, leading to regional convergence when the country reaches a higher level of development. This will stem from the mobility of capital and people, as well as the multiplier and spill-over effects of the growth of the core regions (Friedmann 1972).

The traditional arguments for the support of disadvantaged areas are underpinned by the idea of social solidarity. This can be understood in terms of equality of outcomes or equality of opportunities. In the former, it is argued that all people possess the right to have their important needs satisfied, irrespective of their place of residence in the country. In the latter, the emphasis is on the fact that people's life chances should not be constrained by the place where they live. This approach gives a lot of attention to the mechanisms linking the attributes of particular areas with people's life chances, which may make some areas places of sustained social exclusion.

Territorial justice understood in terms of equality lay at the root of the European Union territorial cohesion policy. It was meant to cope with uneven development and contribute to convergence, both between Member Sstates and between their regions.

On the whole, the rationale behind the public intervention supporting weaker regions and/or fighting regional disparities can be approached, on the one hand, in a normative way – whether it is right or wrong – and, on the other, from a theoretical and practical (instrumental) point of view – whether it can be achieved (it is possible and/or effective) (Pike *et al.* 2006).

What can be challenged here is a traditional widespread belief that reduction in regional disparities is by definition beneficial to less-developed areas. Regional convergence may occur without the development of the disadvantaged regions, for example, when the advanced areas experience crisis or stagnation. Lower territorial inequalities are hardly helpful for the weak regions per se. Moreover, the successful development of the latter does not necessarily lead to regional convergence, if the advanced regions grow at even faster rates. If what really matters is the improvement of social well-being in the less-developed areas, the goals of public policy should be defined and measured in terms of the development of these areas rather than as reduced inter-regional disparities (Domański 2010). This means that the classic dilemma of (economic) efficiency versus (territorial) equality is ill-defined.

The opposition of competitiveness of the national economy and public intervention supporting the weak regions is further questioned in more recent approaches to regional development and policy, called a new paradigm of regional policy (OECD 2009). This is based on the assumption that all areas have endogenous development potential. Low levels of development of certain areas and/or their poor economic performance mean the underutilization of regional/local assets, which, in the long run, has a detrimental impact on the competitiveness of the national economy. Consequently, the major emphasis in regional policy is on the use of the endogenous potential of each region. Thus, the new argument for public support (intervention) in the disadvantaged areas is a better use of their potential, which may be beneficial both to these areas and to the national economy.

The departure from the traditional preoccupation with spatial inequalities (regional convergence) also entails the redefinition of the concept of territorial cohesion, which is increasingly understood in terms of integration of more advanced and less-developed areas rather than in terms of reduced disparities, i.e. equality of outcomes (Bachtler *et al.* 2017; Komornicki and Zaucha 2015).

The second vital problem concerning regional development and policy which has to be discussed here is the relationship between the development of economic activity (economic growth) and social well-being. There is much evidence that long-term trends in the spatial patterns of economic activity and social well-being are not the same.

Agglomeration mechanisms, including external economies of scale based on the existence of a large market, structural diversity, a skilled labour force, accumulated knowledge, and extensive networking, maintain or increase the geographical concentration of economic activities. At the same time, in many developed countries, this is accompanied by a gradual decrease in regional disparities (convergence) in social well-being, for example, in household consumption, access to basic public services, etc. In other words, high standards of living can be found in wide areas beyond the cores of economic growth. The discrepancy between these two trends is strongly highlighted in the *World Development Report 2009* (World Bank 2009). This fact leads its authors to the conclusion that, despite the permanent process of geographical concentration of economic activity (measured, for example, by GDP) and hence uneven economic growth (divergence), development may be more socially inclusive.

The implication is that regional policy should primarily focus on the support for the enhanced standard of living in weak peripheral areas rather than concentrate on regional disparities in economic growth. This can be achieved through the integration of fast-growing areas of economic activity and places of human residence, among other things through the overcoming of infrastructural, institutional, and information barriers. Thus, inhabitants of economically peripheral areas may benefit from a growing concentration of economic activity elsewhere thanks to the growing geographical mobility of society.

The distinction between the spatial distribution of economic activity and the spatial inequalities in social well-being is important and too often has been ignored. However, the universal belief that the convergence in social well-being can be achieved without economic growth at every geographical scale presented by *World Development Report 2009* can be questioned. This is far more true at the intra-regional than the inter-regional scale. The report of the World Bank underestimates negative backwash effects in the form of the out-migration of young educated people and the processes of negative social selection in the regions of low economic activity, which may undermine their long-term development prospects. Therefore, it seems that the objectives of public policy supporting laggard areas should be different at the inter-regional and the intra-regional scale. In the latter, social well-being can be the principal target, whereas in the former this can hardly be achieved without enhanced competitiveness of the regional economy.

Last but not least, there is a long debate on the importance of endogenous and exogenous factors in regional development. The impact of exogenous factors, in particular, has been intensely discussed. One of the contentious problems is the role of transnational corporations (TNCs) in local and regional development, especially in less-developed areas. The question is to what extent they generate positive spill-over effects and become territorially embedded through supplier networks in the areas of their investment (Dicken and Malmberg 2001; Phelps 2000). This is significant in the context of many Polish towns and regions which have become dependent on foreign direct investment in the past two decades.

Another related issue is the so-called 'high road' versus 'low road' of development. The former rests on innovation, skills, and social activation. It finds expression in the upgrading of the regional economy towards high value-added products and services (Gereffi 2008). The latter depends on simple, low value-added activities which are essentially based on low labour costs as well as on poor social and environmental standards.

Public intervention, including European Union and national policies, is a further exogenous factor, the effects of which have to be taken into account.

There is no room here to discuss how the ways in which development is understood and measured have evolved in the previous decades. The broadly understood sustainable development perspective combining economic, environmental, and social goals as it is elaborated in the European strategy for smart, sustainable, and inclusive growth (EC 2010) is adopted here.

Regional changes in Poland since the 1990s: economic performance and social well-being

The analysis of contemporary processes and their effects is divided into two parts. First, changes in economic performance of Polish regions are taken into consideration, and then selected aspects of social well-being are explored. The main scale of the analysis is regional, i.e. the focus is on inter-regional differentiation. In addition, some intra-regional and local disparities are briefly discussed.

An outline of the historical regional differentiation of the country is necessary at the outset. There was no independent Polish state in the nineteenth century. The country was partitioned between Germany, Russia, and Austria, which led to significant differences between various regions of contemporary Poland. The German part was more urbanized and industrialized, with a dense railway network, larger farms, and higher standard of agriculture. Upper Silesia (coal and steel industries) and Lower Silesia were among the most important industrial regions in Europe. This contrasted with more rural eastern and central (Russian) and south-eastern (Austrian) parts, characterized by poor fragmented agriculture and less urbanization. Industrial centres included Łódź (textiles) and other major cities.

Poland regained its independence in 1918. The Second World War resulted in a major shift of the national boundaries of the country. The western and northern territories of contemporary Poland – formerly part of Germany – attracted migrants from the areas lost in the east to the Soviet Union and from other regions; this resulted in a younger population in these territories. State-owned

Soviet-type farming became dominant here, in contrast to the rest of the country where small farmers still prevailed.

Under state socialism, the priority given to military-oriented industrialization favoured mining and manufacturing regions and towns, as most state investment was located there. Rural areas experienced multiple deprivation in terms of jobs and social infrastructure (public services). This lay at the root of mass migration to urban and industrial centres.

The current differentiation in economic performance of the Polish regions can be examined first by using the basic indicator of GDP per capita (Figure 11.1). The central region of Mazowieckie, including the capital city of Warsaw, stands out as the only one representing GDP higher than the EU average. It is followed by three most developed regions of western and south-western Poland: Dolnośląskie (Lower Silesia, including the city of Wrocław), Wielkopolskie (including Poznań), and Śląskie (Upper Silesia). The lowest level (27–30 per

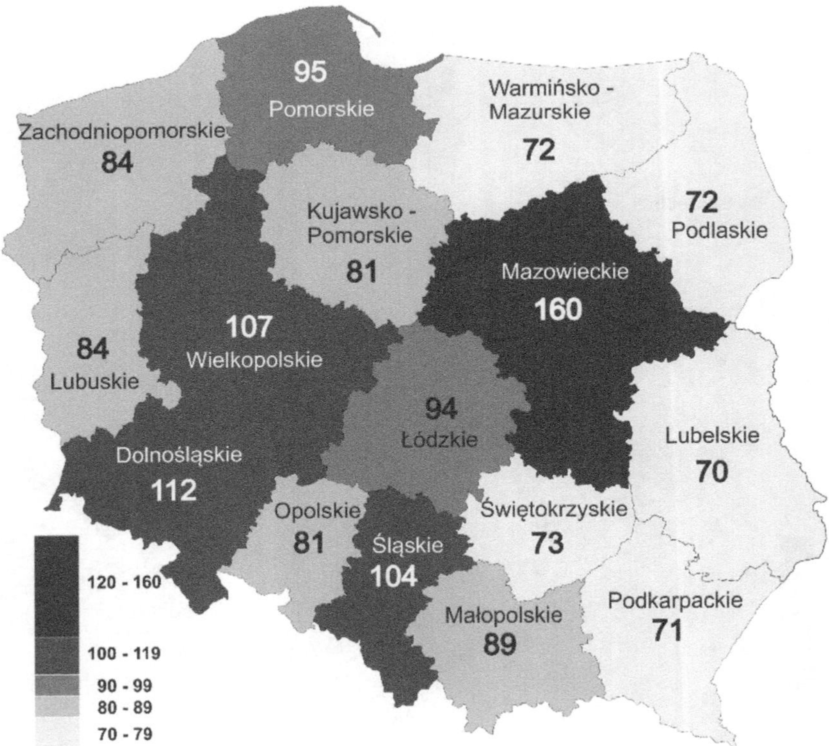

Figure 11.1 Gross domestic product per capita by region in 2014 (Poland = 100).

Source: author's elaboration based on Central Statistical Office of Poland (GUS) data.

cent below the national average) is found in the historically laggard regions of eastern Poland. A closer look taking into account sub-regional differentiation reveals that it is the metropolitan areas which are characterized by the highest GDP per capita (Figure 11.2).

The fastest economic growth since 1995 is shown in the most developed regions: Mazowieckie, Wielkopolskie, and Dolnośląskie (Figure 11.3). Two further regions comprising metropolitan areas have demonstrated the rate of growth above the national average: Łódzkie and Małopolskie (including Cracow). Growth was lower in Pomorskie (including Gdańsk) and Śląskie. At the sub-regional level, metropolitan zones have grown faster than the major cities themselves. It is interesting that relatively high dynamics, similar or higher than in some metropolitan regions, have been achieved by the less-developed eastern regions, especially Podlaskie, Podkarpackie, and Świętokrzyskie. Slower development has taken place in northern regions and the German borderland: Zachodniopomorskie, Kujawsko-Pomorskie, Lubuskie,

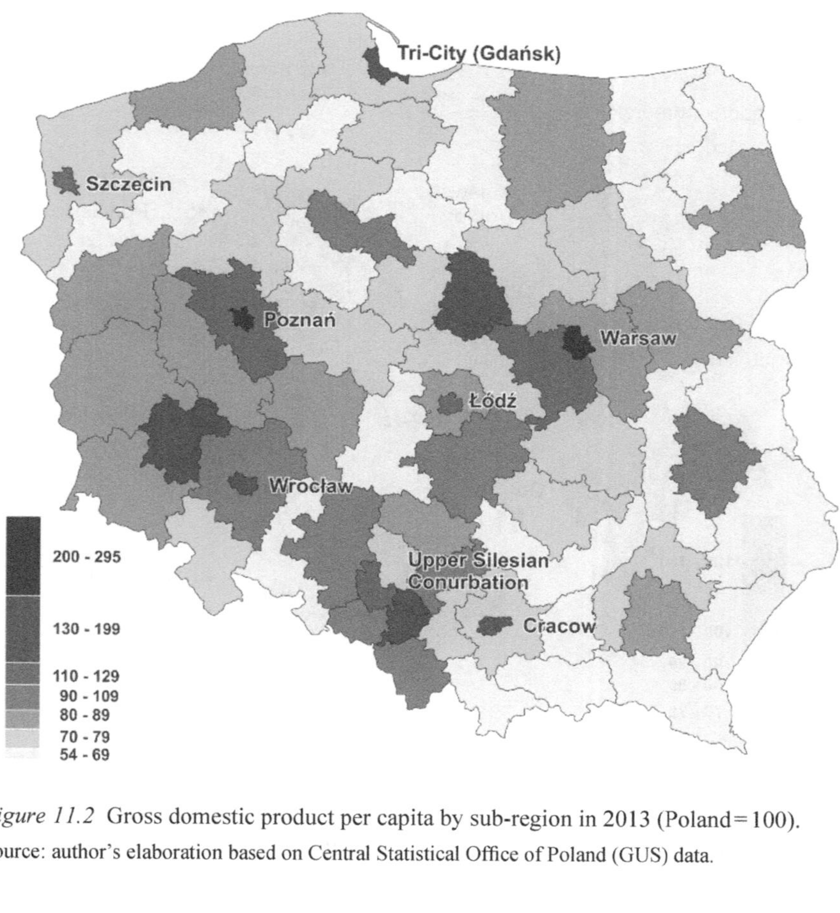

Figure 11.2 Gross domestic product per capita by sub-region in 2013 (Poland = 100).

Source: author's elaboration based on Central Statistical Office of Poland (GUS) data.

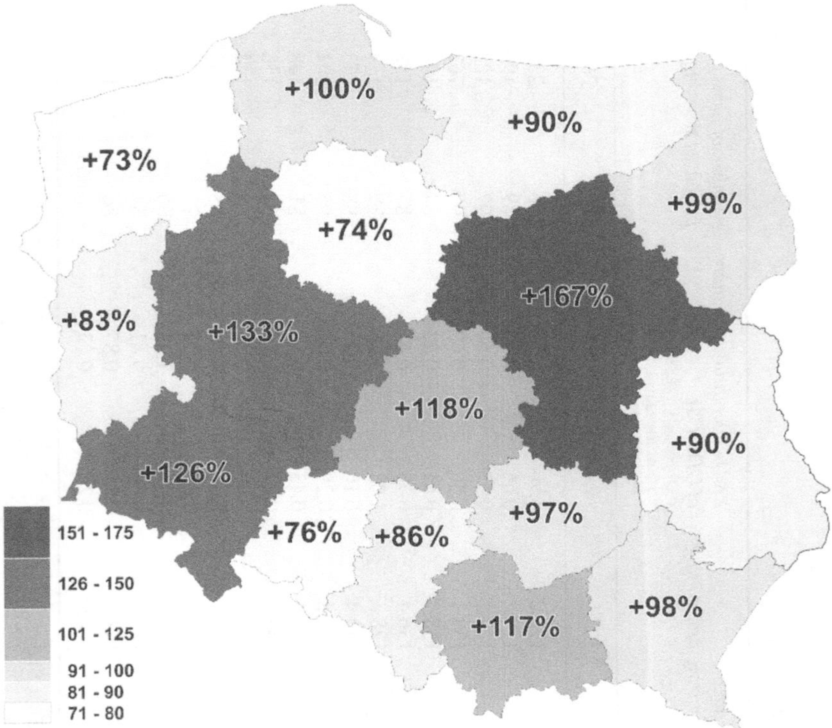

Figure 11.3 Growth of gross domestic product by region, 1995–2014 (constant prices).
Source: author's elaboration based on Central Statistical Office of Poland (GUS) data.

and partly Warmińsko-Mazurskie, as well as in Opolskie, which was plagued by substantial foreign out-migration. However, the growth rate of these regions was also markedly higher than the EU average.

The picture is very similar in productivity in manufacturing and mining measured by value added per employee, with Mazowieckie and Dolnośląskie as leaders (Table 11.1). In general, western and metropolitan regions differ from eastern and northern ones (except for Pomorskie).

Not surprisingly, the most pronounced contrast between metropolitan and non-metropolitan regions can be found in R&D expenditures as share of regional GDP. The capital region of Mazowieckie is the leader again and Małopolskie comes second, thanks to the dominant role of Warsaw and Cracow in R&D. The position of Wielkopolskie, Dolnośląskie, and Śląskie is relatively weaker in this respect. It is worth noting that several northern and some western regions lag behind the eastern ones here, and Podkarpackie in the south-east is ranked third

Table 11.1 Selected indicators of economic performance of Polish regions

Region	*GDP per capita (current prices in thousand zloty)*		*Value added in manufacturing and mining per employee (in thousand zloty)*		*R&D expenditures as share of GDP (%)*		*Number of firms per 1,000 people at working age*	
	1995	*2014*	*2002*	*2014*	*1999*	*2014*	*1995*	*2015*
Mazowieckie	11.2	71.4	68.5	198.2	1.90	1.55	106	233
Dolnośląskie	9.2	50.1	62.1	179.2	0.66	0.65	89	196
Wielkopolskie	8.6	47.9	52.7	129.1	0.57	0.62	97	188
Śląskie	10.4	46.7	60.5	139.1	0.50	0.62	90	163
Pomorskie	8.9	42.4	57.2	138.3	0.64	0.98	84	196
Łódzkie	8.0	42.0	47.9	136.4	0.78	0.67	87	158
Małopolskie	7.6	39.8	51.4	128.3	1.03	1.30	89	173
Lubuskie	8.6	37.7	51.4	140.4	0.10	0.26	98	173
Zachodniopomorskie	9.0	37.6	50.4	122.2	0.29	0.30	95	204
Kujawsko-pomorskie	8.7	36.4	51.8	125.4	0.43	0.31	81	148
Opolskie	8.6	36.4	55.9	143.2	0.27	0.23	59	158
Świętokrzyskie	6.9	32.8	50.7	127.7	0.66	0.35	63	142
Podlaskie	6.7	32.4	52.1	126.3	0.32	0.55	68	132
Warmińsko-mazurskie	7.0	32.0	46.9	114.6	0.33	0.36	75	135
Podkarpackie	6.7	31.7	48.1	117.9	0.62	1.22	60	123
Lubelskie	6.8	31.3	47.9	123.3	0.59	0.61	64	130
Poland	8.7	44.7	55.7	142.5	0.83	0.87	86	174
Gini coefficient	0.067	0.104	0.053	0.067	0.267	0.234	0.063	0.078

Source: author's elaboration based on Central Statistical Office of Poland (GUS) data.

in the country due to the development of the aircraft industry based on the traditions dating back to the 1930s.

A broader view of economic activity is provided by entrepreneurship indicators. The major divergence is between western and eastern Poland (Figure 11.4), reflecting not only a higher level of development and hence a larger market but also demographic differences, with an older population in the East as a consequence of the prolonged migration of young people to other regions. Metropolitan areas, large cities, and medium-sized towns also reveal significant entrepreneurship. The dynamics of new firm creation since 1995 has been above the national average in the developed areas, but also in the eastern, especially the south-eastern regions: Podkarpackie and Świętokrzyskie. As a result, they have reduced the gap in relation to the regions historically dominated by large industrial enterprises: Śląskie and Łódzkie.

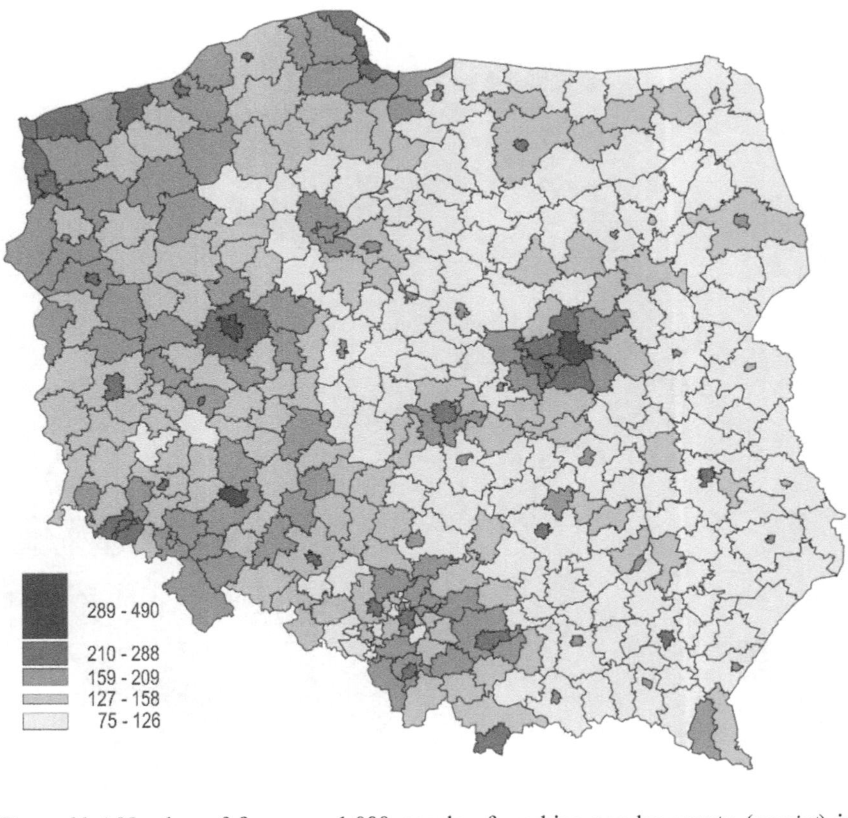

Figure 11.4 Number of firms per 1,000 people of working age by county (*powiat*) in 2015.

Source: author's elaboration based on Central Statistical Office of Poland (GUS) data.

Unemployment rates reflect one of the vital components of social well-being. Since the early years of transformation, they have been the lowest in the metropolitan areas and regions that experienced rapid economic growth, e.g. Wielkopolskie and Mazowieckie. Despite a huge loss of jobs in traditional sectors, unemployment remains moderate in Śląskie and Łódzkie (7–8 per cent). For a long time it was highest in northern regions and partly western borderland, as a result of the collapse of former state-owned farms, poor education, and a young age structure. It is still above the national average now in the North as well as in eastern Poland, where its reduction in recent years has been less radical than elsewhere.

The regional differentiation of the share of people living in poverty (below the nationally defined subsistence minimum) by and large reproduces the historical West-East division of the country (Figure 11.5). It is the highest in Warmińsko-Mazurskie and Świętokorzyskie, the lowest in Śląskie, and very low in Dolnośląskie and Mazowieckie. A more detailed picture given by the share of beneficiaries of social welfare on the commune level confirms the concentration

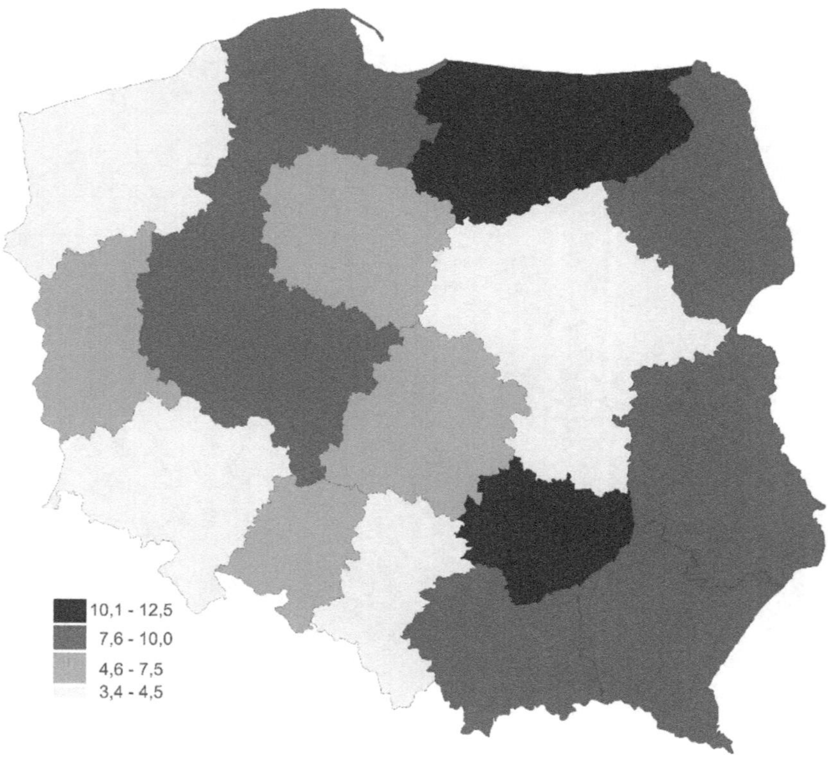

Figure 11.5 Share of people below the subsistence minimum by region in 2015 (%).

Source: author's elaboration based on Central Statistical Office of Poland (GUS) data.

of poverty in the eastern regions and northern territories affected by high unemployment after 1990 (Figure 11.6). It also shows significant local variation within these areas.

The percentage of households furnished with personal computers is higher in regions with metropolitan areas than in rural non-metropolitan ones (Table 11.2). However, the difference between eastern Poland and the rest of the country is generally limited. In Podkarpackie it is almost at the level of Mazowieckie, Małopolskie, Pomorskie, and Śląskie.

It is interesting to examine changes in the educational structure since 1988. The share of people with tertiary education is obviously higher in metropolitan areas, with Mazowieckie, Pomorskie, Małopolskie, and Dolnośląskie being the leaders. Remarkable progress has been achieved by many eastern regions. The same is true of Śląskie, the region of traditional industry, which lagged behind in this respect in the past. A less favourable educational structure is found in some

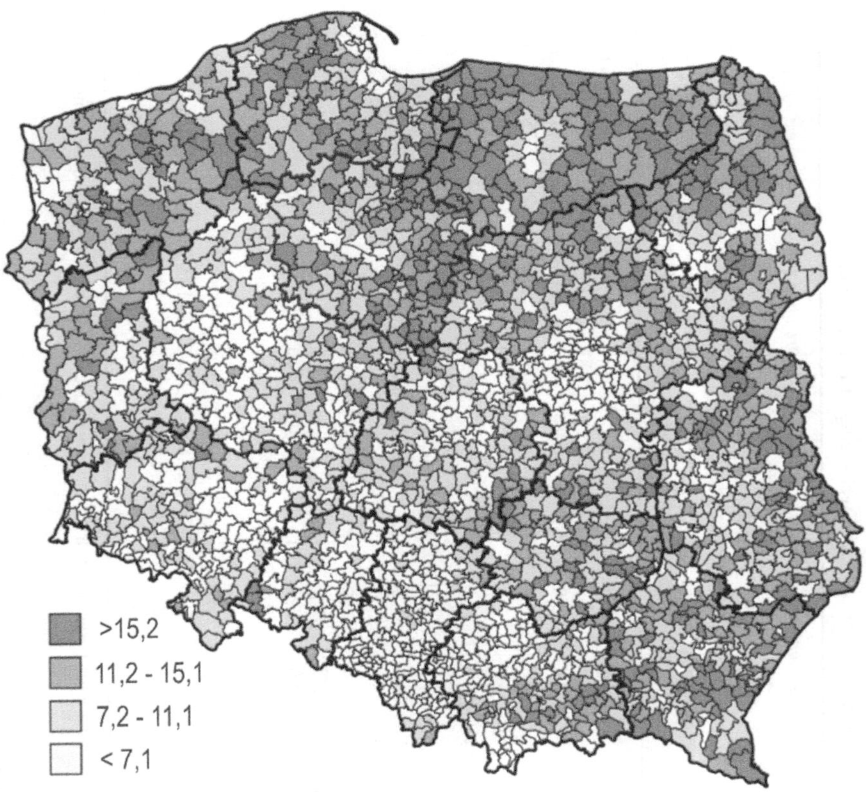

Figure 11.6 Beneficiaries of social welfare by commune in 2015 (%).

Source: author's elaboration based on Central Statistical Office of Poland (GUS) data.

Table 11.2 Selected indicators of social well-being of Polish regions

Region	*Unemployment rate (%)*		*Share of people below subsistence minimum (%)*		*Share of people below legal poverty line (%)*		*Percentage of households furnished with computer (%)*		*Share of people with tertiary education (%)*		*Infant deaths per 1,000 live births*		*Psychological well-being*	*Objective and subjective quality of life*
	1995	*2015*	*2005*	*2015*	*2005*	*2015*	*1999*	*2015*	*1988*[a]	*2011*[b]	*1995*	*2015*	*2015*	*2015*
Mazowieckie	11.6	6.4	9.8	4.1	14.8	8.3	14.5	78.5	10.4	23.6	13.0	3.8	0.01	0.36
Dolnośląskie	16.2	7.0	13.4	4.0	18.7	9.5	13.9	73.8	7.1	16.8	15.3	3.8	–0.02	–0.21
Wielkopolskie	12.6	5.8	13.0	8.9	19.9	16.7	10.6	74.4	6.3	16.4	12.6	4.5	0.11	0.39
Śląskie	10.9	7.2	9.9	3.4	14.2	7.8	12.1	75.9	6.0	15.9	14.6	4.7	0.02	0.04
Pomorskie	16.0	6.6	14.9	8.6	20.4	13.6	13.5	76.2	7.8	17.6	13.9	3.7	0.09	0.33
Łódzkie	13.5	7.7	10.0	5.4	15.1	10.3	10.5	73.4	6.4	16.2	12.8	4.8	–0.13	–0.60
Małopolskie	10.6	7.2	11.3	8.4	17.4	14.3	14.2	76.3	7.6	17.2	12.9	2.8	0.15	0.79
Lubuskie	17.0	6.3	8.8	4.8	14.6	11.4	10.3	75.3	6.1	14.4	11.6	4.1	–0.06	–0.53
Zachodniopomorskie	16.8	7.5	13.1	3.6	19.0	8.1	13.2	72.3	7.2	16.6	16.7	3.6	0.00	–0.52
Kujawsko-pomorskie	16.0	8.0	13.2	6.3	21.3	12.5	10.0	71.3	5.5	14.1	14.4	4.1	0.01	–0.10
Opolskie	12.4	6.5	8.4	6.5	12.0	10.6	9.5	70.7	5.3	13.6	13.4	4.1	–0.06	–0.30
Świętokrzyskie	13.8	10.1	16.2	11.3	24.0	18.6	8.5	67.9	5.6	16.1	12.4	3.8	–0.13	–0.62
Podlaskie	12.0	6.9	13.6	7.8	19.4	13.4	9.6	67.9	6.2	16.0	14.2	4.5	–0.15	–0.47
Warmińsko-mazurskie	21.2	9.4	18.8	12.5	25.1	21.1	6.8	68.4	5.9	14.0	13.1	4.0	–0.03	0.01
Podkarpackie	13.9	11.7	14.9	9.3	22.6	17.1	9.0	75.0	5.7	14.5	11.7	4.1	–0.07	–0.37
Lubelskie	10.6	9.3	14.2	8.6	20.4	14.9	8.0	70.5	6.3	16.2	14.7	3.8	–0.15	–0.52
Poland	13.3	7.5	12.3	6.5	18.1	12.2	11.5	74.2	7.0	17.0	13.6	4.0	0.00	0.00
Gini coefficient	0.078	0.118	0.086	0.180	0.80	0.136	0.089	0.016	0.083	0.056	0.038	0.052	x	x

Source: author's elaboration based on Central Statistical Office of Poland (GUS) data and Czapiński and Panek (2015).

Notes
a people aged 15 and older;
b people aged 13 and older.

northern and western regions, which is confirmed by their poor results in national middle-school tests and secondary school exams.

Infant mortality shows very low variation in Poland. There is neither a classic west-east division, nor a metropolitan vs. non-metropolitan areas differentiation. The relatively worst situation is characteristic of the old industrial regions of Śląskie and Łódzkie, which can be seen as an environmental legacy.

Psychological well-being studied as part of the Social Diagnosis project (Czapiński and Panek 2015) appears to be the highest in Małopolskie, Wielkopolskie and Pomorskie (Figure 11.7). It is about the national average in Śląskie, Mazowieckie and Dolnośląskie, and the lowest in eastern regions and Łódzkie.

Social Diagnosis[2] provides the most comprehensive picture of the objective and subjective quality of life in the country and is based on the sample of 22,200 households and statistical indicators. The best social well-being as shown by the aggregate index is found in Małopolskie; it is also very positive in the developed regions of Wielkopolskie, Mazowieckie, and Pomorskie (Figure 11.8). The study

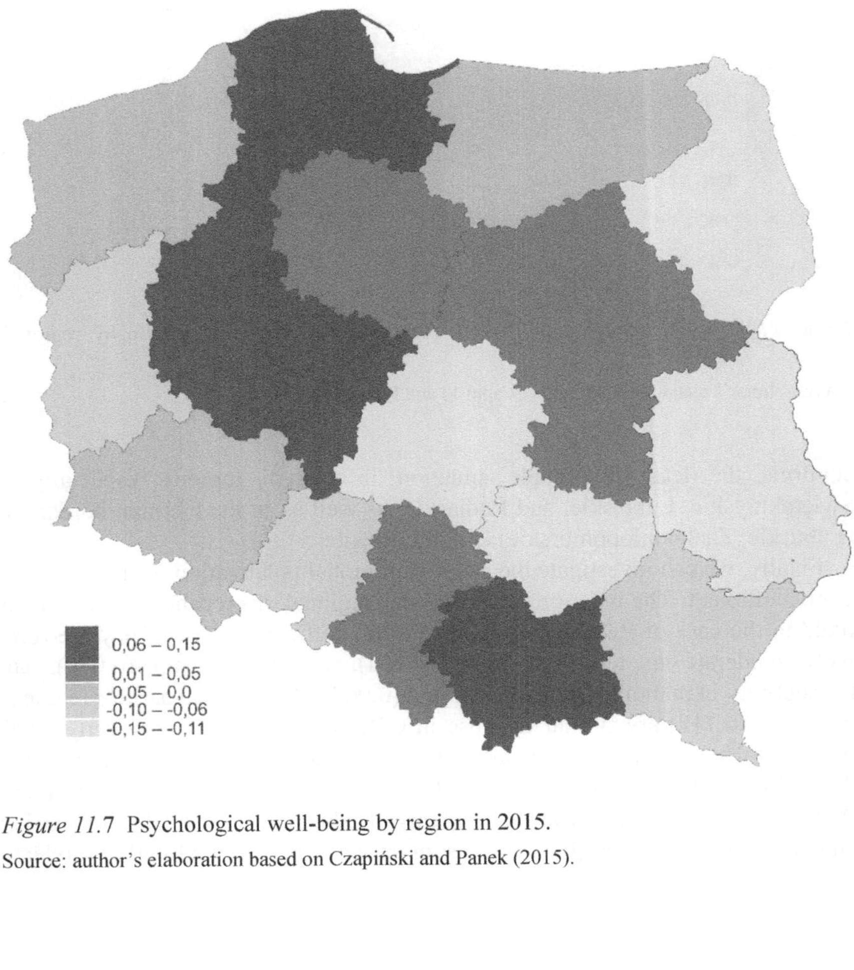

Figure 11.7 Psychological well-being by region in 2015.

Source: author's elaboration based on Czapiński and Panek (2015).

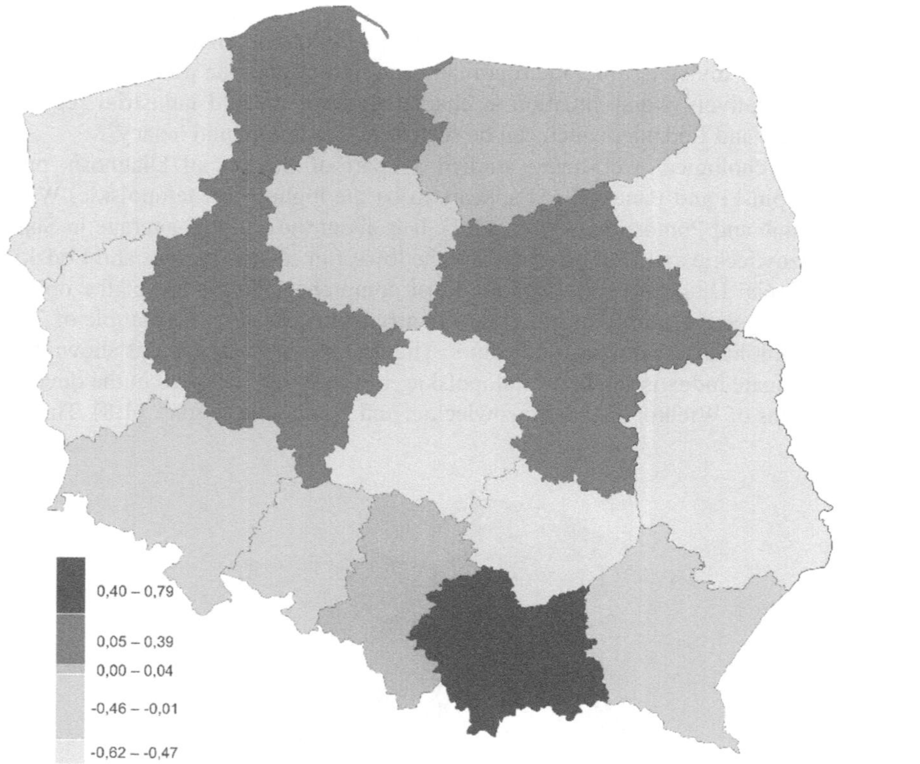

Figure 11.8 Aggregate index of objective and subjective quality of life by region in 2015.

Source: author's elaboration based on Czapiński and Panek (2015).

confirms the least favourable situation in eastern regions, especially in Świętokrzyskie, Lubelskie, and Podlaskie, as well as in the German borderland (Lubuskie, Zachodniopomorskie) and in Łódzkie.

Finally, we can investigate the scope of regional polarization measured by the Gini coefficient. The most pronounced inter-regional discrepancies can be identified in the case of R&D expenditures (Gini coefficient 0.234). They are relatively moderate in terms of GDP (0.104), entrepreneurship (0.078), and productivity in manufacturing and mining (0.067). Regional disparities in unemployment (0.118) are similar to those in GDP and are higher in poverty levels (0.180 in the case of the percentage of people below subsistence minimum and 0.136 for those below legal poverty level). The lowest differentiation among Polish regions is observed in the domains of education (0.056), health (0.052), and computer ownership (0.016). To sum up, there has been a trend of moderate increase of inter-regional disparities in most aspects of economic performance and social well-being. The exception is convergence in educational conditions, computer ownership, as well as R&D expenditures.

At the intra-regional scale, we can see that the differentiation in economic performance is mainly between metropolitan and non-metropolitan areas, as well as between major cities with their suburban zones and peripheral rural areas. On the other hand, there is better intra-regional accessibility (Komornicki *et al.* 2013) and a general improvement in public services, both entailing enhanced social well-being in less-developed areas. Some towns and rural communes in such areas have become places of spectacular success in both competitiveness and social well-being in the previous decades, while others have lagged behind.

We can take a closer look at the processes of change in the Upper Silesian conurbation: a region of traditional industry which has had to face a difficult restructuring process. The dominant sector of coal mining has lost significance, with more than 300,000 jobs gone and a shrinking of the steel and zinc industries. At the same time, the rapid development of consumer and producer services has taken place, furthered by a large regional market; in addition, there was growth of new manufacturing industries, particularly the automotive sector where foreign investment was attracted by good accessibility and technical skills. As a result, unemployment in the region remains low, even though the economic growth rate has been below the national average. The successful restructuring on the regional level was accompanied by increasing local variation. The success of Katowice, Gliwice, Tychy, and some other towns in the conurbation contrasts with the decline of Bytom and the concentration of social problems in some neighbourhoods. This illustrates a new dimension of growing local differentiation in social well-being and the reproduction of social exclusion in certain places.

All things considered, significant improvement in economic performance and social well-being has taken place in less-developed regions. There has also been greater territorial cohesion in terms of economic and social integration at both intra-regional and inter-regional scales. At the same time, there is rather divergence than equalization of spatial disparities at the inter-regional and local levels.

Interpretation of the regional processes and effects in post-socialist Poland

We may begin with the discussion and assessment of the effects of the post-socialist development of Poland from the perspective of regional development and policy, and then seek an explanation of the underlying processes.

From the point of view of inter-regional disparities, there was no reduction of spatial inequalities. They generally had a tendency to increase both in terms of economic performance and social well-being. This reflects the fact that metropolitan regions are the main winners of the fast growth of the Polish economy since 1989. However, if we take into consideration the development of Polish regions which historically lagged behind, there was undoubtedly significant improvement in all spheres. They have reduced the gap vis-à-vis Western European regions, even though they have not caught up with the strongest regions of the country as the latter achieved greater progress.

On the whole, the distance between the least developed regions of eastern Poland and more advanced ones is notably larger in economic efficiency than in non-material aspects of social well-being, especially health, education, and social and psychological well-being.

The general improvement in accessibility and public services, which took place since the 1990s, contributes to greater intra-regional integration of peripheral areas with major urban centres, where economic activities along with higher-order services are concentrated. However, this does not necessarily mean less intra-regional discrepancies. As a matter of fact, there is increasing differentiation between various towns and communes as well as within towns, i.e. at the local scale.

The share of people in poverty and other measures of social deprivation indicate a vast improvement, leading to the conclusion of more socially inclusive development in the territorial dimension in the country. However, social exclusion is a serious problem in some places, for example, certain urban neighbourhoods and rural localities.

The privileged position of metropolitan areas in economic competitiveness can be explained by the size of their market, a pool of skilled labour, and good accessibility in the main, which fosters their economic diversification and leads to enhanced social well-being. This means that the contemporary success of these areas is built upon the leading role of major cities shaped in the past. What is a new feature is the fast development of the outer metropolitan zones around these cities. The pre-socialist legacies of unfavourable economic structures and poor infrastructure, which were maintained and exacerbated by distorted demographic structures under state socialism, represent barriers to the development of non-metropolitan rural areas today. All this means that there is a strong element of continuity in spatial patterns of local and regional development – they appear to be structures of long duration.

Considerable changes were experienced by industrial regions and towns. Their situation has been contingent on the dominant sectors and/or the success of individual enterprises. Many single-industry and one-factory towns were badly affected by deindustrialization. There has been generally successful restructuring of the old industrial regions of Upper Silesia and to somewhat lesser extent of Łódź. The advent of foreign investors has by and large contributed to the enhanced competitiveness of many towns and regions. Delocalization of their subsidiaries from Poland have been very rare so far.

There is much evidence of increased exports of high-value added manufacturing products and services by both foreign subsidiaries and successful domestic companies. This is associated with the significant embeddedness of foreign investors in the growing supplier networks in the country, including other foreign and local firms. However, such functional upgrading and embeddedness, which can be seen as characteristic of the high-road of development, are particularly evident in metropolitan areas and historically more advanced regions, such as Lower and Upper Silesia (Dolnośląskie, Śląskie), Wielkopolskie, and Mazowieckie (Domański, 2011). It can also be identified in the south-eastern region of Podkarpackie, but it is less clear whether this has been the case in other less-developed regions. It seems that the latter more often depend on simple labour-intensive activities. In addition, the embeddedness of foreign firms and the positive spill-over effects of their activity for local enterprises and communities can be more limited here, due to a less diversified regional economy and hence fewer potential suppliers. In a situation of rising wages, this leads to the question whether they are going to follow the trajectory of functional upgrading towards more advanced activities, which already is taking place in metropolitan areas, or whether they will suffer from delocalization of companies to lower-cost locations outside Poland in the future.

The role of public agencies through policies in these processes is interesting. There is little doubt that institutional changes and infrastructural investment undertaken by the national government and supported by the EU funds after 2004 were important factors here. They facilitated enhanced regional competitiveness of the less-developed regions of eastern Poland, which was achieved despite the barriers and legacies discussed earlier. There was even more improvement in social well-being in such areas. Last but not least, there is much evidence that local governments are instrumental in the success of many towns and communes. Different local development trajectories of towns of similar socio-economic conditions are often related to the quality of local governments.

Conclusion

All in all, it is evident that the regional structures of both competitiveness and social well-being cannot be understood without a broader historical perspective. Current patterns and processes of regional and local development are rooted in structures and practices from the pre-socialist past and socialist era, that is, they are clearly path-dependent. Post-socialist transition cannot be reduced to simple notions of 'modernization' or 'Europeanization' – following and copying earlier development paths of Western Europe. The development trajectories of Polish regions and towns are a product of interaction between older structures and newer mechanisms with the influence of various local, national and global agents. They are underpinned by both endogenous and exogenous factors.

The relationship between economic development and social well-being in the regional perspective was based on administrative mechanisms under state socialism. Nowadays it is shaped – reproduced and/or changed – by economic, institutional, demographic, and social structures and mechanisms.

If social justice is primarily understood in terms of reduced social exclusion, we can conclude that the post-socialist development of Poland brought about enhanced competitiveness together with positive social consequences in the previously under-privileged regions, even though the gap between them and metropolitan areas has increased. Thus, competitiveness and solidarity can be seen as being mutually reinforcing rather than contradictory at the regional level in this particular historical period. It does not mean that there are no losers of these processes in social and territorial dimensions. They are evident at the sub-regional and especially the local levels. Further improvement in fighting social exclusion may be more difficult. So far, it has largely been achieved by overcoming infrastructural and institutional legacies from the pre-socialist and socialist times. The remaining areas of social exclusion are determined by a complex nexus of social, economic, and spatial structures, partly rooted in the past and partly generated by contemporary global economy. It follows that existing public policies may not be appropriate to cope with this problem and that new approaches may be needed.

Notes

1 The data refer to 28 countries of the European Union, both in 1990 and 2016.
2 The study takes into account eight important aspects of the life of households and individuals, including income, material affluence, use of modern communication technologies, education, health, medical treatment, stress, mental well-being, lifestyle, pathological behaviour, cultural participation, etc. (Czapiński and Panek 2015).

References

Bachtler, John, Peter Berkowitz, Sally Hardy, and Tatjana Muravska (eds) (2017). *EU Cohesion Policy: reassessing performance and direction*. London: Routledge.

Czapiński Janusz and Tomasz Panek (eds) (2015). *Social diagnosis 2015*: *objective and subjective quality of life in Poland.* Warsaw: The Council for Social Monitoring.

Dicken Peter and Anders Malmberg (2001). 'Firms in territories: a relational perspective', *Economic Geography* 77(4): 345–63.

Domański, Bolesław (2010). 'Should we fight local and regional disparities in economic development in Poland?', *Studia Regionalia* 27: 132–41.

Domański, Bolesław (2011). 'Foreign capital and the development of Polish regions', *Czasopismo Geograficzne* 82(1–2): 173–87.

EC (European Commission) (2010). *Europe 2020: a European strategy for smart, sustainable and inclusive growth.* Luxembourg: Publication Office of the European Union.

Fagerberg, Jan and Bart Verspagen (1996). 'Heading for divergence? Regional growth in Europe reconsidered', *Journal of Common Market Studies* 34(3): 431–48.

Fischer, Manfred and Peter Nijkamp (eds) (1999). *Spatial dynamics of European integration: regional and policy issues at the turn of the century.* Berlin: Springer.

Friedmann, John (1972). 'A general theory of polarized development', in Niles M. Hansen (ed.). *Growth centres in regional economic development*. New York: The Free Press.

Gereffi, Gary (2008). 'Development models and industrial upgrading in China and Mexico', *European Sociological Review* 25(1): 37–51.

Komornicki, Tomasz, Piotr Rosik, Premyslaw Śleszyński, *et al.* (2013). *Impact of the construction of motorways and expressways on socio-economic and territorial development of Poland.* Warsaw: Ministry of Infrastructure and Development.

Komornicki Tomasz and J. Zaucha (2015). 'The concept of territorial cohesion as understood and practiced by Polish regions', Institute for Development Working Paper No. 2. Brighton: ID.

Myrdal, Gunnar (1957). *Economic theory and underdeveloped regions*. London: Duckworth.

OECD (Organisation for Economic Co-operation and Development) (2009). *Investing for growth: building innovative regions*. Paris: OECD.

Phelps, N.A. (2000). 'The locally embedded multinational and institutional culture', *Area* 32(2): 169–78.

Pike, Andy, Andrés Rodríguez-Pose, and John Tomaney (2006). *Local and regional development*. London: Routledge.

Pike, Andy, Andrés Rodríguez-Pose, and John Tomaney (2007). 'What kind of local and regional development and for whom?', *Regional Studies* 41(9): 1253–69.

Smith, David M. and Roger Lee (eds) (2004). *Geographies and moralities: international perspectives on development, justice and place*. Oxford: Blackwell.

Sztompka, Piotr (2004). 'From East-Europeans to Europeans: shifting collective identities and symbolic boundaries in the new Europe', *European Review* 12(4): 481–96.

Vernon, Raymond (1966). 'International investment and international trade in the product cycle', *The Quarterly Journal of Economics* 80(2): 190–207.

World Bank (2009). *World Development Report 2009: reshaping economic geography*. Washington, DC: World Bank.

12 The road towards a genuine Economic and Monetary Union

More competitive and fairer

Annette Bongardt and Francisco Torres

The project of a 'genuine Economic and Monetary Union' (GEMU) advanced against the background of macroeconomic, social, and political tensions facing Economic and Monetary Union (EMU). This chapter asks whether the development of the European Union (EU) towards GEMU is likely to further the European socio-economic model that is anchored in the Treaties, including in its social dimension.[1] EMU constraints have emerged alongside the initial globalisation-driven competitiveness rationale and have become the main driver of reforms. The need to improve the functioning of EMU and deliver results to European citizens resulted in the necessity to increase coordination at the Eurozone level in Member State domains, such as labour markets and social policy (at least).

Since the sovereign debt crisis, the European Central Bank (ECB) has come to insistently call for economic and structural reforms, above all at the Member State level, on the grounds of their critical role for the success of EMU. Progress on those reforms, most notably with a view to price and wage flexibility, is of course important for making EMU function more like an optimum currency area (OCA). But would it also move the EU closer to the European socio-economic model? After all, those reforms will also condition the shape that such a (modernized) European model comes to assume, which in turn makes the matter politically sensitive.

To complicate matters, at the same time as coordination and reform needs grew, the effects of the global financial, economic, and sovereign debt crises stirred up popular contestation. This crystallized around the European model, perceived as an Anglo-Saxon-type model and allegedly driven by the market and at the expense of equity, and led to a backlash against reforms, the currency union, and the European project.

This chapter argues that for GEMU (and the Union) to be sustainable, reforms need to be embedded in a future-oriented European model that is both competitive and fair. To assess whether the EU is on this path, the chapter looks at the state of the European model and asks to what extent it will be furthered by GEMU. It takes stock of the state of GEMU before zooming in on relevant efforts of economic policy coordination, under whose heading matters that shape the European model are addressed.[2] The chapter characterizes the principal features of what is a still not consolidated and incomplete European socio-economic model. It argues that a model that takes into account competitiveness factors in a comprehensive and forward-looking way and is backed by citizens' preferences, is a precondition for an EMU that is sustainable (although it might still fall short of an OCA). A Union that delivers wider benefits for its citizens, including on the European model's social dimension, enhances at the same time the popular support for reforms, for the currency union, and for the European integration project.[3]

The remainder of this chapter is organized as follows. First, it reviews the Maastricht legacy, above all, the need to complete EMU's economic union side, and examines the current state of GEMU and the relevant features of its economic policy coordination strand. Next, it considers whether the European model in its present state serves as a compass for reforms in GEMU. It evaluates EU coordination of structural reforms, discusses the potential and limits to making reforms work for GEMU under constrained decentralization, and highlights the importance of ownership and of a conducive reform narrative therein. Then, it assesses the EU's progress from a single market with a social dimension via OCA requirements to a European social model. It highlights the difficulty of a conducive reform narrative when market correction trails market making in general, and of soft coordination of labour markets and social protection in particular. Finally, it provides a concluding summary of the argument.

The Maastricht legacy and the state of GEMU

The twin global financial and especially the sovereign debt crises brought to the fore the existence of and the urgent need to deal with macroeconomic, social, and political tensions in EMU. Those resulted from flaws in EMU's institutional design, many of which date back to its inception at Maastricht (Torres 2015).

In contrast to the monetary union part of EMU, the Maastricht blueprint had left the economic union side, where there had been a lack of consensus, incomplete.[4] Its completion can be likened to an open compromise. As such, it was dependent on a sufficient convergence of preferences to occur, over time and/or crisis-induced, across Member States. As it stood, it remained insufficiently coordinated. Compared to a stand-alone economic union that has no currency union attached, the good functioning and sustainability of an economic *cum* monetary union make additional demands on the economic union side, notably on labour, product, and financial markets, with regard to flexibility and coordination requirements. Economic and structural reforms would be needed to push the Eurozone more towards an OCA and to facilitate the smooth functioning of monetary policy.[5]

Yet, during EMU's – by many accounts rather successful – first decade, attempts to complete the EMU's governance framework were limited. The lack of perceived urgency arguably contributed to leniency. Insufficient attention was paid to the build-up of macroeconomic disequilibria. The cumulative impact of the global economic and financial crisis (2008–09) and particularly the subsequent sovereign debt crisis, a Eurozone crisis that erupted in 2010, provided a formidable test of EMU's resilience and sustainability. In the sovereign debt crisis, large negative spillovers ran, incidentally rather unexpectedly, from EMU's insufficiently coordinated economic union side into its monetary sphere,[6] putting at stake not only EMU's good functioning but indeed its survival. It became clear that EMU governance was ill prepared to deal with the crisis effects, and that the economic union part of EMU had to be completed at least as far as the prerequisites to sustain the monetary union are concerned.

Economic governance was built up in response to the crises, although this did not occur in a holistic way but was driven by market pressure and limited by political opportunity, occurring through many small, cumulative steps, both inside and outside the Community framework and through various governance mechanisms. In 2012, those piecemeal attempts at governance building culminated in the project of completing EMU by creating a 'genuine EMU' to deal with the EMU's design flaws.[7] Since then, the various EU Presidents' Reports (Juncker *et al.* 2015a, 2015b; Van Rompuy *et al.* 2012) have reiterated the necessity to respond to the Eurozone crisis by completing the EMU's economic union part. This meant seeking progress on four – financial, fiscal, economic, and political – so-called strands as to achieve a 'genuine EMU'. Those four GEMU strands translate, respectively, into a banking union, an integrated budgetary framework, an integrated economic policy framework, and enhanced democratic legitimacy and accountability of EMU governance.

However, attempts to create a GEMU have only made limited progress. Financial integration (a banking union) has progressed substantially, although one-and-a-half of its three pillars are still missing. Fiscal integration did not progress much since 2011. And with regard to an enhanced democratic legitimacy and accountability of EMU governance, the institutional steps taken during the crisis appear not to have been significant. Still, a non-negligible informal bottom-up process of political integration has been occurring through the substantially increased politicization of multi-level governance (Torres 2015). Overall, however, the crisis has thus far failed to mobilize governments and citizens around a new impetus for European integration.

As for the integrated economic policy framework, under whose heading competitiveness issues and structural reforms are discussed, it stands out as the one that has progressed the least during the crisis and especially so since 2012, held back by Member State competences (Bongardt and Torres 2016a, 2016b; Mongelli *et al.* 2016). It is also still far from the level required to sustain EMU. Limited progress on GEMU raises the question of the longer-term political sustainability of both EMU and the political European integration project (Jones and Torres 2015).

Successive Presidents' reports on GEMU claimed that the pursuit of economic policy integration required the creation of stronger incentives for structural reforms in low-productivity countries. The proposal to create incentives for promoting structural reforms for Member States, such as a system of national reform contracts to be signed with EU institutions in exchange for financial support (Van Rompuy *et al.* 2012) was nevertheless abandoned, since it failed to gather the necessary political support across Member States.

In 2015, the Five Presidents' report (Juncker *et al.* 2015b) settled for building on the Euro Plus Pact, notably featuring the creation of a euro-area system of national competitiveness boards to enhance ownership of economic reforms at the national level and prevent divergence above all in the Eurozone (although it is open also to non-euro area countries).

More specifically, during GEMU's first stage (1 July 2015–30 June 2017) concrete progress towards an Economic Union of convergence, growth, and jobs was to rest on the creation of a euro area system of Competitiveness Authorities.[8] The idea behind this innovation was an attempt to improve ownership of reforms and hence strengthen national reform efforts. Loose coordination and non-binding Member State commitments are to be maintained in a first phase, whereas moving to a legal base for commitments is envisaged but postponed to the second stage. In our view, this fact suggests that the Presidents are sceptical as to whether national structural reform through non-binding coordination can deliver reforms of product and labour markets with a view to price and wage flexibility and hence adjustment capacity in the face of asymmetric shocks (Begg *et al.* 2015).

The ECB keeps reminding EMU Member States that it is up to them to enact the economic and structural reforms necessary for EMU's good functioning and sustainability.[9] With its competences limited by treaty to monetary policy, it can only call on Member States, where economic policy competences reside, to tackle the causes of the crises, such as disequilibria associated with competitiveness differentials and insufficient adjustment capacity to asymmetric shocks due to wage-price inflexibility. In the ECB's view, this involves notably reversing the decline in productivity and improving labour market outcomes.[10]

Since, in 2012, at the height of the sovereign debt crisis, ECB President Draghi made the famous – and, as it turned out, credible – commitment to do 'whatever it takes' to defend the common currency, the immediate danger to EMU's survival has been fended off. The ECB also resorted to non-conventional and quasi-fiscal measures to ensure the functioning of the monetary transmission mechanism in the crisis context, as well as the creation of an outright monetary transactions (OMT) facility. The effect was to calm financial markets and lower country risk premiums. ECB actions thereby bought time for Eurozone countries to undertake frequently overdue domestic reforms, which are often time-lagged, and for them to produce effects. As a side-effect, however, they took away some market pressure from Member States to reform.[11]

As for advances on the integrated economic policy framework, in its reflection paper on deepening EMU, the Commission (EC 2017a) proposes advancing in two phases. The first stage (until 2019) would be about completing banking union and capital markets union and the second (until 2025) about completing EMU's architecture, notably complementing the financial union and adding a fiscal stabilization function. It is noteworthy that this broadens the ECB's concern with OCA requirements by putting social considerations on a par with economic ones, with specific recommendations and new social indicators as part of the European Semester, and highlights among other things the need for fair and well-functioning labour markets and welfare states. The Commission (EC 2017b: 47) also made concrete proposals with respect to creating a European Pillar of Social Rights, which is to serve as a compass for a renewed convergence process.

Incidentally, the election in 2017 of pro-European integration President Macron in France and the scheduled British exit from the EU (Brexit) have already put in motion some dynamics that could facilitate both the completion of EMU governance and a change in Member States' national reform narratives (Bongardt and Torres 2016a). On the one hand, the possibility of Brexit has already sharpened European citizens' awareness of the benefits of EU membership. Since 2016, support by EU citizens for the Union, the euro, and for European integration has gone up and stands at high levels (EC 2017c). The UK's potential exit from the EU could come to facilitate progress on GEMU in light of the country's record of trying to obstruct and veto advances in Eurozone governance as well as on issues related to currency union requirements on economic union (such as single market financial regulation motivated by the Eurozone common good of financial stability, or the UK's veto of the Fiscal Compact reinforcing Eurozone governance) and also on social rights (Bongardt and Torres 2016b). On the other hand, issues that are important for the completion of EMU, such as a Eurozone budget and a finance minister possibly accountable to the European Parliament, some form of risk sharing, a European Monetary Fund, and the completion of banking union, are again being tabled. What already has progressed is the European Pillar of Social Rights, which had been launched in 2015 by Commission President Juncker for the Eurozone, and which was agreed at the November 2017 Gothenburg social summit.

The European model as a compass for reforms?

The European Pillar of Social Rights was promoted with a GEMU dimension, which begs the question as to the characteristics of the European socio-economic model and whether it serves as a compass for reforms.

The European model implies that the economy is to serve broader societal – social but also environmental – objectives.[12] It has become fleshed out, by unanimity of the Member States, through the EU's economic agendas, the Lisbon Strategy (2000–10) and its successor for the present decade, the Europe 2020 Strategy (2011–20), aimed at a renewed version of a social market economy for Europe in the twenty-first century. Motivated by common threats facing EU Member States, which derive above all from globalization but also from the realities of the information society, demographic ageing, and climate change, both strategies are geared towards transforming those threats into economic opportunities while making social and environmental protection compatible with the international competitiveness rationale, and indeed turn it into a growth-enhancing factor.

Economic and institutional modernization calls for progress on the areas of innovation, liberalization, entrepreneurship, sustainable development, and employment and social inclusion. The latter social dimension involves reforms to integrate people into the workforce, improve qualifications, and modernize social protection, notably by enshrining the need for long-term sustainability of public finances, adjusting the pension age and significantly reducing the number of people exposed to poverty risk and social exclusion.

The EU's upward move in terms of economic integration to the EMU level increased interdependencies between the members of the monetary union and strengthened the rationale for EU coordination. It gave rise to the need to internalize EMU constraints across Member States' varieties of capitalism and policy areas and meant a qualitative change in European integration.

EU coordination of structural reforms

The Lisbon and Europe 2020 Strategies had been motivated by the competitiveness rationale in a globalization context, rather than by Eurozone constraints. It was spillovers from trade that provided the rationale for EU-level coordination of economic and structural reforms towards common goals. The political economy argument was that peer pressure would help the implementation of those reforms in Member States. In the sovereign debt crisis, the rationale for coordination – centred on the single market and positive (albeit small) spillovers from trade – underwent a dramatic re-evaluation in the Eurozone context when negative and very large spillovers, stemming from insufficient economic coordination, put EMU's good functioning and survival at risk. In the monetary union context, the argument for enhanced EU – read Eurozone, with its heightened interdependencies – coordination became much stronger. Unsurprisingly, peer pressure, which had been largely absent before, also made an appearance. However, although reforms that cater to OCA requirements became more urgent, relevant policy areas, including labour markets and welfare systems, have remained national competences and continue to hinge on loose coordination (constrained decentralization).

The key concerns in a GEMU context are productivity (addressing unsustainable competitiveness differentials) and creating national ownership of reforms. The national competitiveness authorities, which are to foster the implementation of EMU-relevant structural reforms, have the Euro Plus Pact as a reference rather than the Europe 2020 Strategy. The Euro Plus Pact's embodied competitiveness notion is thereby bound to shape the EU model. The Pact is geared towards dealing with monetary union constraints on national economic policymaking and its competitiveness notion falls short of a future-oriented socioeconomic model. In contrast to the Lisbon and Europe 2020 Strategies' broad competitiveness notion, which encompasses the relevant factors for future competitiveness (Gros and Roth 2012), the Euro Plus Pact's focus is narrower and more short-term oriented towards cost competitiveness.

The European Commission (EC 2017a)[13] had advocated that those euro-area national competitiveness boards (open to non-euro members in the EU) should enshrine a broad competitiveness notion more akin to the Lisbon and Europe 2020 Strategies, in that they should go beyond labour unit cost considerations and include factors ranging from productivity to skills, the attractiveness of the business environment, and innovation. However, a divergence of views emerged between the European Commission and the EcoFin Council, for which the preferred designation of those competitiveness authorities – that is, national competitiveness boards (European Commission) versus national productivity boards (Council) – is already indicative. The Council revision of the Commission proposal reduced both the tasks of the Boards and the role of the Commission, besides significantly extending implementation timetables (EP 2016).

The narrower focus (that is, productivity rather than more encompassing competitiveness factors) and the affirmation of national (sovereignty) concerns sit uncomfortably with the improvement of ownership, the effectiveness of non-binding commitments, and the inclusion of wider societal concerns and long-term competitiveness factors. Reforms that are primarily concerned with Eurozone interdependencies and currency union sustainability, rather than being framed in terms of desirable reforms in line with (complementary) socio-economic goals and preferences, carry a large potential for a societal backlash. The European Commission's reflection paper on deepening EMU (EC 2017a) recognizes these concerns, proposing to test new instruments, which include better economic and social convergence standards.

Significantly, the Commission (EC 2018) has hence come to base its assessment of the implementation of structural reforms on broader objectives (those of the Europe 2020 Strategy and of the Broad Economic Policy Guidelines, dropping references to the Euro Plus Pact) and has included the respect of the European social pillar in the European Semester.

Potential and limits to making reforms under constrained decentralization work

Through the European economic agendas, the EU set a modernization agenda aimed at defending the European model by adapting the framework in which markets and agents operate in a forward-looking way to the new competitiveness factors and realities of today's world. The implementation of common European-level objectives and specific targets to which all Member States are committed hinges on the success of soft coordination through the Open Method of Coordination (OMC), aimed at mutual learning of best practice and to be incentivized through benchmarking of Member State performance.

The EU's experience suggests that the competitiveness rationale, which means cost competitiveness in the short run (but is much broader once one takes a long-run view), is unlikely to provide a sufficient motivation for economic reforms at the national level as to prevent economic divergence in the euro area. To be sure, reforms ought to be in the interest of each individual Member State to maintain living standards in a world in which competitiveness factors have changed profoundly. However, those constraints are often neither presented nor (even less so) discussed in terms of desirable reforms in the context of a model of society. Nor is there any common recipe for economic and institutional modernization. The convergence of preferences on institutions is a slow-moving process (Roland 2004). And, with policy competences mostly at the national level, countries need to find their own and most consensual path towards the common agreed objectives and targets.

Nevertheless, soft coordination does have great potential for creating ownership of reform (Bongardt and Torres 2012). With the OMC and decade-long agendas, the Lisbon and Europe 2020 Strategies had the right instruments and long-term frameworks to facilitate the creation of ownership through the convergence of preferences on institutions towards best practice, and hence a consensus, in Member States. The problem has been at the implementation level, since in many Member States the OMC's potential has gone largely unrealized and its record of implementation and enforcement has been weak.

Although the choice of the OMC as a coordination method goes back to Member States' unwillingness to transfer competences to the EU, this soft coordination method allows Member States, with their different varieties of capitalism, and subject to different preferences, traditions, and path-dependent institutions, to trace their own, most consensual path towards common EU aims. Yet, to do so requires Member States' capacity and willingness for mutual learning from best practice and for involving the public in the reform process, as to create ownership of and thus ensure citizens' backing for reforms. EU-wide benchmarking of Member States' performance was geared at informing the public. It was thought that national public pressure would push Member States – in the absence of sanctions in the case of a Member State's non-compliance with its commitments – towards better performance on the most consensual reform path.

In the event, the OMC's effectiveness was hampered by an excessive (subsequently narrowed down) number of targets, and severely weakened when the European Commission had to abandon ranking Member States' performance ('naming and shaming' in what are national policy domains) in the early years of the Lisbon Strategy. However, Member States have differed in their capacity and/or willingness to put available instruments to good use. Progress was uneven across Member States and policy areas (Tilford and Whyte 2010). Some countries made use of annual progress reports on their reform efforts to make continuous improvements, while others ended up producing them merely for the drawer. In addition, public and peer pressure were large absent during the Lisbon Strategy period. The – rather small – positive spillovers from trade did not prove a strong enough incentive for reform. Competitiveness differentials were allowed to build up during the Euro's first decade.

When the sovereign debt crisis, a Eurozone crisis, broke in 2010, it was a watershed also for structural reform with a bearing on the European model. From then on, reform efforts became driven by the Eurozone and the urgency to internalize constraints on the monetary union that originated in insufficient coordination in the economic union sphere.

By that time, it was, however, too late in the process to take in possible lessons in the EU's new economic coordination strategy. The Europe 2020 Strategy, the Lisbon Strategy's successor for the present decade (2011–20), was already well on track very much along the same lines as far as its method (the OMC), broad objectives – smart, inclusive, and sustainable growth – and governance were concerned. The main innovations regarded improved coordination through the European Semester process, thereby bringing together in time the evaluation of Member State progress on the fiscal and structural reform front, and country-specific reports and reform recommendations (Bongardt and Torres 2012). Efforts translated into an attempt to ensure better, tailor-made economic reforms in a strategy that continued to lack a specific Eurozone dimension. Pasimeni (2013) finds that the Europe 2020 Strategy has been comparatively better at integrating the economic and social pillars than at creating synergies with the environmental pillar, which are still not exploited.

The weaknesses of the Europe 2020 Strategy go some way to explaining the coming into existence of the Euro Plus Pact (initially called the Competitiveness Pact or Pact for the Euro) in 2011, only a year later. Against the crisis background, constrained decentralization needed to become more effective in an EMU context. With the Europe 2020 Strategy not catering to specific Eurozone needs, the Euro Plus Pact came to focus on EMU members' greater interdependencies and reforms in monetary union-relevant areas. However, it is likewise hamstrung by weak enforcement (the same OMC, with no sanctions in the case of non-compliance) and by its intergovernmental nature.

Achievements to date remain confined to strengthening incentives for and ownership of reform within the limits of constrained decentralization (EC 2017a). The modifications to the European Semester of economic policy coordination were introduced to strengthen both the Eurozone dimension and ownership of reforms. Greater attention has been given to interdependencies and challenges of the euro area as a whole, with dedicated recommendations and a closer monitoring of spillovers. Broad discussions of reforms are being promoted, giving Member States and stakeholders (national parliaments, social partners, civil society) more opportunities to discuss at all levels. In addition, the EU's financial framework for 2014–20 took a step towards strengthening incentives by establishing a stronger link between the priorities of the European Semester and the use of European Structural and Investment (ESI) Funds, notably with regard to country-specific recommendations. GEMU's economic coordination strand came to feature attempts to bolster structural reforms via national competitiveness authorities to promote the creation of ownership, although those appear fraught by a less encompassing competitiveness notion. In any case, implementation has suffered delays and the second stage of legally binding commitments is at best still some way off. The European Commission has come to set up a Structural Reform Support Service to help implementation in laggard countries. It pools expertise from across Europe and provides technical support for Member States that solicit it, as to promote mutual learning and facilitate the implementation of reforms.

The success of economic reform efforts in the EU and EMU alike is associated with making constrained decentralization work. Apart from the necessary institutional changes to complete GEMU, a better functioning monetary union hinges on adjustment capacity to (asymmetric) shocks, which depend on the capacity and the willingness to implement economic reforms at the Member State level.[14] Proposed remedies – competitiveness authorities or better convergence standards – envisage improving enforcement through incentives or benchmarking. Ownership at the national level hence remains critical for the feasibility and acceptance of reforms and the implementation of common objectives.

On ownership and a reform narrative

The lack of Member States taking ownership of reform has been the Achilles' heel of the EU's economic coordination strategies (the Lisbon and Europe 2020 Strategies and also the Euro Plus Pact) all along and it continues to weaken the Eurozone to date.

Member States had already generally failed, some of them significantly, to take advantage of the Lisbon Strategy's potential to create ownership of often over-due reforms. However, when large negative spillovers flowed from EMU's insufficiently coordinated economic union sphere into its monetary sphere in the Eurozone crisis, those Member States that had made least progress on the Lisbon Strategy's economic and institutional modernization targets – and which therefore had a low growth potential – started to face market pressure. Financial markets started to equate a low growth potential due to delayed institutional modernization with a lower capacity to repay accumulated debts, resulting in higher risk margins. Market pressure made an appearance as a source of (relentless) pressure on Member States to modernize their institutions and effect competitiveness and growth-enhancing structural reforms. According to Schmieding and Schulz (2014), some progress was made on the Euro Plus Pact's account since the eruption of the sovereign debt crisis, as market and peer pressure (largely absent before) and conditionality-induced reforms in adjustment countries in the Eurozone made an appearance and accelerated reforms. Yet, by 2016, reform efforts had lost pace and even stalled in peripheral countries when pressures decreased (Schmieding 2016). When market pressure subsided (somewhat paradoxically, not least due to ECB actions that would buy time for national reforms to be enacted and pay off), so did the perceived urgency to reform.

Of course, building ownership of structural reforms is already difficult in normal times in light of political economy factors.[15] Within a Member State there are winners and losers, a fact that should in theory be more easily dealt with in good economic times. Of course, there are also inter-generational justice aspects (most notably in environmental and welfare state matters) that ought to be accounted for. This was precisely the idea behind the Lisbon process, which was geared towards a broad set of future competitiveness factors, embedded in a process of convergence of preference on institutions in society. In practice, reforms have typically only come about under pressure (when there is little leeway to compensate losers and little time to form a consensus in society). Not least the political cycle – short with regard to the pay-off of most reforms – stands in the way, so that economic reforms are often the product of external (above all, market) pressure and have to be implemented when a country's capacity to compensate losers is, often severely, constrained. Of course, the sequencing of structural reforms with a prioritization of those that have a short-run growth pay-off offers a way to facilitate the implementation of (at least some) structural reforms.[16]

Building ownership becomes even more complicated in a crisis context that adds external sources of pressure for reform, most notably financial market pressure but also peer pressure and, in countries that became subject to adjustment programmes, conditionality. External pressure accelerated reforms in EMU Member States and reforms can already be seen to contribute to growth in the Eurozone (Schmieding 2017).[17] However, if building up EMU governance and ownership under market pressure is challenging, it becomes a double-edged sword in the face of reform conditionality (Nicolaidis and Watson 2016). However, the issue of building national ownership of reform remains pertinent (especially since market pressure has lessened for the time being) and in need of completion, if reforms are to succeed and national reforms are also to be politically sustainable (Schmieding 2016) and the Eurozone is to be resilient and sustainable in the long run.

For the Eurozone, the crunch issue will be whether Member States will have managed to make use of currently favourable conditions to resolve structural problems, so that they and the Eurozone are better prepared to face the next crisis. However, judging by the results of the Lisbon Strategy, aimed at promoting structural reforms in a forward-looking way and in good times (when it is also easier to compensate losers in society) rather than in times of need for urgent corrections, that is – rather tragically – not likely to happen. In our view, a conducive domestic narrative for reform would have to be created, framed in a desirable European socio-economic model of development.

However, the European model is presently still incomplete, notably in its social dimension. It is often perceived as driven by liberalization rather than by social and environmental concerns, which is not particularly helpful either. The same applies to the fact that reforms have at occasions occurred under market pressure but more recently also under peer pressure and/or subject to formal (under adjustment programmes) or informal (ECB letters, peer pressure) conditionality. The Commission heeded the lesson from the sovereign debt crisis that ownership of reform is vital and that equity and social considerations assume particular relevance therein.[18] Only a European model that makes sacrifices look worthwhile can be expected to facilitate necessary reforms in these circumstances and possibly even do so in economically good times.

On a separate but related note, the European model and the reform narrative have not only an internal but also an external dimension. However, as discussed elsewhere (Bongardt and Torres 2017a), European citizens did not trust the EU on enacting the European model in recent advanced trade agreements. Whereas conventional trade agreements did not arouse opposition in the past, advanced ones did. The key issue is that the European model is in many facets (EU food safety, environmental and consumer protection standards, and labour) regulation-driven. Citizens suspected that advanced trade agreements may end up weakening the government's rights or capacity to regulate in the public interest, present or future. There is also some doubt that countries will act in the public interest in the presence of investor protection clauses, even if they are allowed to make standards and regulate according to preferences, because of the potentially high compensation charges they may have to pay for it.[19]

In conclusion, successful reform catering to the competitiveness rationale and EMU constraints requires ownership. This is fostered if Member States put available instruments to good use and foster a public discussion around reform needs and avenues. Governments also need to come clean in their domestic discourses and priorities on the deep economic interdependence of the EU and especially of the Eurozone, adjust their narratives accordingly, and refrain from scapegoating the EU for national policy failures or EMU constraints (Buti and Lacoue-Labarthe 2016). Last but not least, European citizens need to share in the EMU's wider benefits if they are to identify with a European model that makes sacrifices for the Eurozone's sake worthwhile.[20]

From a Single Market with a social dimension via OCA requirements to a European social model?

On a reform narrative when market correction trails market making

With the Single Market, the European integration model changed from trade-driven to regulation-driven. Yet, liberalization does not go necessarily hand-in-hand with EU-level (re-)regulation or a modernization of institutions such as labour markets or the welfare system.

When the EU moved its economic integration objective up another level at Maastricht, from a common market to an economic and monetary union, this implied the need for more coordination and sovereignty-sharing among Member States. In the European reality of mixed economies, it also meant that some features of the European varieties of capitalism became incompatible with EMU constraints, thus requiring reform. Areas like labour markets and social security are cases in point. Yet, in the EU liberalization (market making) has often proved easier than (re-)regulation with common market rules (market correction).[21] Market correction, however, is more in line with the reality of the European mixed economies and the European model.

The reform challenge was aggravated by the fact that public opinion had turned against the Union in the crisis, manifesting resentment with regard to reforms that were arguably fomented by a perceived priority of economics over wider societal (social and environmental) concerns (and distributional consequences). No consensus existed among EU Member States to actively further the European model.[22] Rather unsurprisingly, European integration became contested on the grounds of deregulation and a perceived neglect of European societal values.[23]

The negative integration bias is rooted in differences in governance. The relative ease of single market liberalization through the Community method contrasts with societal concerns advanced through loose coordination with open outcomes. The latter extend to the establishment of conducive market rules and the creation of a favourable business environment, notably for high growth areas like the digital single market but also inclusive and green growth. Fleshing out the European model and implementing concrete actions depends on commitments at the Member State level, where competences for relevant policies and instruments have remained, with no sanctions in the case of non-compliance.[24] The different coordination modes resulted in a wide-ranging liberalization (market making) that was not necessarily accompanied by establishing common rules of the game (market correction), as the convergence of preferences or institutions tends to be a slow-moving process. It follows that the different elements of a European model are not bound to evolve at the same speed. It is hence unsurprising that, in the process, the European socio-economic model should have become more identified with liberalization (neo-liberal policies). Market and peer pressure on Eurozone laggard countries in the sovereign debt crisis (and measures that would restore competitiveness in the short run, above all, wages) aggravated this notion. The idea gained traction that in the EU economics trumps social concerns.

However, whether European regulation is feasible at all depends on sufficient preference convergence. There is either mutual recognition of national rules (negative integration), which implies competition between regulatory systems in the single market, or European regulation (positive integration), with (partial or harmonized) common rules.[25] In the EU, examples of all cases exist. If Member State preferences are diverse, they can be accommodated through the principle of mutual recognition of national standards (the default option),[26] whereas preference convergence is a prerequisite for European regulation. If it is only partial, it covers the establishment of some common rules, leaving areas where there is a lack of consensus to mutual recognition.

Mutual recognition is a fundamental principle of internal market functioning. In practice, it implies competition between (national) regulatory systems. National (home country) regulation is accepted as equivalent in the EU space, provided it is not a barrier to intra-EU trade.[27] Trust is fundamental for facilitating mutual recognition and to counter fears of a race to the bottom of standards. A notion of similarity between countries fosters trust and thereby sustains mutual recognition of national market rules.[28] Political economy problems have arisen when regulatory competition (negative integration) met significant Member State heterogeneity.

With market integration based on the principle of mutual recognition and common rules dependent on trust and shared values, too much heterogeneity in terms of preferences with regard to the model of society can undermine trust among Member States. On the other hand, the participation in common institutions and sovereignty sharing tends to create and strengthen a European identity beyond the various national identities, overcoming the problem of heterogeneous preferences and cultural diversity between Member States.[29] Openness to institutional integration is key to allow for endogenous preference convergence. Time will tell whether this will be the case of the European Social Pillar.

In the EU, the mutual recognition-trust logic is being tested in particular in services, which still lag behind goods markets' integration until today. The European model and the issue of perceived social fairness are the elephant in the room.

The case of services liberalization in the EU illustrates that liberalization cannot be seen out of a societal context, without taking (re-)regulation and impacts on other markets and areas, most notably the labour market or social protection, into account.[30] Services liberalization was resisted due to an anticipated downward impact on labour markets and social standards. The original version of the services directive (the Bolkestein Directive) set out to liberalize in a negative market integration logic, with business services subject to regulation in their home country. Services providers in the EU were thus to be regulated on the basis of mutual recognition, which meant competition between national regulatory systems. The European Commission had had no choice but to base liberalization of the sector on the home country principle, as Member State preferences had not yet sufficiently converged to allow embarking on common or partial European market rules.

With divergent preferences in an ever more heterogeneous EU, regulation and the associated model of society proved not a merely technical issue but a highly contentious and political matter, posing even a threat for the Union. Market rules are not apolitical; they are intertwined with societal values. In an EU that had become much more heterogeneous after the Eastern and Southern enlargement in 2004, they became highly contested. The European model became questioned in light of a feared race to the bottom of standards and contestation reached the EU's political integration project, being widely seen to have contributed to the negative referendum results in France and the Netherlands that buried the European Constitutional Treaty in 2005. The services directive that was subsequently approved in 2006 was a modified version, much watered down in scope and based on some partially shared rules.

The case of the posting of workers directive holds a similar lesson. Its initial 1996 version had also been based on the home country principle, allowing for time-unlimited posting to another EU Member State of employees, who would continue to pay benefits and taxes in their home country. The fact that a posted worker remains affiliated to the social security system of the sending country contributes to a certain remuneration differential with local employees, while the applicable wage can also vary (Fondation Robert Schuman 2016). It gives rise to systems competition perceived as unfair in the face of the large heterogeneity of Member State regulation, putting downward pressure on labour standards. A revised version, agreed in March 2018 by the European Parliament and the Council, aims at fairer pay and improved workers' conditions, correcting the calculation of remunerations (minimum wage, work-related entitlements) and limiting posting duration to 12 (extendable by six) months, after which local (host country) conditions apply.

Soft coordination of labour markets and social protection

It was easy to predict that the single European market and the freedom of movement of people, aggravated by increased labour mobility linked to the EU enlargement and globalization, would put a strain on national labour markets and social systems and would thus put pressure on them to converge (Bertola 2006, 2015).[31] The reason is that the failure to assure common principles resulted in jurisdictional competition between national regulatory systems. Conversely, harmonized policies would better exploit production and employment opportunities offered by market integration. It was hence thought that Member States would embark on some degree of harmonization to avoid a race to the bottom of standards and would try to learn from each other's good practices. In the event, however, the loose approach to economic coordination – with EU-wide performance targets but implementation at the Member State level – encountered difficulties in the EU, not only with regard to market structural but also to welfare state reform.

National social security systems (contribution- or tax-based), built in a different environment and on the presumption of stable populations, need to come to grips at the same time with changed competitiveness factors and the challenge of freedom of movement and often increased labour mobility in the single market. Sustainability constraints of the European social model, or rather its European varieties, need to be taken into account. According to Bentolila and Dolado (2017), the challenge facing social systems is even greater today than two decades ago: heightened globalization and technological progress imply that there is increased demand for social protection but reduced scope for supplying it.[32] The pressure on social systems rendered a possible abuse in the internal market politically sensitive. 'Benefit shopping' made it into (and started to poison) the public debate with regard to reforms of social systems and of European integration. Yet, Member States are able to protect themselves against abuse if they so choose. European Court of Justice case law has come to clarify that, and under which circumstances, Member States are entitled to exclude nationals from another Member State from certain social security benefits.[33]

It is important to note that, despite frequent references to the European (often contrasted with the US) social model, there is no European social model. At the beginning of the Lisbon Strategy there were variations of it (Hemerijk 2002). Sapir (2006) classified them into four varieties of European social models, according to two criteria, efficiency and cohesion.[34] Efficiency is related to the financial sustainability of a social model – and to that extent represents a constraint rather than a choice for society – while cohesion refers to the degree of inequality that a society is willing to accept, and thus subject to a country's preferences on the matter.

However, the Lisbon and Europe 2020 Strategies enshrined targets that set out to make improvement on the two dimensions compatible with each other and growth-enhancing, by bringing people into the workforce (enhancing financial sustainability) and reducing social exclusion (improving equality). The key idea was to create the right incentives to integrate people into the labour market while offering adequate social protection (Bertola 2015). The EU's role in creating a modernized European model is, however, hamstrung, since both the labour markets and the social systems have remained Member State competences. With regard to labour market coordination, the Lisbon Treaty granted the EU a complementary, facilitating role. Its success is especially important in the Eurozone with regard to wage next to price flexibility, as to counter asymmetric shocks in an OCA context.[35]

There was some progress, even if limited. On the one hand, the fact that labour market protection and social protection are substitutes made it possible to achieve a consensus on common principles to guide the modernization and reform of national labour markets and welfare systems in the EU, commonly referred as flexicurity (Council of the EU 2007; EC 2007).[36] Its implementation has, however, been challenging, since it not only requires a solid consensus on the principles but also ambitious structural reforms, above all at the Member State level. Its limited success so far testifies to the difficulty in reforming national (social) models according to common agreed principles across European varieties of capitalism. Schraad-Tischler *et al.* (2017) show that EU Member States' performance on social justice is (still) rather unequal, in the EU as a whole and also in the Eurozone, although it is generally improving in line with post-crisis labour market recovery.[37] If disconnected from social protection, labour market liberalization would be predictably particularly resented. This is the challenge faced by reforms that eye decentralized wage bargaining and the improvement of highly dual labour market protection (Bentolila and Dolado 2017). The 'support' that the EU/Eurozone has been giving came mostly through external pressure or conditionality in the case of adjustment countries.

On the other hand, an EU-wide employment scheme has long since been advocated in the Eurozone crisis as a mechanism to deal with asymmetric shocks; however, unemployment schemes have thus far remained national. Political economy reasons, notably the large differences in unemployment rates in the Eurozone and the EU, have so far stood in the way of such an endeavour.

The crisis effects did lead to a growing awareness and resolve at the EU level of the need to make EMU deliver not only economic but also wider results to citizens, notably by incorporating social concerns. The recent attempts to promote social policy coordination at the Eurozone level are a case in point, whereby a European Social Pillar has been promoted to ensure the sustainability of EMU and with it the political European integration project. One should note that there is also a window of opportunity, as the scheduled British exit from the European Union (Brexit) has made possible advances at the EU level, given the country's long-standing record of opposition to this policy field.[38]

The proposal of a European Pillar of Social Rights, legally a non-binding declaration, illustrates the quest for institutional modernization and further harmonization of basic standards. Launched by Commission President Juncker in his State of Union address 2015, in the context of the discussion on the future of Europe and consubstantiated by the European Commission (EC 2017b), it, in fact, complements GEMU on the competitiveness front. The social pillar narrative goes beyond the wage-price flexibility discourse, concerned with the adjustment capacity to weather (asymmetric) shocks.[39] The aim is to get a wide consensus on a European Pillar of Social rights in the Euro area and labour reforms context.

The pillar is about establishing a number of key principles and rights to support fair and well-functioning labour market and welfare systems, which are to guide participating Member States towards a convergence process towards better working and living conditions.[40] It features three chief categories, namely, equal opportunities and access to the labour market; fair working conditions; and social protection and inclusion. Although primarily intended for Eurozone members, the European Social Pillar was open from the outset to all EU Member States that wanted to take part.

At the Gothenburg social summit of November 2017, EU Member States agreed 20 common principles of a European social pillar for reform to achieve fair and well-functioning labour markets and social systems. Delivery will hinge on the EU institutions, Member States, social partners and other stakeholders. The weak implementation method was maintained.[41] Public and peer pressure is to be strengthened by an online social scoreboard to track performance across EU states.

The European Social Pillar offers the best opportunity yet to foster a consensus around a shared future-oriented European model and create a conducive narrative of reform.

Conclusion

EMU has triggered a qualitative change in European integration, since its constraints need to be internalized across Member States' varieties of capitalism and policy areas. However, reforms in areas such as labour markets and welfare systems hinge on loose coordination. National ownership building therefore remains critical for the support of necessary reforms and for adjustment capacity to shocks.

Attempts to make constrained decentralization more effective have come to broaden the underlying notion of competitiveness. This chapter argues that GEMU needs to be framed in the context of a broad, future-oriented European socio-economic model, as reforms envisaging economic and institutional modernization and the sustainability of both the Eurozone and the European integration project need to be backed by European citizens' societal preferences, in order to be successful. The chapter concludes that the European model is as yet incomplete, most notably in its social dimension, but that there have been significant developments towards a more competitive but also fairer model (most notably the EMU-driven Pillar of Social Rights).

On a last note, this chapter has focused on the economic and social dimension of the European model leaving in the background the environmental dimension, which is as yet less well integrated than the social pillar. Yet, without internalizing environmental effects, economic growth cannot be sustained over time. Only growth that is sustainable provides a credible crisis exit strategy and offers a solution to the problem of legacy costs. Eurobarometer data have consistently shown the importance that EU citizens contribute to a European model providing high environmental protection. What is more, as we discuss elsewhere (Begg *et al.* 2015; Bongardt and Torres 2013b), environmental reforms are a missing link with regard to the sustainability of GEMU and of the EU project, although, if well implemented, they could further both, in line with the European model.

Notes

1 Article 3(3) of the TEU establishes that

> The Union shall establish an internal market. It shall work for the sustainable development of Europe based on balanced economic growth and price stability, a highly competitive social economy, aiming at full employment and social progress, and a high level of protection and improvement of the quality of the environment. It shall promote scientific and technical progress.

2 This chapter does not discuss economic coordination developments related to the Stability and Growth Pact (SGP).

3 As noted by Dustmann *et al.* (2017), economics matters for European citizens' trust in European institutions and for political support for the EU, but it is not the only or even main factor. Europeans want a Union that delivers both on a strong economy and on global public goods. The EU's focus on economic variables will then not automatically restore support for the European project.

4 Given the complexity of the undertaking, a complete design would also have been difficult, if not impossible, to achieve.

5 For a discussion of the prerequisites of transforming EMU – if not into an optimum – into a sustainable currency area, see Bongardt and Torres (2017b).

6 Rather than the other way round, from the monetary into the economic sphere, which was the situation the literature had been cautioning against.

7 However, as Gros (2015) points out, comparing the case of Puerto Rico with Greece, even a GEMU like the US does not protect from regional failures. What differed was adjustment. Unlike the Eurozone, the US left Puerto Rico to the mercy of the markets, albeit without thereby calling into question the survival of the US dollar.

8 It fell short of Sapir and Wolff's (2015) proposal that had advocated more centralization through the establishment of a European Competitiveness Council composed of national competitiveness councils.

9 See, for instance, Draghi (2015).

10 On the need for structural reforms to raise productivity and the benefits thereof for the euro area and other EU policies, see Draghi (2016).

11 See Bongardt and Torres (2016a, 2016b, 2017b) for a more detailed discussion.

12 The European model also enshrines delivering on high environmental standards and quality. For a discussion of environmental sustainability and EU economic governance, which is beyond the scope of this chapter, see Bongardt and Torres (2013a). Economic and environmental concerns are complementary, since economic efficiency reasoning requires that environmental costs are internalized. Nor can economic growth be sustainable if environmental constraints are disregarded.

13 See also https://ec.europa.eu/commission/sites/beta-political/files/factsheet-ncbs_en.pdf, accessed 2 August 2017.

14 The same holds true for promoting sustainable growth and hence for a credible crisis exit strategy. For a more detailed discussion, see Bongardt and Torres (2016a).

15 For Soskice and Hope (2016) the fact that in the Eurozone crisis austerity proved often easier to implement than structural reforms is rooted in different models of development among EU Member States. Note that the comparative political economy literature goes beyond OCA theory, which suggests in which areas reforms should take place to make a currency union like the Eurozone function well. The contribution of the comparative political economy literature on the Eurozone is that it adds insights as to why reforms (especially in the labour market, but not only) might have been stalling despite external pressure.

16 For discussion, see, for instance, Caldera *et al.* (2016). A strong case can be made for the environmental dimension in terms of a crisis exit strategy (Begg *et al.* 2015; Bongardt and Torres 2016a; Pisani-Ferry 2014).

17 Schmieding (2017) argues that Europe is set on growth without significant inflation bottlenecks partly as a result of having progressed significantly due to the structural reforms and other adjustment efforts that were undertaken in major parts of the region. The author concludes that those have helped to make many economies somewhat more flexible, or are promising to do so in the near future.

18 See Papaconstantinou (2016) on the case of Greece. As pointed out by a member of the European Commission at a 2017 conference in Bruges, the Commission regards the authorities' commitment and ownership as the most important ingredient for a programme to work, apart from sufficient administrative capacity. From an economic point of view, it holds that front-loading of adjustment, an ambitious but achievable programme target, and the prompt and forceful strengthening and cleaning of the banking sector are important design features. Other lessons for successful conditionality consider that equity and social considerations should be better and more explicitly taken into account, the usefulness of specific instruments besides fully-fledged macroeconomic adjustment programme, a clear communication strategy, and the possible need for technical assistance at an early stage.

19 One may want to note that the new generation of EU international trade agreements like the Comprehensive Economic and Trade Agreement with Canada (CETA), which are about abolishing non-tariff barriers to trade (given that tariff barriers are already low), magnify the above problems with regulatory competition (a fact which the EU has barely registered). Canada is a G7 member and possibly one of the most similar countries to the EU. Even so, there were protests against CETA by civil society and opposition by the region of Wallonia. Of course, the EU itself is not homogeneous in terms of preferences. Arguably, Canada (or Australia or New Zealand) would be most similar to the UK in terms of regulatory preferences and practices. In the internal market, liberalization is relatively easy whereas re-regulation is more complicated, as it requires sufficient consensus among Member States. It is, therefore, easy for protesters to accuse the EU of prioritizing economics (without regard for distributional consequences and other societal concerns).

20 The European Commission recognizes that EMU's successful completion needs shared objectives and guiding principles. In the words of the European Commission (EC 2017a: 29), 'The euro needs to strengthen its role as a source of shared prosperity, economic and social welfare, based on inclusive and balanced growth and price stability.'

21 The terminology of positive versus negative integration goes back to Tinbergen (1954).

22 Not least because of opposition from the UK, which may possibly, however, leave the EU in 2019.

23 The success of anti-EU populist parties in continental Europe, especially in France, was fomented by opposition to an Anglo-Saxon-type deregulated economic model and a neglect of the European model. It brought home the message of the importance of fairness for the success of the European economy and of the European project.

24 The Single Market and the economic reform strategies also overlap with regard to creating market rules conducive to higher and quality growth areas (as witnessed by the Single Market Act I and II at the beginning of this decade). Yet, there is no functioning transmission mechanism from single market liberalization to market rules (Schäffer and Baumann 2011): a fact that is detrimental to the development of the Single Market in future high growth areas, to the extent that the liberalization of sectors requires conducive market rules (e.g. the digital single market) but also to inclusive growth (emphasizing employment and qualifications and combatting poverty), which aims at transforming the social dimension into a growth-enhancing factor.

25 EU regulation is, above all, risk regulation (Pelkmans 2013). For a discussion of the international dimension and of how trade agreements feed back into European regulation, see Bongardt and Torres (2017a).

26 It is, of course, challenging to distinguish truly heterogeneous preferences from technical or administrative differences, which create frictional barriers to trade that cannot be justified by diverse preferences. The issue of regulation for single market integrity is further discussed in Bongardt (2016). The European Commission has adopted a new approach – market monitoring – to gain in-depth insights into market functioning to help sort out to what extent desirable pro-competitive reforms are held back by Member States in the name of heterogeneity (of technical or administrative differences), which cannot be justified by diverse preferences. With respect to European standards and international trade, see Pelkmans (2013); on the principles of services regulation, see Messerlin (2005).

27 The Commission holds that while 'The current system is mainly focused on products … there is significant potential for further integration both in products and in service markets through the use of standards (for instance, in the digital single market)' (EC 2015: 55).

28 The need for societal acceptability of systems competition was well illustrated by the rejection of the original Bolkestein services directive, based on the home country principle. The issue of regulation for single market integrity is further discussed in Bongardt (2016). In line with the theory of fiscal federalism, only the diversity of preferences is underlying the subsidiarity principle while heterogeneity based on technical or administrative differences is not.

29 It happens that this difference is not greater within than between European Member States (Alesina *et al.* 2017).

30 There are many reasons for this. For example, services include activities that were formerly nationalized and/or national monopolies in some Member States. Services also often need to be regulated in the face of possible market failure (e.g. financial services, network industries, certain professions).

31 The impact was, of course, deferred, as Member States made use of time-limited derogations for labour movement from the new Member States. The UK was an exception, opting to open its labour market immediately in 2004. Ironically, the British choice not to protect its labour market from low-wage competition was to provide a chief argument for the UK's possible exit from the EU.

32 However, Rodrik (2017) holds that in the EU the welfare state was able, regardless of shortcomings, to compensate losers from globalization to a certain extent (through active labour market policies and other), in contrast to what happened in the US.

33 According to the CJEU (2016), a Member State can exclude nationals from other Member States from certain social benefits during the first three months of their residence (judgment in Case C-299/14). A Member State may exclude Union citizens who

go to that State to find work from certain non-contributory social security benefits (Case: C-67/14 Alimanovic, see also Press Release No. 101/15) and that economically inactive EU citizens who go to another Member State solely in order to obtain social assistance may be excluded from certain social benefits (Case: C-333/13 Dano, see also Press Release No. 146/14).

34 The paper shows individual countries' positions at the beginning of the decade of 2000 (that is, the status quo at the beginning of the Lisbon Strategy), with a Mediterranean segment (large inequality, low sustainability), a continental segment (low inequality, low sustainability), an Anglo-Saxon segment (high inequality, high sustainability) and a Nordic segment (low inequality, high sustainability). Bentolila and Dolado (2017) add a fifth segment, Central-Eastern Europe, after the 2004 EU enlargements.

35 For a discussion of the issue of wage flexibility with regard to wage growth, see Buti and Turrini (2017).

36 Integrated flexicurity policies play a key role in modernizing labour markets and contributing to the achievement of the Europe 2020 Strategy's employment rate target of 75 per cent. (http://ec.europa.eu/social/main.jsp?catId=102). The EU regards the principle of flexicurity as a crucial element of the Employment Guidelines and the European Employment Strategy. In conjunction with national governments, social partners and academics, the EU had identified common principles of flexicurity, which are to be implemented through four components: flexible and reliable contractual arrangements; comprehensive life-long learning strategies; effective active labour market policies; and modern social security systems. Flexicurity was inspired by the Danish model; it became consensual with regard to the modernization of social systems (but lost some of its shine when the Danish economy encountered difficulties).

37 For a graphical illustration, of social inclusion, see www.bertelsmann-stiftung.de/de/themen/aktuelle-meldungen/2017/november/eu-arbeitet-sich-aus-der-krise/

38 See, for instance, Chang (2017). It is illustrative that the Commission has resumed work on items like workers' rights and maternity leave, that is, on proposals that had previously been shelved because they would not pass with the UK inside the EU.

39 Product market liberalization is important for price flexibility and the real wage, and hence for the felt impact on living standards.

40 European Commission website, European Pillar of Social Rights, available at: http://ec.europa.eu/social/main.jsp?catId=1226&langId=en. The Commission proposed a wide, inter-institutional (European Parliament, Council and Commission) endorsement. The European Pillar of Social Rights was advanced at the Social Summit for Fair Jobs and Growth in Gothenburg, Sweden, 17 November 2017 (https://ec.europa.eu/commission/priorities/deeper-and-fairer-economic-and-monetary-union/european-pillar-social-rights_en).

41 The UK, which is scheduled to exit the EU in March 2019, did not oppose them.

References

Alesina, Alberto, Guido Tabellini, and Francesco Trebbi (2017). 'Is Europe an optimal political area?', Brookings Papers on Economic Activity. Washington, DC: Brookings Institute.

Begg, Iain, Annette Bongardt, Kalypso Nicolaidis, and Francisco Torres (2015). 'EMU and sustainable integration', *Journal of European Integration* 37(7): 803–16.

Bentolila, Samuel and Juan Dolado (2017). 'Social Europe revisited', *VoxEU*.org, 23 May. Available at: https://voxeu.org/article/social-europe-revisited

Bertola, Giuseppe (2006). 'Social and labour market policies in a growing EU', *Swedish Economic Policy Review* 13: 189–231.

Bertola, Giuseppe (2015). 'Labour and social policy', in Harald Badinger and Volker Nitsch (eds). *Routledge handbook of the economics of European integration*. London: Routledge.

Bongardt, Annette (2015). 'The transformation of the Single European Market: from the Lisbon strategy to Europe 2020', in José M. Magone (ed.). *Routledge handbook of European politics*. London: Routledge, 746–62.

Bongardt, Annette (2016). 'Growth: the possibility of a truly single market', in *EU Essays*. London: IPPR, 68–90.

Bongardt, Annette and Francisco Torres (2012). 'Lisbon Strategy', in Erik Jones, Anand Menon and Stephen Wetherill (eds). *The handbook on the European Union*. Oxford: Oxford University Press, 468–83.

Bongardt, Annette and Francisco Torres (2013a). 'Forging sustainable growth: the issue of convergence of preferences and institutions in EMU', *Intereconomics* 48(2): 72–7.

Bongardt, Annette and Francisco Torres (2013b). 'Economic governance and sustainability', in Amy Verdun and Alfred Tovias (eds). *Mapping European economic integration*. Basingstoke: Palgrave Macmillan, 146–67.

Bongardt, Annette and Francisco Torres (2015). 'EMU and structural reform', in Leila Simona Talani (ed.). *Europe in crisis: a structural analysis*. Basingstoke: Palgrave Macmillan, 37–64.

Bongardt, Annette and Francisco Torres (2016a), 'Economic reform under Europe 2020', *Public Policy Portuguese Journal* 1(1): 57–67.

Bongardt, Annette and Francisco Torres (2016b), 'EMU reform and resilience in a re-dimensioned EU', *Politica Economica* 32(3): 575–96.

Bongardt, Annette and Francisco Torres (2017a). 'Comprehensive Trade Agreements: conditioning globalisation or eroding the European Model?', *Intereconomics* 52(3): 165–70.

Bongardt, Annette and Francisco Torres (2017b). 'EMU as a sustainable currency area', in N. da Costa Cabral *et al.* (eds). *The Euro and the crisis: perspectives for the Eurozone as a monetary and budgetary union*. Cham: Springer, 17–32

Buti, Marco and Muriel Lacoue-Labarthe (2016). 'Europe's incompatible political trinities', *VoxEU.org*, 7 September. Available at: https://voxeu.org/article/europes-incompatible-political-trinities

Buti, Marco and Alessandro Turrini (2017). 'Overcoming Eurozone wage inertia', *VoxEU.org*, 5 October. Available at: https://voxeu.org/article/overcoming-eurozone-wage-inertia

Caldera, Aida, Alain de Serres, and Yashiro Naomitsu (2016). 'Structural reforms in difficult time: the priorities', *VoxEU.Org*, 4 September. Available at: https://voxeu.org/article/structural-reforms-difficult-times

Chang, Michele (2017). 'Can Brexit lead to further integration? The case of economic and monetary union', College of Europe Policy Brief No. 6.17. Bruges: College of Europe.

CJEU (Court of Justice of the European Union) (2016), 'The Court of Justice confirms that nationals of other Member States may be refused certain social benefits in their first three months of residence. Such a refusal does not presuppose an individual assessment'. Press release no. 18/16, Luxembourg, 25 February. Available at: https://curia.europa.eu/jcms/upload/docs/application/pdf/2016-02/cp160018en.pdf

Council of the EU (2007). 'Towards common principles of flexicurity'. Draft Council Conclusions. 15431/07 SOC 476 ECOFIN 483, 23 November.

Draghi, Mario (2015). 'Structural reforms, inflation and monetary policy', speech at the ECB Forum on Central Banking, Sintra, Portugal, 22 May.

Draghi, Mario (2016). 'The productivity challenge for Europe (*Lectio magistralis*)'. Deusto Business School, Madrid, 30 November. Available at: www.ecb.europa.eu/press/key/date/2016/html/sp161130_1.en.html

Dustmann, Christian, Barry Eichengreen, Sebatian Otten, André Sapir, Guido Tabellini, and Gylfi Zoega (2017). *Europe's trust deficit: causes and remedies. monitoring international integration 1*. London: CEPR Press.

EC (European Commission) (2007). 'Towards common principles of flexicurity: more and better jobs through flexibility and security'. COM/2007/0359 final.

EC (European Commission) (2015). 'Proposal for a regulation of the European Parliament and the Council on the establishment of the Structural Reform Support Programme for the period 2017 to 2020 and amending Regulations (EU) No 1305/2013'. COM (2015) 701 final, 2015/0263 (COD).

EC (European Commission) (2017a). 'Reflection paper on the deepening of the Economic and Monetary Union'. COM (2017) 391.

EC (European Commission) (2017b). 'Reflection paper on the social dimension of Europe'. COM (2017) 206.

EC (European Commission) (2017c). *Standard Eurobarometer 87*. Brussels: European Commission.

EC (European Commission) (2018). '2018 European Semester: assessment of progress on structural reforms, prevention and correction of macroeconomic imbalances, and results of in-depth reviews under Regulation (EU) No 1176/2011'. COM (2018) 120 final.

EP (European Parliament) (2016). 'At a glance: the National Productivity Boards'. Directorate-General for Internal Policies and Economic Governance Support Unit, 20 September.

Fondation Robert Schuman (2016). 'The reform of the posted workers directive (European Issue No. 406)'. Available at: www.robert-schuman.eu/en/european-issues/0406-the-reform-of-the-posted-workers-directive

Gros, Daniel (2015). ''Puerto Rico and Greece: a tale of two defaults in a Monetary Union, CEPS High-Level Brief. Brussels: CEPS (updated 30 June 2015).

Gros, Daniel and Felix Roth (2012). *The Europe 2020 Strategy. Can it maintain the EU's competitiveness in the world?* Brussels: Centre for European Policy Studies.

Hemerijk, Anton (2002). 'The self-transformation of the European Social Model(s)', in Gøsta Esping-Anderson (ed.). *Why we need a new welfare state*. Oxford: Oxford University Press, 173–214.

Jones, Erik and Francisco Torres (2015), 'Using interdisciplinary analysis to shape a policy agenda', *Journal of European Integration* 37(7): 875–80.

Juncker, Jean-Claude, with Donald Tusk, Jeroen Dijsselbloem, and Mario Draghi (2015a). 'Preparing for next steps on better economic governance in the Euro area. Analytical Note prepared for the Informal European Council', Brussels, 12 February.

Juncker, Jean-Claude, with Donald Tusk, Jeroen Dijsselbloem, Mario Draghi, and Martin Schulz (2015b). 'Completing Europe's Economic and Monetary Union', Brussels: European Commission, 22 June.

Messerlin, Patrick (2005). 'Liberalising services trade in the EU', *Intereconomics* 40(3): 120–4.

Mongelli, Francesco, Ettore Dorruccci, Demosthenes Ioannou, and Alessio Terzi (2016). 'Responses to the euro area crisis: measuring the path of European institutional integration', in Erik Jones and Francisco Torres (eds). *Governance of the European Monetary Union*. London: Routledge.

Nicolaidis, Kalypso and Max Watson (2016). 'Sharing the Eurocrats' dream: a demoicratic approach to EMU governance', in D.M.J. Chalmers and Christian Joerges (eds). *The end of the Eurocrats' dream: adjusting to European diversity*. Cambridge: Cambridge University Press, 50–77.

OECD (2015). *Economic policy reforms 2015: going for growth*. Paris: OECD.

Papaconstantinou, George (2016). *Game over: the inside story of the Greek crisis*. Athens: Papadopoulos Publishing.

Pasimeni, Paolo (2013). 'The Europe 2020 Index', *Social Indicators Research* 110: 613–35.

Pelkmans, Jacques (2013). 'The economics of single market regulation', in Amy Verdun and Alfred Tovias (eds). *Mapping European economic integration*. Basingstoke: Palgrave Macmillan, 79–104.

Pisani-Ferry, Jean (2014). 'How to climb a mountain with both hands tied', *VoxEU.org*, 7 November. Available at: https://voxeu.org/article/green-policies-promote-eurozone-growth

Rodrik, Dani (2017). 'Too late to compensate free trade's losers'. *Project Syndicate*, 11 April. Available at: www.project-syndicate.org/commentary/free-trade-losers-compensation-too-late-by-dani-rodrik-2017-04?barrier=accessreg

Roland, Gérard (2004). 'Understanding institutional change: fast-moving and slow-moving institutions', *Studies in Comparative International Development* 38(4): 109–31.

Sapir, André (2006). 'Globalisation and the reform of European social models', *Journal of Common Market Studies* 44(2): 369–90.

Sapir, André and Guntram Wolff (2015). 'Euro-area governance: what to reform and how to do it', Bruegel Policy Brief No. 2015/01. Brussels: Bruegel.

Schäffer, Sebastian and Florian Baumann (2011). *Single Market Act – single act for the internal market or revitalisation for the whole project*? Munich: Center for Applied Policy Research.

Schmieding, Holger (2016). *The 2016 Euro Plus Monitor*. London/Brussels: Berenberg and the Lisbon Council.

Schmieding, Holger (2017). *The 2017 Euro Plus Monitor: into a higher gear*. London/ Brussels, Berenberg and Lisbon Council.

Schmieding, Holger and Christian Schulz (2014). *Euro Pact Plus Monitor 2014: leaders and laggards*. Brussels: The Lisbon Council.

Schraad-Tischer, Daniel, Christof Schiller, Sacha Matthias Heller, and Nina Siemer (2017). *Soziale Gerechtigkeit in der EU – Index Report 2017, Social Inclusion Monitor Europe*. Bielefeld: Bertelsmann Stiftung.

Soskice, David and David Hope (2016). 'The Eurozone and political economic institutions', *Annual Review of Political Science* 19(1): 163–85.

Tilford, Simon and Philip Whyte (2010). *The Lisbon Scorecard X: the road to 2020*. London: Centre for European Reform.

Tinbergen, Jan (1954). *International economic integration*. Amsterdam: Elsevier.

Torres, Francisco (2015). 'Political Economic and Monetary Union: EU and domestic constraints', in José M. Magone (ed.). *Routledge handbook of European politics*. London: Routledge, 763–76.

Van Rompuy, Herman, with José Manuel Barroso, Jean-Claude Juncker, and Mario Draghi (2012). *Towards a Genuine Economic and Monetary Union ('Four Presidents' Report' – Report by the Presidents of the European Council, European Commission, Eurogroup and the ECB)*. Brussels, 5 December.

13 Striking a balance between competitiveness and social fairness

What can we expect from the European Pillar of Social Rights?

Susana Muñoz

> Throughout all of my political life I have fought for our unique European economic and social model. I am convinced that Europe will succeed only when its economy is both strong and fair.
>
> (Jean-Claude Juncker, EC 2015)

The interinstitutional proclamation of the European Pillar of Social Rights (EPSR) on 17 November 2017 (European Parliament *et al.* 2017) was a milestone in the process to develop a more social European Union.[1] The Pillar was intended to provide a tangible response to the huge challenges that the EU socio-economic model[2] has been facing since the onset of the multidimensional crisis that has reverberated across the world over the past decade. This crisis has revealed a deep need for the EU to foster economic growth and convergence and to strengthen the social dimension of European integration. In the political guidelines of July 2014, Jean-Claude Juncker pointed to the lack of social fairness in the measures taken to tackle the worst financial and economic crisis facing post-war Europe (Juncker 2014a).[3] Despite the recovery and the economic expansion in the EU, the unemployment rates are high and the number of people suffering from poverty, inequality, and social exclusion is striking. Furthermore, there are significant divergences in the economic and social performance within and across the EU Member States.[4] These wide-reaching social consequences are stunting productivity growth[5] and economic performance in the EU, affecting competitiveness and living standards.[6]

One lesson taught by the crisis has been the need for the EU to 'recreate a process of convergence' among Member States and within societies, 'with productivity, job creation and social fairness at its core' (Juncker 2015). The European Commission, driven by its President, has thus embarked on the development of a 'European pillar of social rights' (EPSR), as first announced in Juncker's State of the Union address in September 2015 (ibid.). The Commission engaged with a wide range of stakeholders in building the EPSR, which was presented on 26 April 2017 (EC 2017d).[7] Alongside the Pillar, the Commission adopted a number of accompanying legislative and non-legislative initiatives and also published its reflection paper on Europe's social dimension (EC 2017b) in line with the White Paper on the future of Europe (EC 2017c). In Bratislava, the leaders of the 27 EU Member States stressed that economic and social insecurity needs to be tackled as a matter of priority (European Council 2016). The Rome Declaration of 25 March 2017 emphasises the commitment to work towards a social Europe based on sustainable growth, which promotes economic and social progress, as well as cohesion and convergence, while upholding the integrity of the internal market (European Council 2017a). Social rights have therefore returned to centre stage as a key component of the fairer, more social Europe required by the future EU27.

The solemnly proclaimed EPSR raises high expectations and important questions related to its nature as a *pillar* endowed with a foundational basis,[8] its pan-*European* scope, its truly *social* dimension, its core of fundamental social *rights*, and its effective implementation. Our analysis aims to provide a critical assessment of the EPSR in the light of its potential contribution to foster social fairness and inclusive competitiveness in the EU. This chapter concludes with some reflections on the Pillar's challenges and opportunities.

Why a *pillar*? The legal and political nature of the EPSR

Background

The roots of the Pillar may be found in the context of the debate on the achievement of a genuine Economic and Monetary Union (EMU) in 2012. The Four Presidents' Report of December 2012 puts forward an 'integrated economic policy framework' to guide the policies of Member States towards strong and sustainable economic growth and employment. It states that 'in order to remain a highly attractive social market economy and to preserve the European social models, it is important for the Union to be globally competitive and to avoid excessive divergences in competitiveness among EMU members' (Van Rompuy *et al.* 2012: 13).

The political initiative of the Pillar began to take shape following the appointment of the new European Commission in 2014. In the political guidelines for the Commission, Jean-Claude Juncker proposed an agenda for a renewed EU focused on ten policy areas, the first being 'a new boost for jobs, growth and investment' and the fifth 'a deeper and fairer Economic and Monetary Union'. The reform of EMU would be pursued 'always with Europe's social dimension in mind' (Juncker 2014a). In his statement to the European Parliament ahead of the vote on the College, the President-elect of the Commission expressed his determination 'for Europe to have a social triple-A rating: that is just as important as an economic and financial triple-A rating' (Juncker 2014b).

One immediate measure proposed by the Five Presidents' Report of June 2015 is to move towards an 'Economic Union of convergence, growth and jobs' based on four 'pillars': (1) the creation of a euro area system of Competitiveness Authorities; (2) a strengthened implementation of the Macroeconomic Imbalance

Procedure; (3) a greater focus on employment and social performance; and (4) stronger coordination of economic policies within a revamped European Semester. The third pillar is based on the ambition to earn a 'social triple-A' and is also presented as an 'economic necessity' (Juncker *et al.* 2015). Without mentioning social rights, this pillar looks ahead to the EPSR.

The full name was first used by President Juncker in his 2015 State of the Union address in connection with 'a fair and truly pan-European labour market':

> I will want to develop a European pillar of social rights, which takes account of the changing realities of Europe's societies and the world of work. And which can serve as a compass for the renewed convergence within the euro area.
>
> (Juncker 2015)

On 6 October 2015, the College of Commissioners discussed, for the first time, the concept of the 'Pillar of Social Rights' during a debate on the economic and social dimension of the Single Market. The pillar would be 'a self-standing reference document, of a legal nature, setting out key principles and values shared at EU level' (EC 2015, 2016a).

A preliminary outline of the Pillar, followed by a broad open consultation, was published in the Commission Communication of 8 March 2016 (EC 2016c, 2016d).[9] Since then, the nature of the EPSR has given rise to intense debate.[10] The 2016 Communication was unclear on what exactly was meant by a 'pillar' in this context: it talked of 'a number of essential principles to support well-functioning and fair labour markets and welfare systems' intended to become 'a reference framework' (EC 2016c: 7). In January 2017, a high-level conference took place to conclude the consultation and define the future direction of the Pillar.[11] The Commission's final proposal of 26 April 2017 (EC 2017d, 2017e) takes into account the substantial response to the consultation[12] and specifies the legal nature of the Pillar. The 2017 Commission Communication reiterates that the Pillar establishes a 'framework for guiding future action' by the participating Member States (EC 2017a: 6). Finally, the EPSR signed and proclaimed by the European Parliament, the Council and the Commission on 17 November 2017 (European Parliament *et al.* 2017) maintains the Pillar's objective of serving as a 'guide' to efficient employment and social outcomes and the improved enactment and implementation of social rights.[13]

Legal form and political value

The Pillar was presented on 26 April 2017 in two legal forms with identical content: as a Commission recommendation and as a proposal for an interinstitutional proclamation (EC 2017d, 2017e). The recommendation was adopted on the basis of Article 292 TFEU and took effect on the date of publication. In making a proposal for a joint proclamation, the Commission followed the example of the EU Charter of Fundamental Rights, which was solemnly proclaimed on two occasions – on 7 December 2000 in Nice and on 12 December 2007 in Strasbourg – by the European Parliament, the Council and the Commission (European Parliament *et al.* 2000, 2007).[14] The form and wording of the proclamation have thus been interpreted as a sign of constitutional purpose (Council of the EU 2017b: 3).

The European Parliament had supported the choice of an interinstitutional agreement on the adoption of the Pillar, while also calling for a social protocol to be introduced into the Treaties when they are revised (EP 2017: §31, §47). Although the proclamation is an atypical act of a political nature (Council of the EU 2017b: 6) and is not an interinstitutional agreement under Article 295 TFEU, most of the MEPs agreed with the Commission's social package presented in April 2017. Beyond some references to the Pillar as a 'vague concept' or a mere 'declaration of principles or good intentions', the EPSR has been recognised as the basis laying down the minimum standards for EU-wide social rights (EP 2017b). The Council also welcomed the proclamation as

> our chance to reconnect the EU with its citizens. Having all Member States standing together on a set of common social values offers a unique opportunity to show that we deliver on a fairer and more social Europe, as foreseen by the Treaty.
>
> (Council of the EU 2017c: 6)

Against this backdrop, criticism has been levelled against the absence of a legally binding document. Given the expectations raised by the use of the term 'rights', a mere repeat of soft coordination initiatives would create a backlash (Vandenbroucke 2017a: 14). Concern has been expressed about the fact that 'the Pillar remains fundamentally a framework of voluntary principles' (EAPN 2017: 5).

Neither the Commission recommendation nor the proclamation have binding force. As an interinstitutional proclamation, the Pillar does not resemble any other legal act provided for in the Treaties. Nevertheless, this was undoubtedly a more pragmatic and realistic option, given the difficulties of achieving an agreement on the enforceability of the principles and rights enshrined in the Pillar and the diversity of national views and social realities. The precedent of the EU Charter of Fundamental Rights is enlightening enough.[15] The adoption of any fundamental rights instrument aspires to some binding legal force. Nevertheless, the rationale of this Commission's initiative does not demonstrate a readiness for a new bill of rights. On the other hand, despite the lack of binding force, the Pillar has significant political value and may have a legal impact which should be reflected in the effective implementation of its content through various legislative and non-legislative mechanisms.[16]

A dynamic instrument

Another important aspect of the Pillar is that it was designed as a dynamic instrument that provides sufficient flexibility and room for manoeuvre for players at all levels to act according to their competences and to update their legislative instruments in the light of their own situation and socio-economic environment. The Commission has emphasised that the Pillar is part of a gradual, long-term process.[17] This evolving approach reflects the rationale of an instrument which is intended to take account of changing social realities (EC 2016c: 7). But at the same time this pragmatic process generates higher expectations concerning its effective implementation.

Indeed, the EPSR has been held up as a symbol of strong political commitment in this regard. This so-called 'catalogue of principles' has been referred to as both a 'programme of principles' and a 'programme of action' (Juncker 2017b). As its name suggests, the Pillar is intended to provide essential and reliable (social-based) support for the various policy areas it covers. A great deal of effort is required on the part of all stakeholders to make the Pillar enforceable. Questions then arise as to whether this 'guide' actually contributes to the effectiveness of social rights, rather than being a mere high-sounding proclamation.

The *European* scope of the EPSR

According to the 2016 Commission Communication, the Pillar will be developed within the euro area but other EU Member States will be able to join in if they wish to do so (EC 2016c: 7). This initial restricted scope was based on the specific needs and challenges facing the euro area. Nevertheless, social issues involve all EU Member States, and the potential negative effects of a multi-speed Union could aggravate socio-economic inequalities and increase social dumping (Caniard and Weber 2016: 16–17; Lörcher and Schömann 2016: 18).

The Pillar's scope is not primarily pan-European but *euro area-oriented*. This choice has been criticised because it emphasises the economic rather than the social objectives of the initiative. The European Parliament, therefore, notes that 'standards to be articulated by the Pillar should apply to all countries participating in the single market … and that legislation, governance mechanisms and financial instruments relevant for their achievement should apply to all EU Member States' (EP 2017a: §2). For the EESC, the Pillar 'must offer a positive project for all and should apply to all EU Member States, while acknowledging that the Eurozone may need particular instruments/mechanisms' (EESC 2017a: 3).

In its final proposal of 26 April 2017, the Commission adjusted its initial approach, instead emphasising the applicability of the Pillar to all EU Member States that wish to be part of it. The proclaimed Pillar is clearly 'addressed to all Member States', although it is 'notably conceived for the euro area', because a stronger focus on employment and social performance is particularly important to increase resilience and deepen EMU (European Parliament *et al.* 2017: recital 13).

The solemn proclamation of the Pillar does not contain any explicit reference to its addressees, such as that provided for in Article 51(1) of the EU Charter of Fundamental Rights. But it may be inferred from its preamble that the Pillar is intended for the EU and its Member States, which share the responsibility for delivering on the Pillar within their respective competences. The social partners at all levels have 'a crucial role to play' in this regard (European Parliament *et al.* 2017: recitals 17, 20).[18]

The principle of conferral, which sets the limits of Union competences, and the principles of subsidiarity and proportionality, which govern the use of these competences, are thus relevant for both the Pillar's scope and implementation.

When considering the wide range of areas covered by the Pillar, the EU has either legislative competences or coordinating competences in connection with economic, employment, social, and public health policies.[19] The proclamation of the Pillar does not establish new powers and tasks for the EU or modify the powers and tasks as conferred by the Treaties (recital 18), and neither does it alter the Member States' competences to implement the Pillar if they wish to join. The decision on this political commitment belongs to each Member State, regardless of whether or not it is member of the euro area. All EU Member States are also expected to act as members of the Council, and the Council may adopt measures specific to the euro area Member States in limited circumstances (in particular, Articles 136–8 TFEU).

The Pillar's content concerns both EU citizens and third country nationals with legal residence. The principles referring to workers are applicable to all those in employment, 'regardless of their employment status, modality and duration' (European Parliament *et al.* 2017: recital 15). The EESC is of the view that 'this initiative should include all citizens, covering all phases of the life-cycle. The Committee is concerned about the lack of reference to asylum seekers and migrants' (EESC 2017a: 6).

The purpose of the EPSR is not to harmonise policies related to the areas covered by the Pillar according to a 'one-size-fits-all' approach. The focus is on providing a reference framework for the EU Member States. In light of the existing economic and social divergences between them, the euro area appears to be a pragmatic starting point for its implementation, albeit an ambitious one. As a matter of principle, the application of the Pillar to all EU Member States should be encouraged.[20]

Is the Pillar truly *social*? The rationale and purpose of the EPSR

The EPSR initiative is designed to strengthen the foundations of EMU in line with the EU's social mission and objectives as laid down in Article 3 TEU, namely, to promote its values and the well-being of its peoples and to work for sustainable development based on balanced economic growth and price stability, a highly competitive social market economy aiming at full employment and social progress (European Parliament *et al.* 2017: recital 1).

The drafters of the Treaty of Lisbon were consistent with the 'affirmation of social objectives as equivalent, not subordinate, to economic objectives' as an integral part of the spirit in which the EU was conceived and of the direction in which it should develop (The European Convention 2003: 8). The central idea of the 'highly competitive social market economy' is the existence of a complementarity between market freedom and social fairness, generating high levels of competitiveness and living standards.[21] The social market economy provides a framework within which competitiveness contributes to social fairness and, at the same time, social fairness stimulates competitiveness. There is, therefore, a feedback process in which an appropriate balance needs to be ensured.[22]

In the past decade, the implementation of far-reaching measures to tackle the crisis gave rise to growing socio-economic imbalances in the EU, within and across Member States, that require a different structural socio-economic framework.

The Commission's action in building the Pillar is based on its conviction that 'economic development should result in greater social progress and cohesion', and that social policy should be considered a 'productive factor, which reduces inequality, maximises job creation and allows Europe's human capital to thrive' (EC 2016c: 2). As outlined in its 2016 Communication, the Pillar meets a twofold need: overcoming and looking beyond the crisis, and moving towards a deeper and fairer EMU (EC 2016c: 3). For the Commission, the principles included in the preliminary version of the Pillar addressed key concerns for a deeper and fairer EMU, such as 'the need to boost competitiveness, to increase participation in the labour market, develop adequate social protection floors, make full use of people's potential, ensure the sustainability of public finances and increase the adjustment capacity and resilience of economic structures' (EC 2016d: 2). Nevertheless, economic and social performances are presented as 'two sides of the same coin' (EC 2016c: 4). This begs the question of whether the Commission is seeking an appropriate balance between economic and social aspects in the process of building the EPSR.

The text of this Communication reveals tension between the economic and social aspects of the Pillar. Against this backdrop, criticism has been raised as to the Pillar's genuine role. Some authors have suggested that it is 'embedded in a deep economic rhetoric' in which economic growth is the main goal, while the social dimension of EMU is more technical than really founded on the values and principles of the Treaties. In their view, the Commission thus embarked on an 'unconvincing development of a "highly competitive social market economy"' (Lörcher and Schömann 2016: 18–20). The European Trade Union Confederation has emphasised that fundamental social rights must take precedence over economic freedoms and has recognised that the status quo was not acceptable (ETUC 2016: 3). On the other hand, European employers have stressed that solely focusing on 'social rights' is not the right approach because 'the social dimension of the EU is much broader than this'. For BusinessEurope, the focus must be on increasing the contribution of Social Europe to Europe's global competitiveness (Business Europe 2016). Other stakeholders have pointed out that only a 'balanced economic and social strategy' aimed at reducing inequality and sharing prosperity will make the Pillar successful (EAPN 2016: 3).

Building on the results of the public consultation, the Commission adapted the wording in its 2017 Communication and specified that the Pillar should be 'a compass for a renewed process of convergence towards better working and living conditions among participating Member States' (EC 2017a: 2). It confirmed that the EU's economic and social challenges are interlinked, while stressing the 'specific meaning' of these challenges for the completion of EMU (ibid.: 5). The EPSR thus emphasises that economic and social progress are intertwined, and the establishment of the Pillar 'should be part of wider efforts to build a more inclusive and sustainable growth model by improving Europe's competitiveness' (European Parliament *et al.* 2017: recital 11). The aim of the Pillar is 'to serve as a guide towards efficient employment and social outcomes when responding to current and future challenges which are directly aimed at fulfilling people's essential needs, and ensuring better enactment and implementation of social rights' (European Parliament *et al.* 2017: recital 12). This multifaceted purpose, while challenging, reflects a proclamation designed to address the needs and expectations expressed by the relevant stakeholders. In the specific process of deepening EMU driven by the Commission, the Pillar is seen as a tool and social fairness is enshrined as an overarching objective. EMU is presented as a means to an end: jobs, growth, social fairness, economic convergence, and financial stability (EC 2017f: 10, 18, 32, 2017g: 13).

Since the Social Summit in Gothenburg, the Heads of State or Government have highlighted the importance of the social dimension of the various EU policies in building the common future of the Union. Delivering on the EPSR as a shared political commitment and responsibility of the EU and its Member States and making swift progress on social questions at EU level are some of the core issues discussed at recent meetings of the European Council (European Council 2017b: 2, 2018: 2).

Economic and social aspects of European integration are interlinked and mutually enriching. The EPSR includes both dimensions without ranking them in any order of importance. While it is true that the origins of the Pillar can be linked to the priority of completing EMU, the emphasis placed on its social dimension and the recent developments in favour of a 'more social Europe' have confirmed the need to take a genuinely integrated approach and pursue economic and social integration at both EU and national levels as an 'interconnected endeavour' (Schiek 2017: 612–13).

A catalogue of 'social *rights*'? The nature of the Pillar's content and its potential contribution to a fairer and more socially balanced competitiveness

Principles, rights, standards

The EPSR

> expresses principles and rights essential for fair and well-functioning labour markets and welfare systems in twenty-first-century Europe. It reaffirms some of the rights already present in the Union *acquis*. It adds new

> principles which address the challenges arising from societal, technological, and economic developments. For them to be legally enforceable, the principles and rights first require dedicated measures or legislation to be adopted at the appropriate level.
>
> (European Parliament *et al.* 2017: recital 14)

The Pillar does not clarify the notion of 'social rights' in this context. It is important to note how the Pillar has changed since its 2016 preliminary version, which contained 'essential principles' selected both for their economic and social importance for the performance of participating Member States.[23] The wording of this version differed from the first Commission reference to 'a consolidated and clear set of social rights' based on various national, EU, and international legal instruments (EC 2015).

It may indeed be assumed that a pillar of 'social rights' requires a rights-based approach, which seemed to be lacking in the 2016 version (Lörcher and Schömann 2016: 31–2). Following the public consultation, the Commission placed more emphasis on the fact that the Pillar is about 'delivering new and more effective rights for citizens' (EC 2017a: 4). The final version adopted this rights-based approach where relevant,[24] and the wording was updated to express the rights more clearly,[25] in line with the title of the initiative. While this development is more consistent with the goal of establishing a pillar of social rights, it does raise the risk of confusion in the use of principles and rights that are not justiciable. Like the first outline, the EPSR does not contain a legally binding framework.

The EPSR enshrines 20 key principles and rights organised into three chapters: (1) equal opportunities and access to the labour market; (2) fair working conditions; and (3) social protection and inclusion.[26] Unlike the first outline, a preamble lays down the legal basis of the Pillar and refers to the provisions of the TEU, the TFEU, and the EU Charter of Fundamental Rights. Compared to the first outline, some of the 20 policy areas have been changed and restructured. The rights are said to reaffirm some of the rights already present in the EU *acquis*, whereas the principles are said to be new and tend to address the challenges arising from societal, technological, and economic developments. The distinction between them is not always clear and can lead to confusion,[27] inasmuch as each 'principle/right' is not identifiable as such and may contain various related rights.[28]

The Pillar renders more visible and more explicit a number of rights that already exist in the EU *acquis* – for instance, the right for women and men to receive equal pay for work of equal value (Principle 2b) or the right for workers or their representatives to be informed and consulted on matters relevant to them, in particular on the transfer, restructuring, and merger of undertakings and on collective redundancies (Principle 8b). In many cases, the Pillar goes beyond the existing *acquis*, e.g. by focusing the general right to education and training throughout life on quality and inclusiveness (Principle 1), by introducing procedural and substantive safeguards for workers in the event of dismissals

(Principle 7), or by providing rights related to work-life balance for all people in employment with caring responsibilities (Principle 9). At the same time, the Pillar complements the *acquis* with new principles, some of which include new rights within the EU. This is the case, e.g. for the right to fair wages that provide for a decent standard of living for all workers (Principle 6a), the right to adequate social protection for the self-employed, under comparable conditions to workers, regardless of the type and duration of their employment relationship (Principle 12), and the right to adequate minimum income benefits (Principle 14). On the other hand, some principles of the preliminary outline have been omitted, such as the principle that health care systems shall encourage the cost-effective provision of care, and the principle that all workers shall be ensured adequately paid sick leave during periods of illness. Finally, some important areas are missing in the final version, such as the rights of asylum seekers and migrants, a dedicated principle on youth, and a reference to the environment.

Overall, this content can be seen as 'quite modern and exciting' (Hendrickx 2018: 5). On the other hand, the Pillar's content received criticism for a lack of uniformity, disappointing substance, or lack of ambition,[29] and even overreach on the part of the EU. Questions may also be raised as to the implementation of some of the principles/rights, given that the EU – which may act only within the limits of the powers and tasks conferred by the Treaties – will not be able to deliver on principles and rights that the Member States are not in a position to put into practice. The effective enforcement of principles/rights is therefore a key issue (Caniard and Weber 2016: 19–25; Frazer and Marlier 2016: 29–33).

The Commission stresses that the Pillar builds on the strong body of law which exists at the EU and international level as well as on existing best practices across Europe. It refers to the values enshrined in the Rome Treaties and to the work of international organisations such as the United Nations, the ILO, and the Council of Europe. In particular, the Pillar draws on the 1961 European Social Charter, the 1996 Revised European Social Charter, the 1989 Community Charter of the Fundamental Social Rights of Workers, and the European Code of Social Security. The EU 'social *acquis*' developed over the last 30 years, the EU Charter of Fundamental Rights, new legislation, and the Court of Justice case law are also part of the Pillar's foundations. Finally, the UN Sustainable Development Goals for 2030 are mentioned (EC 2017a: 6).[30]

These explicit references to the legal foundations of the Pillar respond to the criticism levelled at its 'scant respect for international and European treaties' (Lörcher and Schömann 2016: 24)[31] and the absence of overall vision and overarching values and principles in the first outline (Frazer and Marlier 2016: 11). Despite the addition of these references, the connection between the Pillar and existing international, European, and national legal sources of fundamental social rights raises questions. In this respect, the Council of Europe and the ILO welcomed the EPSR initiative as a means of strengthening cooperation and synergies between systems for the protection of social rights (Council of Europe 2016; ILO 2016). Implementing the Pillar should result in consistency with the key texts of these organisations. This approach could provide an enhanced pan-European dimension of the Pillar in the pursuit of converging social protection standards.

In his most recent State of the Union address on 13 September 2017, Jean-Claude Juncker stressed the need to agree, at the very least, on 'a European Social Standards Union in which we have a common understanding of what is socially fair in our single market'. The EPSR solemnly proclaimed two months later was seen as 'a strong pillar of social standards' (Juncker 2017). This shift in discourse with a new emphasis on social standards is remarkable.

The EPSR is not another bill of social rights within the multilevel system for the protection of fundamental rights in Europe. It may be argued that a number of social rights are missing (Deakin 2017: 205–6; Lörcher and Schömann 2016: 26; Sabato and Vanhercke 2017: 93), that the proposal is disappointing,[32] and that there is room for more ambitious accompanying initiatives. But the Pillar's main purpose is not to be a 'restatement of social rights'; its emphasis on social policy as a contribution to sustainable economic development can be seen as 'the right approach' (Deakin 2017: 210).

The Pillar is not intended to replace existing instruments for the protection of social rights at the national or European level. Moreover, the lack of enforcement of social rights is a recurrent issue which requires integrated solutions at various levels. Despite its shortcomings, the Pillar makes more explicit and adds new elements to a number of principles and rights already expressed in various forms in the EU and in the international legal *acquis*. At the same time, the Pillar is about delivering 'new and more effective rights for citizens' in relevant fields linked to emerging social challenges and the changing world of work. The Pillar alone, in the form of a solemn proclamation, is unable to meet this ambitious goal. The focus is on strengthening the enforcement of existing rights and delivering on the new social standards enshrined in the Pillar through appropriate implementation.

Further insights into competitiveness

While promoting social fairness, the Pillar as a whole should be an enabler for inclusive competitiveness. A number of principles/rights may have particular potential for boosting competitiveness. This is the case for: the right to quality and inclusive education, training and life-long learning (Principle 1); the transition towards open-ended forms of employment (Principle 5a); the prevention of employment relationships that lead to precarious working conditions, including by prohibiting abuse of atypical contracts (Principle 5d); fair wages and adequate minimum wages (Principle 6); the information about employment conditions and protection in case of dismissals (Principles 7a and 7b); work-life balance (Principle 9); healthy, safe, and well-adapted work environment (Principle 10); adequate social protection (Principle 12); the right for unemployed to adequate activation support from public employment services to (re)integrate in the labour market and adequate unemployment benefits of reasonable duration (Principle 13); the right for everyone lacking sufficient resources to adequate minimum income benefits, combined with incentives to (re)integrate into the labour market for people who can work (Principle 14).

Analysing the Pillar's content in more detail, it is interesting to assess the approach taken in a particular area, such as wage policy. This example illustrates the challenges, limits, and opportunities of this initiative.

Recently, real wage growth has lagged behind productivity growth. During the crisis, part of the 'competitiveness problem' in the euro area was linked to wage and productivity developments (Draghi 2013). In particular, setting up a monetary union and single currency without commensurate coordination of economic and social policy, especially wage policy, gave rise to wage inflation and loss of competitiveness and hence to the imbalances that precipitated the crisis (Deakin 2017: 204). Fairer and stronger wage coordination in the euro area was required to address the social impact of the crisis. Indeed, wage increases in line with productivity goals to ensure higher standards of living contribute to competitiveness while tackling inequalities. It is a 'solidaristic means' (ibid.: 204) of maintaining competitiveness, since it allows the benefits of a strong economic performance to be widely shared (Dahan 2017). Another important issue is wage dispersion, which damages equality, productivity, and competitiveness. Most Member States have a national statutory minimum wage and a few Member States have different wage floors set through collective agreements.

Against this backdrop, the Pillar sets out the *right to fair wages* that provide for a decent standard of living for all workers (Principle 6a), which is not enshrined in the EU Charter of Fundamental Rights. The Pillar is thus aligned with the 1989 Community Charter of the Fundamental Social Rights of Workers (Right 5) and the 1961 European Social Charter (1996 Revised European Social Charter) (Article 4). Principle 6b refers to *adequate minimum wages* that shall be ensured in a way that provide for the satisfaction of the needs of the worker and his/her family and in the light of national economic and social conditions. Economic conditions may include the need to keep wage development in line with productivity; the evolution of the standards of living are an example of social conditions. The Pillar also foresees the need to safeguard access to employment and incentives to seek work and recognises the role of minimum wages in preventing in-work poverty. Finally, all wages shall be *set in a transparent and predictable way* according to national practices and respecting the autonomy of the social partners (Principle 6c). The Pillar takes into consideration the diversity of Member States wage policies. It advocates transparency through well-established consultation procedures. A way of ensuring predictability is defining rules such as adjustment to the cost of living for minimum wages.[33]

According to Article 153(5) TFEU, the provisions of Article 153 TFEU shall not apply to pay. The Union has no legislative competence in this field. The EU and Member States are required to work together on a coordinated strategy for employment (Article 145 TFEU) and the Union shall contribute to a high level of employment by encouraging cooperation and by supporting and complementing Member States' action (Article 147 TFEU). Despite the limitations of this framework, the Pillar takes a leap forward by reinforcing standards on wages and complementing the EU *acquis*. Given the Pillar's nature and in line with the Treaties, the initiative in this matter lies with Member States and social partners. In order to deliver on Principle 6, the following standards should at least be considered: a fair wage must be above the poverty line in a given country, i.e. 50 per cent of the national average wage, and the minimum or lowest net remuneration or wage must not fall below 60 per cent of the net average wage.[34] This objective should be determined by legislative measures or collective agreements.

At the EU level, the European Employment Strategy is implemented through the European Semester. The guidelines for national employment policies will be amended by a Council decision to align with the Pillar's principles. In particular, the standards set out in Principle 6 will be included in Guideline 5, according to which Member States should encourage wage-setting mechanisms, allowing for the responsiveness of wages to productivity developments while ensuring fair wages. Member States and social partners should ensure adequate minimum wage levels, taking into account their impact on competitiveness, job creation, and in-work poverty (EC 2017h). Wage developments are addressed in country-specific recommendations within the European Semester. In line with Principle 6, particular attention should be paid to Member States in which the poverty threshold is not reached.

For the period 2018–19, the Council acknowledges that there is a case for further supporting wage growth in the euro area while fostering economic and social convergence and increasing growth. Following the Pillar's principles, it recommends that euro area Member States take action to pursue policies supporting sustainable and inclusive growth, e.g. by creating the conditions to promote wage growth respecting the role of social partners (in countries with large current account surpluses), and to implement reforms aimed at effective social dialogue and wage bargaining, shifting taxes away from labour, etc. (Council of the EU 2018).

Progress has therefore been made since the Pillar's proclamation, which suggests that it may help deliver a more inclusive competitiveness. This potential needs to be further harnessed at various levels.

The Pillar's potential: implementation and follow-up

The implementation of the EPSR is 'a shared political commitment and responsibility' (European Parliament *et al.* 2017: recital 17). The Pillar gives full consideration to the political and legal constraints deriving from the fact that Member States are primarily responsible for the definition of their employment and social policy and also bear most of the financial burden in the areas covered. The Pillar should be implemented by both the EU and the Member States within their respective competences, taking due account of different socio-economic environments and the diversity of national systems, including the role of social partners, and in accordance with the principle of subsidiarity and proportionality.

The EPSR was devised as a programme of action. Its development has been included in the 2016, 2017, and 2018 Commission Work Programmes.[35] The

Commission was invited by the European Council in December 2017 to propose 'appropriate monitoring' of the Pillar's implementation (European Council 2017b). The Commission presented its views in its Communication of 13 March 2018 (EC 2018b). The main idea is to continue to make use of existing tools and processes while strengthening the monitoring in the European Semester. Given the importance of ensuring tangible progress on the ground, the Commission also provided further details about each principle/right presented in three main sections: existing EU law, scope and changes introduced by the Pillar, and implementation (suggestions addressed to Member States and social partners, as well as recent and ongoing initiatives at EU level).[36]

As proposed by the Commission, various instruments are available at EU level: (1) EU law; (2) social dialogue; (3) policy guidance and recommendations, monitoring progress; and (4) financial support. Other avenues may also be explored with a view to enhancing the operational effectiveness of the Pillar.

A wide range of instruments

First of all, given that the Pillar is not legally binding, further legislative initiatives are necessary in order to ensure the enforcement of a number of principles and rights. To this end, on 26 April 2017, the Commission adopted alongside the Pillar's final proposal a first series of accompanying legislative and non-legislative initiatives related to work-life balance,[37] the information of workers,[38] access to social protection,[39] and working time.[40] An important focus of the Pillar's follow-up is the effective implementation of existing legislation. The Commission envisages a wide range of measures such as support to improve awareness of rights, enforcement mechanisms, and interpretative guidance. Further legislative or non-legislative EU initiatives may follow in the Commission Work Programmes.[41] Not all the principles and rights enshrined in the Pillar may require further legislation at EU level, and some aspects may be interpreted as falling outside the Union's powers and tasks (European Parliament *et al.* 2017: recital 18).[42] Therefore, the Member States' commitment to implement the Pillar remains crucial.

Second, the involvement of the social partners is essential to the delivery of social rights. The promotion of dialogue between management and labour is a common objective of the Union and its Member States. The EU recognises and promotes the role of the social partners. They are to be consulted in the policy areas covered by Article 153 TFEU and may request implementation of their agreements at the EU level (Articles 151–5 TFEU). They may also support the Pillar's implementation via collective bargaining at national level and/or by identifying and exchanging good practices across Member States. Enhanced dialogue between social partners at various levels is essential in this context, since no single model exists and there are significant differences in socio-economic performances of Member States.

Third, implementation of the Pillar requires policy guidance and recommendation and monitoring progress. Social issues have been mainstreamed and reinforced in the European Semester for economic policy coordination in recent years. The 2018 European Semester has become an essential tool by taking account of the situations of each Member State and providing political impetus and coordination in the areas covered by the Pillar. Its content is thus reflected in some key components of the European Semester, such as: (1) the Annual Growth Survey 2018 (EC 2017i: 3);[43] (2) the Joint Employment Report (JER) 2018 that monitors Member States' performance, notably through the Social Scoreboard accompanying the Pillar (EC 2017j: 2,19–26);[44] (3) the Employment Guidelines amended to align with the Pillar, with a view to improving the EU's competitiveness and foster social cohesion (EC 2017k); (4) the Country Reports; and (5) the country-specific recommendations.

The European Semester should support the development of the Pillar (EP 2018: §8, §9). Following the JER's adoption by the EPSCO Council in March 2018 (Council of the EU 2018b: 6), the headline indicators should become useful tools for upward social convergence in the EU. Their impact and outcomes remain to be seen.

Finally, financial support is the cornerstone of the EPSR's implementation. Investment in the areas covered by the Pillar is vital if the initiative is to succeed. It is expected that EU funds will continue to support its implementation, in particular, the European Social Fund but also the European Structural and Investment Funds and other key financial programmes such as the Youth Employment Initiative, Erasmus+, the European Globalisation Adjustment Fund, and the Fund for European Aid to the Most Deprived. The Pillar will also be a reference for the post-2020 EU financial programming period.[45]

Further avenues

While the various implementation instruments proposed by the Commission are steps in the right direction, they need to be embedded in strong governance driven by a converging political approach at EU, national, regional, and local level in order to ensure that the Pillar has real impact. To this end, the Council has emphasised the importance of a 'strong ownership' at Member State level, with Ministers for Employment and Social Affairs taking a leading role and the EPSCO Council playing a central part in the governance and implementation of the Pillar (Council of the EU 2017d: 4). All EU Member States agree that improvements need to be made to employment and social conditions, but there are 'different starting points, different national circumstances and that we will move at different speeds' (Council of the EU 2017c: 6).

Implementation and impact remain major conditions for the Pillar's success. The means of enforcement envisaged by the Commission have been criticised for their legal weakness (Rasnača 2017a). The Pillar also faces major risks, such as the risk of failure due to the principle of subsidiarity in social policy areas, the risk of remaining a 'paper tiger' 'without Juncker' (Vanhercke *et al*. 2017: 211), the risk of merely frustrating citizens, and the risk of backfiring. Its ability to deliver tangible results has been questioned (Dhéret 2017; Rasnača 2017b;

Vandenbroucke 2017b). In itself, the Pillar will be insufficient to bring tangible benefits to European citizens (Fernandes 2017).

In the absence of political motivation to follow up on the Pillar, judicial enforcement has been explored as a potential option, since the courts at both EU and national level would be able to rely on its 'rather promising (protective)' principles when interpreting EU law — in the same way as the EU Charter of Fundamental Rights was endorsed prior to the entry into force of the Treaty of Lisbon (Rasnača 2017a). But considering the essential differences between the Charter and the Pillar, the prospects for judicial enforcement of the latter appear to be a distant hope.[46]

The Commission is committed to mainstreaming the Pillar's priorities in all EU policies. Alongside the social dimension of the Single Market, particular attention should be paid to EMU.[47] The Pillar may provide useful 'guidance towards more binding standards for the euro area' (EC 2017: 9–10).[48] Opportunities to promote minimum social standards at transnational or regional level may also be seized. The possibility of using the enhanced cooperation mechanism (Article 20 TEU) was also suggested as a means to build a solid EPSR (EP 2017: §2). Other strategies such as the extension of Union's legislative competences and the 'reconstruction' of the EU legislative procedure would require Treaty amendments (Weiss 2017).

Notwithstanding the many difficulties, the Pillar represents a major step forward and has the potential to be a 'new start' for social Europe, paving the way towards 'a new and long overdue "Social Agenda"' (Sabato and Vanhercke 2017: 74). Its effective implementation involves both EU law and 'soft' governance mechanisms, according to the division of competences and the very diverse socio-economic environments in the areas covered by the Pillar. It is thus fundamental to reach a consensus on who should do what in these areas. A clear roadmap accompanying the Pillar appears to be essential (EESC 2017b: 6,15; EP 2017a: §47; Vanhercke *et al.* 2017: 211).[49] The Commission proposes strengthening the monitoring of the Pillar's implementation via the European Semester. It is to be hoped that governance will be strong enough to bring about changes in the Member States so as to overcome the 'deficit in common purpose' (Vandenbroucke 2017a: 46) on the Union's social foundations.

Conclusion

The EPSR provides a meaningful response to the process of building a deeper, fairer Union that is better equipped to tackle the devastating consequences of the recent crisis and to face the future. It is the result of a concerted effort to strengthen the social dimension of the EU as a whole. The Juncker initiative generated positive momentum, with many relevant stakeholders expressing their support. The Pillar thus raised high expectations, and its success will rely on the effective implementation of the social standards it lays down. This will require joint efforts and involve a wide range of players at European, national, regional, and local level. Substantial differences in socio-economic performance within and among the Member States justify a cautious approach. Delivering on the Pillar is part of an evolving process: it is not an outcome but a beginning.

Although the EPSR is not a legally binding instrument for the protection of social rights, it nevertheless has both a political and a legal impact. Its main added value lies in its integrated, dynamic, and action-oriented approach. It is designed to be a useful tool that, as well as raising awareness of the need to take into account social principles and rights, also complements and develops the EU's social *acquis* and reinforces standards which may provide a fairer and more socially balanced competitiveness in the EU.

This was a timely initiative at a crucial moment for the future of the Europe of 27. To achieve the ambitious goals of a 'European Social Standards Union', there is an overriding need to build a consensus, at both EU and national level, around the future social foundations of the Union. Major challenges still lie ahead.

Notes

1 The EPSR was signed and solemnly proclaimed by the European Parliament, the Council and the Commission in Gothenburg, Sweden, at the Social Summit for Fair Jobs and Growth.

2 This multi-layered concept allows for a diversity of national economic and social models in the EU with shared values and objectives. It also refers to the link between economic and social aspects in connection with the 'social market economy' set out in Article 3(3) TEU as part of the Union's objectives. On the whole, the third paragraph of Article 3 TEU was considered 'an acceptable compromise' to encapsulate the 'European social model' (Ziller 2014).

3 Since the start of its term, this Commission has focused on 'social fairness' instead of 'social justice', despite the latter being mentioned in Article 3(3) TEU. It does not provide a definition of 'social fairness' or an explanation of the grounds for this approach. In my understanding, 'social fairness' pursues the aim of tackling social inequalities by creating the conditions for equal opportunities so as to guarantee each individual the same ability to participate in social life. This principle should underpin 'social justice' and social inclusion. In Rawls' conception of justice as fairness, the principle of 'fair equality of opportunity' means that 'all should have a fair chance to attain [positions]' and '[t]he expectations of those with the same abilities and aspirations should not be affected by their social class' (Rawls 1999: 63). I do not address in this chapter the vast academic debate on social justice. On the need for a conception of justice based on a specific understanding of the EU, see Vandenbroucke (2017a).

4 In February 2018, there were around 17.6 million unemployed people in the EU, 1.4 million more than in the first quarter 2008 before rising in the wake of the crisis; the unemployment rate was 20.8 per cent in Greece and 2.4 per cent in the Czech Republic. In 2016, 23.5 per cent of the EU28 total population was at risk of poverty or social exclusion (source: Eurostat). See also EC (2018a).

5 Productivity growth in the EU remains modest: 0.8 per cent in the third quarter of 2017 (EC 2018a: 39–40).

6 Competitiveness is a multifaceted and continuously evolving concept. This chapter takes inspiration from the enlightening work of the Competitiveness Advisory Group:

> Competitiveness implies elements of productivity, efficiency, profitability. But it is not an end in itself or a target. It is a powerful means to achieve rising standards

of living and increasing social welfare – a tool for achieving targets.... Economic competition is thus the *ally*, not the enemy, of social dialogue

(CAG 1995: 2–3; author's emphasis)

7 The Pillar was presented in the form of a Commission Recommendation on the European Pillar of Social Rights (EC 2017d), together with a proposal for an Interinstitutional Proclamation on the European Pillar of Social Rights (EC 2017e). The Pillar is accompanied by three Staff Working Documents. One document provides more detailed explanations on each of the principles and rights set out in the Pillar (SWD(2017) 201 final). Another document establishes a 'social scoreboard' to monitor progress on the ground (SWD(2017) 200 final). The third document is a report of the public consultation (SWD(2017) 206 final). See also EC (2017a).

8 The word 'pillar' (*socle* in French, meaning 'base' or 'foundation') suggests an essential and reliable support. My understanding of this pillar is linked to the social aspect as a cross-cutting and foundational component of the EU. In this sense, the EPSR should support the various policies underpinning the Union's objectives, in line with the horizontal social clause of Article 9 TFEU.

9 The Communication was accompanied by two Staff Working Documents (SWD(2016) 50 final; SWD(2016) 51 final).

10 For an overview on the key stakeholder and institutional views on the preliminary outline of the Pillar, see Sabato and Vanhercke (2017).

11 See http://ec.europa.eu/social/main.jsp?langId=en&catId=88&eventsId=1187&furtherEvents=yes

12 Up to the end of 2016, the Commission consulted stakeholders at the EU, national, regional, and local level. The main stakeholders involved were citizens, Member States, EU institutions, social partners, civil society, the European research community and other organisations like the Council of Europe, the ILO, the IMF, the OECD, and the World Bank. More than 60 meetings and events at EU and national level, involving more than 2,500 participants, were organised. The Commission received around 200 position papers, as well as 16,560 replies to its online questionnaire. See SWD(2017) 206 final at 4–7.

13 Recital 12. The Commission's proposal for an interinstitutional proclamation of the Pillar was slightly adapted only in the preamble by the Council on 23 October 2017 (Council of the EU 2017).

14 This solemn proclamation is separate from the Community Charter of the Fundamental Social Rights of Workers which was adopted as a declaration by the Heads of State or Government of 11 Member States of the European Community on 9 December 1989.

15 The Charter only became legally binding, with the same legal value as the EU Treaties, with the entry into force of the Treaty of Lisbon on 1 December 2009.

16 On the spreading significance and the real power and coercion exercised via soft law, see Dawson (2017).

17 Allan Larsson, Special Adviser to European Commission President for the EPSR, states that it 'is not going to be a quick fix: it should go deep and have an impact over a long period of time' (EC 2016b: 11). See also Marianne Thyssen's address to the European Parliament debate (EP 2017b).

18 In the Commission recommendation, the responsibility to implement the Pillar is also shared by the social partners, but this was seen as interfering with their autonomy (Council of the EU 2017b: 8).

19 As mentioned in Recital 6, the TFEU contains provisions laying down the powers of the Union relating *inter alia* to the freedom of movement of workers (Articles 45–8), the right of establishment (Articles 49–55), social policy (Articles 151–61), the promotion of dialogue between management and labour (Article 154), including agreements concluded and implemented at Union level (Article 155), equal pay for men

and women for equal work (Article 157), the contribution to the development of quality education and vocational training (Articles 165, 166), Union action complementing national policies and fostering cooperation in the field of health (Article 168), economic, social, and territorial cohesion (Articles 174–8), the formulation, and the surveillance of the implementation, of the broad guidelines of the economic policies (Article 121), the formulation and the examination of the implementation of the employment guidelines (Article 148) and more generally, the approximation of legislation (Articles 114–17). Other examples of provisions relating to EU's coordinating competences are provided for in Articles 2(3), 5(1), 5(2), 5(3), 120, 121, 134, 145, 150, 156 TFEU.

20 For instance, the European Trade Union Confederation urges all EU Member States to join the Pillar (ETUC 2017).

21 The social market economy was defined as 'a regulative policy which aims to combine, on the basis of a competitive economy, free initiative and social progress' (Müller-Armack 1956). On the origins and evolution of the social market economy and the perspective of a new European social order, see Velo and Velo (2013).

22 The duality of economic and social dimensions is a constant feature of the European integration project. Their coexistence, interconnections, and asymmetric or conflictual relationship have given rise to a significant body of academic literature and political debate with divergent opinions; see the emblematic analysis by Scharpf (2010). On the structural imbalance in favour of 'the economic', see Garben (2017).

23 For a detailed comparison between the preliminary outline of March 2016 (EC 2016d) and the final proposal of April 2017 (EC 2017d), see Sabato and Vanhercke (2017: 84–93).

24 For instance, Principle 2 on gender quality states: 'a. Equality of treatment and opportunities between woman and men *must be* ensured and fostered … b. Women and men *have the right to* equal pay for work of equal value' (author's emphasis).

25 Principles have been relabelled as rights. For instance, Principle 1 was changed from 'All persons *shall have access to* quality education …' to 'Everyone *has the right to* quality and inclusive education …'; in Principle 14, 'adequate minimum income benefits *shall be ensured* for those who lack sufficient resources for a decent standard of living' was changed to 'everyone lacking sufficient resources *has the right to* adequate minimum income benefits ensuring a life in dignity at all stages of life, and effective access to enabling goods and services' (author's emphasis).

26 Chapter I contains: 1. Education, training and life-long learning; 2. Gender equality; 3. Equal opportunities; 4. Active support to employment. Chapter II contains: 5. Secure and adaptable employment; 6. Wages; 7. Information about employment conditions and protection in case of dismissals; 8. Social dialogue and involvement of workers; 9. Work-life balance; 10. Healthy, safe and well-adapted work environment and data protection. Chapter III contains: 11. Childcare and support to children; 12. Social protection; 13. Unemployment benefits; 14. Minimum income; 15. Old-age income and pensions; 16. Health care; 17. Inclusion of people with disabilities; 18. Long-term care; 19. Housing and assistance for the homeless; 20. Access to essential services.

27 The distinction between rights (which must be respected) and principles (which must be observed) drawn in the Charter of Fundamental Rights of the EU is not relevant here. Neither the rights nor the principles of the Pillar are directly enforceable as an integral part of the interinstitutional proclamation. On this ambiguous wording, see Council of the EU (2017b: 5). See also EESC (2017b: 10).

28 For instance, Principle 4 under the title 'Active support to employment' involves at least three 'rights': (1) the right to timely and tailor-made assistance to improve employment or self-employment prospects (Principle 4a); (2) the right for young people to continued education, apprenticeship, traineeship, or a job offer of good standing within 4 months of becoming unemployed or leaving education (Principle

4b); and (3) the right for unemployed people to personalised, continuous, and consistent support (Principle 4c).

29 In comparison with earlier instruments such as the Community Charter of the Fundamental Social Rights of Workers of 9 December 1989 (Deakin 2017: 194).

30 More specifically, the Pillar's preamble refers to Article 3 TEU, Articles 9, 151 and 152 TFEU, the EU Charter of Fundamental Rights and several TFEU provisions in the fields covered by the Pillar (Recitals 1–6).

31 In the 2016 Commission Communication, the social rights and principles laid down in international law are presented as possible sources of 'inspiration' (SWD(2016) 50 final, at 17).

32 See, for instance, the opinion of Gabriele Bischoff, President of the EESC Workers' Group, in Martin (2017).

33 SWD(2018) 67 final, at 33.

34 See, for instance, the following decisions of the European Committee of Social Rights: *GENOP-DEI and ADEDY v. Greece*, Complaint No. 66/2011, decision on the merits of 23 March 2017, §57 and *GSEE v. Greece*, Complaint No. 111/2014, decision on the merits of 23 March 2017, §187.

35 Commission Work Programme 2016, *No time for business as usual*, 27.10.2015, COM(2015) 610 final, at 9. Commission Work Programme 2017, *Delivering a Europe that protects, empowers and defends*, 25.10.2016. COM(2016) 710 final, at 10. Commission Work Programme 2018, *An agenda for a more united, stronger and more democratic Europe*, 24.10.2017, COM(2017) 650 final, at 7.

36 SWD(2018) 67 final of 13.3.2018. It updates the document SWD(2017) 201 final and details progress made at EU level since April 2017.

37 COM(2017) 252 final and COM(2017) 253 final.

38 C(2017) 2611 final and SWD(2017) 205 final.

39 C(2017) 2610 final.

40 C(2017) 2601 final.

41 See, for instance, new initiatives for 2018 included in the 'social fairness package' as part of 'a deeper and fairer Internal Market with a strengthened industrial base', such as the proposal for a regulation of the European Parliament and the Council establishing a European Labour Authority of 13.3.2018 (COM(2018) 131 final) and the proposal for a Council recommendation on access to social protection for workers and the self-employed of 13.3.2018 (COM(2018) 132 final). The Commission is working on an initiative on a European Social Security Number (COM(2017) 650 final, n. 113, ANNEX 1, at 3). Other priority pending proposals are related to the revision of the Written Statement Directive, the coordination of social security systems and work-life balance for parents and carers, the revision of the posting of workers directive, the European Accessibility Act and the legal framework of the European Solidarity Corps (ANNEX 3). The European Council has recently invited the Council to examine the initiatives presented under the 'social fairness package' (European Council 2018).

42 The Pillar does not entail an extension of the Union's powers and tasks. Potential conflicts or divergences are not excluded. For instance, interpretation of the broad scope of the extension of the principle of equality between women and men to 'all areas' (Principle 2) may be needed (Council of the EU 2017b: 10).

43 The Pillar is integrated by prioritising reforms designed to help the labour force acquire skills and promote equal opportunities in the labour market, fair working conditions, increasing labour productivity to support wage growth and adequate and sustainable social protection systems.

44 The analysis on the basis of 14 headline indicators that assess employment and social trends shows at least one 'critical situation' for 17 Member States (SWD(2017) 200 final). An interactive tool on the Social Scoreboard is available at https://composite-indicators.jrc.ec.europa.eu/social-scoreboard/#. For an assessment of these indicators, see the background analysis of Galgóczi *et al.* (2017).

45 The EU budget will need to deliver on the Pillar's 'full implementation' (EC 2018c: 7). A comprehensive proposal for the future Multiannual Financial Framework for the period 2021–27 is expected in May 2018.
46 On the significant caveats regarding the enforceability of the social rights (rights or principles) enshrined in the Charter, see Kornezov (2017).
47 Surprisingly, there is only one reference to the Pillar in the roadmap for completing EMU (EC 2017g).
48 See also Rasnača and Theodoropoulou (2017).
49 Note also the Action Programme relating to the implementation of the Community Charter of basic social rights for workers, presented by the Commission in 1989 (COM (89) 568 final). By contrast, this Commission's approach builds on a wide variety of existing instruments and monitoring under the European Semester.

References

BusinessEurope (2016). 'European Pillar of Social Rights – BusinessEurope contribution to the debate', 24 August 2016. Available at: www.businesseurope.eu/publications/european-pillar-social-rights-businesseurope-contribution-debate

CAG (Competitiveness Advisory Group) (1995). 'Enhancing European competitiveness: first report to the President of the Commission, the Prime Ministers and Heads of State'. Luxembourg: OOPEC. Available at: http://aei.pitt.edu/2866/1/2866.pdf

Caniard, Étienne and Emelyn Weber (2016). 'La construction d'une Europe dotée d'un socle des droits sociaux. Avis du Conseil économique, social et environnemental de la République française'. Paris: CESE. Available at: www.lecese.fr/sites/default/files/pdf/Avis/2016/2016_15_europe_socle_droits_sociaux.pdf

Council of Europe (2016). Opinion of the Secretary General of the Council of Europe on the European Union initiative to establish a European Pillar of Social Rights', 2 December 2016. Available at: https://rm.coe.int/16806dd0bc

Council of the EU (2017a). 'Proposal for an Interinstitutional Proclamation on the European Pillar of Social Rights', 20 October 2017. 13129/17. Available at: http://data.consilium.europa.eu/doc/document/ST-13129-2017-INIT/en/pdf

Council of the EU (2017b). 'Opinion of the Legal Service', 19 September 2017. 12077/17. Available at: http://data.consilium.europa.eu/doc/document/ST-12077-2017-INIT/en/pdf

Council of the EU (2017c). 'Outcome of the Council Meeting Employment, Social Policy, Health and Consumer Affairs', 15–16 June 2017. 10376/17.

Council of the EU (2017d). 'European Pillar of Social Rights: joint SPC-EMCO Opinion of 31 May 2017', 2 June 2017. 9498/17.

Council of the EU (2018a). 'Council recommendation on the economic policy of the euro area', 23 January 2018. 32/18.

Council of the EU (2018b). 'Outcome of the Council Meeting, Employment, Social Policy, Health and Consumer Affairs', 15 March 2018. 7132/18.

Dahan, Samuel (2017). '(Re-)designing institutions for EMU wage setting: strengthened coordination between monetary and economic institutions', *European Labour Law Journal* 8(4): 281–305.

Dawson, Mark (2017). 'Integration through soft law: no competence needed? Juridical and bio-power in the realm of soft law', in Sacha Garben and Inge Govaere (eds). *The division of competences between the EU and the Member States: reflections on the past, the present and the future.* Oxford: Hart, 235–50.

Deakin, Simon (2017). 'What follows austerity? From social pillar to new deal', in Frank Vandenbroucke, Catherine Barnard, and Geert De Baere (eds). *A European Social Union after the crisis*. Cambridge: Cambridge University Press, 192–210.
Dhéret, Claire (2017). 'European social rights need more than a proclamation: recommendations for an ambitious social summit'. Brussels: EPC. Available at: www.epc.eu/pub_details.php?cat_id=4andpub_id=8067
Draghi, Mario (2013). 'Euro area economic situation and the foundations for growth', 14 March 2013. Available at: www.ecb.europa.eu/press/key/date/2013/html/sp130315.en.pdf?2d8f825dcf65b5ce0794ec5bd17a8b7a
EAPN (European Anti-Poverty Network) (2016). 'Last chance for social Europe? EAPN statement on European Pillar of Social Rights'. Available at: www.eapn.eu/wp-content/uploads/2016/09/EAPN-2016-EAPN-Position-European-Pillar-Social-Rights-600.pdf
EAPN (European Anti-Poverty Network) (2017). 'Make social rights the beating heart of Europe! EAPN response to the European Pillar of Social Rights'. Available at: www.eapn.eu/wp-content/uploads/2017/09/EAPN-2017-EAPN-Response-European-Pillar-Social-Rights-1314.pdf
EC (European Commission) (2015). 'College holds orientation debate on the economic and social dimension of the Single Market'. Press release IP/15/5763. Available at: http://europa.eu/rapid/press-release_IP-15-5763_en.htm
EC (European Commission) (2016a). 'Frequently asked questions: the European Pillar of Social Rights'. MEMO/16/64. Available at: http://europa.eu/rapid/press-release_MEMO-16-64_en.htm
EC (European Commission) (2016b). 'The future European Social Pillar in context', *Social Agenda* 46(12): 10–13.
EC (European Commission) (2016c). 'Launching a consultation on a European Pillar of Social Rights'. COM(2016) 127 final.
EC (European Commission) (2016d). 'Annex: first preliminary outline of a European Pillar of Social Rights'. COM(2016) 127 final ANNEX 1.
EC (European Commission) (2017a). 'Establishing a European Pillar of Social Rights'. COM(2017) 250 final.
EC (European Commission) (2017b). 'Reflection paper on the social dimension of Europe'. COM(2017) 206.
EC (European Commission) (2017c). 'White Paper on the future of Europe: reflections and scenarios for the EU27 by 2025'. COM(2017) 2025.
EC (European Commission) (2017d). 'Commission Recommendation on the European Pillar of Social Rights'. C(2017) 2600 final.
EC (European Commission) (2017e). 'Proposal for an Interinstitutional Proclamation on the European Pillar of Social Rights'. COM(2017) 251 final.
EC (European Commission) (2017f). 'Reflection paper on the deepening of the Economic and Monetary Union'. COM(2017) 291.
EC (European Commission) (2017g). 'Further steps towards completing Europe's Economic and Monetary Union: a roadmap'. COM(2017) 821 final.
EC (European Commission) (2017h). 'Proposal for a Council Decision on guidelines for the employment policies of the Member States'. COM(2017) 677 final and ANNEX.
EC (European Commission) (2017i). 'Annual Growth Survey 2018'. COM(2017) 690 final.
EC (European Commission) (2017j). 'Draft Joint Employment Report'. COM(2017) 674 final.
EC (European Commission) (2017k). 'Annex to the Proposal for a Council decision on guidelines for the employment policies of the Member States'. COM(2017) 677 final.

EC (European Commission) (2018a). 'Employment and Social Developments in Europe: quarterly review', February 2018. Luxembourg: Publications Office of the European Union.
EC (European Commission) (2018b). 'Monitoring the implementation of the European Pillar of Social Rights'. COM(2018) 130 final.
EC (European Commission) (2018c). 'A new, modern Multiannual Financial Framework for a European Union that delivers efficiently on its priorities post-2020'. The European Commission's contribution to the Informal Leaders' meeting on 23 February 2018. COM(2018) 98 final.
EESC (European Economic and Social Committee) (2017a). 'Opinion on the European Pillar of Social Rights', 25 January 2017. SOC/542.
EESC (European Economic and Social Committee) (2017b). 'Impact of the social dimension and the European Pillar of Social Rights on the Future of the European Union', 19 October 2017. SOC/564.
EP (European Parliament) (2017a). 'Resolution of 19 January 2017 on a European Pillar of Social Rights'. 2016/2095(INI).
EP (European Parliament) (2017b). 'Decision adopted on the European Pillar of Social Rights and work-life balance initiative (debate)'. 26.04.2017.
EP (European Parliament) (2018). 'Resolution of 14 March 2018 on the European Semester for economic policy coordination: employment and social aspects in the Annual Growth Survey 2018'. 2017/2260(INI).
ETUC (European Trade Union Confederation) (2016). 'Position on the European Pillar of Social Rights, working for a better deal for all workers'. Available at: www.etuc.org/sites/www.etuc.org/files/document/files/european_pillar_of_social_rights_.pdf
ETUC (European Trade Union Confederation) (2017). 'No future without a more social Europe'. Press release. 26.04.2017. Available at: www.etuc.org/press/no-future-without-more-social-europe#.WuiJxpe-nIU
European Council (2016). 'Bratislava Declaration and Roadmap', 16 September 2016. Available at: www.consilium.europa.eu/media/21250/160916-bratislava-declaration-and-roadmapen16.pdf
European Council (2017a). 'The Rome Declaration', 25 March 2017. Press release 149/17. Available at: www.consilium.europa.eu/en/press/press-releases/2017/03/25/rome-declaration/
European Council (2017b). 'Conclusions', 14 December 2017. EUCO 19/1/17 REV 1.
European Council (2018). 'Conclusions', 22 March 2018. EUCO 1/18.
European Parliament, Council of the European Union and European Commission (2000). 'Charter of fundamental rights of the European Union', *Official Journal of the European Union* 2000/C 364/01.
European Parliament, Council of the European Union and European Commission (2007). 'Charter of fundamental rights of the European Union', *Official Journal of the European Union* 2007/C 303/01.
European Parliament, Council of the European Union and European Commission (2017). 'Interinstitutional proclamation on the European Pillar of Social Rights', *Official Journal of the European Union* 2017/C 428/09.
Fernandes, Sofia (2017). 'Göteborg et le socle européen des droits sociaux: vers un "triple A social"'? Paris: Institut Jacques Delors. Available at: https://institutdelors.eu/wp-content/uploads/2017/11/goteborgetleseds-fernandes-tribune-nov17.pdf
Frazer, Hugh and Éric Marlier (eds) (2016). 'Towards a European Pillar of effective social rights: submission to the European Commission', Brussels: ESPN.

Galgóczi, Béla, Aline Hoffmann, Maria Jepsen, *et al.* (2017). *The Social Scoreboard revisited*. Brussels: ETUI.
Garben, Sacha (2017). 'The constitutional (im)balance between "the market" and "the social" in the European Union', *European Constitutional Law Review* 13(1): 23–61.
Hendrickx, Frank (2018). 'The European Social Pillar: a first evaluation', *European Labour Law Journal* 9(1): 3–6.
ILO (International Labour Organization) (2016). *Building a social pillar for European convergence*. Geneva: ILO.
Juncker, Jean-Claude (2014a). 'A New Start for Europe: my agenda for jobs, growth, fairness and democratic change. Political guidelines for the next European Commission'. Available at: https://ec.europa.eu/commission/sites/beta-political/files/juncker-political-guidelines-speech_en.pdf
Juncker, Jean-Claude (2014b). 'Setting Europe in motion: President-elect Juncker's main messages from his speech before the European Parliament'. Available at: http://europa.eu/rapid/press-release_SPEECH-14-705_en.htm
Juncker, Jean-Claude (2015). 'State of the Union 2015: time for honesty, unity and solidarity'. Available at: http://europa.eu/rapid/press-release_SPEECH-15-5614_en.htm
Juncker, Jean-Claude (2017a). 'State of the Union address 2017'. Available at: http://europa.eu/rapid/press-release_SPEECH-17-3165_en.htm
Juncker, Jean-Claude (2017b). 'Opening remarks at the press conference following the Social Summit for Fair Jobs and Growth'. Available at: http://europa.eu/rapid/press-release_SPEECH-17-4730_en.htm
Juncker, Jean-Claude, Donald Tusk, Jeroen Dijsselbloem, *et al.* (2015). 'Completing Europe's Economic and Monetary Union'. Brussels: European Commission. Available at: https://ec.europa.eu/commission/sites/beta-political/files/5-presidents-report_en.pdf
Kornezov, Alexander (2017). 'Social rights, the Charter, and the ECHR: caveats, austerity, and other disasters', in Frank Vandenbroucke, Catherine Barnard, and Geert De Baere (eds). *A European Social Union after the crisis*. Cambridge: Cambridge University Press, 407–32.
Lörcher, Klaus and Isabelle Schömann (2016). 'The European pillar of social rights: critical legal analysis and proposals'. Brussels: ETUI. Available at: www.etui.org/content/download/23792/198154/file/16+The+European+pillar+os+social+rights+Lorcher+Schoemann+WEB+version.pdf
Martin, David (2017). 'Can the EU deliver on its Pillar of Social Rights?', *Deutsche Welle*, 27 April. Available at: http://p.dw.com/p/2c2Fv
Müller-Armack, Alfred (1956). 'Soziale Marktwirtschaft', in Erwin von Beckerath *et al.* (eds). *Handwörterbuch der Sozialwissenschaften*. Stuttgart: Fischer, Mohr, Vandenhoeck & Ruprecht, 390–2.
Rasnača, Zane (2017a). '(Any) relevance of the European Pillar of Social Rights for EU law?' *European Law Blog*, 17 November 2017. Available at: https://europeanlawblog.eu/2017/11/17/any-relevance-of-the-european-pillar-of-social-rights-for-eu-law/
Rasnača, Zane (2017b). *Bridging the gaps or falling short? The European Pillar of Social Rights and what it can bring to EU-level policymaking*. Brussels: ETUI.
Rasnača, Zane and Sotiria Theodoropoulou (2017). 'Strengthening the EU's social dimension: using the EMU to make the most out of the Social Pillar'. Brussels: ETUI. Available at: www.etui.org/content/download/33061/306553/file/EMU+and+Social+Pillar+Rasnaca+Theodoropoulou+Policy+Brief+2017-05.pdf
Rawls, John (1999). *A Theory of Justice*. Rev. edn. Cambridge, MA: The Belknap Press.

Sabato, Sebastiano and Bart Vanhercke (2017). 'Towards a European Pillar of Social Rights: from a preliminary outline to a Commission Recommendation', in Bart Vanhercke, Sebastiano Sabato, and Denis Bouget (eds). *Social policy in the European Union: state of play 2017.* Brussels: ETUI, 73–96.

Scharpf, Fritz W. (2010). 'The socio-economic asymmetries of European integration, or why the EU cannot be a "social market economy"', *Socio-Economic Review* 8: 211–50.

Schiek, Dagmar (2017). 'Towards more resilience for a social EU – the constitutionally conditioned internal market', *European Constitutional Law Review* 13(4): 611–40.

The European Convention (2003). 'Final Report of Working Group XI on Social Europe'. CONV 516/1/03 REV 1. Available at: http://european-convention.europa.eu/pdf/reg/en/03/cv00/cv00516-re01.en03.pdf

Vandenbroucke, Frank (2017a). 'The idea of a European Social Union: a normative introduction', in Frank Vandenbroucke, Catherine Barnard, and Geert De Baere (eds). *A European Social Union after the crisis*. Cambridge: Cambridge University Press, 3–46.

Vandenbroucke, Frank (2017b). 'From the Gothenburg Social Summit to a European Social Union', *Social Europe*, 27 November 2017. Available at: www.socialeurope.eu/gothenburg-social-summit-european-social-union

Vanhercke, Bart, Sebastiano Sabato, and Denis Bouget (2017). 'Conclusions: social policy in the EU: high hopes but low yields', in Bart Vanhercke, Sebastiano Sabato, and Denis Bouget (eds). *Social policy in the European Union: state of play 2017.* Brussels: ETUI, 201–14.

Van Rompuy, Herman, José Manuel Barroso, Jean-Claude Juncker, and Mario Draghi (2012). 'Towards a genuine Economic and Monetary Union'. Available at: www.consilium.europa.eu/media/23818/134069.pdf

Velo, Dario and Francesco Velo (2013). *A social market economy and European economic monetary union*. Bern: Peter Lang.

Weiss, Manfred (2017). 'The future of labour law in Europe: rise or fall of the European social model?', *European Labour Law Journal* 8(4): 344–56.

Ziller, Jacques (2014). 'Social market economy as an objective according to Article 3 of the Treaty of the European Union', in José Maria Gil-Robles, Fausto de Quadros, and Dario Velo (eds). *The European Union and social market economy*. Bari: Cacucci Editore, 133–69.

14 Conclusion

Paolo Chiocchetti and Frédéric Allemand

This book has endeavoured to offer a pluralist and interdisciplinary exploration of the impact of competitiveness and solidarity on contemporary European societies and policy-making. The broad-ranging investigation of key theoretical and empirical issues conducted in its 12 chapters has yielded several important findings.

First of all, the importance of competitiveness and solidarity as key concepts for the analysis of societal and policy problems across disciplinary boundaries and policy areas has been fully corroborated. Despite their relatively recent fortune, their politically-charged nature, and their conceptual ambiguities, they can help illuminate crucial aspects of contemporary social life and can serve as useful guiding principles for theory-making, law-making, and policy-making in virtually every field of the social sciences and the humanities.

Second, the book offers the most comprehensive analysis to date of the different ways in which competitiveness, solidarity, and their relationship can be theorised and applied to empirical research and policy-making. While the polysemy of the term competitiveness was discussed at length in the earlier literature, an in-depth assessment of its variegated and often contradictory broader implications was missing or only lightly sketched in. The book lays the foundations of a systematic analysis of these issues, showing that competitiveness and solidarity are often antagonistic, may sometimes be mutually reinforcing, and can in extreme cases be conceptualised as coinciding. In addition, it sheds new light on the conceptual complexity and policy relevance of the relationship between competitiveness and solidarity, pointing to promising avenues to make the European Union simultaneously more economically successful and socially fairer.

Third, two important methodological consequences can be derived from the latter finding. On the one hand, scholars and practitioners should handle the polysemic terms of competitiveness and solidarity with the utmost care, defining them with explicitness and precision and leaving no ambiguity about their intended meaning. On the other hand, scholars and practitioners should be aware that their relationship cannot be reduced to a simple and unilateral one. Neither the idea of an invariably corrosive effect of competition on solidarity, ultimately leading to hellish visions of a dog-eat-dog world, of a Darwinian survival of the fittest, and of a Hobbesian *bellum omnium contra omnes*, nor the idea of an automatic synergy between the two, ultimately leading to heavenly visions of a world of perfect competition where there are no losers but only winners, does justice to the richness of their interaction.

Fourth, all our contributors have broadly confirmed that competitiveness and solidarity represent highly regarded and deeply entrenched principles, both in the European Union and in its Member States, which means all seek to find a productive balance between the two through a variety of different institutional settlements and policy solutions. While deeply pessimistic views on the future of social cohesion and of the welfare state were rare, however, most contributors did find a certain asymmetry in contemporary European and national policies to the benefit of competitiveness and to the detriment of solidarity, which threatens both the achievement of valuable social goals and the political sustainability of the European integration process.

Finally, the 12 chapters offer important contributions to the specialist research in a variety of disciplines and issues, notably in European Union studies, economics and political economy, law, political science, sociology, history, geography, federalism theory, economic policy and governance, social policy, regional development, and the solidarity economy, while also providing useful overviews of specific disciplinary fields for a non-specialist audience.

As was to be expected, the contributors could not reach a consensus on the kind of institutional and policy solutions necessary to enhance the economic success, the social fairness, and the political and environmental sustainability of the European socio-economic model(s). For some contributors, an intelligent use of self-reinforcing forms of 'competitive solidarity' (e.g. high-road industrial strategies, the social investment perspective in social policy, export-led growth, the performance-enhancing effect of internal and external competition) can ensure the type of development that is at the same time more competitive and more solidary. For other contributors, the current imbalance against solidarity cannot be overcome by competition and growth alone, but it requires the deployment of various degrees of 'protective solidarity' based on market-correcting policies: less competition, more solidarity. For a third group, the achievement of the above-mentioned societal goals seems to require a transcendence of existing models of competitive market economy and a move towards alternative models based on cooperation and economic democracy, be they state-led or civil society-led. This disagreement is inevitable, as policy choices rest not only on the intrinsic quality and empirical efficacy of policy designs but also on the goals and broader societal preferences of their proponents. It is also a desirable and necessary element of a dynamic and democratic society. In fact, the contemporary debates on public policy-making and on the future of the European Union would greatly benefit from an explicit acknowledgement of the political dimension of policy choices and a broadening of the boundaries of acceptable orientations.

The findings of the book also provide an indication of some promising avenues for future research on competitiveness and solidarity.

On the one hand, the potential and pitfalls of models and policy designs based on 'competitive solidarity' should be explored more in depth. Theoretically, it is not entirely clear why models such as high-road development and the social investment state should not aspire to levels of redistribution and social protection even higher than those of the Keynesian welfare state: a radical interpretation of their fundamental principles (the pursuit of social welfare and beyond GDP goals, equality of opportunity) could justify massive doses of market-correcting intervention to level the playing field of competition (e.g. initial wealth and acquired advantages, social networks, talents) and to continually protect and restore the position of the losers. Empirically, more quantitative and qualitative research on the actual constraints, returns, and externalities of policy designs based on 'competitive solidarity' is needed.

On the other hand, the relevance of alternative models and policy designs based on 'protective solidarity' or 'radical solidarity' should be re-assessed. Over the last three decades, scholarly criticism of neo-liberal and third-way policy orientation has been growing louder: concrete alternative proposals, however, have often been impressively vague or have remained untested. Further scholarly reflection and practical experimentation and evaluation in this field, from self-managed initiatives to public policies at the local, regional, national, and international level, might provide important insights for strengthening and reorienting the current models of economic production and distribution, social interaction, and political participation in Europe and beyond.

Finally, more research should be done on the connections between the macro-level of public policies, institutions and social outcomes and the micro-level of individual/group ideas, attitudes, and behaviour. A stronger engagement with the body of research produced on this issues by psychologists, sociologists, experimental economists, philosophers, anthropologists, historians, and natural scientists may help illuminate the micro-foundations both of dysfunctional solutions (e.g. unbridled competition, populist backlashes, 'exclusive solidarity') and of balanced and mutually-reinforcing forms of 'competitive solidarity'.

In any case, the tensions between competitiveness and solidarity are bound to remain for a long time at the forefront of the theoretical and public policy discussion – in the European Union and beyond.

Index

For Product Safety Concerns and Information please contact our
EU representative GPSR@taylorandfrancis.com Taylor & Francis
Verlag GmbH, Kaufingerstraße 24, 80331 München, Germany